Bearing Witness
to
African American Literature

African American Life Series

A complete listing of the books in this series can be found online at wsupress.wayne.edu

Series Editors

Melba Joyce Boyd
Department of Africana Studies, Wayne State University

Bearing Witness to African American Literature

Validating and Valorizing
Its Authority, Authenticity,
and Agency

BERNARD W. BELL

Wayne State University Press
Detroit

© 2012 by Wayne State University Press, Detroit, Michigan 48201. All rights reserved.
No part of this book may be reproduced without formal permission.

16 15 14 13 12   5 4 3 2 1

Library of Congress Cataloging-in-Publication Data

Bell, Bernard W.
Bearing witness to African American literature : validating and valorizing its authority, authenticity, and agency / Bernard W. Bell.
  p. cm. — (African American life series)
Includes bibliographical references and index.
ISBN 978-0-8143-3714-1 (pbk. : alk. paper) — ISBN 978-0-8143-3715-8 (e-book)
1. American literature—African American authors—History and criticism. 2. African Americans—Intellectual life. 3. African Americans in literature. I. Title.

PS153.N5B45 2012
810.9'896073—dc23   2011045232

Designed by Charles Sutherland
Typeset by E.T. Lowe
Composed in Bodoni and Minion Pro

CONTENTS

Preface
Every Tongue Got to Confess   vii

Introduction
Memoir: On Becoming an African American Scholar Activist   1

1. Double Consciousness as the Sign of African American Difference   25
    I. The African American Jeremiad and Frederick Douglass's Fourth of July 1852 Speech   25
    II. Genealogical Shifts in Du Bois's Discourse on Double Consciousness as the Sign of African American Difference   41
    III. Booker T. and W. E. B.: The Authority, Authenticity, and Agency of African American Double Consciousness   63

2. The Roots and Branches of the African American Literary Tradition   73
    I. The African American Literary Tradition   73
    II. African American Writers   85
    III. The Image of Africa in the Afro-American Novel   111
    IV. Jean Toomer's "Blue Meridian": The Poet as Prophet of a New Order of Man   126
    V. The Legacy of James Baldwin: The Artist as Redemptive Lover and Righteous Witness   137

3. Modern and Contemporary African American Vernacular and Literary Voices   149
    I. The Blues Voices in John Edgar Wideman's *Two Cities*   149
    II. Clarence Major's Homecoming Voice in *Such Was the Season*   154
    III. Charles Johnson's Philosophical Fiction: Slave Revolt in the Quest for Unity of Being in *Middle Passage*   163
    IV. Trey Ellis's Voice of the New Black Aesthetic in *Platitudes*   169

4. Womanist African American Vernacular and Literary Voices 185
    I. Ann Petry's Demythologizing of American Culture and Afro-American Character 185
    II. Nails, Snails, and Puppy-Dog Tails: Black Male Stereotypes in the Fiction of Toni Morrison, Alice Walker, and Terry McMillan 195
    III. The Liberating Literary and African American Vernacular Voices of Gayl Jones 206
    IV. Toni Morrison's Blues People in a Jazz World 218
    V. *Beloved:* A Womanist Neo–Slave Narrative; or, Multivocal Remembrances of Things Past 227

5. Bearing Witness to the Changing Same: Representations of Black American Identity in American and African American Literature 239
    I. Three Vernacular Theories for Teaching African American Literature for the Twenty-First Century 239
    II. Mark Twain's "Nigger" Jim: The Tragic Face behind the Minstrel Mask 260
    III. "The Negro" as Metonym, Metaphor, and Marginal Man in William Faulkner's *Go Down, Moses* 275
    IV. William Styron's Nat Turner: A White Southerner's Meditation on a Legendary Slave Revolt 283
    V. Deconstructing the American Melting Pot and Literary Mainstream: Validating and Valorizing African American Literature in the College Curriculum 292

Works Cited 309

Index 323

PREFACE

Every Tongue Got to Confess

WHILE THE ORIGINS OF OUR GENETIC COUSINS IN AFRICA AND THE LESSONS OF our genealogical African ancestors remind us that "I am because we are, and since we are therefore I am" (Hord and Lee 8), the resilience, resourcefulness, and motherwit of our African American elders, preachers, and extended family teach us that "every tongue got to confess; everybody got to stand in judgment for theyself; every tub got to stand on its own bottom" (Hurston 30). General readers as well as specialists in American and African American Studies will therefore find this judiciously edited collection of interdisciplinary, code-switching critical examinations of the authority, authenticity, and agency of American and African American literature, language, and culture a provocative testimony of the personal and professional development of my roles and responsibilities as a revisionist African American scholar and activist.

The highlights of this development began in 1963 with research on Melville's "Benito Cereno" for the late poet, critic, and professor Sterling A. Brown, my mentor, and participation with him in the historic civil rights March on Washington. My post-civil rights scholarly and activist roles and responsibilities continued to develop in 1968 with a critical review of William Styron's *The Confessions of Nat Turner* in the *Michigan Quarterly Review*; in 1969 with cofounding the W. E. B. Du Bois Department of Afro-American Studies at the University of Massachusetts; in 1970 with chairmanship of the executive committee of the consortium of departments of African American Studies at Amherst, Smith, Mount Holyoke, and Hampshire Colleges, as well as the University of Massachusetts; in 1972 with editing *Modern and Contemporary Afro-American Poetry*, an anthology representing, in the depth and breadth necessary to appreciate, the rich, complex diversity of some of the best poetry by black Americans from the 1920s through the 1960s; and in 1974 with publication in the landmark black Broadside Critics Series of my seminal theory of the relationship of the folk philosophy and cultural nationalism of Johann Gottfried von Herder to the flowering of a black American poetic tradition in *The Folk Roots of Contemporary Afro-American Poetry.*

Post–civil rights collections of lectures and essays by African American academic humanists and literary scholars who edited their books themselves range from the integrationist aesthetic of Blyden Jackson's *The Waiting Years* (1976), which declares in the first of fifteen essays published between 1946 and 1976 that Negro "writing has been too often execrable" (34); to the more sanguine, influential, and intellectually provocative ten essays published between 1985 and 1991 in Henry Louis Gates Jr.'s *Loose Canons* (1992) that examine "the implications of the nationalistic eruptions and politics of identity" (xii) in the cultural and canon reformation wars; and the equally celebrated eclectic poststructuralist, psychoanalytic, and feminist seventeen essays that appeared between 1977 and 2001 in response to the emergence of "'Black Studies' [. . .] and 'Women's Studies'" (ix) in Hortense Spillers's *Black, White, and in Color* (2003). Spillers's essays were the subject of two academic symposia, one at the University of Pennsylvania in 2000 and the other at Johns Hopkins University in 2001. The twenty-three lectures and essays produced between 1957 and 1989 in Richard K. Barksdale's *Praisesong of Survival* (1992) and the twenty-one produced between 1962 and 1986 in Ruth T. Sheffey's *Trajectory* (1989) more traditionally represent their legacy of achievements as educators and literary critics as they close their professional careers. In contrast, the twenty-three lectures and essays that I first presented to the public between 1968 and 2008 before collecting them here in *Bearing Witness to African American Literature* develop a revision of W. E. B. Du Bois's theory and trope of double consciousness as central to our African American hybrid cultural identity; create an original theory of residually oral forms (oratory, including the vernacular; myth, including ritual, legend, tale, and song) for reading the African American novel; advocate an African Americentric vernacular and literary tradition; and deconstruct the myths of the American melting pot and literary mainstream. Contemporary specialists, students, and general readers should therefore remember, as Sir Francis Bacon states, "Some books are to be tasted, others to be swallowed, and some few to be chewed and digested" (114). African American readers should also be mindful not only that they must chew the fish but spit out the bones before swallowing food for thought but also that if they don't stand for something in the struggle to reconcile the ironies and paradoxes of their identities as a biracial, bicultural people, they'll surely fall for anything in their quest for power, status, and wholeness.

More specifically, this collection of interdisciplinary lectures and essays is a response to the call and encouragement of colleagues, graduate students, and everyday people, as well as to the critical success of my two prize-winning major studies of African American literature and culture—*The Contemporary African American Novel: Its Folk Roots and Modern Literary Branches* (2005) and *The Afro-American Novel and Its Tradition* (1987)—to make available under one cover the out-of-print, unprinted, or scattered oral and written record of my journey. The lectures and essays in this book trace, with occasional minor revisions, the different voices that chart my journey speaking truth to power, peers, and people around the world in Africa, Asia, and Europe, as well as the United States. This journey ranges from participating in the culture wars as a graduate student activist in the Black Studies movement of the twentieth century to participation in the transcultural globalization movement of the twenty-first century as an international scholar and Fulbright cultural ambassador several times in Spain, Portugal, and China. Delivered to or published for a variety of audiences, the selections range spatially from Morgan State University to Harvard University, from *Black World* to the *World & I*, from the *College Language Association Journal* and *Phylon* to the *Mark Twain Journal* and *Michigan Quarterly Review*, from *American Dialog* and *American Book Review* to the *Massachusetts Review* and *African American Review*, from the Second World Black and African Festival of Arts and Culture to Peking University and Beijing Foreign Studies University, and from the Universities of Salamanca, Valladolid, Coimbra, Lisbon, Oporto, Freiburg, and Heidelberg to the Sorbonne. The talks and testifying in this book thus bear witness to my authority, authenticity, and agency as a revisionist African American literary and cultural theorist, historian, and critic.

"I am a witness," James Baldwin confessed to an interviewer in 1984. "In the church in which I was raised you were supposed to bear witness to the truth. Now, later on, you wonder what in the world the truth is, but you do know what a lie is." As a Manchild of the Promised Land who also graduated from De Witt Clinton High School in the Bronx, I, like Baldwin in this particular role, am a "witness to whence I came, where I am. Witness to what I've seen and the possibilities that I think I see" (qtd. in Lester 22). As a scholar and activist, my primary purpose in the lectures and essays in the five chapters of this book was and is to count my blessings as I spread the good news about keeping faith with the folk roots of the modern institutional origins and the contemporary challenges of African American literary studies in the emerging new world.

Although this book has been in progress for several years as a testament to the price of the journey for the many thousand gone and as a contribution in some small measure to improving the understanding and appreciation of the richly diverse ironies and paradoxes of African American hybrid identities and vernacular theories of literature, I am indebted to my colleague Keith Gilyard, a distinguished scholar and poet, for his encouragement and inspiration in the final stages of this project for its structure. In addition, my research assistants Phyllisa Smith Deroze and Sarah Rude provided inexpendable diligent service in the fact-checking, proofreading, digital completion of this book.

INTRODUCTION

Memoir: On Becoming an African American Scholar Activist

Like the mother who reminds her son and many of us black men by her example of resilience and resourcefulness in Langston Hughes's poem "Mother to Son," "Life for me ain't been no crystal stair." But I wasn't motivated to write "On Becoming an African American Scholar Activist" to tell yet another story of the death of too many black men at an early age. Nor did I write it back at the dawn of the twenty-first century for vanity. Instead, because I believed in 2004 that The Contemporary African American Novel: Its Folk Roots and Modern Literary Branches *would be my last, if not my best, major literary study—it won an American Book Award and three other prestigious awards—I wrote it as the introduction to the book. It is therefore a meditation on my role and responsibility as a humanist educator, literary critic, and elder to pass on the lessons of my life in reconciling the tensions of my African American biracial and bicultural identities to my extended family and the next generation. I was also inspired as a grandfather by the following memorable lines attributed to poet Robert Hayden:*

> *It is time to call the children*
> *Into the evening quiet of the living room*
> *And teach them the lessons of their blood.*

So, "On Becoming an African American Scholar Activist" is also a testament of my legacy to my young grandchildren Larissa, Damani, Akili, Khari, Aisha, and Lyndon of personal and social responsibility to strive for a higher quality of life for others as well as for themselves.

"Everything now, we must assume, is in our hands," African American gay novelist, playwright, and essayist James Baldwin reminded us in the biblical and black spiritual jeremiad at the end of *The Fire Next Time* (1963); "we have no right to assume otherwise. If we—and now I mean the relatively conscious whites and the relatively conscious blacks, who must, like lovers, insist on, or create, the consciousness of the others, do not falter in our duty now, we may be able, handful that we are, to end the racial nightmare and achieve our country, and change the history of the world" (119). Like many black American men of the pre–World War II generation who are what some readers of Marxist Antonio Gramsci's *Prison Notebooks* (1971) might call organic intellectuals and agents of social change,[1] my soul looks back in wonder at how we collectively and individually got over the life crises of our sociohistorical separation from primary communities, our sociopsychological liminal or transitional experience with hybrid identities, and our ultimate sociocultural reincorporation.[2]

In our rites of passage many of us have come this far mainly by faith, resourcefulness, and resilience in challenging the legacy of slavery and social hierarchy that subjected and continues in many ways to subject Negroes with one drop of black blood, especially those whose skin was darker than a brown paper bag, to racial prejudice, discrimination, and exclusion. For example, in *The Future of the Race* (1996), Henry Louis Gates Jr., the distinguished brown-skinned critic and chair of the African American Studies Department at Harvard University, tells the following story about the brown paper bag ritual that he encountered as a student at Yale in the 1960s:

> Some of the brothers who came from private schools in New Orleans held a "bag party." As a classmate explained it to me, a bag party was a New Orleans custom wherein a brown paper bag was stuck on the door. Anyone darker than the bag was denied entrance. That was one cultural legacy that would be put to rest in a hurry—we all made sure of that. But in a manner of speaking, it was replaced by an opposite test whereby those who were deemed "not black enough" ideologically were to be shunned. I was not so sure this was an improvement. (Gates and West 18–19)

Thus, African Americans, especially native-born male intellectuals and agents of progressive social change, owe an immense debt to our primary racial, ethnic, and national communities. We are especially obligated to the ancestors and elders on whose shoulders we stand, for our modern and contemporary survival strategies for reconciling the tensions of our dual racial and cultural identities and for our distinctive vernacular theories of an African American cultural and literary tradition. "The whole history of the progress of human liberty shows that all concessions, yet made to her august claims, have been born of earnest struggle. [. . .] This struggle," Frederick Douglass wrote in a letter to white abolitionist Gerrit Smith in 1849, "may be a moral one; or it may be a physical one; or it may be both moral and physical; but it must be a struggle" (qtd. in Barbour 42).

When I was a latchkey kid in grammar school during World War II, I would occasionally upset my brown-skinned, working-class, single mother by visiting my equally brown-skinned but estranged father and my short, wiry, witty paternal grandfather, who lived at 1915 North Capitol Street, only two blocks from my school in northwest Washington, D.C. Although I rarely saw my father during these after-school visits and never developed a relationship with him, Grandpa Weaver loved to tell me stories, and I loved to listen. Often, these stories would be about his strategies for resisting antiblack racism in the army during World War I and in his everyday experiences with the tragicomic ironies of "separate but equal" racial segregation in the army and the nation's capital. Wryly critical of the ways of black and white folks, he sometimes began the stories with the same popular black folk saying: "If you're white, you're all right. If you're brown, stick around. But if you're black, oh brother, get back, get back!" Most folks in our primary speech community knew from their everyday experiences that racial prejudice and segregation actually meant an unequal and unjust division of power, privilege, preference, and resources. So, he would underscore this fact by usually closing the storytelling sessions in his living room or on the front porch of his two-story red brick home with the trenchant vernacular moral lesson of courage, resilience, and resourcefulness: " 'Member, son, it takes shit, grit, and motherwit to survive in dis man's world."

Also, before migrating to Harlem and the South Bronx at the end of World War II, my mother and I used to make frequent visits to kinfolk outside the District of Columbia in Norbeck, Maryland, especially in the summer. Usually during these visits, my mother's oldest and most maternal sister, Aunt Gretna, would affectionately call me "Benniewix" and welcome me with a big hug before strengthening our family bond with my favorite communal and spiritual ritual. While she was baking bread in the oven of a huge wood-burning stove in her equally huge kitchen, she would tell me and her daughter, Little Gretna, who was a year younger than I, stories about having Jesus in our lives, and she would hum spirituals. After taking two or three pans out of the oven and piling butter on the big, fluffy, golden brown chunks of hot white bread for us, she would say, "Don't y'all forget yo blessing.

And 'member, de Lord helps dem dat helps demselves." Aunt Gretna's tall, dark-skinned husband, Uncle Jim, a construction worker and the protector and provider of the family who, unlike my uncles Angel and David, brought his paycheck home every Friday and with whom she shared authority, would sometimes walk through the kitchen on these occasions. When he overheard her, he would say in his usual soft-spoken manner with a smile on his face, "Ya think long, ya think wrong," reminding us that she didn't mean for us to help ourselves to another chunk of bread without her permission. These anecdotes are examples of the bidialectalism and residually oral forms of the African American vernacular roots of my authenticity, authority, and agency, key terms indicating a significantly, predominantly, or exclusively black American identity formation and primary reference group orientation that will be defined more fully in chapter 1. These are the sociolinguistic, cognitive, and affective roots of my double consciousness, ambivalence, and code-switching as a modern African American organic intellectual, as well as an African American vernacular critic, literary scholar, and social activist in the tradition of W. E. B. Du Bois and Sterling A. Brown, two of my elders, ancestors, and primary intellectual role models.

Grounded in the specific experiences of enslaved black people of primarily West and Central African ancestry and culture with antiblack racism in the United States (Holloway 1–18) and rooted in the hybrid cultural heritage of our African American folk and vernacular tradition, *The Contemporary African American Novel: Its Folk Roots and Modern Literary Branches* is a sequel to *The Afro-American Novel and Its Tradition* (1987). The mixed heritage of African American folk and our vernacular tradition has deep historical roots in South Carolina, the Georgia Sea Islands, and Louisiana that have been transplanted and have developed contemporary branches nationally, especially in northern and midwestern industrialized cities. In *The Souls of Black Folk* (1903), Great Barrington–born W. E. B. Du Bois, who bore witness as a visibly mixed black New England Brahmin to the lives of black peasants, sharecroppers, and farmers as a teacher in Tennessee and who wrote a thesis on it as a doctoral student in Berlin, identifies the folk struggling up from slavery at the end of the nineteenth century as "the black artisan" (Du Bois 17, 55–64; Lewis 143). In *The New Negro* (1925), Philadelphia-born Alain Locke, a similarly light-skinned black intellectual educated at Harvard and the University of Berlin, calls the modern transplanted and transformed folk of Harlem in the 1920s "the New Negro," "the migrant masses," and "the Negro . . . peasant matrix of that section of America that has most undervalued him" (3, 4, 15). In *The Big Sea* (1940), the light-skinned black poet Langston Hughes, born in Joplin, Missouri, and educated at Lincoln ("black Princeton") University, simply refers to the folk of the Harlem Renaissance as "ordinary Negroes" (228). The *Oxford English Dictionary* reminds us that the term "vernacular" has shifted from its Latin root *verna,* meaning "a home-born slave," to include "a language or dialect: That is naturally spoken by the people of a particular country or district" and "arts, or features of these: Native or peculiar to a particular country or locality."[3] As a literary history that deploys the biologically and culturally mixed heritage of black folk in the United States, both southern rural and northern urban, as a dominant trope, and as a critical study that reaffirms the strategic essentialism of African American literature and hybrid identity formations, this book is more dialectic and cyclical than linear despite the designated time frames in the chapter headings.

The Contemporary African American Novel: Its Folk Roots and Modern Literary Branches is not only a diachronic but also a synchronic critical study that charts frequently concurrent and overlapping residual and emergent as well as dominant cultural, narrative, and aesthetic movements. For example, as one aspect of the African American aesthetic that moves cyclically from residual to emergent, the blues aesthetic "arises as a late nineteenth-century/early twentieth-century secular thrust of the African-American musical culture, whose oldest musical and lyrical heritage was Africa but whose changing contemporary expression summed up their [African American] lives and history in the West."[4] This book, therefore, begins with a critique of contemporary cultural and literary theories and ideologies for representing and reading the authenticity, authority, and agency of African American culture and character. This critique illuminates why and how the dominant African American aesthetic focuses on the nature and function of the shifting grounds for discovering and constructing truth, ethics, and politics as well as beauty in art and literature primarily by, for, and about black Americans. Chapters 2–8 will identify and examine closely the relationship of class and cultural formations to the pattern of residual, emergent, and dominant African American narrative and aesthetic movements. These chapters revise, expand, and enrich the coverage of women and contemporary male writers by including homosexual romances and novels as well as science fiction and detective novels that, like other subgenres in the narrative tradition, are written by and about biracial, bicultural African Americans speaking for themselves. More than literary history, *The Contemporary African American Novel: Its Folk Roots and Modern Literary Branches* is also a theoretical and methodological study of the rhetoric, dialectics, and dialogics of the African American novel and romance, especially their constructions of cultural and political identities.

More specifically, this book is a call for a reinvigorated discourse on the liberating impact of vernacular and literary cultural production by African American novelists and on continuity and change in the tradition of the African American novel. I began it in the 1990s as a response to the impact of Eurocentric postmodernism and postcolonialism on my vernacular theory of contemporary African American novelists and novels, especially critiques of vernacular criticism and cultural nationalism that categorically repudiate all master narratives and boundaries, heuristic as well as historical, as inherently fixed and essentialist. "Too often," as poststructuralist feminist critic Diana Fuss clearly and persuasively demonstrates, "constructionists presume that the category of the social automatically escapes essentialism, in contradistinction to the way the category of the natural is presupposed to be inevitably entrapped within it. But there is no compelling reason to assume that the natural is, in essence, essentialist and that the social is, in essence, constructionist" (6). Finally, this book is a response to the overwhelmingly positive critical reception of *The Afro-American Novel and Its Tradition*. The questions raised in that book concerning the politics of identity remain inextricably linked to the poetics and rhetoric of the African American novel, as well as to the lessons learned from my elders and ancestors about southern down-home Jim Crow survival rituals and northern school of hard knocks in storefront churches, barbershops, schoolyards, basement parties, rooftop gang rituals, and the ebony tower. My modern streetwise urban elders and peers, who used to call me "Schoolboy" and went out of their way to keep me out of harm's way, included pimps, prostitutes, pushers, junkies, number runners, pickpockets, shoplifters, gamblers, and everyday hustlers, who generally considered themselves players in the game of life, as well as some preachers, teachers, and cultural and social welfare workers, who were like coaches, trainers, and referees in the game.

In situating the authenticity, authority, and agency of my identity as an African American cultural and literary critic, I assume, like most black Americans in the United States of my pre–World War II and Jazz Age generation, that the world is interpreted from the vantage point of different, often still separated, and unequal racial and ethnic spaces and communities. My generation bore witness to the sounds of the big bands of Cab Calloway, Count Basie, and Duke Ellington as well as to the demonstrations by African Americans protesting Italy's fascist invasion of Ethiopia in 1935 and support along with Germany of the right-wing general Francisco Franco in the Spanish Civil War of 1936–39. Many postmodern and some postcolonial theorists, as illustrated in chapter 1, advocate seeing the world from multiple transnational and transcultural subject positions while paradoxically and often unconsciously grounding the subjectivities of themselves and others in the ethnocentric norms of their own Anglocentric or Eurocentric background, primary speech community, and predominantly white middle-class living space. Afro-British cultural critic Paul Gilroy, for example, constructs his diasporic theory of the black Atlantic and cultural hybridity by focusing on "the special relationships between 'race,' culture, nationality, and ethnicity which have a bearing on the histories and political cultures of Britain's black citizens" (3). In contrast, the dynamics of my identity formation and cultural productions are explicitly grounded in the African Americentric core of my sociohistorical, sociocultural, and sociopsychological double consciousness and code-switching, or blending of Standard American English (SAE) and African American Vernacular English (AAVE) vocabulary, pronunciation, grammar, and tropes, as a revisionist African American male vernacular cultural and literary critic.[5] In the field of cultural production, according to sociologist Pierre Bourdieu, symbolic and cultural capital are particularly important. Whereas symbolic capital refers to the "degree of accumulated prestige, celebrity, consecration or honour and is founded on a dialectic of knowledge [. . .] and recognition [. . .] cultural capital [. . .] is a form of knowledge, an internalized code or a cognitive acquisition which equips the social agent with empathy towards, appreciation for or competence in deciphering cultural relations and cultural artifacts" (qtd. in R. Johnson 7). African and African American revisionist cultural and literary critics use our dual heritage to contest and complicate Eurocentric master narratives and myths of the natural, universal superiority of Western culture and the innate purity, unity, and dominance of white people, especially men. We also express our ambivalence in Eurocentric, Afrocentric, or African Americentric types of modernism and postmodernism that acknowledge the limitations and possibilities of cultural relativism and provisional truths in the quest for personal and collective freedom, literacy, and wholeness.

Because they will be explained more fully in chapter 1, let me here just briefly define the terms "Eurocentric," "Afrocentric," and "African Americentric" as unstable, shifting geopolitical and philosophical concepts that basically indicate whether Europe or Africa or the United States is at the center of one's vision of the world and method of interpreting it and literary texts. The history of imperialism and the Atlantic slave trade as well as of foreign-born immigration and native-born migration clearly indicates that the relation of the lighter peoples of the world to the darker is marked by racial and cultural mixture. Rather than indicating a direct, mechanistic correlation between a writer's social position and the type of literary text that he or she produces, the dominant aesthetic tradition of the African American novel reveals that the text is not only an indirect, imaginative representation and construction of the racial, class, and gender identity formation or position of the author and of the group to which he or she implies a primary commitment. The text is also a product of the complex conditions of the production, circulation, and consumption of socially significant symbolic acts and goods for a marketplace of different types of consumers and resisting readers.

I deploy rhetorical, dialectical, and dialogical critical strategies to reexamine and reconstruct the relationship between conventionally classified—but far from pure, static, and mutually exclusive—black and white cultures, especially their vernacular and literary traditions, mainly in the United States. As elaborated more fully in chapter 2, my critical theory and analyses of the culture of Americans of sub-Saharan black African descent are grounded primarily in the sociohistorical and sociocultural specificity of the dynamic pattern of our everyday and mythic experiences in antagonistic cooperation with the dominant white social formation in the United States. I am therefore committed to an aesthetic that imaginatively seeks to challenge and change insidious contemporary language and other institutional manifestations of the hegemonic, hierarchic system of antiblack racism in the United States. Contemporary antiblack racism includes racial profiling, racial brutality by police officers, racial discrimination in the justice system and media, and racial residential and economic redlining, which are fostered by negative stereotypes and representations of nonwhite people, sometimes expressed by ourselves, that serve to maintain and perpetuate the power, preferential treatment, and privileges of the white ruling class and its nonwhite supporters.

In other words, like Bourdieu's theory and rigorous analysis of the cultural field, my analysis adapts a radical contextualization of literary texts:

> It takes into consideration not only works themselves, seen relationally within the space of available possibilities and within the historical development of such possibilities, but also producers of works in terms of their strategies and trajectories, based on their individual and class habitus, as well as their objective position within the field. It also entails an analysis of the structure of the field itself, which includes the positions occupied by producers (e.g. writers, artists) as well as those occupied by all the instances of consecration and legitimation which make cultural products what they are (the public, publishers, critics, galleries, acade-

mies and so forth). Finally, it involves an analysis of the position of the [literary] field within the broader field of power. (R. Johnson 9)

More specifically for this study, although my analytic method includes the social conditions of the production, circulation, and consumption of novels as symbolic texts and acts, I am primarily committed to the validation and valorization of the authentic everyday voices and previously excluded experiences of ordinary black Americans in the revisionist tradition of black and white social scientists, humanists, and artists. This tradition includes Anna Julia Cooper, Carter G. Woodson, John B. Cade, Charles S. Johnson, Lawrence D. Reddick, Melville J. Herskovits, Benjamin A. Botkin, Kenneth M. Stampp, John Hope Franklin, Norman R. Yetman, George P. Rawick, and John W. Blassingame, as well as Du Bois and Brown.

Highlighting the problems of the authenticity, authority, and agency of African American voices, the self-liberated slave John Little told an interviewer in 1855 after escaping to Canada, "Tisn't he who has stood and looked on, that can tell you what slavery is—'tis he who has endured" (qtd. in Yetman 1). How do auditors and readers assess the authenticity and authority of the pronunciation, vocabulary, and grammar of this and similar voices that were and are usually recorded, interpreted, and published by white interviewers and editors? How do readers and critics move beyond the popular cultural legacy of the cacography, malapropisms, anachronisms, anomalies, and distorted syntax of African American language, culture, and character spawned by the plantation and blackface minstrel traditions? White authorities and masters, too often with the complicity and collusion of members of the oppressed group, not only controlled the past, they also controlled and control the vernacular, popular, and written histories. "Seldom before or since has racism been so pervasive and so academically respectable in America as during the early years of the twentieth century," writes sociologist Norman Yetman. "The assumption of the innate and inherited inferiority of non–Anglo Saxon racial and ethnic groups permeated and dominated intellectual as well as popular thought. Social, scientific, and historical thought both mirrored and reinforced this racism" (341).

For example, in twentieth-century historiography and popular culture in the United States, Ulrich B. Phillips's *American Negro Slavery* (1918) and *Life and Labor in the Old South* (1929) and Stanley Elkins's *Slavery* (1959) provoked early revisionist scholarship by providing academic respectability for the negative stereotypes of black Americans as biologically and culturally inferior. These stereotypes were first popularized onstage in the 1830s in the minstrel tradition of blackfaced white men mocking black culture, language, and character. They were also popular in pre–Civil War writings by such authors as George Tucker, William A. Caruthers, Nathaniel B. Tucker, John E. Cooke, and John Pendleton Kennedy. But they had their most significant impact and influence on the post-Reconstruction writings of Thomas Nelson Page and Joel Chandler Harris, who either sympathetically supported or nostalgically glorified the plantation tradition of the Old South. In their romanticized representations of the Old South from the perspective of the white planter class, slavery was a paternalistic agricultural economic system. Influenced by his Southern heritage to devalue and dismiss the testimonies, the oral history, of ex-slaves as unintelligent, unintelligible, and unreliable, Phillips valorized the popular representations of African Americans as descendants of culturally, morally, and intellectually deficient contented slaves in his comprehensive study of American slavery. Because "the typical Negroes" were naturally "impulsive and inconstant, sociable and amorous, voluble, dilatory, and negligent, but robust, amiable, obedient and contented," Phillips writes, "they have been the world's premium slaves" (8).

According to Elkins, slavery in the United States was a closed social system, more like Nazi concentration camps than like slavery in Latin America and the Caribbean, in which enslaved Africans and their descendants were infantile laborers and Sambos who were "docile but irresponsible, loyal but lazy, humble but chronically given to lying and stealing" (82). This thesis was a counterdiscourse not only to the revisionist scholarship of John Hope Franklin's classic comprehensive black history *From Slavery to Freedom* (1947) and Kenneth Stampp's history of American slavery *The Peculiar Institution* (1959) but also to earlier revisionist scholarship inspired by the Harvard-educated black historians W. E. B. Du Bois and Carter G. Woodson. In 1896, Du Bois published *The Suppression of the African Slave Trade to the United States of America, 1638–1870*, followed in 1924 by *The Gift of the Black Folk* and in 1935 by *Black Reconstruction in America*. In 1915 Woodson founded the Association for the Study of Negro Life and History, followed in 1916 by the *Journal of Negro History*, and in 1922 he published *The Negro in Our History*. In the 1920s and 1930s black and white revisionist scholars and cultural workers in the United States began to recover, reclaim, and reassess missing or misrepresented texts and absent black voices for the reconstruction of a more diverse and democratic usable American past.

It is also very important to remember that in 1896 the *Plessy v. Ferguson* U.S. Supreme Court decision, which will be examined more closely later in this book, transformed the southern ritual and trope of Jim Crow into a national reality. Ironically, in his landmark conciliatory speech on race relations at the Atlanta Cotton Exposition in 1895, especially his dramatic racial simile of the relationship of the fingers to the hand, Booker T. Washington ostensibly persuaded the white ruling class that southern black folks like himself would accept separate but equal racial segregation as the law of the land. "In all things that are purely social," Washington told white leaders of politics and commerce, "we can be as separate as the fingers, yet one as the hand in all things essential to mutual progress" (154). *Plessy v. Ferguson* established that racial segregation was reasonable and legal where separate but equal public facilities were provided. Racially segregated and unequal public facilities, as were generally the rule rather than the exception, were thus a violation of federal law that was rarely if ever prosecuted. Segregation and antiblack racism also challenged black Americans to create and maintain alternative, often parallel, social and cultural systems for survival as a people.

In the tradition of African American cultural resistance and resiliency, as quiet as it is kept, the first major projects to collect and preserve the life stories of ex-slaves were at black institutions, Fisk University in Tennessee in 1928 and Southern University in Louisiana in 1929, under the direction of such sociologists as Charles S. Johnson at Fisk and such historians as John B. Cade at Southern. Although the interviews collected by black staff members of Johnson's Social Science Institute were a major source for his analysis in *Shadow of the Plantation* (1934), the first major study to reveal the plantation system from the slaves' point of view, the interviews were not published until the 1970s. Also in 1934, Lawrence Reddick, a graduate student participant in the Fisk project and a faculty member at Kentucky State College, led a Federal Emergency Relief Administration (FERA) pilot project of twelve "Black white-collar workers" who collected approximately 250 interviews in Indiana and Kentucky. Because of their allegedly inadequate interviewing experience, the proposal for a more ambitious project was disapproved until the Federal Writers' Project (FWP) established a similar study. Reddick's ambitious but unrealized proposal to employ five hundred black college-educated workers to interview the surviving ex-slave population systematically was supported by Johnson and cosponsored by Woodson and the Association for the Study of Negro Life and History (Yetman 341–45). The interviews directed at Southern University by Cade were summarized in 1935 in the article "Out of the Mouths of Ex-Slaves" (294–337), but the more than 400 interviews with ex-slaves in thirteen states that he directed while at Prairie View State College during 1935–38 remain unpublished.

Although we hear the stories of ex-slaves filtered through the voices and inscribed by the pens of African American historians, including Du Bois's revisionist classic study *Black Reconstruction in America* (1935), the voices of enslaved Africans and African Americans were not generally valued in white American historiography until the Black Studies movement inspired revisionist scholarship in the 1960s. This was the case even though more than two thousand interviews with those who endured slavery, as well as commentaries and autobiographies by them, were compiled in seventeen states by the FWP in 1936–39. During this period, Henry G. Alsberg was the national director of the FWP; George Cronyn, the associate director; Sterling A. Brown (1936–38), the national editor for Negro affairs; and John Lomax (1936–37) and Benjamin Botkin (1937–39), the national folklore editors for this project. Because of his prestige, Lomax, probably the most distinguished southern white folklorist and popularizer of American folk songs, was primarily responsible in 1937 for systematically extending the Slave Narrative Collection program through the different states. "The interview method of collecting folklore and a corollary emphasis upon the collection of life-history materials, both of which he introduced, became a hall mark of Writers' Project research," Yetman notes (348).[6]

As a nationally respected Howard University associate professor, published poet and essayist, and scholar of black and white American poetry, fiction, and drama, Brown, the "light, bright, damned-near white" son and grandson of ex-slaves (S. N. Brown 6), who wryly called himself the black sheep of his family, was exceptionally well qualified for his responsibilities of coordinating "all the Writers' Project's studies by and about Blacks [. . .] and monitoring the number of Blacks employed in the Project" (Gabbin 70). At the beginning of their careers, such now distinguished black writers as Roi Ottley, Willard Motley, Frank Yerby, Zora Neale Hurston, Margaret Walker, Arna Bontemps, Claude McKay, Richard Wright, and Ralph Ellison were employed on state projects during Brown's tenure as national editor. But we should not forget that most of the interviewers were unemployed white artists and writers with obvious class, racial, and regional biases that distorted the collection of the ex-slave narratives and the writing of guidebooks in states such as Texas, Mississippi, and South Carolina. Alsberg, Brown, and Botkin therefore provided specific, detailed guidelines to the state field collectors and directors and revised the interviewers' questionnaires designed by folklorist Alan Lomax in order to improve "the level of authenticity and honesty in their presentation of this material" (Gabbin 72). But Texas and Mississippi state directors either extensively revised or failed to send interviews to the national office that questioned the popular legend of slavery as a benign paternalistic Southern social system of benevolent white masters and contented black slaves. Interested readers will find in Robert Gordon and Bruce Nemerov's *Lost Delta Found* (2005) the voices of the black assistants (musicologist John W. Work, sociologist Lewis Wade Jones, and graduate student Samuel C. Adams) that Alan Lomax silenced as the "other guy" in the pioneer discovery and recording of blues artist Muddy Waters in the Fisk University–Library of Congress Coahama County Study, 1941–1942 (xv).

Because of the popularity of blackface minstrel stereotypes created by white performers to ridicule black character and culture while reifying the myth of white supremacy, these guidelines and questionnaires were especially needed for the recording and interpretation of the ex-slaves' unique Gullah dialect and culture in the coastal areas of South Carolina and Georgia. Based on his experience with and respect for authentic black folk speech, developed primarily while he was a teacher in Virginia, and demonstrated in his published poetry and criticism, especially a seminal article in 1933 on black stereotypes in American literature, Brown also recommended that "truth to idiom be paramount, and exact truth to pronunciation secondary" (qtd. in Gabbin 73). Even so, the racial, regional, class, and gender biases of many of the interviewers and state editors resulted in either violations of or uneven adherence to Brown's standard of authenticity.

As my venerable teacher, mentor, and friend, Brown, who was a social realist and modernist in critical theory and poetic practice, is most important in my rites of passage in becoming an African Americentric scholar and activist. Unlike the focus on the African past and African Diaspora of many Afrocentrics, my primary scholarly comparative methodology focuses on the double consciousness and hybrid identity formations resulting from the acculturative process in the United States that transformed Africans into African Americans. This is not a philosophical issue of whether identity is the product of either nature or nurture. Rather, it is the anthropological proposition that identity is a complex dialectic process that takes place between nature and nurture. Other important revisionists who influenced me in my journey as an African Americentric scholar include the anthropologist Melville J. Herskovits, who, along with Brown, was prominent among the consultants on African American culture to Gunnar Myrdal's landmark controversial study, *An American Dilemma* (1944). Herskovits's *Myth of the Negro Past* (1941) is a provocative, valuable, revisionist, seminal study of African cultural survivals in the United States and Caribbean that reconstructs Du Bois's sociopsychological concept and introduces the African acculturative process of retention, reinterpretation, and syncretism. Continuing the revisionist tradition in 1945, Botkin edited

Lay My Burden Down, the first modest folk history of excerpts and selections from narratives in the Slave Narrative Collection of the FWP. Even more impressive are Kenneth Stampp's *Peculiar Institution* (1956) and Charles Nichols's *Many Thousand Gone* (1963), classic histories by a white and a black scholar that challenged traditional historiography by including black voices across the nation telling their stories from the social margins about the legacy of slavery.

Elkins's comparative study of slavery in Latin America, the Caribbean, and Nazi concentration camps was primarily a response to Stampp's displacement of the moral and scholarly authority of Phillips and the Sambo identity with evidence from the testimonies of former plantation slaves themselves. Challenging the assumptions and extending the evidence of Phillips, this testimony from the traditionally devalued and unacknowledged voices of the peculiar institution supported Stampp's thesis that enslaved black Americans "were merely ordinary human beings, that innately Negroes *are,* after all, only white men with black skins, nothing more, nothing less" (vii). But my rites of passage into manhood as an African American revisionist scholar, vernacular theorist, modernist critic, and social activist challenged the authority of this well-intentioned declaration of the norms of Negro identity.

In the 1970s several books recovered and reassessed the voices in the Slave Narrative Collection of the FWP for the pedagogical, cultural, and research projects fostered by the Black Studies movement. These include Yetman's valuable *Life under the "Peculiar Institution"* (1970), Rawick's impressive nineteen-volume *From Sundown to Sunup* (1972), and Blassingame's provocative *Slave Community* (1972) and *Slave Testimony* (1977). These revisionist studies challenged the standard representation of African American character and culture as deviant and deficient by the historiography of Phillips and Elkins. Elkins's *Slavery* was an important influence on the controversial representation of Nat Turner and his slave revolt in 1831 as deviant in William Styron's 1968 Pulitzer Prize–winning *Confessions of Nat Turner.* In response to the misrepresentation of African American culture and character by Elkins and Styron, I wrote the first articles in my rites of passage as a revisionist scholar and activist in 1968.

According to family legend, however, my rites of passage into manhood began during the economic depression of the 1930s below the Mason-Dixon line, the eighteenth-century geographical boundary between Maryland and Pennsylvania that marked the political and cultural line between the North and South. Born and raised in early childhood in the racially segregated black speech communities and public schools of Washington, D.C., and Norbeck, Maryland, where neither the outdated books and inadequate supplies nor the curriculum and physical plant were the equal of facilities and resources in white schools, I am the only son of a single black mother. A high school graduate and avid reader, she insisted that I read such authors as Paul Laurence Dunbar, Langston Hughes, Louisa May Alcott, Robert Louis Stevenson, Mark Twain, and Edgar Allan Poe, as well as the comic books that I usually preferred to read. With my migration to New York during World War II, I learned the urban strategies of survival as a manchild in the mean streets and racially nonsegregated public schools of the Promised Land in the increasingly black and Puerto Rican speech communities of the South Bronx. I was nevertheless required in grade school to participate in speech therapy classes to correct my African American Vernacular English (AAVE). My after-school hustles (delivering groceries; shining shoes; washing cars and windows; cleaning fish in a Jewish market and hallways in my housing project; playing blackjack; pitching nickels and dimes; shooting dice; shoplifting; snatching handbags; and watching out for cops at gambling dens) and my mother's monthly welfare checks helped us to survive the hard times. But I was fortunate to escape the fate of many of my peers in such gangs as the Happy Gents, Coppians, Slicksters, Puerto Rican Tigers, and Irish Dukes. Graduating from De Witt Clinton High School at seventeen, I entered the liminal stage of my rites of passage into manhood by joining the military and learning the strategies of killing and survival as a U.S. Marine in Europe and the Far East during the Korean War. In the late 1950s I returned to revitalize the core black culture of my identity by reintegrating into the predominantly African American community of the nation's capital, especially the Northeast Housing Projects on Benning Road. I became a husband, a father of three sons, and a graduate of the predominantly black Howard University, as well as a D.C. high school teacher, scholar activist, doctoral student, and ultimately a faculty member in the Black Studies movement of 1968–69 at the University of Massachusetts in Amherst.

Actually, my authority and agency as an African American scholar and activist began to transform my consciousness and commitment during the Mississippi Freedom Rides and Schools in 1962 with the inspiration of Sterling Brown, whom I affectionately and respectfully called "Prof." As a Korean War veteran who had to take remedial English in order to matriculate at Howard University under the GI Bill and as the first college student in my family, I realized that I was not the turn-the-other-cheek type of person required to participate in nonviolent civil rights demonstrations. But while working as a graduate research assistant with Prof at Howard on the critical debate of whether Herman Melville's "Benito Cereno" was most meaningfully read as a realistic or allegorical short story of a black slave revolt at sea, I became deeply involved in revisionist scholarship on slavery and in theories of social realism and modernism. It was also in his office during this time that I first met Student Nonviolent Coordinating Committee (SNCC) activists Michael Thelwell, Stokely Carmichael, Charlie Cobb, Courtland Cox, and Cleveland Sellers, who were undergraduate college students recruiting volunteers for the Civil Rights movement and Freedom Schools in Alabama and Mississippi.

Inspired by my research and Prof's profound spiritual, political, and scholarly identification with southern rural and urban working-class blacks, as well as with young undergraduate student activists and future SNCC leaders in the Black Power movement of the mid-1960s, I became more politically active as a cultural worker and critic. Because I was an ex-marine who did not believe in nonviolence, and because I was a father who drove a cab and worked as an airline chef to support my wife and three sons, I was neither willing nor able to participate in street demonstrations. But I did participate with Prof and other student activists in supporting lectures, forums, and meetings on the Howard campus and in the city concerning everything from sit-ins, Freedom Schools, and voting registration drives to poetry readings, agitprop theater, and other cultural performances. This phase of my agency as a scholar of African American social neorealism and modernism culminated with Prof and me participating in the extraordinary 1963 March on Washington and paying tribute to the legendary and venerable pioneer African American scholar and activist W. E. B. Du Bois at the news of his death during the march.

The next stage of my rites of passage as a revisionist African Americentric literary and cultural critic committed to validating and valorizing black American voices from the bottom and margins of society was the completion of a master's thesis, "Anger in the Novels of Ralph Ellison, John O. Killens and James Baldwin," at Howard University in 1966. After accepting a fellowship in 1967 to study with Professor Sidney Kaplan, a 1949 Bancroft Prize–winning specialist in American and African American Studies, at the University of Massachusetts, I began achieving national recognition in 1968 and 1969 with my publication of scholarly book reviews in the *Michigan Quarterly Review* and *American Dialog*. These essays challenged the pseudo-Freudian Stanley Elkins–influenced representation by William Styron of the Virginia slave revolt of 1831 and of its legendary messianic leader, Nat Turner, as an aberrant act by a sexually repressed violent predator of white women.

During the same period, two major academic and political developments resonated deeply in my life. The first was the completion of my doctoral dissertation,

"The Afro-American Novel and Its Tradition," under the direction of Professor Kaplan. The second was the impact on me of Ralph Ellison's *Shadow and Act* (1964), Frantz Fanon's *Wretched of the Earth* (1968), and Harold Cruse's *Crisis of the Negro Intellectual* (1968) and of my participation as a Phi Kappa Phi honors graduate student in the historically neglected Black Studies movement at the University of Massachusetts in transforming me into a postcolonial African Americentric vernacular theorist, literary critic, and social activist. Even more remarkable than San Francisco State University, the University of Massachusetts movement established departments, rather than programs, of African American Studies at the elite private institutions of Amherst, Smith, Mount Holyoke, and Hampshire Colleges, as well as a department named in honor of W. E. B. Du Bois at the Amherst campus of the public University of Massachusetts. As a graduate student and faculty member, I not only cofounded the W. E. B. Du Bois Department of African American Studies at the University of Massachusetts but also served as interim chairman of the department and as the first chairman of the Five-College Executive Committee of African American Studies.

Although generally neglected in major reports by the Ford Foundation and books by specialists such as Thomas Sowell, Nick Aaron Ford, and Perry A. Hall on the Black Studies movement,[7] the Du Bois Department of African American Studies was arguably the most politically and intellectually diverse and dynamic radical development in a white institution of higher education at that time on the East Coast if not in the nation. Under the charismatic leadership of Michael Thelwell, a prize-winning Jamaican writer, SNCC political activist, and compelling orator, and under my academic and administrative leadership, our faculty included a diversity of radical academic, social, and cultural activists of the era. Most of the following national and international important faculty were recruited by Thelwell: Algerian resistance fighter and first Algerian ambassador to the United States Cherif Guellal; Marxist historian, literary executor of the W. E. B. Du Bois Papers, and political activist Herbert Aptheker; father of the African modern novel Chinua Achebe; SNCC organizer and political activist Ivanhoe Donaldson; anthropologist and scholar activist Johnetta Cole; prize-winning historian and scholar activist John Bracey; founder of modern jazz and virtuoso drummer Max Roach; avant-garde jazz saxophonist, poet, and playwright Archie Shepp; award-winning playwright and director Paul Carter Harrison; award-winning graphic artist Nelsen Stevens; and award-winning cultural critic and Americanist scholar Sidney Kaplan.[8] As a faculty member in the Department of English at the University of Massachusetts for twenty-four years as well as in the W. E. B. Du Bois Department of African American Studies during its most turbulent initial two years, I also founded the Black Faculty Association and chaired the Minority Faculty Association in order to increase the recruitment, retention, and power of black and nonwhite minority faculty.

My participation in the African American Studies movement to challenge and change the literary canon, academic curriculum, and critical pedagogy continued in the 1970s. In 1971 I published a pioneering essay on Jean Toomer, "A Key to the Poems in *Cane*," in the *College Language Association Journal*, and in 1972 I edited the anthology *Modern and Contemporary Afro-American Poetry* as a pedagogical collection of poems that reveals in some depth the vitality and versatility of some of the best modern and contemporary African American poets. As one of the Broadside Press critics, I also published a pioneering monograph on Johann Gottfried von Herder and African American vernacular poetic theory and practice in 1974, *The Folk Roots of Contemporary Afro-American Poetry*. I joined the Department of English at Pennsylvania State University (PSU) in 1991 and coordinated the development of an undergraduate and graduate program in African American literature that ranked among the nation's top programs of its type in the mid-1990s. I was also active at PSU in developing the African and African American Studies Department, in negotiating mutually agreeable terms in 2001 between black student demonstrators and the university president for implementing a more vigorous diversity plan at the university, and in organizing the Africana Research Center.

I have been blessed with invitations to lecture and teach in the United States, Europe, Africa, and the People's Republic of China (PRC) at such universities and colleges as Harvard, Clark, Iowa, Amherst, Smith, Chicago, Morgan State, Freiburg, Heidelberg, Lisbon, Coimbra, Salamanca, Valladolid, Balboa, La Mancha, Sorbonne, Peking, Beijing Foreign Studies, Sichuan International Studies, Sichuan Normal, Mianyang Teachers, and Southwest University of Science and Technology. I have authored, edited, or coedited eight books and published more than sixty articles nationally and internationally. For these achievements I have received the honor of several awards as a scholar and activist. They include the American Book Award (2005), College Language Association Creative Scholarship Award (2006, 1989), *Choice* Academic Book of Year (2006), induction into the International Literary Hall of Fame for Writers of African Descent (2000), and Du Bois/Garvey Pan African Unity Award (1999). Internationally, I have been honored to serve as a visiting professor at the University of Freiburg in Germany in 1974–75, as a member of the Colloquium at the Second World Black and African Festival of Arts and Culture in Lagos, Nigeria, in 1977, and as a senior Fulbright-Hays scholar at the University of Coimbra in Portugal in 1982–83, at the University of Salamanca in

Spain in 1996, at Beijing Foreign Studies University in 2004, and at the Southwest University of Science and Technology in 2006 in the People's Republic of China.

But I still draw strength as an African Americentric scholar and critic from memories of the sociocultural rituals and stories of my primary speech community. Particularly indelible are memories of those about the souls and ways of black folk recounted by my single mother, paternal grandfather, and kinfolk in Washington and by my aunts, uncles, cousins, and up-South extended family in Maryland. Equally strong are memories of the survival strategies of my black peers and elders in the turbulent streets of the South Bronx, where I and thousands of black southerners and Puerto Ricans migrated after World War II. Even though my wife, sons, and I have lived for many years in predominantly white communities, these memories were enriched and extended further by vital links with my wife's family in North and South Carolina, especially my sage septuagenarian cousin Tea Baby, who is more appropriately and respectfully known as Mother McClellan to other Church of God in Christ members. These links with and memories of traditional and contemporary southern black American speech communities and culture are also invigorated by my wife's tragicomic stories about her family's strategies for surviving intraracial and interracial color lines in getting an education and religion, as well as working in cotton fields and white folks' homes during her childhood in Monroe, North Carolina, before moving to Philadelphia and Washington, D.C.

As a boy, I was nurtured primarily in exclusively black storytelling sessions while participating in the vibrant culture of an up-South rural community. This culture included church revivals and camp meetings, picnics, apple orchard and corn-field raids, skinny-dipping in water holes, fruit and vegetable picking, wood-sawing and water-hauling chores, chicken and fish-fry parties, hog-slopping and hog-killing rituals, squirrel and rabbit hunting, horseshoe games, and caddying with black men from 7th and T Streets at the nearby whites-only golf club across the road from my Aunt Gretna's house in Norbeck. Later, from 169th Street and Brook Avenue to 174th and Claremont Parkway in the South Bronx, the black Baptist church, schoolyards, front stoops, rooftops, street corners, pool halls, gambling dens, barbershops, community centers, and house parties became the primary sites for sustained and substantive immersion with my predominantly black peers and elders in the African American urban oral tradition. In the predominantly white United States Marine Corps, I traveled to many countries and reconstructed my identity within and against the different cultures and languages of the peoples of Puerto Rico, Spain, France, Italy, Sicily, Turkey, Greece, Algeria, and Japan. And as a student at Howard University, working at night as a cab driver and airline chef,

I drank deeply from the reservoir of knowledge and the inspirational example of such distinguished and varied black educators and scholars as E. Franklin Frazier, Rayford Logan, Kelly Miller, Frank Snowden, William Banner, Arthur P. Davis, Chancellor Williams, Owen Dodson, John Lovell, Jose Ferrer Canales, Margaret Butcher, and Dorothy Porter, as well as Prof.

This autobiographical sketch does not mean that I intend to flip the script in this book either to demonize whiteness and matriarchy or to deify blackness and patriarchy. Nor is it intended as an immodest advertisement for myself and an intemperate sweeping indictment of the black bourgeoisie, Whitey, Oreos, neoconservative blacks, radical Afrocentrics, angry black feminists, transnational Anglocentrics, multicultural buppies, or platinum-album-selling rappers and their associates for the victimization of ostensibly powerless black folks. It certainly doesn't mean that only black folks can understand black culture or teach black literature. Rather, this autobiographical sketch seeks to offer a useful personal model of rites of passage—the three major phases of separation, transition or liminality, and incorporation that mark the acculturative and socialization processes in an individual's life—for assessing the authenticity, authority, and agency of a revisionist African Americentric critic and text. The language, knowledge, and power of my voice emanate from the storytelling lessons and scholarly legacy of my ancestors and elders as well as from the post–civil rights sensibility of many people, especially men, in the United States of sub-Saharan black African descent and bicultural national heritage. This model is an interdependent configuration of chromosomes, color, ethnicity, class, gender, geography, age, culture, sexuality, consciousness, commitment, conscience, and choice. But it assumes that an Afrocentric or African Americentric critic and text will be significantly grounded in and will manifest a viable link to, or politically activist knowledge of, the sociohistorical and sociopsychological dynamics of traditional and contemporary black American culture, language, and character. It also assumes that the critic will be as formally educated in and committed to the interdisciplinary field of African American Studies, including membership in and professional support for its major historical institutions, as he or she is or would be in any traditional discipline. In such cases, however, a modern black Afrocentric or African Americentric native-born speaker and code-switching critic would arguably manifest more authenticity, authority, and agency in interpreting ethnic commonplaces and nuances in the language of literature by, about, and primarily for African American readers than would a modern or contemporary white critic.

My rites of passage as a native-born African Americentric critic and cultural worker therefore map the roots and branches of the authenticity, authority, and agency of my identity and of the struggle of African Americans through vernacular and literary cultural production to affirm their humanity, to resist domination, and to attain their full civil rights as citizens with dignity in the United States. "Power concedes nothing without a demand," Frederick Douglass reminded a white abolitionist in an 1849 letter. "It never did, and it never will. Find out just what people will submit to, and you have found out the exact amount of injustice and wrong which will be imposed upon them; and these will continue till they are resisted with either words or blows, or with both" (qtd. in Barbour 42). In their everyday struggle for identity, status, and power to fit into or to change an unjust and unequal social system, the authors and texts under examination in this book illuminate the complexity and paradoxes of our hybrid identity formations. The authors and novels that I examine here reveal that a change in the tradition of the African American novel is under way. They also reveal how our identities are both a product of and a process in a specific time and place of a core of ethnic beliefs and values derived from the complex, dynamic relationship of our chromosomes, color, ethnicity, class, gender, geography, age, culture, sexuality, consciousness, commitment, conscience, and choice. When I was inducted into the International Literary Hall of Fame for Writers of African Descent at the Gwendolyn Brooks Center in Chicago in 2000, my soul clapped hands and sang, to borrow a phrase from William Butler Yeats and Paule Marshall, as I heard the voices of my elders and ancestors rising above the praise songs of my contemporary community of writers and cultural workers: "Boy, you've done good. You're sure enough a credit to the race. But don't ya git weary 'cause the Lord ain't through with you yet!"

Notes

1. According to the introduction to political theorist Antonio Gramsci's *Selections from the Prison Notebooks*, "organic intellectuals are distinguished less by their profession, which may be any job characteristic of their class, than by their function in directing the ideas and aspirations of the class to which they organically belong." Gramsci adds, "When one distinguishes between intellectuals and non-intellectuals, one is referring in reality only to the immediate social function of the professional category of the intellectuals, that is, one has in mind the direction in which their specific professional activity is weighed, whether towards intellectual elaboration or towards muscular-nervous effort. This means that, although one can speak of intellectuals, one cannot speak of non-intellectuals,

because non-intellectuals do not exist. [...] Each man, finally, outside his professional activity, carries on some form of intellectual activity, that is, he is a 'philosopher,' an artist, a man of taste, he participates in a particular conception of the world, has a conscious line of moral conduct, and therefore contributes to sustain a conception of the world, or to modify it, that is, to being into being new modes of thought. [...] In the modern world, technical education, closely bound to industrial labour even at the most primitive and unqualified level must form the basis of the new type of intellectual." Antonio Gramsci, *Selections from the Prison Notebooks,* trans. and ed. with an intro. by Quintin Hoare and Geoffrey Nowell-Smith (London: Lawrence, 1971) 4, 9.

2. For the anthropological meanings and significance of rites of passage, see Arnold van Gennep, *The Rites of Passage,* trans. Monika B. Vizedom and Gabrielle L. Caffee (Chicago: U of Chicago P, 1960) ch. 1; and Victor W. Turner, *The Ritual Process: Structure and Anti-Structure* (Middlesex, England: Penguin, 1974) ch. 3.

3. *Compact OED* 3614. See also Baker 2; and Barbara E. Johnson, "Response," *Afro-American Literary Study in the 1990s,* ed. Houston A. Baker Jr. and Patricia Redmond (Chicago: U of Chicago P, 1989) 42.

4. "The Blues reflects earlier developments of an African-American speech and continuing musical experience now given new forms as reflection of the post–Civil War African American culture that was no longer limited as severely to religious reference or the social restraints of slavery. [...] By the nineteenth century the diverse Africans had become African Americans and the Blues, from spiritual and work song, through hollers and shouts and arhoolies, jumped out to celebrate black entrance into a less repressive, less specialized would—less harsh, more uncertain, but still tragic and depriving in too many ways." Amiri Baraka, "The 'Blues Aesthetic' and the 'Black Aesthetic': Aesthetics as the Continuing Political History of a Culture," *Black Music Research Journal* (Fall 1991): 101–02.

5. I have adapted this term from Stephen Soitos's neologism "Euro-Americentric" in *The Blues Detective: A Study of African American Detective Fiction* (Amherst: U of Massachusetts P, 1996).

6. For an antiessentialist interpretation of the Slave Narrative Collection that highlights how biases of the national administrators, state editors, and white interviewers influenced the authenticity, authority, and agency of the interviews, see Sharon Ann Musher, "Contesting 'The Way the Almighty Wants It': Crafting Memories of Ex-Slaves in the Slave Narrative Collection," *American Quarterly* (March 2001): 1–31.

7. See, for example, Thomas Sowell, *Black Education: Myths and Tragedies* (New York: McKay, 1972); Nick Aaron Ford, *Black Studies: Threat-or-Challenge?* (Port Washington, NY: Kennikat, 1973); and Perry A. Hall, *In the Vineyard: Working in African American Studies* (Knoxville: U of Tennessee P, 1999).

8. Additional faculty included African and African American historian and social activist Playthell Benjamin; political scientist and social activist William Strickland;

political scientist, cultural critic, and activist Acklyn Lynch; SNCC activist and social critic Julius Lester; Black Panther Party and League of Revolutionary Black Workers organizer, historian, and social activist Ernest Mkalimoto; social scientist and activist Chester Davis; art historian, artist, and designer Olufemi Richards, literary historians Eugene and Esther Terry; African historian and Swahili instructor Dovi Afesi; and sculptor Ray Miles.

1

Double Consciousness as the Sign of African American Difference

I

The African American Jeremiad and Frederick Douglass's Fourth of July 1852 Speech

In 1991 I was flattered to be the only American scholar to receive an invitation from Professor Paul Goetsch, head of the Department of English, University of Freiburg, West Germany, to join his coeditor Gerd Hurm and my interdisciplinary former German colleagues with a contribution to The Fourth of July: Political Oratory and Literary Reactions, 1776–1876 *(1992), a collection on the tensions between orality and literacy associated with the Declaration of Independence. The seeds for this invitation were planted during my appointment for a year in 1974 as an exchange visiting lecturer of American and African American literature between the Departments of English at Freiburg University and the University of Massachusetts where I was an assistant professor. I initially had some reservations and considerable anxiety about whether I was doing the right thing in culturally transplanting my reluctant wife and three athletic young sons from the Happy Valley of Amherst, Massachusetts, to the Black Forest area of southern Germany. But our gracious and generous reception by new acquaintances and previous exchange professors not only quickly allayed our anxieties but also exceeded our expectations for exciting cultural adventures. My intellectual style and interdisciplinary methodology also significantly benefited from lecturing at various teaching colleges and at the University of Heidelberg, where I first interacted with several young international scholars and critics, including Werner Sollors while he was completing his habilitation on Amiri Baraka. But two experiences had the most dynamic, valuable, and memorable impact on my pedagogy and research. The first was my introduction in enlightening academic and informal exchanges with students and colleagues such as Paul Goetsch, Herbert Pilch, Kurt Müller, Karl Müller, Gunter Jarfe, Willi Erzgräber, Rita Stoephosius, Jurgen Freund, and especially Berndt Ostendorf in cafés, classrooms, lecture halls, and dinner parties. The most intriguing exchanges focused on the reader-response criticism and reception theories developed at the University of Constance by Hans Robert Jauss and Wolfgang Iser. The second were equally provocative exchanges about nineteenth- and twentieth-century American and African American folk and popular culture, especially the global impact of blues and jazz. These cultural and interdisciplinary exchanges culminated in the publication of* The Folk Roots of Contemporary Afro-American Poetry *(1974), the early drafts of chapters of* The Afro-American Novel and Its Tradition *(1987), and the essay "The African American Jeremiad and Frederick Douglass's Fourth of July 1852 Speech."*

"The legend has it," says an African American contemporary celebrant of Jubilee, "that a Negro got a mule in Washington and arrived in [each?] town on June 19th with the Emancipation Proclamation. So that July 4th is whites' Independence and June'teen [is] Negro Independence Day." Expressing his cultural dualism as an American of African descent, another celebrant states, "Well, as a patriot and a citizen I celebrate the 4th of July, but from a race standpoint I still like the 19th of June" (qtd. in Wiggins xii).[1] Many African Americans in Texas celebrate the day that they call Juneteenth because General Gordon Granger landed in Galveston, Texas, on June 19, 1865, and read a federal order freeing all the slaves in east Texas.

"For a significant number of Afro-Americans, their particular local independence observance—whose date varied from region to region—was 'the biggest day in the United States' and held more cultural significance for them than July 4th. In 1863 Frederick Douglass called January 1 'the most memorable day in American Annals' before concluding that—'The fourth of July was great but the first of January, when we consider it in all its relations and bearings is incomparably greater'" (Wiggins xi). For postbellum Americans of African descent, January 1 was racially and ethnically more significant than July 4. Whereas the latter marked the signing in 1776 of the Declaration of Independence by the legendary Founding Fathers of the nation, the former marked the promulgation in 1863 by Abraham Lincoln, the legendary Moses of black liberation, of the Emancipation Proclamation. That the primary purpose of this presidential act and document, which freed slaves in only the seceding states, was military rather than humanitarian is apparent in Lincoln's issuance on September 22, 1862, of his preliminary proclamation. This document gave the states that had seceded from the Union one hundred days to renounce their rebellious, proslavery, states' rights secession and to resume without penalty their constitutional rights and responsibilities as a nation (Quarles 14–19). Lincoln's speeches and letters even more explicitly reveal that his primary mission was saving the Union, not freeing slaves.[2] Although the ironic tensions between white and black messianic traditions are more apparent to our generation than to Lincoln's, Douglass's 1863 article illuminates some of the historical irony and paradox of the state of mind of Americans of African descent.

African American Double Consciousness

W. E. B. Du Bois, the legendary nineteenth-century black intellectual and champion of civil rights, first articulated the theory and trope of double consciousness in March 1897. "Am I an American or am I a Negro? Can I be both? Or is it my duty to cease to be a Negro as soon as possible and be an American?" Du Bois asks in "The Conservation of Races," a speech to the American Negro Academy. "Does my black blood place upon me any more obligation to assert my nationality than German, or Irish, or Italian blood would [. . .]? Have we in America a distinct mission as a race, a distinct sphere of action and an opportunity for race development, or is self-obliteration the highest end to which Negro blood dare aspire?" (Lester, *Seventh Son* 182–83). With a disdain for racial demagogues and a messianic resolve for moral reform, Du Bois combines a biological and social definition of race in this appeal to the "Talented Tenth," the exceptionally gifted and morally qualified black male and female cultural elite, to choose racial solidarity over racial assimilation in realizing "that broader humanity which freely recognizes differences in men, but sternly deprecates inequality in their opportunities of development" (Lester, *Seventh Son* 182–83). Du Bois believed that the mission of the Talented Tenth was to be the torchbearers of racial justice and social equality for black Americans, and that the mission of black Americans was to be the vanguard for social and spiritual change in the world.

Five months after addressing the American Negro Academy, Du Bois published "The Strivings of the Negro People," a more poetic description for a primarily white audience of the complex fate of being a black American, in the August 1897 issue of *Atlantic Monthly*. This essay, with a revised title and text that sharpen its personal, racial, and political tone, appears as "Of Our Spiritual Strivings" in *The Souls of Black Folk*. After describing his initiation in primary school into the world of color prejudice and discrimination, and after discovering that he was "shut out from their world by a vast veil" that engendered contempt and longing for "dazzling opportunities" beyond the veil, Du Bois provides us with his classic definition of the sociopsychological tensions in the identity formation of Negroes:

> After the Egyptian and Indian, the Greek and Roman, the Teuton and Mongolian, the Negro is a sort of seventh son, born with a veil, and gifted with second-sight in this American world—a world which yields him no true self-consciousness, but only lets him see himself through the revelation of the other world. It is a peculiar sensation this double consciousness, this sense of always looking at one's self through the eyes of others, of measuring one's soul by the tape of a world that looks on in amused contempt and pity. One ever feels his twoness—an American, a Negro; two souls, two thoughts, two unreconciled strivings; two warring ideals in one dark body, whose dogged strength alone keeps it from being torn asunder. (16–17)

In each of these discourses, the sociopsychological and sociocultural condition of African Americans was not the same fate of all ethnic immigrants and hyphenated Americans. Rather, it was the complex double vision of Americans of sub-Saharan African descent whose humanity and culture had been historically devalued and marginalized by people of European and British descent and cultures. African Americans were both people of African descent and nonpeople to the majority of white people; they were part of the society yet alienated from it; they were among the first settlers to build the nation, but they are among the last to have their full first-class citizenship guaranteed by the nation. African Americans were therefore destined to function on two levels of reality, and their attitudes toward national assimilation and racial solidarity or separatism were largely determined by the degree of alienation from or faith in the principles and practices of the ruling class of white Anglo-Saxon Protestants.

According to Du Bois, then, double consciousness was a product of institutionalized racism and a dialectic process in American society between the bearers, on one hand, of residually oral sub-Saharan African cultures and, on the other, of industrialized Western print cultures. For many contemporary African Americans, the compelling tension of this biracial, bicultural state of mind is the striving to reconcile one's ancestral African past—however remote, mythic, or spiritual—with one's American present, one's ascribed status and identity with one's achieved status and identity. (Double consciousness thus signifies the biracial, bicultural way of seeing and being in the world with others, especially other Americans of African descent.) It is the dominant ontological and epistemological process of African and North American cultural syncretism whose dynamic resilience and resourcefulness was forged primarily in the social crucible of slavery and institutionalized racism. It is most frequently expressed in the irony, paradoxes, and parody of African American folk and formal art. This sociocultural and sociopsychological dualism is eloquently dramatized in Frederick Douglass's speech in Rochester, New York, on July 5, 1852, an outstanding example of the African American jeremiad.

The Sacred and Secular Origins of the American Jeremiad

Cultural historians in the United States have revealed that the messianic rhetoric of the American and African American jeremiad has its origins in the Judeo-Christian tradition, King James Bible, and Puritanism of New England. Perry Miller, Henry Nash Smith, R. W. B. Lewis, Sacvan Bercovitch, Ernest Tuveson, David Noble, Wilson J. Moses, and David Howard-Pitney trace the providential interpretation of American history and America's self-righteous mission of saving the world and establishing the kingdom of God on earth to sacred and secular myths of origin.[3] Derived from the Hebrew *mashiah,* which means anointed, the Messiah, according to the *Oxford English Dictionary,* is "the Hebrew title [. . .] applied in the O.T. prophetic writings to a promised deliverer of the Jewish nation, and hence applied to Jesus of Nazareth as the fulfillment of that promise [. . .] an expected liberator or savior of an oppressed people or country" (*Compact OED* 375). In *Black Messiahs and Uncle Toms,* Wilson Jeremiah Moses, a distinguished black historian, concisely summarizes the Judeo-Christian tradition of messianism:

> The belief in a messiah grew out of the Hebrews' experience of oppression at the hands of the great Middle-Eastern empires. It symbolized their hopes for an improvement in the fortunes of their nation and the restoration of their ancient ideals. The messiah would usher in a messianic

age. The chosen people would revolt against their political oppressors and revitalize the conservative values advocated by the prophets.

Messianic ideas were adapted by early Christians, who saw Jesus of Nazareth as the long-awaited messiah (*Christos* in Greek means anointed one). After the death of Jesus, the early Christians began to await his second coming, at which time he would inaugurate a messianic era of a thousand years' duration. This belief came to be known as millenarianism or chiliasm, from the Latin *millenarias* and the Greek *chilios* (a thousand). [...] A messianic people are a chosen or anointed people who will lead the rest of the world in the direction of righteousness. The messianic people traditionally see themselves as a conscience for the rest of the human race—sometimes as a suffering servant or a sacrificial lamb, sometimes as an avenging angel. (4–5)

The term *jeremiad* means a "lamentation; a writing or speech in a strain of grief or distress; a doleful complaint; a complaining tirade" (*Compact OED* 1505). It is derived from the Old Testament prophet Jeremiah, who predicted between the sixth and seventh centuries BC the destruction of Jerusalem by the Babylonians as divine punishment for the violations by Israelites of the Mosaic covenant. Jeremiah also prophesied the future redemption and restoration of Israel after its atonement.

Perry Miller's *The New England Mind: The Seventeenth Century* reveals the Puritan roots of Americans' secular myth of themselves as a chosen people whose exodus from corruption and bondage in the Catholic Old World of Europe to a spiritual rebirth in the promised land of the Protestant New World in America. In *The American Jeremiad* Sacvan Bercovitch identifies the American jeremiad as the crucial rhetorical ritual that has characterized the major writings of Anglo-American culture since the Puritan era. According to Bercovitch,

> this rhetorical ritual began with the promise. The exodus of the Puritans as a New Israel was leading toward the millennium. The second element of the jeremiad, however, was the assertion of declension. Although the Puritans as a Chosen People had crossed the frontier threshold from the medieval past in which history had no meaning, they, as individuals and as a group, had not fully accepted their responsibility to make history a progressive path toward the future kingdom. They were slothful. They were distracted and pursued false and evil values. And they received divine punishments for their failures to act as a Chosen People. This pro-

> gressive jeremiad [. . .] established great tension in the community of saints as the distance between the perfection of the promise and the imperfection of daily activity was examined and deplored. The preachers of the jeremiad concluded their criticism with the third and final part of the jeremiad: a prophecy that the Chosen People would accept their responsibility, reject their sinful life-styles which looked too similar to those of the corrupt medieval past, and construct the environment for the kingdom in the immediate future. (Qtd. in Noble 5)

Spreading from the New England Puritans to all colonial Protestants in the eighteenth century, the Puritan jeremiad became political and American by 1776. "The promise was a virtuous republic," writes David W. Noble. "The Revolution was the exodus from the Egyptian bondage of monarchy. And the new citizen saints found themselves living in a state of declension, the gap between the ideal republic and their imperfect political experience. But political prophets pointed out their failings, explained their sufferings as punishment for those failures, and pointed toward the fulfillment of the promise in the future" (6).

More important for black Americans, Moses underscores the evolution of two varieties of American messianism: hard-line and soft-line. The former "eventually developed into the doctrine of white racial supremacy, ruthless expansionism, religious intolerance, and economic insensitivity," and the latter grew "out of the unrealized ideals of the Jeffersonian tradition and the American enlightenment, which came to emphasize America's mission to preserve the inalienable rights of man." According to soft-line messianism, "the American mission was not to dominate the rest of the world, forcing it into the paths of righteousness, but to serve as an example of the spiritual perfection that human nature could aspire to in an atmosphere of political freedom" (*Black Messiahs* 8).

The most ironic illustration of the problematics and fusion of these two varieties of messianism is Thomas Jefferson's expression of the American jeremiad in *Notes on the State of Virginia*:

> And can the liberties of a nation be thought secure when we have removed their only firm basis, a conviction in the minds of the people that these liberties are the gift of God? That they are not to be violated but with his wrath? Indeed I tremble for my country when I reflect that God is just; that his justice cannot sleep forever; that considering numbers, nature and natural means only, a revolution of the wheel of fortune, an

exchange of situation is among possible events; that it may become probable by supernatural interference! The Almighty has no attribute which can take side with us in such a contest. (Qtd. in Moses, *Black Messiahs* 31–32)

Although Jefferson felt guilty and fearful about the American national sin of slavery, *Notes* also reveals his belief in white supremacy. Such racist ironic analogies by a father of children with a young slave girl as well as by a Founding Father of the nation as blacks prefer white mates "as uniformly as in the preference of the Oranootan [sic] for the black woman over those of his own species" (qtd. in Moses, *Black Messiahs* 40) provoked classic black jeremiads by Othello, Banneker, and Walker.

The African American Jeremiad

In *Black Messiahs and Uncle Toms* Moses defines the African American jeremiad as "mainly a pre–Civil war," ingenious adaptation of messianic traditions in the form of "constant warnings issued by blacks to whites, concerning the judgment that was to come for the sin of slavery" (30–31). Diverse scholars in various social science and humanist disciplines from W. E. B. Du Bois, Melville J. Herskovits, and E. Franklin Frazier to Lawrence Levine, Albert J. Raboteau, and Orlando Patterson persuasively argue that evidence of the retention of African religious traits by black people is stronger for the Caribbean than for the United States.[4] "The religion of black slaves in the United States," as historian Moses notes, "was similar to both that of West Africans and that of Europeans. These similarities may be attributed to African retentions, syncretic tendencies, and spontaneous parallel evolution" (28). A dramatic, historical example of the sociocultural, sociopsychological dualism of black Americans is the connection between revolutionary black nationalism and African religious survivals. This is apparent, on one hand, in the role of conjuring by Gullah Jack, a leader in the 1822 slave revolt of Denmark Vesey, and, on the other hand, in the messianic avenging angel mission that Nat Turner assumed in his 1831 revolt.

Some scholars believe that the African American jeremiadic tradition begins in 1788 with "Essay on Negro Slavery" by a free black from Maryland who used the pen name "Othello." Adapting the American jeremiad and warning of God's wrathful judgment for the American national sin of slavery, he wrote, "Beware Americans! Pause—and consider the difference between the mild effulgence of approving Providence and the angry countenance of incensed divinity" (qtd. in Moses, *Black Messiahs* 33). Benjamin Banneker's letter in 1791, Richard Allen and Absalom Jones's "Address to Those Who Keep Slaves, and Approve the Practice" in 1794, Prince Hall's speech "Charge Delivered to the African Lodge at Menotomy" in 1797, and especially David Walker's "Walker's Appeal in Four Articles Together with a Preamble to the Colored Citizens of the World but in Particular and Very Expressly to Those of the United States of America" in 1829 are African American jeremiadic responses to the racial injustices and social inequality expressed in Jefferson's *Notes on the State of Virginia*.

A North Carolina free black who moved to Boston and owned a secondhand clothing store, Walker begins his jeremiad with an allusion to the transgressions of natural and divine laws by Jefferson and the miscegenation laws that "held us up as descending originally from the tribes of Monkeys or Orang-Outangs." Because of their hypocrisy, oppression, and sin, Walker prophesies, "Americans, unless you speedily alter your course, you and your *Country are gone!!!!!!* [. . .] I call God—I call angels—I call men, to witness that your DESTRUCTION *is at hand*, and will be speedily consummated unless you REPENT" (qtd. in Moses, *Black Messiahs* 33). Walker closes his essay with the jeremiadic hope that Americans will repent and restore the covenant. "And wo, wo, to you if we have to obtain our freedom by fighting. Throw away your fears and prejudices then, and enlighten us and treat us like men, and we will like you more than we now hate you. Treat us like men [. . .] and we yet, under God, will become a united and happy people" (qtd. in Moses, *Black Messiahs* 46). Antebellum black abolitionists continued the theme and motifs of the jeremiadic tradition.

That Most Foul and Fiendish of All Human Decrees

"By that most foul and fiendish of all human decrees," Douglass thunders in his July 5, 1852, jeremiad, "the liberty and person of every man are put in peril. [. . .] In glaring violation of justice, in shameless disregard of the forms of administering law, in cunning arrangement to entrap the defenseless, and in diabolical intent this Fugitive Slave Law stands alone in the annals of tyrannical legislation. I doubt if there be another nation on the globe having the brass and the baseness to put such a law on the statute book" (375). For Northern abolitionists like Horace Mann, Charles Sumner, and Gerrit Smith as well as blacks, fugitive and free, the Fugitive Slave Law provisions of the Compromise of 1850, the most extreme political effort to avoid Southern secession over the protection and expansion of slavery, were the most shockingly flagrant violation of constitutional and Christian principles. For Southerners and proslavery advocates, it was the culmination of their struggle for the rigorous enforcement of their property rights as guaranteed by the Fugitive Slave Act of 1793 and article 4, section 2, clause 3 of the Constitution: "No person held to service or labor in one State, under the laws thereof, escaping into another, shall be delivered up on claim of the party, to whom such service or labor may be due."

Some arguments for the unconstitutionality of the Fugitive Slave Act are "(1) that the Congress had no power to enact laws to guarantee the compact between the states on reclaiming fugitive slaves, (2) that suspects were denied the right of trial by jury, (3) that suspects were denied the right to confront and cross examine witnesses, and (4) that commissioners were not salaried but paid fees which were doubled for cases decided in favor of slave catchers" (Campbell 27–28). Also bitterly denounced were the provisions compelling all citizens to assist in capturing suspects, imposing fines and imprisonment for concealing or rescuing fugitives. The intensive, ruthless manhunts by slave catchers struck fear in the souls of blacks of being kidnapped. They also provoked the defiance of the law by militant abolitionists, including the rescues of Shadrack in Boston and Jerry McHenry in Syracuse. Defiance was similarly manifested in the personal liberty laws of some Northern states that prohibited the use of local jails for confining suspects. The Fugitive Slave Act thus heightened the sectional crisis of the 1850s, the emigration mood of blacks, especially to Canada, and the jeremiads by abolitionists at public meetings and in editorial comments.

What to the Slave Is the Fourth of July?

Having accepted the invitation of the Rochester Ladies' Anti-Slavery Society to give a Fourth of July address on July 5, 1852, Douglass spoke to a gathering of between five hundred and six hundred people in Corinthian Hall in Rochester, New York. The motifs and leitmotifs, structure and style, of this speech are eloquent illustrations of the purpose and passion of the African American jeremiad. According to literary critic William L. Andrews, "the temptation to indulge in the excesses of the American jeremiad had become particularly strong for American Independence Day orators. Social and political discord prompted orators from Maine to South Carolina to lament current trends and call the nation back to the sacred text of the Constitution and the ideal of controlled progress that it sanctioned as the only means of achieving America's predestined political millennium" (167). In adapting the American jeremiad, Douglass improvises on the triadic structure of promise, declension, and prophesied restoration.

Douglass opens with an apologia whose ironic tone, diction, and syntax are more in the tradition of the slave narrative than of the exordium of classic oratory. Disarming his probably white audience, who paid 12½ cents to hear him, by addressing them as "Friends and Fellow Citizens," he proceeds to catalog his ostensible limitations as a speaker on such a "large, and out of the common way" theme for him. His apologies for the "quailing sensation," "distrust of my ability," and "limited powers of speech" culminate with the understatement, "The little experience I have had in addressing public meetings, in country school houses, avails me nothing on the present occasion." Confessing that he has "often had the privilege to speak in this beautiful Hall, and to address many who now honor me with their presence," he still suffers "embarrassment" because of "the distance between this platform and the slave plantation, from which I escaped." With mock humility and initial balanced prepositional phrases, he professes that "with little experience and with less learning, I have been able to throw my thoughts hastily and imperfectly together" (360). By this use of repetition, irony, and parody, Douglass expresses his double consciousness. He was not only a free black American in the North and former fugitive slave in 1838 from the South whose legal freedom was bought in 1846 by two British female abolitionists but also an internationally celebrated orator, abolitionist, and writer as well as, according to the Fugitive Slave Act of 1850, a commodity threatened with summary enslavement by unscrupulous slave catchers. In this manner Douglass problematizes time, space, race, class, and gender, dramatizing the paradox of being both a part of and apart from his white friends and fellow citizens.

In outlining the facts concerning the promise of America's birth, Douglass, assuming the voice of a black Jeremiah, continues the ironic tension between himself and his audience as he draws biblical analogies between "your National Independence," "your political freedom," and "what the Passover was to the emancipated people of God." The "great deliverance" of "the American Colonies" from the "tyranny of England" is compared to that of the Israelites from bondage in Egypt. Wryly improvising on the youth, promise, and hope of "the Republic of America," Douglass plays with lexical and syntactic variations of 1776 and his age, seventy-six. "Seventy-six years, though a good old age for a man, is but a mere speck in the life of a nation. Three score years and ten is the allotted time for individual men; but nations number their years by thousands" (360). Were it not for the nation's youth, the black Jeremiah tells his audience, "its future might be shrouded in sorrow." He also employs the unadorned diction of parental authority to construct a multivalent conceit of a tyrannical British Pharaoh:

> Your fathers esteemed the English Government as the home government; and England as the fatherland. This home government [. . .] although a considerable distance from your home, did, in the exercise of its parental prerogatives, impose upon its colonial children, such restraints, burdens and limitations, as, in its mature Judgement, it deemed wise, right and proper. But, your fathers [. . .] presumed to differ from the home government in respect to the wisdom and the justice of some of those burdens and restraints. (361)

After reviewing the facts of the birth of the nation, warning that "from the round top of your ship of state, dark and threatening clouds may be seen," Douglass leaves "the great deeds of your fathers to other gentlemen" and turns his attention to the present. "The accepted time with God and His cause," the black Jeremiah declares, "is the ever-living now. [. . .] We have to do with the past only as we can make it useful to the present and to the future" (364, 366).

Like "the children of Jacob," who invoke the name of Abraham and his covenant with God "when they had long lost Abraham's faith and spirit," the children of the Republic of America invoke the name of Washington, Douglass declares in the declension section of his jeremiad. "Yet his monument is built up by the price of human blood, and the traders in the bodies and souls of men shout—'We have Washington to our father'" (367). With mock innocence, punctuated throughout the speech by his ironic direct address to the audience as "fellow-citizens," the black Jeremiah asks a series of questions that rhythmically blends political and religious imagery:

> What have I, or those I represent, to do with your national independence? Are the great principles of political freedom and of natural justice, embodied in that Declaration of Independence, extended to us? and am I, therefore, called upon to bring our humble offering to the national altar, and to confess the benefits and express devout gratitude for the blessings resulting from your independence to us? Would to God, both for your sakes and ours, that an affirmative answer could be truthfully returned to these questions. (367)

Such is not the case, however; he answers sadly: "I am not included within the pale of this glorious anniversary! Your high independence only reveals the immeasurable distance between us. The blessings in which you, this day, rejoice, are not enjoyed in common. The rich inheritance of justice, liberty, prosperity and independence, bequeathed by your fathers, is shared by you, not by me" (368).

Hyperbolically indicting his white audience for the "inhuman mockery and sacrilegious irony" of asking him to speak on the Fourth of July, Douglass takes up "the plaintive lament of a peeled and woe-smitten people." Quoting Psalm 137:1–6, which includes the poignant line, "How can we sing the Lord's song in a strange land?" our black Jeremiah warns America of the danger of following "the example of a nation whose crimes [. . .] were thrown down by the breath of the Almighty, burying that nation in irrevocable ruin!" (368).

Douglass then delivers a "blasting reproach [. . .] and stern rebuke" to his fellow citizens:

> Standing, there, identified with the American bondsman, making his wrongs mine, I do not hesitate to declare, with all my soul, that the character and conduct of this nation never looked blacker to me than on this 4th of July! Whether we turn to the declarations of the past or to the professions of the present, the conduct of the nation seems equally hideous and revolting. America is false to the past, false to the present, and solemnly binds herself to be false to the future. Standing with God and the crushed and bleeding slave on this occasion, I will, in the name of humanity which is outraged, in the name of liberty which is fettered, in the name of the constitution and the Bible, which are disregarded and trampled upon, dare to call in question and to denounce, with all the emphasis I can command, every-thing that serves to perpetuate slavery—the great sin and shame of America! (368–69)

Repetition with a difference, especially the balanced pairing of similar ideas in forms, heightens the passion and power of this jeremiadic indictment of white fellow citizens for not keeping faith with the sacred promise and secular mission of America. With "scorching irony" and the compelling repetition of "your" at the beginning of more than six successive clauses that stress American "bombast, fraud, deception, impiety, and hypocrisy," Douglass then answers the question, "What, to the American slave, is your 4th of July?"

Focusing on his personal experience as a slave in Baltimore, Douglass next ranges from personal invective to biblical prophecy and Garrisonian rhetorical resolve in his indictment of "flesh-mongers," "inhuman, disgraceful, and scandalous [...] lawmakers," and "DOCTORS OF DIVINITY" for their silent or eloquent support of the slave trade in general and the Fugitive Slave Act of 1850 in particular (372–75). "The Bible addresses all such persons," he warns by invoking Matthew 23:23, "as 'scribes, pharisees, hypocrites, who pay tithe of *mint, anise* and *cummin*, and have omitted the weightier matters of the law, Judgment, mercy and faith'" (376–77). Condemning the "popular church, and the popular worship of our land and nation" as "an abomination in the sight of God," Douglass also invokes Isaiah 1:13–17: "Yea! when ye make many prayers, I will not hear. YOUR HANDS ARE FULL OF BLOOD; cease to do evil, learn to do well; seek Judgement; relieve the oppressed; judge for the fatherless; plead for the widow" (378). Unlike the American church, the English church "true to its mission of ameliorating, elevating and improving the condition of mankind, came forward promptly, bound up the wounds of the West Indian slave, and restored him to his liberty" (381).

Reviewing in his peroration the flagrant contradictions between American principles and practices, Douglass recites a litany of parallel, antithetical propositions in complex and compound-complex sentences. Shifting the directives from "Fellow-citizens" to "Americans" and repeating the third-person pronominal "you" in initial and "your" in intermediary positions in each sentence, he closes this litany with the simple yet profound ironic restatement of the nation's unfulfilled promise and mission by Jefferson himself:

> You declare that you "hold these truths to be self-evident that all men are created equal; and are endowed by their Creator with certain inalienable rights; and that among these are, life, liberty, and the pursuit of happiness"; and yet, you hold securely, in a bondage which, according to your own Thomas Jefferson, "is worse than ages of that which your fathers rose in rebellion to oppose," a seventh part of the inhabitants of your country.

This, in turn, is followed by more than a dozen simple sentences, emphatically beginning and ending with the indefinite pronoun "it," that catalog and magnify the apocalyptic consequences of slavery: "It is a curse to the earth that supports it" (383).

Before identifying the path to redemption and restoration of the promise of America as a beacon of liberty and democracy to the world, Douglass intones a final jeremiad that imagistically reinforces the perversion of natural and moral law: "Oh! be warned! be warned! a horrible reptile is coiled up in your nation's bosom; the venomous creature is nursing at the tender breast of your youthful republic; *for the love of God, tear away,* and fling from you the hideous monster, and *let the weight of twenty millions crush and destroy it forever!*" (383–84). The length, structure, and tone of the prophecy of restoration that concludes Douglass's jeremiad of July 5, 1852, reveal the depth of his faith in the promise of America. Only about five pages long, it begins with a strong affirmation of the Constitution of the United States as a "GLORIOUS LIBERTY DOCUMENT." Although this faith in the Constitution led to a bitter break in the late 1840s with the paternalism of William Lloyd Garrison, the radical abolitionist who inspired Douglass to become a lecturer for the Massachusetts Anti-Slavery Society in 1841 and who believed that the Constitution was a slave document, Douglass's final words of hope quote Garrison's "The Triumph of Freedom."

But Douglass's hope is not based solely on the belief "that every American citizen has a right to form an opinion of the constitution, and to propagate that opinion, and to use all honorable means to make his opinion the prevailing one" (385). His conviction that "the doom of slavery is certain" also draws "encouragement from the Declaration of Independence, the great principles it contains [. . .] the genius of American Institutions" and "the obvious tendencies of the age" (386–87). The major tendency is that

> no nation can now shut itself up from the surrounding world, and trot round in the same old path of its fathers without interference. [. . .] The far off and almost fabulous Pacific rolls in grandeur at our feet. The Celestial Empire, the mystery of ages, is being solved. The fiat of the Almighty, "*Let there be light,*" has not yet spent its force. No abuse, no outrage whether in taste, sport or avarice, can now hide itself from the all-pervading light. [. . .] *Africa must rise and put on her yet unwoven garment.* "*Ethiopia shall stretch out her hand unto God.*" (387)

This invocation of Psalms 68:31—"Princes shall come out of Egypt; Ethiopia shall soon stretch out her hands unto God"—has been interpreted as prophesying that not only will Christianity spread to Africa and Africans but also that Africans will become the chosen people. The juxtaposition of this prophecy with the concluding invocation of Garrison's "God speed the year of jubilee. [. . .] That year will come, and freedom's reign, / To man his plundered rights again / Restore"

(387) is dramatic, decisive evidence of Douglass's mixed heritage and the double consciousness of the African American jeremiadic tradition (Moses, "Poetics of Ethiopianism" 411–26).

Notes

1. Bracketed inserts in quotations are Wiggins's. This is the standard study on African American celebrations of their emancipation from slavery. For a concise identification of the different states and dates as well as the divergent reasons for emancipation celebrations, see Wiggins xix–xx.

2. See, for example, Letter from Abraham Lincoln to Horace Greenly, August 22, 1862, *Collected Works of Abraham Lincoln,* ed. Roy P. Basler, vol. 5 (New Brunswick: Rutgers UP, 1953) 388–89.

3. See Perry Miller, *The New England Mind: The Seventeenth Century* (New York: Macmillan, 1939); Henry Nash Smith, *Virgin Land: The American West as Symbol and Myth* (Cambridge, MA: Vintage, 1950); R. W. B. Lewis, *The American Adam: Innocence, Tragedy, and Tradition in the Nineteenth Century* (Chicago: U of Chicago P, 1955); Sacvan Bercovitch, *The American Jeremiad* (Madison: U of Wisconsin P, 1978); Ernest L. Tuveson, *Redeemer Nation: The Idea of America's Millennial Role* (Chicago: U of Chicago P, 1968); David W. Noble, *The End of American History: Democracy, Capitalism, and the Metaphor of Two Worlds in Anglo-American Historical Writing, 1880–1890* (Minneapolis: U of Minnesota P, 1985); Moses, *Black Messiahs*; and David Howard-Pitney, *The Afro-American Jeremiad: Appeals for Justice in America* (Philadelphia: Temple UP, 1990). I am indebted to Moses, *Black Messiahs* for much of the following discussion of this tradition.

4. See W. E. B. Du Bois, *The Negro Church* (Atlanta, GA: Atlanta UP, 1903); Melville J. Herskovits, *The Myth of the Negro Past* (Boston: Beacon, 1958); E. Franklin Frazier, *The Negro Church in America* (New York: Schocken, 1964); Levine, *Black Culture*; Albert J. Raboteau, *Slave Religion* (New York: Oxford UP, 1978); and Orlando Patterson, *The Sociology of Slavery* (Rutherford, NJ: Fairleigh, 1969).

II

Genealogical Shifts in Du Bois's Discourse on Double Consciousness as the Sign of African American Difference

Because I began adapting W. E. B. Du Bois's theory and trope of double consciousness in the 1970s as one of the cornerstones of my own indigenous African American cultural and critical theories of literature, I begin this collection with "Genealogical Shifts in Du Bois's Discourse on Double Consciousness as the Sign of African American Difference." This essay had its origins in four scholarly events. The first were my scholarly challenges as a visiting lecturer in 1974–75 at the University of Freiburg and as an author in 1974 who traced the circumstantial influence on W. E. B. Du Bois of elements of Johann Gottfried von Herder's folk philosophy in The Folk Roots of Contemporary Afro-American Poetry, *a seminal publication in Dudley Randall's Broadside Critics Series. The second was an invitation in 1984 from the distinguished scholar and critic of African American literature William L. Andrews to contribute one of the three original essays among more than a dozen reprinted reviews and essays to his* Critical Essays of W. E. B. Du Bois *(1985). In my essay "W. E. B. Du Bois's Struggle to Reconcile Folk and High Art," I used newly acquired unpublished manuscripts in the Du Bois Papers in the University of Massachusetts Archives. The third was the reconstruction in my prize-winning 1987 critical study* The Afro-American Novel and Its Tradition *of Du Bois's famous theory and trope as the sociohistorical and sociopsychological root of the biracial and bicultural identities of African Americans, not a psychotic or schizophrenic way of being in the world with others. And the fourth scholarly inspiration for "Genealogical Shifts" was an invitation from my colleagues Emily Grosholz and James Stewart to present a lecture and coedit the publication of the lectures presented at the conference "The Thought of W. E. B. Du Bois" that they organized at Penn State University in March 1992. My lecture, "Looking Through a Glass Darkly: The Philosophical Legacy of Du Boisian Double Consciousness," was revised and expanded into "Genealogical Shifts," which first appeared in 1996 in* W. E. B. Du Bois on Race and Culture: Philosophy, Politics, and Poetics, *a multivocal collection of thirteen responses by distinguished scholars in different disciplines to the philosophy, politics, and rhetoric of Du Bois's examination of the concept of race.*

HOW VALID AND VIABLE TODAY IS W. E. B. DU BOIS'S NINETEENTH-CENTURY discourse on double consciousness as the sign of African American racial and cultural difference? Had Du Bois "considered the issue of gender," states black historian Darlene Clark Hines, "instead of writing, 'One ever feels his twoness,' he would have mused about how one ever feels her 'fiveness': Negro, American, woman, poor, black woman" (338). Prominent white feminists such as Catherine MacKinnon and black feminists such as bell hooks contend that patriarchy is the central problem in the social construction of contemporary human identities. Clearly, inquiries into processes of subject construction and the politics of differences, as critic Joan W. Scott reminds us, should examine "the relationships between discourse, cognition, and reality, the relevance of the position of situatedness of subjects to the knowledge they produce and the effects of difference on knowledge" (28). Although race, ethnicity, gender, and class are interrelated major forces in the construction of human subjects, history has vindicated Du Bois's prediction that the problem of the twentieth century is the problem of the color line. Contemporary global ethnic conflicts also suggest that the correlative problem of biculturalism will be central to identity formations in the twenty-first century.

Although sensitive in different degrees to the historical representation of the black subject as male, Ralph Ellison, Larry Neal, Robert Stepto, Berndt Ostendorf, Henry Louis Gates Jr., Mary Helen Washington, Barbara Johnson, and this author are but a few of the many artists, scholars, and critics who have reformulated the rhetoric, dialectics, and dialogics of Du Bois's biracial and bicultural trope to map the quest in contemporary literary criticism for a truth that acknowledges and synthesizes the souls and art of black folk.[1] As an African American revisionist theorist of the relationship between vernacular and literary traditions, I will not, however, in this essay focus exclusively on Du Bois's contemporary impact on cultural studies, critics, and workers. Rather, I will first trace the historical origins and discursive shifts in Du Bois's ideological construction of double consciousness as the sign of African American racial and ethnic difference. Secondly I will analyze its dialectic and dialogic use as a theme and trope in two of his earliest narratives in which the protagonists are represented as "epitomized expressions" of African Americans: the unpublished "A Fellow of Harvard" and the published "Of the Coming of John."

Since Aristotle's *Rhetoric*, Plato's *Phaedrus* and *Gorgias* and, more recently, Bakhtin's *The Dialogic Imagination*, the distinction among rhetorical, dialectical, and dialogical discourse has been a topic of contention among their different advocates. In "Dialogics as an Art of Discourse in Literary Criticism," Don Bialostosky provides the most lucid and cogent explanation of these distinctions, which I have found useful for my examination of Du Bois's discourse on the unique psychological dualism of African Americans. In Bialostosky's account,

> dialectic concerns impersonal relations among terms that are independent of those who hold them—relations of confirmation and contradiction, antithesis and synthesis, and the like. Rhetoric concerns relations of practical agreement and disagreement among persons—relations that may be effected, despite ideological differences in the formation of consensuses among divergent interests and parties. Dialogics concerns the relations among persons articulating their ideas in response to one another, discovering their mutual affinities and oppositions, their provocations to reply, their desires to hear more, or their wishes to change the subject. [. . .] dialectic aims at discovering the truth of ideas or theses, rhetoric at determining the decisions of people, and dialogics at articulating the meaning of people's ideas, our own and those of others. As dialectic strives for conviction on a question and rhetoric for persuasion of an audience, dialogics strives for comprehensive responsiveness and responsibility to the consequential person—ideas of a time, culture, community, or discipline—that is, for the fullest articulation of someone's ideas with the actual and possible ideas of others. (789)

For our examination of the shifts in Du Bois's discourse, the most important distinction here is between dialectics and dialogics. Although both are interpretive strategies that involve oppositional forces, the former signifies the dynamics of an historical process of inquiry for a truth that synthesizes partial views and the latter the dynamics of a rhetorical process that acknowledges and articulates different voices.

Etymologically, according to the *Oxford English Dictionary*, consciousness is derived from the Latin *conscius*, which denotes "knowing something with others, knowing in oneself." Its linguistic origin thus suggests an epistemological relationship among language, knowledge, and power. Its first literary attestation in English as internal knowledge or conviction occurred in 1632. As an ontological concept inscribed in British philosophical discourse of 1678 with the suffix "-ness," it signified "the state or faculty of being and volition" (*Compact OED* 522).

In "W. E. B. Du Bois and the Idea of Double Consciousness," historian Dickson D. Bruce Jr. perceptively identifies the two main sources that probably influenced Du Bois's use of the term. The first was the product of European romanticism and American transcendentalism, and the second was a product of the emerging field of psychology (229–309). In 1843, for example, Ralph Waldo Emerson used the term "double consciousness" in "The Transcendentalist" to explain the dialectic tension between the self and the world, the soul and nature. "The double consciousness plaguing the Transcendentalist," Bruce writes, "summarized the downward pull of life in society—including the social forces inhibiting genuine self-realization—and the upward pull of communion with the Divine; the apparent chaos of things-as-they-are and the unity of Nature comprehended by universal law; and the demanding, cold rationality of commercial society and the search for Truth, Beauty and Goodness—especially Beauty—that ennobled the soul" (300–01). Although it is also probable, as critics contend, that both Emerson and Du Bois were familiar with the reference in Goethe's *Faust* to "Two souls, alas! Reside within my breast," Du Bois's use of the allusion is distinctively African American, as black historian Wilson J. Moses reveals in "The Poetics of Ethiopianism."[2]

The *OED* identifies the rise of double consciousness as a diagnostic term in psychological discourse in 1882 as "a condition which has been described as a double personality, showing in some measure two separate and independent trains of thought and two independent mental capabilities in the same individual." But the term actually appeared as early as 1817 in a psychological case study of Mary Reynolds titled "A Double Consciousness, or a Duality of Person in the Same Individual" (Mitchell 185–86; Plumerm 807–12). In 1890, as black literary biographer and critic Arnold Rampersad noted, William James, who possibly introduced the concept to Du Bois at Harvard, explored the idea in *The Principles of Psychology*; and in the English translation of the 1893 German text of psychologist Oswald Kulpe the term is defined as a "general derangement of memory" that "is characterized by the existence of a more or less complete separation of two aggregates of conscious processes, which alternate at certain intervals or can be called up in irregular sequence by favourable conditions. The two aggregates are oftentimes of entirely opposite character."[3] As an idea and a term, double consciousness is therefore derived from philosophical discourses on European romanticism and American transcendentalism as well as from medical and psychological discourses on personality disorders that Du Bois probably encountered and from which he arguably appropriated the phrase as a student at Harvard between 1888 and 1890 or the University of Berlin between 1892 and 1894.

Why and how, then, is double consciousness the sign of the distinctiveness of African American culture and character and not merely of the potential for disorder and pathology, as in the dominant European and American discourses, of particular individuals? In "The Conservation of Races," a speech he presented in March 1897 as a founding member of the American Negro Academy, a newly formed organization of black male intellectuals and activists, Du Bois first articulated his African American transformation of psychological dualism in his theory of racial and national identity:

> Here, then, is the dilemma, and it is a puzzling one, I admit. No Negro who has given earnest thought to the situation of his people in America has failed at some time in life, to find himself at these cross-roads; has failed to ask himself at some time in life: what, after all, am I? Am I an American or am I a Negro? Can I be both? Or is it my duty to cease to be a Negro as soon as possible and be an American? If I strive as a Negro, am I not perpetuating the very cleft that threatens and separates black and white America? Is not my only possible practical aim the subduction of all that is Negro in me to the American? Does my black blood place upon me any more obligation to assert my nationality than German, or Irish, or Italian blood would? It is such an incessant self-questioning and the hesitation that arises from it, that is making the present period a time of vacillation and contradiction for the American Negro; combined race action is stifled, race responsibility is shirked, race enterprises languish, and the best talent, the best energy of the Negro people cannot be marshaled to do the bidding of the race. [. . .] Have we in America a distinct mission as a race, a distinct sphere of action and an opportunity for race development, or is self-obliteration the highest end to which Negro blood dare aspire? (182)

Here the dual state of mind is implicitly ascribed to Negroes who have given earnest thought to their racial, national, and, a more modern cultural construction, ethnic identity as a people in America.

With a disdain for racial demagogues and a resolve for moral uplift, Du Bois rhetorically combines a biological, patriarchal, and social definition of race in this appeal to the "Talented Tenth," the exceptionally gifted and morally qualified male and female black cultural elite, to choose racial solidarity over racial assimilation in realizing "that broader humanity which freely recognizes differences in men, but sternly deprecates inequality in their opportunities of development" ("Conservation of Races" 183). But the tension between rhetorical and dialectical discourses is apparent in this speech, because, as black philosopher Lucius Outlaw persuasively argues in *W. E. B Du Bois on Race and Culture,* Du Bois's "The Conservation of Races" is "a decidedly *political* project [. . .] which is very much concerned with altering the negative valorizations of the Negro race" (28).

It is apparent by his references to blood in this speech a year after the *Plessy v. Ferguson* Supreme Court decision and two years after Booker T. Washington's Atlanta Cotton Exposition speech, both supporting separate but equal racial policies, that with this audience of black intellectuals Du Bois stresses biological as well as spiritual and cultural factors in explaining "the riddle" of the racial distinctiveness of African Americans. "We are Americans, not only in birth and by citizenship, but by our political ideals, our language, our religion. Farther than that our Americanism does not go," he states. "At that point we are Negroes, members of a vast historic race that from the very dawn of creation has slept, but awakens in the dark forests of its African fatherland" ("Conservation of Races" 182–83). In other words, despite the survival of Africanisms in late nineteenth-century America, especially in the Deep South through the anthropological process of syncretism, most Americans of African descent were born in the United States, spoke African American Vernacular English (AAVE), a nonstandard dialect of Standard American English, subscribed to the democratic ideal, and believed that God endowed all people with inalienable rights to life, liberty, and the pursuit of happiness. The faith of black Americans in a transcendent truth, which at times and in different ways was both a curse and a blessing, is of paramount importance in our intraracial as well as interracial struggle against all forms of domination.

If Negroes are Americans by birth, geography, ideals, language, and religion, what, then, are the criteria that define African American difference for Du Bois? "We are the first fruits of this new nation, the harbinger of that black tomorrow which is yet destined to soften the whiteness of the Teutonic today," Du Bois lyricizes. Using the language of dialectics in stressing African spirituality over Teutonic nationalism and American materialism, he underscores the distinctive complexity of his transformation of psychological dualism by identifying the presence of

African Americans and their three general cultural traits and gifts to America that were apparent to him as well as to Alexander Crummell, Anna Julia Cooper, and other black intellectuals by 1897: "We are that people whose subtle sense of song has given America its only American music, its only American fairy tales, its only touch of pathos and humor amid its money-getting plutocracy" ("Conservation of Races" 183). Moving beyond a superficial, essentializing concept of racial and national identity, Du Bois engages in a radical, racialized counterdiscourse to the hegemonic ideology of white supremacy that subordinates the will and well-being of blacks individually and collectively to those of the dominant group.

Despite the complicity and disingenuity of too many of those "who have been reared and trained under the individualistic philosophy of the Declaration of Independence and the laissez-faire philosophy of Adam Smith," Du Bois states in "The Conservation of Races," "the history of the world is the history, not of individuals, but of groups, not of nations, but of races, and he who ignores or seeks to override the race idea in human history, ignores and overrides the central thought of all history." In an effort to reconcile the biological and sociocultural tensions in his definitions of race, he elaborates:

> Although the wonderful developments of human history teach that the grosser physical differences of color, hair and bone go but a short way toward explaining the different roles which groups of men have played in human progress, yet there are differences—subtle, delicate, and elusive though they may be—which have silently but definitely separated men into groups [. . .] which, while they perhaps transcend scientific definition, nevertheless, are clearly defined to the eye of the historian and sociologist. (178)

Race, he continues, may be thus defined biologically and socioculturally as

> a vast family of human beings, generally of common blood and language, always of common history, traditions, and impulses, who are both voluntarily and involuntarily striving together for the accomplishments of certain more or less vividly conceived ideals of life [. . .] yet no mere physical distinctions would really define or explain the deeper differences, the cohesiveness, and continuity of these groups. The deeper differences are spiritual, physical, differences—undoubtedly based on the physical, but infinitely transcending them.

Equally important as the deeper yet transcendent spirituality of racial differences for Du Bois is the belief that "for the development of Negro genius, of Negro literature and art, of Negro spirit, only Negroes bound and welded together, Negroes inspired by one vast ideal, can work out in its fullness the great message we have for humanity" (178–81). Clearly, then, the distinctiveness of African American double consciousness is a dynamic, rather than merely static and essentialist, residual African spirituality expressed in "the great message" of African American folk and formal art.

"The Talented Tenth," Du Bois's first call for a black "aristocracy of talent and character" to inspire and lead the self-liberating struggle of the most socially exploited and marginalized class of black Americans, was published in 1903 in *The Negro Problem* (33–75; Lester 385–403). Edited by Booker T. Washington, this book also included essays by other representative black Americans of the period. In his essay, Du Bois boldly proclaimed that the mission of the Talented Tenth was to be the messengers of moral integrity, racial justice, and social equality for black Americans and that the mission of black Americans was to be the crusaders for spiritual and social change in the world. In 1948, influenced by subsequent ideological, technological, and geopolitical developments as well as by the unrelenting criticism of his apparent advocacy of cultural elitism, Du Bois, in an address to the Grand Boulé, a national black social fraternity, reformulated his earlier concept of the Talented Tenth and blacks as a group. "This group," he explained, "was not simply a physical entity, a black people, or people descended from black folk. It was, what all races really are, a cultural group [. . .] 15,000,000 men and women, who for three centuries have shared some common experiences and common suffering; and have worked all those days and nights together for their own survival and progress; that this complex of habits and manners could not and must not be lost. It must be conserved for the benefit of the Negro people themselves, and for mankind" ("The Talented Tenth: The Reexamination," reel 80, frame 190). Du Bois thus argues that the principal defining characteristic, mission, and message of a people is the cultural expression of their shared struggle for survival and progress for themselves and mankind.

It is important to remember that Du Bois's thoughts and feelings on socialized ambivalence, race, and nationalism were shaped at the end of the nineteenth century. As Rampersad notes, Du Bois probably drew on the psychology and philosophy of his teachers and time, including the orthodox religious philosophy of James McCosh at Fisk and the pragmatism and phenomenology of William James at Harvard (74). Profoundly impressed by German nationalism and culture while studying in Germany between 1892 and 1894, Du Bois was startled by an imperious, aristocratic professor's remark in a lecture on America: "Die Mulattin sind niedrig! Sie fuhlen sich niedrig!" (Mulattoes are inferior! They feel themselves inferior!) Reflecting on this period at ninety years old, Du Bois writes, "I began to feel that dichotomy which all my life has characterized my thought: how far can love for my oppressed race accord with love for the oppressing country? And when these loyalties diverge, where shall my soul find refuge?" (*Autobiography* 165, 169).

It was also in a solitary ritual celebration of his twenty-fifth birthday that he sought to resolve his sociocultural and sociopsychological dualism. "I am firmly convinced that my own best development is not one and the same with the best development of the world and here I am willing to sacrifice," he writes in his posthumously published autobiography. "That sacrifice to the world's good became too soon sickly sentimentality. I therefore take the world that the Unknown lay in my hands, and work for the rise of the Negro people, taking for granted that their best development means the best development of the world" (171). For Du Bois, the age of social Darwinism and disinterested scientific truth culminated ironically and paradoxically in the 1890s with the triumph of Booker T. Washington's accommodationist support of social segregation and industrial education for the mutual benefits of racial and economic advancement; with the "separate but equal" *Plessy v. Ferguson* Supreme Court decision; with the triumph of hegemonic white nationalism and Jim Crow law; with the rape, lynching, and disfranchisement of many thousands of blacks, especially in the Deep South; and with the resurgence after the Spanish-American War of American military, economic, and cultural domination of nonwhite peoples in several nations.

Five months after addressing the American Negro Academy, Du Bois shifted his rhetoric on double consciousness in the publication of "Strivings of the Negro People," a more poetic description of the complex fate of being a black American for a primarily white audience, in the August 1897 issue of *Atlantic Monthly*. This essay, shifted again slightly to sharpen the nuances of its personal and political tone, appears as "Of Our Spiritual Strivings" in the multivoiced *The Souls of Black Folk*. After introducing his classic racialized metaphor of the veil in describing his initiation in primary school into the world of color prejudice and discrimination, and after discovering that he was "shut out from their world by a vast veil" that engendered contempt and longing for the "dazzling opportunities" beyond the veil, Du Bois provides us with his equally classic, often-quoted definition of the psychological dualism of Negroes:

> After the Egyptian and Indian, the Greek and Roman, the Teuton and Mongolian, the Negro is a sort of seventh son, born with a veil, and gifted with second-sight in this American world—a world which yields him no true self-consciousness, but only lets him see himself through the revelation of the other world. It is a peculiar sensation this double consciousness, this sense of always looking at one's self through the eyes of others, of measuring one's soul by the tape of a world that looks on in amused contempt and pity. One ever feels his twoness—an American, a Negro; two souls, two thoughts, two unreconciled strivings; two warring ideals in one dark body, whose dogged strength alone keeps it from being torn asunder.
>
> The history of the American Negro is the history of this strife,—this longing to attain self-conscious manhood, to merge his double self into a better and truer self. In this merging he wishes neither of the older selves to be lost. He would not Africanize America, for America has too much to teach the world and Africa. He would not bleach his soul in a flood of white Americanism, for he knows that Negro blood has a message for the world. He simply wishes to make it possible for a man to be both a Negro and American, without being cursed and spit upon by his fellows, without having the doors of Opportunity closed roughly in his face.

The end of the black American's strivings, Du Bois continues, is "to be a co-worker in the kingdom of culture, to escape both death and isolation, to husband and use his best powers and his latent genius" (*Souls of Black Folk* 16–17).

Clearly, in each of the shifts in these texts, African American psychological dualism was not the fate of all ethnic immigrants or hyphenated Americans. Rather, it was the complex double vision of Americans of African descent whose humanity and culture had been historically devalued and marginalized primarily by people of European and British descent but on occasions with the complicity of members of their own racial or ethnic group. African Americans were both people of mixed African ancestry and nonpeople to the majority of whites; we were a fundamental part of American society yet segregated apart within it. We were among the first people to build the nation, but twentieth-century America only began to renew national policies reluctantly and significantly in the 1950s and 1960s to redress the violations of our civil rights as full first-class citizens.

African Americans—especially southerners, intellectuals, artists, and professionals —were therefore impelled by a complex combination of custom, law, circumstances, and choice to function primarily on two levels of a pervasively, perversely, and paradoxically racialized reality. Although it is true that our human personalities are complex and contradictory, our attitudes as black Americans toward racial integration and separatism were largely determined by the degree of alienation from or faith in the principles and practices of the ruling class of white Anglo-Saxon and Euro-American Protestants.[4]

In addition to being a dialectic and a dialogic process in American society between the bearers of vestigial vernacular sub-Saharan African cultures, double consciousness is an ambivalent expression of industrialized Western print cultures. It is, for most contemporary African Americans, the quest to synthesize one's sense of being an outsider with that of being an insider and one's ascribed status and identity with one's achieved status and identity. In other words, African American hybridity thus signifies a biracial, bicultural state of being in the world with others, an existential site of socialized ambivalence and emancipatory possibilities of personal and social transformation.

Although on the surface both "The Conservation of Races" and "Of Our Spiritual Strivings" illuminate the paradox, dualism, and dialectic of the experiences of black Americans, of being "an outcast and a stranger in mine own house," the differences in the moral and political tone of the two discourses reflect the primary racial differences in audiences. While adhering to the nineteenth-century masculinist grammatical convention of privileging the male pronoun as the generic marker for representing both sexes, "Of Our Spiritual Strivings" distinctively racializes the tone with the pronoun "Our," the metaphor of the veil, and the multiple leitmotifs of sight and insight, visibility and invisibility, slavery and freedom. By metaphorically encouraging the reader's participation in the public discourse on race, the rhetorical and dialectic tension in the text is foregrounded in its representation of the sociopsychological and sociocultural differences and struggles between the worlds of whites and nonwhites.

"In 'Strivings,'" historian Thomas C. Holt contends, "blacks are not so much aliens as alienated. It is not cultural difference but cultural disfranchisement that shapes their struggle" (304). Actually, cultural and racial differences inscribed in eighteenth- and nineteenth-century legal statutes as "black codes" and implemented in juridical decisions reinforced the hegemonic power of the white ruling class, fostered anxiety and paranoia about challenges to that power, and perpetuated until the 1960s the paradoxical political and cultural disfranchisement of black American citizens. Chesnutt's *The Marrow of Tradition,* Johnson's *The Autobiography of an Ex-Colored Man,* Toomer's *Cane,* Wright's *Native Son,* Ellison's *Invisible*

Man, Baldwin's *Go Tell It on the Mountain,* and Morrison's *Beloved* readily come to mind as improvisational variations on Du Boisian themes and tropes of double consciousness.

In an apparent revision of Du Bois's sociopsychological metaphor and of sociologist Robert E. Park's 1928 theory of the marginal man as a racial and cultural hybrid or Creole, socialized ambivalence was defined in 1937 by anthropologist Melville J. Herskovits in *Life in a Haitian Valley* as the anthropological adjustment to the sociopsychological conflict that results from the contradictory imperatives of European and African cultural traditions primarily in colonial and neocolonial situations (295–96). In the United States, this ambivalence is expressed in both the mixed emotions of many Americans of African descent about ideologies of social integration, cultural assimilation, and black cultural nationalism and in our shifting identification between white and black cultural systems as a result of institutionalized racism. Double vision, an apparent rewriting of Du Bois's metaphor by Ralph Ellison in *Shadow and Act* (1964), is a fluid, ambivalent, laughing-to-keep-from-crying perspective toward life as expressed in the innovative use of irony and parody in African American folklore and formal art (136–37).

Much of this irony and parody was and is a creative way of managing the legacy of systemic American racism. Although there is no valid scientific evidence of a biological relationship between culture and race, as African philosopher Anthony Appiah argues in "The Uncompleted Argument: Du Bois and the Illusion of Race," it is nevertheless the perception of biological and cultural differences (color, hair, religion, language, beliefs, and values) ascribed to and socially inscribed as race in popular and formal texts by the white American majority that served as the principal basis for the incremental regional social subjugation, exploitation, and exclusion of African captives and African Americans (32). More than mere prejudice, as African American sociologist William J. Wilson reminds us, racism is "an ideology of racial domination or exploitation that (1) incorporates beliefs in a particular race's cultural and/or inherent biological inferiority and (2) uses such beliefs to justify and prescribe inferior or unequal treatment for that group" (32).

Historically, the increasing demand for cheap labor in the United States led to the construction of political statutes and racist acts in the late seventeenth century and the reification of a pseudoscientific and theological racist ideology by the late nineteenth century that—in paradoxical contravention of the letter and spirit of the Declaration of Independence, the Constitution of the United States, and the Bible—restricted or nullified the civil rights of nonwhite persons and immorally devalued our human rights as subjects. De facto and de jure racism clearly prevented the equal participation of blacks in the dominant white culture and literary discourse, so that our need for empowering symbols and values had to be satisfied and sustained by the resourcefulness, resilience, and creativity of our indigenous ethnic group.

"What seems clear upon reading the texts created by black writers in English or the critical texts that responded to these black writings," as black literary critic Henry Louis Gates brilliantly demonstrates in a recent study that illuminates the kinship of the trope to the Yoruba and African American trickster and toast traditions of Esu-Elegbara and the Signifying Monkey,

> is that the production of literature was taken to be the central arena in which persons of African descent could, or could not, establish and redefine their status within the human community. Black people [. . .] had to represent themselves as "speaking subjects" before they could even begin to destroy their status as objects, as commodities, within Western culture. In addition to all of the myriad reasons for which human beings write books, this particular reason seems to have been paramount for the black slave. (*Signifying Monkey* 129)

It is in this racially and ethnically specific context that we can best understand the shift from the rhetoric and dialectics of Du Boisian double consciousness in his speeches and essays to the dialectics and dialogics in two of his contemporaneous narratives.

A close examination of Du Bois's earliest unpublished and published fiction, "A Fellow of Harvard" and "Of the Coming of John," reveals that they are semiautobiographical narratives that illuminate the socialized ambivalence of the writer's dialectic and dialogic use of the sign of the hybrid identity of Americans of African descent. "A Fellow of Harvard" is the incomplete unpublished manuscript of a novel. It consists of fragments of three versions. The first is a two-page plot outline, dated Berlin, December 7, 1892, in which the idea of duality is expressed intratextually in the romantic tension between the idealism and spirituality of the self and the provincialism and materialism of the world. The author/narrator describes the nameless hero as "a Western boy of N.E. ancestry—somewhat eccentric from childhood." His eccentricity, like Du Bois's, is his driving ambition to excel intellectually and psychologically to become "a fellow of Harvard" even though his local school committee awards him a prize for a year at "x—coll." Supported by a hometown church that encourages him to enter the ministry, he leaves the college in disgust with its "narrowness" before graduation and "writes a capital brochure which secures him aid at Harvard where he enters as a junior" (reel 87, frame 156). Intertextually and dialogically, the correlation between the voices of the author/narrator and the nameless protagonist in this fragment and the voices in this fragment with the divergent views we hear in Du Bois's autobiographies and *The Souls of Black Folk* indicate that they are morally, culturally, psychologically, and politically close, although temporally and spatially distant.

Also like Du Bois, the protagonist struggles with uneven success to maintain his fellowship status but manages to receive a European fellowship. In Europe, he is not a good student but becomes "an avowed socialist" and returns to America without completing his thesis. His efforts to find a teaching position are unsuccessful, except at "a Southern Negro school where his eccentricities get him [in] trouble with the blacks & his radicalism with the whites." After completing and publishing his thesis with "brilliant success," he secures and loses another college position because his politics and "ideals clash with the mammonism & materialism of his surroundings." With his dismissal and the ridicule of his published masterpiece, "He already [a] monomaniac becomes hopelessly insane and dies 'a fellow of Harvard'" (frame 756). In the plot outline, then, Du Boisian double consciousness is clearly more of a personal and artistic emancipatory effort than a group sociopsychological condition and more of a curse than a blessing to the semiautobiographical, fictive, nonconforming African American idealist and political radical in the Victorian era.

The second fragment is eight pages of a multivoiced chapter in which the protagonist, George Smith, is a "smart but odd" sixteen-year-old boy in a small western town whose father and townsmen wonder if he will apply his genius to a trade or a profession as a livelihood. Du Bois employs conventional dialogue in Standard African American dialect for the parents and interior dialogue for George to dramatize the implied author's support in stylized Standard American English for liberal college education over industrial education as the better preparation to attain full freedom, literacy, dignity, and civil rights for post-Reconstruction black Americans. Expressing sympathy for industrial education in the major generational and educational conflict in the plot and black communities of that era, a member of the local chapter of the locomotive engineers states in frustration, "No sooner a workman make himself respectable than off his sons go to the kid gloved professors or to college. Education is a good thing—a good thing of course, but somehow it don't work out right. If we could educate our sons for farmers or for tradesmen—it would be all right, but that's just what they won't be—and I'm blessed if I see my way out of the thing" (frames 759, 760).

When asked by his father what he "goin't do for a living," George sinks into reflection and interior dialogue with himself on the vagueness and flux of his plans for the future. "Now what a question to put to a sixteen year old boy, a living? The thought had scarcely occurred to him—yes it had occurred but not in that way, or no, not in that in 'living' there was a touch of the sordid, the shadow of a breathless scramble for bread—and he shrank from that—he feared it—it had no part in his dreams, in his great airy castles" (frames 759, 760). Dramatizing the choice between industrial and higher liberal education during the 1890s of the best path up from slavery as the horns of the dilemma of social stratification for blacks as individuals and a group, this fragment ends abruptly with George's interior self-questioning.

The longest fragment of the three versions of "A Fellow of Harvard" is forty-seven handwritten pages and dated April 14, probably 1893. Du Bois's use of psychological dualism in this narrative is clearly derived from the redemptive vestiges of African spirituality and the unredemptive impact of American racism and materialism. The first of seven planned but uncompleted chapters focuses on a southern revival meeting that dramatizes the cultural syncretism of African and American belief systems and the economic exploitation and racial discrimination of sharecropping that divide the world and consciousness of John Johnson, the black protagonist. His "holy mission from his own flesh & blood [. . .] from a prophet of the high God"—from his African great-grandfather who was a legendary preacher and conjuror—was "to lead the people he loved into the promised land" (frame 783). Through description and dialogue, black myth-legend, music, and speech, Du Bois establishes the origins of African American spirituality in the rural southern black revival meetings and the legacy of such blends of African and non-African religious beliefs and practices as Christian fundamentalism, Southern goophering (i.e., conjuring, hoodoo, or mystical syncretic powers), and root healing or folk medicine. (As Zora Neale Hurston explains in *Mules and Men*, "Nearly all of the conjure doctors practice 'roots,' but some of the root doctors are not hoodoo doctors" [340].)

Demonstrating the authority and authenticity of his use of the African American vernacular tradition, Du Bois begins the heteroglossic chapter with "a strange song rolling down the valley in rythmic [sic] cadence" to which a black sharecropper responds in dialect: "Reckon the big meetin's begun." As the voices of men, women, and children that began in sorrowful cadence rise in powerful triumph and communion, an approaching church member responds, "Lord, but the spirrit [sic] seem to be a moving right pretty." Holding center stage in this spiritual drama of "simple true hearted folk" is the minister, whose enthralling chanted sermon and wounds-of-Jesus call to join the church establishes the dominant messianic motif of the narrative: "There he hangs on the tree [. . .] I have seen his wounds [. . .] see from his side the crimson stream is rippling down the mountain [. . .] see see it is pouring in the door, it is rushing thro the windows, can you not feel it, its warm hands are clasping at you O my little ones come to Jesus, come to Jesus here ye the song—" (frame 772). In response to this call, the teenaged protagonist John and his even younger sister, Tildy, "git religion."

But young John was still dissatisfied by the world about him. "From his cradle he had looked out upon a double world [. . .] a white one and a black one and the first meant to him all that was overbearing unfortunate and hateful, the second all that was lovable and dear to him." He was troubled, however, that "he could not trace this line throughout the world. Not only did the two worlds seem to grow together at the top when the sun glare[d] bright and rosy o'er the eastern hills and drank up the dew in the meadow of black & white, and washed Capt. Thornton & Sam Johnson and the black cow and George's dog—not only here was the world necessarily [?] one, but at other unexpected places the two worlds faded into one" (frame 772). Most troubling was the thought that God was not "black and kinky haired" as he had learned from his mother's African American myth-legends about his own mission as God's messenger and warrior but white as in the Bible.

Throughout the chapter the color symbolism and dialectic between residual African cultural elements and Christian messianic myth-legend reinforce the capacity of double consciousness to evoke the ambiguity and irony of the protagonist's experiences as a young American of African ancestry. The symbolism and voices we experience as readers are more dialectic than dialogic because the language situates the characters in a specific historical and ideological context that highlights interracial and intraracial class and color conflicts. The language also proposes a synthesis of antithetical elements to achieve sociocultural emancipation and enlightenment by affirming a transcendent messianic truth. Taunted by the son of a white, post-Reconstruction plantation owner about his plans to go to Phillips Exeter Academy, to write books, and to become a Fellow at Harvard, John, foreshadowing Du Bois's advocacy of a Talented Tenth, is motivated by personal pride and moral commitment to lead his people in their struggle for freedom, justice, dignity, and literacy. After his family is threatened with lynching because he beats Captain Thornton's son in a fight, his mother reveals that his legendary African great-grandfather and she have sacrificed to provide him with the legacy of resources, spiritual and material, necessary for him to fulfill his mission as God's avenging messenger and his people's messiah.

Du Bois dramatically sustains his imaginative reconciliation of the narrator's double consciousness in the concluding pages of "A Fellow of Harvard." After killing the white overseer who cut him with a whip, John's great-grandfather, "William John Thoms, the grandson of the prince Chiawba of Africa," a powerful preacher, and a "goopher man" who "c'd heal the sick & no magic ever worked agin him," disappeared. But young John's legendary ancestor left a legacy of courage, goopher charms, a written will, and crumpled instructions to locate a buried inheritance. "I remember his big form as he stood at the door," John's mother, Matilda, tells him proudly in passing on her grandfather's patrimony; "he only hand this to father and said 'give it yo first granson, when he is ready to gird on the sword of God & go forth & smite his enemies'" (frames 780, 781). With no discernible irony, the implied author represents John faithfully following the instructions at midnight, using the goopher charms, and finding a grave containing a skeleton, an anvil, and two hundred dollars in gold and silver. Matilda then pridefully gives her son the hundred dollars in silver that she has saved to send him to school and "into the great wicked world for to fight for his people agin the hosts of the devil." Rather than closure, the final chapter leaves the reader with John telling his little sister, Tildy, that he is going over the mountain to the great city "to be a great man—perhaps a preacher, perhaps perhaps, a Fellow of Harvard" (frame 786). The resolution of the racial and cultural conflicts is thus inscribed as the hopeful synthesis of masters of both the spoken and written word: the preacher and the professor.

Prefaced biculturally with an excerpt from a poem by Elizabeth Barrett Browning and three moving bars of music from a black spiritual, "Of the Coming of John" is Du Bois's most effectively developed short fictive orchestration of his turn-of-the-century motifs of double consciousness. The stylization of black and white voices dramatizes for the implied author and the protagonist, John Jones, the dominance of the problem of the color line over problems of gender, class, and culture. As in the earlier thirteen chapters of *The Souls of Black Folk*, however, the tension between dialectic and dialogic discourse in "Of the Coming of John" is apparent.

Although, as Frederic Jameson stresses in his reading of Mikhail Bakhtin, "the normal form of the dialogical is essentially an *antagonistic* one, and [. . .] the dialogue of class struggle is one in which two opposing discourses fight it out within the general unity of a shared code," within the master code of the Christian religion "the basic formal requirement of dialectical analysis is maintained and its elements are still restructured in terms of *contradiction*" (84–86). This reading of Bakhtin's theory of dialogics is also useful in interpreting "Of the Coming of John," which is ultimately a univocal rather than multivocal text in its deep structure. On this level the Du Boisian matrix of music, speech, and symbolism in the narrative illuminates the class and cultural as well as racial conflicts in the historical struggle of blacks for social equality with whites.

Anthropologically, the protagonist's identity crisis of double consciousness is dramatized by the ritual process of his separation, liminality, and reintegration with his primary racial and ethnic community. The major racial, class, and cultural dualisms are constructed in the tragedies of two Johns: one black and the other white. Before the protagonist's separation from his hometown to pursue higher education, John Jones is accepted by both the white and black communities as a black, good-natured, respectful plow-hand and childhood playmate of John Henderson, the white, bigoted son of wealthy Judge Henderson. Socialized in the ethics of Jim Crow, they become conscious in the liminal stage of their college educations of radically different responses to continuing their traditionally structured system of social power and privilege. In their futile efforts to reintegrate with their communities they turn on, rather than to, each other. Their lives end tragically in murder and suicide over white John's sexual assault of black John's sister, Jennie, a house servant to Judge Henderson.

The opening and closing episodes of the triadically structured narrative are situated in Georgia. Following the contrapuntal cultural and racial referents of the lyrical epigraphs, the first voice we hear is that of a first-person plural male narrator/observer. He introduces us to the multileveled ironies of the separate but equal community within a community of southern white Jonestown, where he is a faculty member and the protagonist is a student on the black campus of Wells Institute. Speaking Standard American English with the authority and norms of the collective voice of the aspiring black middle class, the nameless narrator's discourse is disrupted and subverted by white voices of authority. Judge Henderson and other white folk of the protagonist's hometown of Altamaha (Atlanta), paternalistically disapprove of higher education and social equality for John Jones—"'It'll spoil him,—ruin him,' they said" (Du Bois, *Souls of Black Folk* 167)—and other blacks. But for the Judge's white son, John, to go to Princeton is both desirable and good. "'It'll make a man of him,' said the Judge, 'college is the place.'" Although the coming home of both Johns to their "Southern village" was eagerly awaited with pride and hope, "neither world thought the other world's thoughts, save with a vague unrest" (168). In the closing episodes, about which I will later say more, an omniscient narrator assumes the authority of orchestrating the multiple black and white southern dialect voices.

But it is in the climactic liminal episode in a New York opera hall that the protagonist experiences the inspirational beauty and harmony of the cultural synthesis of European folk and formal art in Wagner's *Lohengrin* and in the disruptive power of the veil, Du Bois's classic metaphor for institutionalized racism, in the American North. Before he arrives in New York, however, we witness the protagonist's transformation in body and soul as a result of his college education and discovery of "the Veil that lay between him and the white world." Differences, restraints, and slights that he had felt natural, ignored, or laughed at as a boy in his hometown, such as the Jim Crow cars caused by "the color-line that hemmed in him and his," now evoked sarcasm and a vague bitterness from him (Du Bois, *Souls of Black Folk* 170). Ambivalent about his plans to return home to be a leader of his people, he welcomed the offer at graduation to travel north to sing spirituals during the summer vacation with the school quartet.

In New York he is so overwhelmed by the material elegance and cultural richness of the white world around him that he is swept into an opera hall with a young white couple beside whom he is seated in the hall, subsequently recognizing the male in the couple as his boyhood playmate. Before suffering the indignity, injustice, and irony of being ejected because of his race at the angry insistence of the white John, the black John was enthralled by "a world so different from his, so strangely more beautiful than anything he had ever known, that he sat in dreamland, and started when, after a hush, rose high and clear the music of Lohengrin's swan. [. . .] A deep longing swelled in all his heart to rise with that clear music out of the dirt and dust of that low life that held him prisoned and befouled" (Du Bois, *Souls of Black Folk* 171).

Based on a German legend from the Middle Ages, *Lohengrin* was written to the composer's own libretto and established the Wagnerian organic style of the interplay of ethereal and earthly leitmotifs in his romantic operatic dramas. The transmutation of the embedded folk narrative text of "*Lohengrin*" into the aristocratic text of the opera captivates the protagonist and ironically dramatizes Du Bois's subconscious complicity in the exploitative pattern of transcultural appropriation by which the dominant culture revitalizes itself and perpetuates the single voice and values of a hegemonic class. The changing movements and swelling harmony of *Lohengrin* stirred the soul of the protagonist and made his identity crisis more acute. "If he could only live up in the free air where birds sang and setting suns had no touch of blood," he exclaimed more plaintively than rebelliously to himself and God. "Who had called him to be the slave and butt of all? And if he had called, what right had he to call when a world like this lay open before men?" As the movement of the harmony changed and grew fuller, "he felt with the music the movement of power within him. If he but had some master-work, some life-service, hard,—aye, bitter hard, but without the cringing and sickening servility, without the cruel hurt that hardened his heart and soul. When at last a soft sorrow crept across the violins, there came to him the vision of a far-off home,—the great eyes of his sister, and the dark drawn face of his mother." Hurrying from the hall and calling himself "a natural-born fool," John immediately writes his family that he is coming home. On the train south, he seeks through interior monologue to reconcile the ironic tension of his double consciousness with a biblical imperative: "Here is my duty to Altamaha plain before me; perhaps they'll let me help settle the Negro problems there,—perhaps they won't. 'I will go in to the King, which is not according to the law; and if I perish, I perish'" (Du Bois, *Souls of Black Folk* 172–73).

Distanced emotionally and intellectually as well as spatially from the orthodox Christian codes of Altamaha, the protagonist is unsuccessful in his effort to reintegrate himself with his primary community in the final episodes of the narrative. The abstract, impersonal, methodical tenor and tone of his coming home speech at the Baptist church to foster a black unity that transcended religious and denominational antagonisms alienated him from his community and evoked the scorn of the folks in the Amen corner. "'Today,' he said with a smile, 'the world cares little whether a man be Baptist or Methodist, or indeed a churchman at all, so long as he is good and true. What difference does it make whether a man be baptized in a river or washbowl, or not at all? Let's leave all that littleness, and look higher'" (Du Bois, *Souls of Black Folk* 174). However, the college-educated John Jones no longer fits in. "He had come to save his people, and before he left the depot he had hurt them," he thinks after being sent by Judge Henderson to his back door. "He sought to teach them at the church, and had outraged their deepest feelings. He had schooled himself to be respectful to the Judge, and then blundered into his front door" (175–76). On the surface level, John seems to accept the situation of hegemonic white rule. Judge Henderson reminds him that this means that "in this country the Negro must remain subordinate, and can never expect to be the equal of white men [. . .] by God! we'll hold them under if we have to lynch every Nigger in the land." Although in order to teach at the black school he acquiesces to the Judge's bigoted injunction to "teach the darkies to be faithful servants and laborers as your fathers were" (176), the protagonist is summarily dismissed and the school closed by the Judge after he discovers that John has appropriated the text of the French Revolution to subvert the rule of whites and revoiced the text of social equality and independence to empower his black students.

Du Bois ends his narrative of double consciousness on a paradoxical and pyrrhic note with the spiritual and moral triumph but physical and psychological defeat of the protagonist. Resolved to leave Altamaha after his dismissal by Judge Henderson, John Jones is enraged to find near the bluff of the sea his young sister, Jennie, struggling in the arms of Judge Henderson's bored, "little spoiled and self-indulgent," "headstrong" son, John Henderson. Without a single word, the protagonist kills his sister's attacker with a tree limb and "all the pent-up hatred of his great black arm." In utter despair he tells his mother that he is "going away,—I'm going to be free" (*Souls of Black Folk* 179), and he returns to the site of the fatal encounter in the pine trees high above the sea. Hearing the noise of galloping horses merging with "the faint sweet music" of the opera hall, the protagonist jumps into the sea, humming the "Song of the Bride"—"Freulig gefuhrt, ziehet dahin" (Joyfully led, pass along to that place)—and pitying "that haggard white-haired man, whose eyes flashed red with fury" as he rushed to lynch him (180). That in the final resolution of his double consciousness by suicide the protagonist not only hums the German lyrics to a Wagnerian aria but also pities his chief white antagonist is both a paradoxical and pyrrhic triumph of the romantic over the realistic and the spiritual over the material. This shift from rhetoric to dialectics and dialogics in Du Bois's discourse on the theme and trope of double consciousness foreshadows the dominant contradictions and complementarities in his subsequent texts, especially his messianic self-representation as an epitomized expression of the African American racial spirit in *Darkwater* and *Dusk of Dawn*.

We should thus celebrate Du Bois as the preeminent exemplar of the black scholar/activist whose life and legacy of double consciousness are a sociocultural and sociopsychological sign of the distinctive, complex fate of being an African American, especially a black intellectual or artist. As demonstrated by its resurgence in African American literary criticism,[5] Du Boisian double consciousness, in short, continues to be a vital and viable rhetorical sign: first, of the dynamics of continuity and change in the biracial, bicultural state of being in the world with others; second, of the existential site of socialized cultural ambivalence and emancipatory possibilities of personal and social transformation; and third, of an epistemological mode of critical inquiry for interpreting the rich complexity of African American culture, especially literature.

Notes

1. See Ellison, *Shadow and Act*; Larry Neal, "And Shine Swam On," *Black Fire: An Anthology of African-American Writing*, ed. LeRoi Jones and Larry Neal (New York: Morrow, 1968) 638–56; Robert B. Stepto, *From Behind the Veil: A Study of Afro-American Narrative* (Urbana: U of Illinois P, 1979); Gates, *Signifying Monkey*; Berndt Ostendorf, *Black Literature in White America* (Totowa, NJ: Barnes and Noble, 1982); Mary Helen Washington, ed., *Invented Lives: Narratives of Black Women, 1860–1960* (Garden City, NY: Anchor, 1987); Barbara Johnson, "Metaphor, Metonomy and Voice in *Their Eyes Were Watching God*," *Black Literature and Theory*, ed. Henry Louis Gates Jr. (New York: Methuen, 1984) 205–19; and Bell, *Afro-American Novel*.

2. See Bruce 301–02. See also Johann Wolfgang von Goethe, *Faust*, trans. Bayard Taylor (New York: Arden, n.d.) 68; Werner Sollors, "Of Mules and Mares in a Land of Difference; or, Quadrupeds All?" *American Quarterly* 42 (1990): 182; Joel Porte, "Emerson, Thoreau, and the Double Consciousness," *New England Quarterly* 41 (1968): 41, 50; Du Bois, "Strivings" 197; and Moses, "Poetics of Ethiopianism" 411–26.

3. *Compact OED* 522; Bruce 303; and Kulpe 217. See also Rampersad 74.

4. As we are reminded by the responses of twenty black intellectuals and artists in Early, *Lure and Loathing*, the consensus of contemporary critics acknowledges the validity but questions the viability of Du Boisian double consciousness. Some argue that it is no longer useful because it reduces the complexity and diversity of African American character to a schizoid male construct that reinforces racial stereotypes. But those who dismiss the usefulness of double consciousness as a contemporary interpretive metaphor implicitly or explicitly acknowledge that racism was, if not is, a stifling dominant force in their lives. Also, the alleged declining significance of race in America is, as the Rodney King case so tragically reminds us, at best a premature, if not fallacious, assumption and an unconvincing, if not illogical, conclusion.

5. In addition to the texts identified in note 2, see Eric Sundquist, *To Wake the Nations* (Cambridge: Belknap, 1993); Denise Heinze, *The Dilemma of "Double Consciousness": Toni Morrison's Novels* (Athens: U of Georgia P, 1993); and Sandra Adell, *Double-Consciousness/Double Bind: Theoretical Issues in Twentieth-Century Black Literature* (Urbana: U of Illinois P, 1994).

III

Booker T. and W. E. B.: The Authority, Authenticity, and Agency of African American Double Consciousness

In all things purely social we can be as separate as the five fingers, and yet one as the hand in all things essential to mutual progress.

Booker T. Washington, "Atlanta Compromise"

"It seems to me," said Booker T.,
"That all you folks have missed the boat.
Who shout about the right to vote,
And spend vain days and sleepless nights
In uproar over civil rights.
Just keep your mouths shut, do not grouse,
But work, and save, and buy a house."

"I don't agree," said W. E. B.
"For what can poverty avail
If dignity and justice fail?
Unless you help to make the laws,
They'll steal your house with trumped-up clause.
A rope's as tight, a fire as hot,
No matter how much cash you've got.
Speak soft, and try your little plan,
But as for me, I'll be a man."

Dudley Randall, "Booker T. and W. E. B."

Even before including Dudley Randall's classic poem "Booker T. and W. E. B." in my teaching in the 1960s and in Modern and Contemporary Afro-American Poetry *in 1972, a sizeable collection of poets and poems whose power and wisdom illuminated for me the diversity of human experience and quickened my sense of understanding of the emerging new world, "Booker T.*

and W. E. B." has been one of my favorite poems. As the major epigraph to "Booker T. and W. E. B.: The Authority, Authenticity, and Agency of African American Double Consciousness" reveals, the poem dramatically represents in a wry vernacular voice the ideological and tactical conflict between the two dominant black American race leaders at the turn of the twentieth century. This essay had its genesis in my scholarly resistance to the provocative argument of my former colleague, Harvard Professor William J. Wilson, the most frequently cited African American social scientist in the nation, in his prizewinning 1978 study The Declining Significance of Race. *My resistance to elevating class over race consciousness became more vigorous in 1993 with the disingenuous denial by "twenty leading African American intellectuals" of the validity of the authority, authenticity, and agency of African American double consciousness in black critic Gerald Early's* Lure and Loathing. *It intensified in 1997 in response to arguments by white former* New York Daily News *political columnist Jim Sleeper's article "Toward an End of Blackness" and by black Harvard law professor Randall Kennedy's "My Race Problem—and Ours." Sleeper argued unconvincingly for "the surrender of race consciousness," and Kennedy argued absurdly that "neither racial pride nor racial kinship offers guidance that is intellectually, morally, or politically satisfactory." These debates in the media and the academy about whether race matters in the twentieth century culminated in my lecture "Booker T. and W. E. B.: The Authority, Authenticity, and Agency of African American Double Consciousness" as the keynote address at Morgan State University on April 7, 1999. The lecture also appeared in print later the same year in* Black Nationalist: Reconsidering Du Bois, Garvey, Booker T. and Nkrumah.

QUIET AS IT IS KEPT NOWADAYS AMONG THE ELDERS, FAMILY LEGEND SAYS THAT we Bells have Cherokee ancestry and possibly some Dutch or German. Even so, I thank God, the omniscient, omnipotent authority and authenticator; my mother, a single parent and the essential agent of my color, class, culture, and character; and the United States Marine Corps, the transcultural and transformative agent of my consciousness and character, for making me a black man. The historical resonance of this affirmation of my racial and gender identity probably emanates in part from the legend that Frederick Douglass stressed the contrast between himself and Martin Delany, his partner and fellow abolitionist in 1847 on the *North Star*, with the remark that "[I] thank God for making me a man simply; but Delany always thanks him for making him a *black man*" (qtd. in Harding 149). As black historian and civil rights activist Vincent Harding reminds us, Douglass was "far less conscious of his African roots than Delany, far less assertive concerning his black identity." Like Delany, I thank God for making me a black man, even though I haven't retraced my roots to Africa. I therefore reject arguments for "the surrender of race consciousness" like those in white former *New York Daily News* political columnist Jim Sleeper's "Toward an End of Blackness" and in black Harvard law professor Randall Kennedy's "My Race Problem—and Ours." According to Kennedy's ahistorical, unpersuasive argument, *"Neither racial pride nor racial kinship offers guidance that is intellectually, morally, or politically satisfactory"* (56).

In other words, as the range of responses by "twenty leading African-American intellectuals" to W. E. B. Du Bois's theory and trope of double consciousness in Gerald Early's *Lure and Loathing* (1993) demonstrate, it is now both fashionable and profitable to deny or repudiate the agency, authority, and authenticity of African American double consciousness. In narratology, an agent is the representation of a human being who acts and influences events. But as it is used here, agency, to paraphrase philosopher Charles Taylor, is the sociocultural and sociopsychological process by which the individual assumes a responsible political position in maintaining or changing the systems of language and power by which he or she constructs and represents a personal and group identity or subjectivity of authenticity and authority (Prince, ch. 1).

Although in *Sincerity and Authenticity* literary critic Lionel Trilling explains authenticity "as a criterion of art and as a quality of the personal life which may be either enhanced or diminished by art" (134), Charles Taylor defines authenticity more broadly in *The Ethics of Authenticity*, dividing the concept into two categories. In category Λ, authenticity "involves (i) creation and construction as well as discovery, (ii) originality, and frequently (iii) opposition to the rules of society and even potentially to what we recognize as morality." But in category B, authenticity also "requires (i) openness to horizons of significance (for otherwise the creation loses the background that can save it from insignificance) and (ii) a self-definition in dialogue. That these demands may be in tension has to be allowed," Taylor notes. "But what must be wrong is a simple privileging of one over the other, of (A), say, at the expense of (B), or vice versa." Authenticity thus implies both transcending or overcoming restrictive material conditions and transgressing or violating social and moral boundaries (66–67).

In contrast, authority is basically the power to influence or command thought, opinion, or behavior. "The grounds on which legitimate authority often rest," social scientist Marvin E. Olsen reminds us in "Power as a Social Process," "are (a) traditional values, beliefs, norms, and customs, (b) legal prerogatives established through more-or-less rational agreements and (c) special expertise or knowledge relevant to the situation. To the extent that an actor draws legitimacy from all three sources [. . .] his authority is especially strong" (7). Contrary to the new critical orthodoxy, this neither implies nor infers that black culture and character are static or one-dimensional. Innateness and immutability are the salient features in neither term nor in the dynamic relationship among language, knowledge, and power in the social construction of identity, including the strategic use of essentialism.

In *Reflecting Black: African American Cultural Criticism* (1993) cultural critic, black public intellectual, and ordained minister Michael Dyson attempts to move beyond essentialism and authenticity by defining essence as "an immutable, history transcending characteristic of, for instance, art objects, religions, and cultures. [. . .] While one may cherish black cultural norms, values and ideas—or even wish to protect them from rejection, irrelevance, or extinction—such desires," he writes and I certainly agree, "must not be realized through appeals to an unvarying racial or cultural essence that remains unaffected by vicissitudes or chance" (xvi–xvii). But who, besides apparently the most extreme white racist—and black Afrocentrists—are these nameless people who argue for "an unvarying racial or cultural essence?"

Certainly, Booker T. Washington, who was born a slave in 1856 in the Old Dominion and believed that his father was white, and W. E. B. Du Bois, who was born in 1868 a free New England Brahmin and claimed French Huguenot ancestry on his father's side, were neither racial nor cultural purists and essentialists. During the post-Reconstruction era of rising industrial expansion, material progress, and white terrorism in the New South, the conflict between Washington and Du Bois as to whether industrial training or higher education was necessary to achieve their major objectives seemed irreconcilable. But the difference between these two leaders was more fundamentally a matter of agency, authority, and authenticity as manifested in their different backgrounds, personalities, and strategies. Both aspired to move their race up from slavery to economic, cultural, and political freedom, literacy, and unity. But Washington chose the rural southern strategy of accommodationism and benevolent despotism, inspired by the gospel of manual labor, property ownership, and the toothbrush preached by his New England schoolteachers; and Du Bois preferred the strategy of promoting an urban, aristocratic concept of a "Talented Tenth," his cosmopolitan term for the exceptionally qualified men and women of the race, the cultural elite, to lead the masses in their common struggle for full American citizenship and social equality.

Since the 1960s, I have certainly not been alone in arguing in my scholarship and pedagogy that the unique pattern of experiences of black people in North America, from the myths of Africa as the heart of darkness and of Europe as the originary site of white supremacy to the legendary realities of antiblack racism, has generated racially and ethnically different cultures. African American culture provides the material and symbolic modalities, especially double consciousness, by which Americans of African descent and heritage in the United States cope with the contradictions between the principles and practices of white American citizens, as well as with the paradoxes between the ideals of middle-class white Americans and the realities of all classes of black Americans, especially in the South. Major African American literary theorists and critics Houston Baker and Henry Gates privilege the blues and black speech, respectively, while Jewish American prize-winning cultural historian and critic Lawrence Levine stresses the spirituals as essential to an understanding and expression of African American culture and consciousness. In contrast, I advocate the five residually oral forms of oratory, myth, legend, tale, and song. As senior scholars of American and African American culture and literature, we therefore all ground our critical theories and practice in the everyday experiences and vernacular tradition of Americans of African descent and hybrid cultural identities.

Although I believe that my explanation of genealogical shifts in Du Bois's discourse on double consciousness as the sign of African American difference has been clear, if not absolutely convincing, some people still find it difficult to understand why and how double consciousness was distinctively African American. The fact is that double consciousness, like all language, is a racially, ethnically, and politically contested term that is neither static nor merely a reflection of reality. As linguists Edward Sapir and Benjamin Lee Whorf have argued, our language habits shape reality and our interpretation of it. W. E. B. Du Bois appropriated the concept of double consciousness and deployed it as a distinctive trope at the turn of the twentieth century. This was the era of the legal sanction of Jim Crow and white American nationalism in the *Plessy v. Ferguson* Supreme Court decision of 1896 and the resurgence of Western imperialism with the military and commercial occupation of Cuba, as well as the annexation of Puerto Rico, Guam, Hawaii, and the Philippines, after the Spanish-American War of 1898. Du Bois's compelling trope situates "the Negro" sociohistorically, sociopsychologically, and socioculturally as "a sort of seventh son, born with a veil, and gifted with second-sight in this American world—a world which yields him no true self-consciousness, but only lets him see himself through the revelation of the other world" (*Souls of Black Folk* 16). The network of understandings that defines black American culture and informs black American consciousness evolves from the unique pattern of experiences of black people in North America, experiences, as sociologist Robert Blauner convincingly argues, "that no other national or racial minority or lower class group shared" (352). These experiences—of Africa, the transatlantic or Middle Passage, slavery, Southern plantation tradition, emancipation, Reconstruction, post-Reconstruction, northern migration, urbanization, and racism—have produced a residue of shared memories and frames, of reference for black Americans.

Unlike the first white immigrants and indentured servants, captive Africans, too many folks naively deny or willfully dismiss as irrelevant, were the only group to be deprived systematically of their Old World cultural links and social support systems in order to transform them into slaves for life. Fugitive slave laws and the Black Codes made even free-born blacks justifiably anxious about their freedom and their lives in the United States. The twentieth-century debate over whether President Clinton and the nation ought to apologize to black Americans for slavery was, for many black folks of my generation, too little, too late in the context of federal and state resistance to and nullification of affirmative action policies, laws, and practices. Even more chilling were and are the brutal and murderous acts committed with apparent impunity against black people by too many law enforcement officers, including the brutal beating and tazing in Los Angeles of Rodney King in 1991, the sodomizing in New York City of Abner Louima in 1997, and the multiple shooting in New York City of unarmed Amadou Diallo in 1999.

It seems as though these are not only times that try the souls of black folk but also times that an increasing number of black and white intellectuals are questioning Ralph Ellison's more representative updated reconstruction of Du Boisian double consciousness. For Ellison and many thousands gone,

> being a Negro American has to do with the memory of slavery and the hope of emancipation and the betrayal by allies and the revenge and contempt inflicted by our former masters after the Reconstruction and the myths, both Northern and Southern, which are propagated in justification of that betrayal. It involves, too, a special attitude toward the waves of immigrants who have come later and passed us by. It has to do with a special perspective on the national ideals and national conduct, and

> with a tragicomic attitude toward the universe. [. . .] It involves a rugged initiation into the mysteries and rites of color. [. . .] It imposes the uneasy burden and occasional joy of a complex double vision, a fluid, ambivalent response to men and events which represents, at its finest, a profoundly civilized adjustment to the cost of being human in this modern world. (*Shadow and Act* 136–37)

But what are the specific times and places, histories and cultures, of African American identities?

Digging into the slave past of black people of sub-Saharan West and Central African ancestry and heritage in the United States, black cultural workers of the 1960s, like many of their elders of the 1920s, discovered that the roots of African American vernacular culture were embedded in the Old South, especially the Georgia and South Carolina Sea Islands and the Mississippi delta. As anthropologist William S. Pollitzer reveals in "The Relationship of the Gullah-Speaking People of Coastal South Carolina and Georgia to Their African Ancestors," the culture in these sites is a unique hybrid blend of a significant number of Bantu-speaking Central African survivals with elements of Native American as well as white Anglo- and Euro-American cultures (58–65). And despite the contemporary transformation of the indigenous Gullah culture on several of those islands by the resurrection of a plantation tradition of resorts for the white rich and famous, they bloom perennially in the verbal, musical, and ritualistic expressions—the socially symbolic acts—of contemporary rural and urban black Americans. In 1790, when the first census was taken in the colonies, 91 percent of the black population (690,000) lived in the South. As late as 1910, 89 percent still lived there. With the outbreak of World War I, my black ancestors began pouring into northern and western cities: Chicago, Detroit, California, Philadelphia, Pittsburgh, New York, and Boston. They fled the South for the North, the fields and farms for the shops and factories. They came talking our talk and walking our walk. They came singing our songs and telling our stories—"Walk together children; don't you get weary." They came expressing the sociohistorical, sociopsychological, and sociocultural authority and authenticity of our African American hybrid identities. Even so, according to 1998 U.S. Census Bureau statistics, 55 percent of black Americans still lived in the South. Six of the ten states with the largest African American populations were in the South: Texas (2.4 million), Florida (2.3 million), Georgia (2.1 million), North Carolina (1.6 million), Maryland (1.4 million), and Louisiana (1.4 million). In addition, the five top states or state equivalents with the largest percentage of African Americans in their total population were southern: Washington, D.C.

(63 percent), Mississippi (36 percent), Louisiana (32 percent), South Carolina (30 percent), and Georgia (28 percent). It is neither surprising nor suspect therefore that the six black professionals in black Harvard sociologist Sara Lawrence-Lightfoot's *I've Known Rivers* (1994) testify to the power of ancestry and the imperative of periodic returns to family cultural origins. This, in part, validates and valorizes the centrality of roots, return, and the journey home in the construction of the identities of black folks.

In "How It Feels to Be a Problem: Du Bois, Fanon, and the Impossible Life, of the Black Intellectual," cultural critic Ross Posnock joins what he calls "a growing chorus of thinkers writing postmodernism's obituary!" and proclaims in a tortured, distorted reading of Du Bois "the reemergence of the cosmopolitan and the universal, ideas stigmatized by the bias of the postmodern toward the particular and local." He argues that "identity politics [. . .] particularly in the form of a fetish of racial authenticity, of roots" has so dominated African American intellectual history by whites and blacks that it "has made it difficult to discern that the black creative intellectual at the turn of the century emerged as a social type by resisting the lure of the prevailing ideology of the authentic" (323–24).

According to Posnock, the "foremost proponent of authenticity was Booker T. Washington, whose mostly white funded Tuskegee machine normalized blackness as contented submission to a utilitarian life of agrarian labor." In contrast, Posnock writes, "W. E. B. Du Bois, the crucial theorist and embodiment of the black intellectual, helped construct this new social type by insisting on the implicitly Dreyfusardian notion of the intellectual as bearer of the universal or, in Du Bois's terms, as 'co-worker in the kingdom of culture', [. . .] a deracialized realm 'above the Veil'" (324–25). Contrary to Posnock's misreading and misquoting of Du Bois and Fanon, as well as black novelists Charles W. Chesnutt and Sutton Griggs in an attempt to celebrate their alleged legacy of moving from racial authenticity to deracinated universality, Du Bois was indeed lyrical and metaphorical. "The history of the American Negro," Du Bois writes in *The Souls of Black Folk*, "is the history of this strife—this longing to attain self-conscious manhood, to merge his double self into a better and truer self. In this merging he wishes neither of the older selves to be lost. He would not Africanize America, for America has too much to teach the world and Africa. He would not bleach his Negro soul in a flood of white Americanism, for he knows that Negro blood has a message for the world. He simply wishes to make it possible for a man to be both a Negro and an American, without being cursed and spit upon by his fellows, without having the doors of opportunity closed roughly in his face" (17). The cardinal message of "Negro blood" as expressed in the ancestral voices of the Sorrow Songs and inscribed in history in

Martin Luther King's "I Have a Dream" speech is, in Du Bois's words, "a faith in the ultimate justice of things. [...] That sometime, somewhere, men will judge men by their souls and not by their skins" (189).

As I pointed out in "Genealogical Shifts in Du Bois's Discourse on Double Consciousness as the Sign of African American Difference," in the discursive shifts in Du Bois's texts from the 1890s to the 1940s, the African American paradoxical sense of being in the world with others was not the fate of all ethnic immigrants and hyphenated Americans. Rather, it was the complex double vision of black Americans of sub-Saharan West and Central African descent whose lives had been historically and paradoxically devalued and marginalized by institutionalized racism, slavery, and rituals of lynching primarily by people of European and British descent but on occasions with the complicity of members of our own racial and ethnic group. Although it is true that our identities are complex, contradictory, and diverse, our attitudes as black Americans toward racial integration and separatism were largely determined by the degree of alienation from or faith in the principles and practices of the ruling class of white Anglo-Saxon and Euro-American Protestants. The major principles and practices, of course, are freedom, democracy, individualism, capitalism, and justice. Based on the legendary one-drop rule, African Americans were both people of African ancestry and nonpeople to the majority of whites; we were an essential part of American society yet segregated apart within it. We were among the first people with whose sweat, blood, and tears the nation was built. But only in response to the civil rights and Black Power struggles did twentieth-century America begin reluctantly and radically in the 1950s and 1960s to address the problem of the color line and to redress the violations of our civil rights as full first-class citizens.

For Du Bois, then, the conflicting state of mind of being a black American was a mixed blessing. It was an ancestral gift for making sense of the mystery of life in the cosmic scheme of things and a product of institutionalized racism. For many contemporary African Americans, it is still the striving to reconcile one's ancestral African diasporic slave past with one's American present and one's ascribed status and identity with one's socially and culturally constructed status and identity. Rather than a sociocultural conflict that has been immutably internalized as incipient personal pathology, African American psychic dualism thus signifies a biracial, bicultural state of being in the world with others, an existential site of socialized cultural ambivalence and emancipatory possibilities of transformation, and a dynamic epistemological mode of critical inquiry for African Americans.

2

The Roots and Branches of the African American Literary Tradition

I

The African American Literary Tradition

Because of the international critical respect for the challenging theory, historical scope, and interdisciplinary methodology of The Afro-American Novel and Its Tradition, *my first major literary study in 1987, I was invited in 1990 by British editors to contribute an historical and critical essay on African American literature to the* Encyclopedia of Literature and Criticism, *edited by Martin Coyle, Peter Garside, Malcolm Kelsall, and John Peck. The initial title of the reference book was* Literature and Criticism: A New Century Guide, *which was changed apparently because of the scholarly length, breadth, and depth of its more than ninety essays. Rather than a conventional survey of African American literature, "The African American Literary Tradition" stresses the distinctive dual African and European biological and cultural heritages of most people of sub-Saharan African descent in the United States. It illuminates how their struggle for freedom and equality in a nation paradoxically and ironically founded on freedom and slavery fostered the double-voiced texts that discerning readers should discover in the complex relationship of their vernacular to their literary tradition.*

"ANYONE WHO ANALYZES BLACK LITERATURE," WRITES LITERARY CRITIC HENRY Louis Gates Jr., "must do so as a comparativist [. . .] because our canonical texts have complex double formal antecedents, the Western and the black" (*Signifying*

Monkey xxiv). This has long been the considered judgment and is now the prevailing wisdom of most African Americanists. Because of the distinctive history and acculturation of Africans in the British colonies in North America, the literary tradition of African Americans is most meaningfully assessed in the context of the tension between their attitudes toward their dual African and European cultural heritages on one hand and their oral and literary heritages on the other. Every American writer of African descent works within and against the dual tradition—oral and literary, African and European, male and female—that each inherits as part of his or her North American cultural legacy and in which, however marginally, each participates in the elusive quest for status, power, and identity. Each writer's contribution and significance are therefore influenced by his or her relationship to past and present writers, as well as by the relationship of his or her texts to others in the tradition, both in the narrow Eurocentric sense of literary formalism and in the broader Afrocentric cultural sense.

While a Eurocentric worldview privileges Greece, Rome, and Europe as the birthplace of civilization and the universal standard of cultural excellence, an Afrocentric worldview, as the neo-hoodoo aesthetician Ishmael Reed's novel *Mumbo Jumbo* (1972) brilliantly illustrates, stresses ancient Africa, including Egypt, as the more historically and archaeologically valid cradle of mankind and cultural diversity. It is generally accepted by scientists that human beings evolved in East Africa at least two million years ago, moved into Europe and Asia about one million years ago, and finally came to the Americas over the Bering Strait some twelve thousand years ago. Pulitzer Prize–winning novelist Alice Walker employs magical realism in *The Temple of My Familiar* (1989) to re-create the primordial sub-Saharan African mother of us all, whether, like paleontologists or fundamentalists, we call her Lucy or Eve.

According to T. S. Eliot's Eurocentric perspective in "Tradition and the Individual Talent," "the historical sense compels a man to write not merely with his own generation in his bones, but with a feeling that the whole of the literature of Europe from Homer and within it the whole of the literature of his own country has a simultaneous existence and composes a simultaneous order" (49). From a dual African and European perspective, as Richard Wright states in "Blueprint for Negro Writing": "Eliot, Stein, Joyce, Proust, Hemingway, and Anderson; Gorky, Barbusse, Nexo, and Jack London no less than the folklore of the Negro himself should form the heritage of the Negro writer. Every iota of gain in human thought and sensibility should be ready grist for his mill, no matter how far-fetched they may seem in their immediate implications" (60).

The point here is not that black literary texts are self-reflexive, self-sufficient intertextual sign systems. Nor is it that all black writers choose to invoke African muses and to employ exclusively black sources in creating their texts. But that black literary texts are sign systems whose referents are nonliterary as well as literary texts that illumine the meaning of the shared experience of black Americans and the complex double consciousness that, as turn-of-the-century aesthete and social scientist W. E. B. Du Bois explains in *The Souls of Black Folk* (1903), a landmark collection of essays, is the special burden and blessing of our African American identity.

In clarification of the group's historical determination to define and name themselves, "Negro," first capitalized as a proper noun by the *New York Times* newspaper in 1930 as a result of a campaign by the NAACP, is a socioeconomic term that was popular in the United States from about 1880 to 1960 for designating both the freeborn and enslaved American descendants of sub-Saharan African peoples. During the Black Power and Black Arts movements of the 1960s, "black," previously considered a racial linguistic marker and badge of inferiority, became popular as a more prideful assertion of racial and ethnic identity that affirmed both political and cultural distinctiveness. "Afro-American" and "African American," the most accurate terms for the racial and cultural hybrid identity of the nation's largest minority group prior to the twenty-first century, were also popular in the 1960s in affirming the common legacy of nonwhite people of African descent in the United States, associating them with a specific place and past. Until 1831 when the first convention of "People of Color" was held in Philadelphia to protest the revival of organized efforts by the American Colonization Society to send free blacks back to Africa, the most popular formal self-conscious institutional group identity of free blacks was African: for example, the Free African Society (1787), New York African Free School (1787), African Mason Lodge (1787), First African Baptist Church of Savannah (1788), and African Methodist Episcopal Church (1794).

"Language," literary critics Rene Wellek and Austin Warren remind us, "is the material of literature as stone or bronze is of sculpture, paints of pictures, or sounds of music. But one should realize that language is not mere inert matter like stone but is itself a creation of men and is thus charged with the cultural heritage of a linguistic group" (22). African American culture is the symbolic and material expression by blacks in the United States of our relationship to nature, to our racial and ethnic community, and to whites as we seek to adapt to our environment in order to survive and thrive, both individually and collectively. We find the roots of this culture in the Deep South in the syncretism of residual Africanisms with elements of European and Native American culture and in the dynamics of gender, class, and ethnic differences. Culture thus signifies the constitutive social process by which people create specific, different ways of life as they adapt to environmental conditions and historical circumstances. For black Americans this process of acculturation has been shaped by a distinctive history: Africa, slavery, the Middle Passage, the Southern plantation, the Emancipation Proclamation, the Thirteenth, Fourteenth, and Fifteenth Amendments to the Constitution, Reconstruction, post-Reconstruction, northern migration, industrialization, urbanization, and, most important, antiblack racism. The unique configuration of these historical experiences generated the interrelated processes of double consciousness, socialized ambivalence, and double vision that best explain the complex, creative dynamics of African American ethnic culture and character.

Du Bois defined the African American experience as the complex sociocultural and sociopsychological duality of Americans of sub-Saharan African descent whose humanity and culture were paradoxically and institutionally commodified, devalued, and marginalized by people of West European and British descent (*Souls of Black Folk* 16–17). Socialized ambivalence signifies an identification shifting between the values of the superordinate white and subordinate black cultural systems as a result of institutionalized antiblack racism. Double vision refers to a tragicomic, wry perspective toward life as expressed in the use of irony, paradox, and parody in African American folklore and formal art.

Some literary historians identify the beginning of the African American literary tradition as the teenage New England slave Lucy Terry's "Bar's Fight," a 1746 verse account of an Indian raid in Deerfield, Massachusetts, which was not published until 1855. Grounded in an indigenous black American vernacular expressive tradition, a more meaningful and appropriate typology of valued writing by and about African Americans divides the literature into documentary, autobiography/biography, and imaginative genres (novels, poems, and plays).

Our African American literary tradition begins with the irony of appeals by African peoples for freedom from the oppression of white British colonists. The early petitions of enslaved Africans for permission to purchase their freedom and to return to Africa invoke the same principle that the white colonists invoked in laying the philosophical foundation for their separation from England. Perhaps the most historically revealing was dated May 25, 1774—less than a week before the British blockaded the Port of Boston in retaliation for the Boston Tea Party of December 1773. It reads: "That your Petitioners apprehind we have in common with all other men a natural right to our freedoms without Being depriv'd of them by our fellow men we are a freeborn Pepel and have never forfeited this Blessing by aney compact or agreement whatever" (Aptheker, *Documentary History* 7–9). The irony of this moving document speaks volumes about the priority given by blacks, who were defined by law as commodities rather than subjects, to forging personal identities or subjectivities on the basis of their common condition and the evolving consciousness of a people in transition from an oral to a literate culture.

As most readers are probably aware, many letters, speeches, essays, and tracts by black Americans calling for freedom, justice, and brotherhood are also valued literary documents. These include astronomer and poet Benjamin Banneker's 1791 letter demonstrating his artistic and scientific attainments to Thomas Jefferson while challenging his racist beliefs in *Notes on the State of Virginia;* clothier and abolitionist David Walker's 1829 revolutionary pamphlet calling for blacks to end slavery by any means necessary; abolitionist orator and journalist Frederick Douglass's eloquent speech, delivered to the Rochester Antislavery Sewing Society on July 5, 1852, on the hypocrisy of the celebration of American independence; and doctor, journalist, and novelist Martin Delany's 1852 *The Condition, Elevation, and Destiny of the Colored People of the United States, Politically Considered,* which promoted the emigration of African Americans to nonwhite nations.

Beginning in 1760 with Briton Hammon's *A Narrative of the Uncommon Suffering and Surprizing Deliverance of Briton Hammon a Negro Man, Servant to General Winslow* and ending in 1901 with Booker T. Washington's *Up from Slavery,* slave or emancipatory narratives and black autobiographies provided dramatic, often messianic, and occasionally jeremiadic first-person testimonies of the discovery of antiblack racism in the secondary acculturative process of interacting with whites. Emancipatory narratives, most of which were published between 1830 and 1865, are the personal accounts of physical and psychological bondage and freedom. Some, like *Narratives of the Sufferings of Lewis and Milton Clarke* (1846) and *The Life of Josiah Henson* (1849), were dictated to white amanuenses and editors who controlled how the facts would be recorded and interpreted. But most were written by the self-emancipated men and women themselves, some of whom had already told their stories dozens of times from an antislavery platform. The most celebrated, highlighted by wry, self-authenticating subtitles, are Olaudah Equiano's *The Interesting Narrative of the Life of Olaudah Equiano, or Gustavus Vassa, the African, Written by Himself* (1789), Frederick Douglass's *Narrative of the Life of Frederick Douglass, an American Slave, Written by Himself* (1845), and Harriet Jacobs's (Linda Brent's) *Incidents in the Life of a Slave Girl, Written by Herself* (1861), whose factual details and authorship were authenticated in 1985 by literary critic and historian Jean Yellin. The problems of authority, authenticity, and agency are addressed in Equiano's, Douglass's, and Jacobs's autobiographies by the explicitly bold assertion of racial identity in the titles that the narratives are written by the authors themselves.

The general pattern of narratives by Frederick Douglass, William W. Brown, J. W. C. Pennington, Solomon Northrop, William and Ellen Craft, and Harriet Jacobs begins with the enslaved subject's realization of the evils of the institution, first attempts at resistance and flight, cunning victories over oppression, and detailed descriptions of different types of brutal physical and depressive spiritual bondage. The narratives end with a successful flight north and an activist role in the "true" religion, rather than the religion that the master class used to justify slavery, and in abolitionist politics. Many read like moral and political allegories. And though the narrators' appeals are mainly to the moral conscience of whites, they clearly express a resolute faith in the humanity of blacks and the righteousness of their struggle for freedom, literacy, and wholeness, both as individuals and as an ethnic group.

Institutionalized antiblack racism and sexism, as most intriguingly illustrated in the narratives by Douglass and Jacobs, at some point frustrated the individual's efforts to realize his or her potential wholeness or balance as an American citizen of African descent. Impelled by the resiliency of significant elements of African cultural survivals and by personal resistance to class, racial, or sexual domination, these individuals turned primarily to their kinship network or ethnic community for survival strategies. Within the ethnic group the individual was disciplined to internalize these sociopsychological tensions and to transform the aborted social energy into cultural energy and expression. Over a long period of time this process of acculturation has settled in the deep consciousness of the individuals who directly experienced it as both self-protective and compensatory cultural behavior, the double consciousness that African American writers, sometimes self-consciously but often unconsciously, illumine for readers. As this experience is expressed symbolically in the spoken and written word, both African American dialect and Standard American English, it becomes accessible and, perhaps, strongly meaningful to a double audience: individuals within and outside of the primary speech community and ethnic group who have never gone through it.

While it has long been known to most African Americanists that William Wells Brown became the father of the African American novel with the London publication in 1853 of *Clotel*, it was not until 1982 that Harriet E. Wilson was discovered to have become the mother of the African American novel with the Boston publication in 1859 of *Our Nig*. Rather than the "great American novel" or a popular romance of the "Feminine Fifties," like Emma Southworth's multi-million-copy-selling *The Hidden Hand, Our Nig*, as its ironic and parodic title suggests, is an intriguing synthesis of the European American sentimental novel and the African American emancipatory narrative, of fiction and fact, of romance and autobiography that is, unlike most emancipatory narratives, addressed primarily to a black audience. Based on the author's life as an indentured servant in New England, its ironic and parodic style is derived from its racial and ethnic double consciousness.

Like its mixed European American stepbrother, the African American novel is a hybrid form. Rather than the culmination of an evolutionary process in the narrative tradition, it is the product of social and cultural forces that shape the author's attitude toward life and that fuel the dialectical process between romantic and mimetic narrative impulses. In contrast to the European American novel, however, the African American novel has its roots in the combined oral and literary traditions of African American culture. It is one of the symbolic literary forms of discourse that black Americans have appropriated from Western culture and adapted in their quest for status, power, and identity in a racist, white, patriarchal North American social arena. The African American novel, in other words, is not a solipsistic, self-referential linguistic system; it is a symbolic sociocultural act. "Precisely because successive Western cultures have privileged written art over oral or musical forms," Gates reminds us, "the writing of black people in Western language has, at all points, remained political, implicitly or explicitly, regardless of its intent or its subject" (*Signifying Monkey* 132). In this sense, the nineteenth-century romances and novels of William Wells Brown, Martin Delany, Francis E. W. Harper, Harriet Wilson, and Sutton Griggs were both private and public linguistic enactments of human relationships reflecting ethical as well as aesthetic decisions inside and outside of the text. They were imaginative literary weapons in the struggle for freedom, literacy, and integrity.

Twentieth-century novelists such as Richard Wright, Zora Neale Hurston, Ralph Ellison, James Baldwin, John A. Williams, William Melvin Kelley, Ernest Gaines, Toni Morrison, Alice Walker, John Edgar Wideman, and Ishmael Reed also employ the novel and romance as symbolic acts to explore the disparity between European American myths and African American reality. But they do not approach the narrative tradition from the same ideological perspective as their white contemporaries, black predecessors, or one another. Among other things, radical social and cultural change has encouraged the movement toward more individualism in the novelists and more experimentation in their aesthetics. Most modern and postmodern African American novelists nevertheless share in a common tradition. This occurs mainly because as members of the largest nonwhite ethnic group in the United States prior to the twenty-first century, African American novelists—except those who have been estranged by birth or acculturation, by circumstances or choice from African American communities and culture—develop their personal and national identities within and against the distinctive pattern of values, orientations to life, and shared ancestral memories they acquired from and contribute to African American culture.

As much as, if not more than, their white contemporaries, nineteenth-century black novelists tapped the roots of their indigenous racial and ethnic culture for matter and method. But the worldview of the racially terrorized and devalued, politically disfranchised, and economically exploited was and is hardly the same as those who dominate and abuse them. Because the distinctiveness of each group's historical experience creates a different cultural frame of reference within which it views and interprets reality, there will inevitably be corresponding differences in the meaning of the archetypal patterns they employ to reconstruct their individual and collective experiences and subjectivities. White and black novelists of the nineteenth and twentieth centuries, for example, both draw on aspects of the Judeo-Christian tradition—especially messianic and jeremiadic themes, symbols, and rituals—for terms to order their experiences. But since, more often than not, the white man's mythic heaven is the black man's mythic hell, black American writers generally express strong ambivalence toward its values, whether by symbolic acts of silence or speech, submission or rebellion. Also, in contrast to the search for innocence and the Adamic vision that inform the Euro-American novel, we usually find the Manichaean drama of white versus black, an apocalyptic vision of a new world order, and the quest to reconcile the double consciousness of Afro-American identity embedded in the texts of nineteenth- and twentieth-century African American novels.

In the twentieth century, for example, Hurston's rewriting of the sentimental romance in *Their Eyes Were Watching God* (1937) celebrates the liberating possibilities of love, storytelling, and autonomy for black women. Wright's rewriting of the myths of the "bad nigger" and the American Dream in *Native Son* (1940) continues to overwhelm readers with the power of its naturalistic truth. Reed's rediscovery and parodic revitalization of such traditional narrative forms as the western in *Yellow Back Radio Broke-Down* (1969), the detective novel in *Mumbo Jumbo* (1972), and the emancipatory narrative in *Flight to Canada* (1976) intrigue us by their bold experimentation with and celebration of an Afrocentric aesthetic. We are also intrigued by Alice Walker's adaptation of the epistolary method in the Pulitzer Prize–winning *The Color Purple* (1982), whose theme is a rewriting of Janie Crawford's dreams in Hurston's romance of what an independent black woman ought to be. And we are left spellbound by Toni Morrison's Pulitzer Prize–winning *Beloved* (1987): a Gothic neo–slave narrative and postmodern romance that speaks in many compelling voices of the historical rape of black women and of the concord of sensibilities that African American people share.

Thematically and structurally, therefore, from Brown and Wilson to Reed and Morrison, the tradition of the African American novel is dominated by the struggle for freedom from all forms of oppression and by the personal odyssey to realize the full potential of one's complex bicultural identity as an African American. This prototypical journey—deriving its sociocultural consciousness from the group experience of black Americans and its mythopoeic force from the interplay of Eurocentric and Afrocentric symbolic systems—begins in physical or psychological bondage and ends in some ambiguous form of deliverance or vision of a new world of mutual respect and justice for peoples of color. In short, the Afro-American canonical story is the quest, frequently with apocalyptic undertones, for freedom, literacy, and wholeness—personal and communal—grounded in social reality and ritualized in symbolic acts of African American speech, music, and religion.

Like the poetry of all national and ethnic groups, Afro-American poetry has its roots in the historical experience of the group's relationship to nature and society. As I illustrate in *The Folk Roots of Contemporary Afro-American Poetry* (1974), it is to the unknown black bards of the spirituals and folk songs—a unique fusion of an ancient African cosmic sensibility and an inchoate Protestant American culture—that North America is indebted for its most priceless music, those sorrowful and joyous songs whose encoded message subtly yet forcefully decried oppression and celebrated the possibilities of the human spirit. And whatever is racial or ethnic in the poetry of black poets is attributable to the power and wisdom of early black music and the double consciousness that it expresses.

The colonial period was the age of Phillis Wheatley, the first slave and second woman in America to publish a book of poems. The Senegambian-born Boston slave's heroic couplets and Christian piety reflect the preoccupation of the few "privileged" black poets of the eighteenth century with neoclassical conventions and biblical symbolism refracted through the prism of an evolving double consciousness. Although Thomas Jefferson considered her poetry beneath the dignity of criticism, many of her contemporaries interpreted *Poems on Various Subjects, Religious and Moral* (1773) as indisputable evidence of the mental equality of blacks. While her neoclassicism nearly stifles her personal voice and ethnic identity, pride in her African heritage is apparent in her self-image in several poems, such as "Ethiop," "Afric's Muse," and "vent'rous Afric."

The most popular antebellum black poet was Francis Ellen Watkins Harper. Her first book, *Poems on Miscellaneous Subjects* (1854), clearly illustrates that her purpose and passion are one: to promote the causes of abolition, Christianity, feminism, and temperance. Her use of abolitionist conventions and Standard English reflects the tension between her ethnic and national consciousness as she sought to explore the burning social issues of the nation and reconcile her personal double consciousness. The postbellum and post-Reconstruction period was the age of Paul Laurence Dunbar, the Ohio-born poet whose ambiguous use of black speech and music is the culmination of the identity crisis of many late nineteenth-century black poets. His dilemma of being torn between the impulse to explore and expand the forms of Afro-American folklore and the desire to master Euro-American conventions is equally representative. If the antebellum popularity of slave narratives marks the first flowering of Afro-American literature, then Dunbar's publication of *Oak and Ivy* (1893) and *Majors and Minors* (1895) marks the second renaissance. The muted cry of anguish we hear and sense beneath Dunbar's mask of humor, which is the theme of "We Wear the Mask," is due in part to white critics' unjustly ignoring the majority of his poems in Standard English and only praising the pathos and humor of what he refers to in "The Poet" as "a jingle in a broken tongue," literary dialect established by the conventions of minstrelsy and the plantation tradition.

The third awakening of Afro-American art and letters, during the 1920s, was dominated by the prolific, versatile Langston Hughes, who is popularly considered the poet laureate of black America. This period is also known as the Negro Renaissance, Harlem Renaissance, and New Negro movement. It was the period in which Harlem was the national stage for the meteoric rise of such artists as Claude McKay, Jean Toomer, Countee Cullen, Bill Robinson, Florence Mills, Josephine Baker, Ethel Waters, Paul Robeson, Roland Hayes, Aaron Douglass, Louis Armstrong, Bessie Smith, Duke Ellington, and Hughes. Many artists of the decade, like Hughes, turned to Africa and Afro-American folklore for a sense of tradition. Hughes's first book of verse, *The Weary Blues* (1926), focuses on the nightlife of the Harlem cabarets and captures the sights and sounds of the Jazz Age. Besides introducing jazz and blues rhythms into poetry, Hughes took the world for his audience, but, for the most part, his subject was the black urban working class. His music was the sound of Lenox Avenue in New York, Seventh Street in the District of Columbia, and South State Street in Chicago. And his language has been aptly called Harlemese: vibrant, rhythmic, direct, racy urban black speech.

In contrast to the rebellious poetry of the 1920s and 1930s, the verse of the 1940s by Robert Hayden, Margaret Walker, Melvin Tolson, Gwendolyn Brooks, and Owen Dodson seems sedate. This is not to suggest that racial themes, social protest, and experiments in prosody are absent in their work, especially Walker's "For My People," Hayden's "Runagate Runagate," and Brooks's *Annie Allen* (1949), for which she was awarded the Pulitzer Prize in 1950. Products of an era of American criticism that repudiated didacticism in literature and advocated the concept of art for art's sake, the black poets of the 1940s labored diligently and in many cases successfully to perfect their craftsmanship.

The black poets of the 1950s were nomadic, bohemian bards whose audiences were the predominantly white patrons of Greenwich Village coffee houses and San Francisco bistros. Amiri Baraka (LeRoi Jones), Bob Kaufman, and Ted Joans were among the most prominent of this black beat generation. Their chief themes were alienation, jazz, war, and death; their language was iconoclastic; and their style surrealistic. Too avant-garde for the traditional literary establishment, they gave public readings and appeared in underground magazines such as *Beatitude, Big Table,* and *Evergreen Review.*

Rising like a phoenix out of the ashes of Watts, New York, Newark, Chicago, and Atlanta came the poets of the Black Arts movement of the 1960s, including Haki Madhubuti (Don Lee), Nikki Giovanni, Sonia Sanchez, Etheridge Knight, Askia Toure, Clarence Major, and Larry Neal. Because the Black Arts and Black Power concepts both relate broadly to the Afro-American's desire for self-determination and nationhood, both are nationalistic. With Baraka, the multitalented writer, as the drum major of the movement, this generation of poets—most of them under thirty-five years old—set out to create a New Black Aesthetic and nation. Their credo was art for people's sake, and their goal was black unity and liberation. The movement was toward Islam rather than Christianity, pan-Africanism rather than Americanism, and a black aesthetic—especially a revitalizing use of Africa, the blues, and the urban black vernacular—rather than a white.

Black poetry of the 1970s and 1980s—as illustrated by Alice Walker, Sterling Plumpp, Carolyn Rodgers, June Jordan, Michael Harper, Maya Angelou, Jayne Cortez, Rita Dove, Eugene Redmond, Ishmael Reed, and Al Young—continues to illumine the tension between Eurocentric and Afrocentric aesthetic values. Regardless of the sociopolitical convictions of individual contemporary African American poets, many of their poems reveal a romantic interest in and realistic evaluation of black folk values, a celebration of the black masses and of musicians as heroes, and a validation of the poetic qualities of black speech and music. The diverse styles, structures, and themes of their poems, in short, attest to the complexity of their bicultural identity as African Americans.

Like documentary, autobiographical, fictive, and poetic African American literature, black theater literature, especially after the realism of Lorraine Hansberry's *A Raisin in the Sun* (1959) and beginning with the expressionism of Amiri Baraka's *Dutchman* (1964), dramatizes the tension between Eurocentric and Afrocentric sensibilities and conventions. "In an effort to locate a specific culturally derived voice," playwright and director Paul Carter Harrison writes,

> Afro-Americans began to shape an aesthetic that reflected both the African legacy and their cumulative experience in a highly technological society. The aesthetic formulations seemed crude in the beginning, song-dance-drum—those civilizing forces of ritual—appearing quaint and exotic next to the formal canons of Western dramaturgy. However, after the discovery of oral and literary traditions among the Yoruba and the Akan, and of the ontological system of the Dogon, the rudimentary apprehension of drum as iconographic reference—the rhythmical analogue to the human voice—was elaborated into a more sophisticated aesthetic principle. (xliv)

Baraka's *Dutchman* (1964) and *The Slave* (1964), Joseph Walker's *River Niger* (1972), James Baldwin's *Blues for Mister Charlie* (1964), Ron Milner's *What the Wine Sellers Buy* (1974), Paul Carter Harrison's *The Great Mac Daddy* (1972), and Ntozake Shange's *for colored girls who have considered suicide / when the rainbow's enuf* (1974)—are among the major plays that chart this development by Douglas Turner Ward's Negro Ensemble Company and Woodie King's New Federal Theater as well as by traditional American theater institutions, both on and off Broadway. Among the coveted awards received by African Americans is the Pulitzer Prize for plays such as *No Place to Be Somebody* (1970) by Charles Gordone, *A Soldier's Play* (1982) by Charlie Fuller, and *Fences* (1987) by August Wilson.

The consensus of contemporary specialists in the fields of African American literary history and criticism is that the African American literary tradition is best understood and appreciated by interpreting its merits within the context of its own indigenous nature and function. Important contemporary critical studies include Robert Stepto's *From Behind the Veil* (1979), which emphasizes the intertextuality of call-and-response in canonical black texts; Barbara Christian's *Black Women Novelists* (1980), which traces the impact of stereotypic images on the narrative tradition of black women; Keith Beyerman's *Fingering the Jagged Grain* (1985), which highlights the use of black folk materials in recent black fiction; and Melvin Dixon's *Ride Out the Wilderness* (1987), which argues for spatial ethnic tropes as the distinctive feature of Afro-American literature. The consensus of senior critics is that the most significant historical, cultural, and critical studies include Houston Baker's *Blues, Ideology, and Afro-American Literature* (1984), which focuses on the blues as the key black vernacular trope; Bernard Bell's *The Afro-American Novel and Its Tradition* (1987), with its theory of the novel as a socially symbolic act that formally encodes and wryly illumines the biracial, bicultural, residually oral tradition of African Americans; Hazel Carby's *Reconstructing Womanhood* (1987), which analyzes the influence of black feminist discourse on the literary conventions of early black American women; Henry Gates's *The Signifying Monkey* (1988), which privileges signifying and pastiche as the prototypical black vernacular and literary tropes; and William Andrew's *To Tell a Free Story* (1988), which illumines the uniquely self-liberating and empowering rhetorical strategies of black autobiography. Best interpreted in its own indigenous bicultural context, African American literature revitalizes the language and challenges people to realize the richness and diversity of their human potential.

II

African American Writers

In 1973 I was invited by Professor Everett Emerson, then editor of Early American Literature, *the major academic journal in that period of literature, and my colleague at the University of Massachusetts, to write a chapter on African American writers for* American Literature 1764–1789: The Revolutionary Years *(1977), a literary history by a new generation of critics and scholars. My chapter went through the usual many drafts and revisions, primarily for its excessive length and radical tone. The revisions extended into 1975 while I was in Germany resisting as tactfully as possible requests to change my African Americentric style that challenged rather than confirmed the interpretations of earlier writers. "Tyler, Parrington, Commager, Murdock, Miller, and Jones," the esteemed Americanist scholar Professor Robert Spiller observed in his review of the book, "are almost forgotten and never deferred to." Spiller also noted, "Except for the chapters on the Loyalists, the travelers, and the blacks, there is little novelty in the material."*

Although I mention the neglect of African American writers in Moses Coit Tyler's classic nineteenth-century Eurocentric cultural and intellectual histories of American literature in my conclusion, it is significant that Professor Spiller recognized the newness of my chapter, "the only minority representation" in the Emerson book, as a Choice reviewer similarly observed. Twenty-first-century general readers and students will find scholarly studies in the 1980s and 1990s by Catherine Obianuju Acholonu and Vincent Carretta that provocatively debate the issues of Equiano's birth, nationality, and name. Hopefully, readers will also find this essay interesting and informative.

As Jefferson originally penned it, the Declaration of Independence included a strong statement of grievance against the British king for having "waged cruel war against human nature itself." Though the passage attacking slavery was deleted from the declaration, the work remains, as Edwin Gittleman reveals in his 1974 article, a slave narrative, for Jefferson conceived of Americans as living the lives of slaves under British tyranny. While he hated slavery in every form, Jefferson did not see the black victims of absolute slavery as fully human. If the enlightened Jefferson was not able to embrace the principle of equality for enslaved Africans, other Americans were even more racist in their sentiments. Nevertheless, some notable black writers developed in revolutionary America, who are now beginning to receive their due.

Because of the distinctive history and acculturation of Africans in the English colonies during the revolutionary period, their literary gifts are most meaningfully assessed in the context of the tension between African American attitudes toward integration and separatism on the one hand and the oral and literate cultural heritages on the other. Most modern historians accept the fact that American slaves were the descendants of peoples with a history and culture. Since culture is basically the symbolic and material resources developed in the process of interaction between the individual, his society, and his environment, it is neither acquired nor lost overnight, whether as the result of conditions imposed by the slave system or by the urban ghettoes. That the African slave's way of life did change radically with his introduction to a new environment and social system goes without saying. But the change was seldom rapid, never uniform, and generally accretive and syncretic rather than a sloughing off of Old World values and survival techniques with the adoption of New World values.

Too many students of American character and culture overlook the fact that the first black people did not arrive in the colonies with a group identity as slaves and "neegars" but with specific African identities. The majority of the captives were Ibo, Ewe, Biafada, Bakongo, Wolof, Bambara, Ibibio, Serer, and Arada. Unlike the first white immigrants, they were the only involuntary servants brought to seventeenth-century Virginia in chains and systematically deprived of their Old World cultural heritage and social systems in order to transform them into better slaves and servants. This development was the result of the interaction between slavery and racism, for the increasing demand for cheap labor led to political acts and a social ideology that severely restricted the human and civil rights of blacks. Prior to the end of the seventeenth century, free blacks in Virginia could acquire property, vote, and even intermarry with whites. But with the racialization and growth of slavery the black codes of the eighteenth century reduced them to a quasifree lower caste. Christian principles prevented neither southerners nor northerners from arrogating to themselves supreme power over other human beings, yet in practice Africans in the non-slave-based economies of the North fared better than their southern brothers. Many colonial slaves and free blacks in New England, for example, were taught to read and write in order to make them better Christians and more efficient porters, clerks, and messengers. It is also important to remember that the names of such eighteenth-century organizations as the African Society (1787), the New York African Free School (1787), the African Mason Lodge (1787), and the African Methodist Episcopal Church (1794) established the first formal self-conscious group identity of free blacks as African.

While Egyptian, Ethiopian, and Arabic script were known in parts of Africa for centuries, eighteenth-century Africa was mainly an oral culture. As Olaudah Equiano, the European African abolitionist, tells us in his classic slave narrative, the spoken word, music, and dance were at the center of a communal, profoundly religious way of life. In contrast, industrialized Europe and England had moved beyond the oral stage and medieval thinking to a reverence for print and human enlightenment. The literary tradition and its attendant values, especially reading and writing, were cherished as the exclusive heritage of civilized man. Until the twentieth century these two modes of perceiving, organizing, and communicating experience were believed by Europeans to be related to different stages of development of the mind. But as Claude Lévi-Strauss notes, these alternative approaches are actually "two strategic levels at which nature is accessible to scientific enquiry: one roughly adapted to that of perception and imagination: the other at a remove from it [. . .] one very close to, and the other at a remove from sensible intuition" (15). Each has its own advantages. While a literate orientation heralds the advancement of technology and abstract learning, an oral orientation reinforces the primacy of events and disciplined yet improvisational acts of a group nature. One culture conceives of man as the measure of all things; the other conceives of him as a deeply religious being, living in harmony with a mystical, organic universe.

By 1764 the institution of racialized slavery had been established in the colonies for more than a hundred years, and by 1789 the compulsion of whites to remake blacks into harmless, civilized Christians was a matter of record. As Vernon Loggins observes, Cotton Mather's *Rules for the Societies of Negroes*, written in 1693, was typical of the general attitude of the Puritan and Anglican divines, whose interest in Christianizing blacks was to make them more honest, useful servants. Freedom in the form of manumission or a privileged status was the reward for those considered acceptably acculturated. The deprivation of educational, economic, and political opportunities for the majority of blacks, however, made cultural assimilation the prize of precious few. In addition, the process of adopting the dominant, antiblack racist Anglo-Saxon cultural pattern of the revolutionary period resulted in the ethnic double consciousness that W. E. B. Du Bois eloquently described in *The Souls of Black Folk*. African Americans were both people of African descent and nonpeople to the majority of whites; they were part of the society yet alienated from it; they were among the first colonists to build the nation, but the nation has yet to grant and guarantee them first-class citizenship. African Americans were therefore destined to function on two levels of reality, and their attitudes toward integration and separatism were largely determined by the degree of alienation from or faith in the principles of the dominant white Anglo-Saxon Protestant society.

Integration may be defined as the dual processes of cultural and social assimilation. While cultural assimilation during the revolutionary era involved essentially learning the English language, the Bible, the classics, the popular English and neoclassical writers, and colonial behavior patterns, social assimilation, in contrast, meant full participation in the organizations and institutions of the emerging nation. Fear for their physical and psychological security led white colonists to redefine Africans as a distinctive group of subhumans who ought to be culturally but not socially assimilated, especially in southern colonies where their numbers were a cause of alarm. This was particularly true of Virginia where there were only 300 blacks in the mid-seventeenth century but 120,156 blacks and 173,316 whites by the mid-eighteenth. Consequently, in 1662 the colony imposed a fine for interracial fornication; in 1691 it banned interracial marriages; and in 1723 it deprived free blacks of the right to vote. In seventeenth-century New England, where the black population was never more than 20,000, blacks were excluded from the militia; nevertheless, from the French and Indian wars to the Battle of Bunker Hill slaves and free blacks alike took up arms in the struggle for American independence (Franklin 57, 66, 89).

Although confrontations with British soldiers, like that of Crispus Attucks, the fugitive slave and New England seaman, who was among the five colonists killed in the Boston Massacre, may be interpreted as integrationist acts of patriotism, the early petitions of slaves for permission to purchase their freedom and to return to Africa affirm their desire for separatism. In truth, however, the major loyalty of colonial blacks was not so much to a place or a people as it was to the principle of freedom, the principle the white colonists themselves expressed in terms of the natural rights of man as they laid the philosophical foundation for their separation from England. At least three petitions from New England slaves in 1773 sounded a similar note. The first was in January to Governor Hutchinson and the general court from "many Slaves, living in the Town of Boston, and other Towns in the Province [. . .] who have had every Day of their Lives imbittered with this most intollerable Reflection, That, let their Behavior be what it will, nor their Children to all Generations shall ever be able to do, or to possess and enjoy any Thing, no, not even *Life itself,* but in a Manner as the *Beasts that perish.* We have no Property! We have no Wives! No Children! We have no City! No Country!" The author of the petition was, ironically, Felix. The second, a letter addressed to delegates of the House of Representatives by four slaves—Peter Bestes, Sambo Freeman, Felix Holbrook, and Chester Joie—"In behalf of our fellow slaves in this province and by order of their Committee," came in April. After expressing "a high degree of satisfaction" with the legislative efforts of the colony "to free themselves from slavery," the letter boldly asserts, "We expect great things from men who have made such a noble stand against the designs of *their fellow-men* to enslave them" and goes on to request "one day in a week to work for themselves, to enable them to earn money to purchase the residue of their time." Seeing no relief from degrading prejudice and discrimination in America, they were willing to submit to the law "until we leave the province [. . .] as soon as we can from our Joynt labours procure money to transport ourselves to some part of the coast of Africa, where we propose a settlement" (Aptheker 6–8). The third petition addressed to Governor Hutchinson arrived in June and echoes the sentiments of James Otis's 1764 protest in the *Rights of the British Colonies:* "Your Petitioners apprehend they have in common with other men a naturel right to be free and without molestation to injoy such property as they may acquire by their industry, or by any other means not detrimental to their fellow men" (qtd. in S. Kaplan 13). None of these petitioners were granted relief by the courts, the legislature, or the governor.

Perhaps the most historically revealing petition for freedom was dated May 25, 1774—less than a week before the British blockaded the Port of Boston in retalation for the Boston Tea Party of December 1773—and addressed to Governor Thomas Gage and the General Court of Massachusetts by "a Grate Number of Blackes of this Province who by divine permission are held in a state of Slavery within the bowels of a free and christian Country." As the hegemonic colonial orthography and grammar, as well as the counterhegemonic use of irony and paradox in the above and the following lengthy quotations reveal, this moving document seeks to demonstrate the priority given by blacks to the forging of personal and collective identities on the basis of their common condition and the evolving consciousness of a people in transition from an oral to a literate culture:

> That your Petitioners apprehind we have in common with all other men a naturel right to our freedoms without Being depriv'd of them by our fellow men as we are a freeborn Pepel and have never forfeited this Blessing by aney compact or agreement whatever. But we were unjustly dragged by the cruel hand of power from our dearest frinds and sum of us stolen from the bosoms of our tender Parents and from a Populous Pleasant and plentiful country and Brought hither to be made slaves for Life in a Christian land. [. . .] How can the master be said to Beare my Borden when he Beares me down whith the Have chanes of Slavery and operson against my will. [. . .] and as we cannot serve our God as we ought whilst in this situation. Nither can we reap an equal benefet from the laws of the Land which doth not justifi but condemns Slavery or if there had bin aney Law to hold us in Bondage we are Humbely of the Opinion ther never was aney to inslave our children for life when Born in a free Countrey. We therfor Bage your Excellency and Honours will give this its deer weight and consideration and that you will accordingly cause an act of the legislative to be pessed that we may obtain our Natural right our freedoms and our children be set at lebety at the yeare of twenty one. (Aptheker 7–9)

As in the past, the legislature voted to let the question "subside"—did they find the petition unintelligible? unacceptable? inexpedient?—but subside it did not.

Despite the scores of antislavery petitions by blacks—some in the eloquent prose of the period, others acceptable, all intelligible—Quakers, and other groups, the Founding Fathers chose political and economic expediency over principle when they deleted all reference to slavery from the final draft of the Declaration of Independence. According to Jefferson, the condemnation of slavery was deleted in deference to the economic interests of Georgia and South Carolina, who argued for the continuation of the slave trade. To compound this fracture between principle and practice, between the emerging national belief in the inalienable rights of man and colonial laws, between the antislavery, industrial North and the proslavery, agrarian South, the Constitutional Convention of 1787 disingenuously sanctioned slavery without using the terms *slave* and *slavery*. For example, article 1, section 2 declared that representation in Congress and taxes were to be determined by the numbers of free persons in each state "and excluding Indians not taxed, three fifths of all other persons." In addition, article 1, section 9 stated that prior to 1808 "The Migration or Importation of such Persons as any of the states now existing shall think proper to admit, shall not be prohibited," thus extending the slave trade for twenty years; and article 4, section 2 stated that "No Person held to Service or Labour in one State [. . .] escaping into another, shall [. . .] be discharged from such Service or Labour, but shall be delivered up on claim of the Party to whom such Service or Labour may be due" (qtd. in Syrett 105, 109, 113). If it is true that the fathers of the Constitution were dedicated to the principle of freedom, it is no less true, as the eminent African American historian John Hope Franklin reminds us in his classic *From Slavery to Freedom* (1947), that they were even more dedicated to the political, ethnocentric, socioeconomic proposition that "government should rest upon the dominion of property" (100).

Although the antislavery movement was set back by the Three-Fifths Compromise of the ruling class and its political repudiation of the natural rights of blacks, many African Americans felt that the preamble to the Declaration of Independence still held out the promise of "Life, Liberty and the pursuit of Happiness" for them as well as whites. For them the Revolutionary War had been a struggle more for personal freedom than for political independence. And at the end of the war, hundreds of the 5,000 blacks who fought for the patriots were freed by the states even though some masters contested the promises of manumission. By 1790 there were nearly 4 million whites and slightly more than 750,000 blacks in the United States. In the southern states there were 641,691 slaves and 32,048 free blacks. The mid-Atlantic states had approximately 36,000 slaves and 14,000 free blacks. In contrast, New England had only 3,700 slaves in a black population of more than 13,000. While

Vermont and Massachusetts reported no slaves at all, Connecticut had 2,600. The only city able to boast no slaves was Boston. Its 761 blacks were free (Franklin 102–03).

By virtue of his unique situation as a slave or quasifree person in a society that was growing painfully aware of its paradoxical role as the oppressed and the oppressor, the African American writer's struggle for independence provides a classic metaphor for the psychological and political schism of the new nation. Even more than the slave petitions for freedom, the writings of two African Americans and a European African reveal how individual processes of cultural and social assimilation in a basically hostile white Anglo-Saxon literate society fostered the duality or doubleness of early black identity. For Jupiter Hammon, Phillis Wheatley, and Olaudah Equiano, the necessity of functioning on two planes of reality was a challenge that each met in terms of his or her own unique situation and gifts.

1

In the case of Jupiter Hammon, whose publication in 1760 of the broadside poem "An Evening Thought" marks the formal birth of African American literature, we see the influence of the Bible and slavery in shaping an otherworldly view of liberty and equality that fostered a passive social vision. What little is known about his life is found in scraps of information in letters and in the poetry and prose itself. Born a slave on October 17, 1711, Hammon was owned by the Lloyds, a merchant family of Long Island. A dutiful, intelligent servant, he was apparently encouraged in his efforts to read and write by Henry Lloyd, his first master, for in one of his discourses he refers to the English divines, Burkitt and Beveridge, whose works were in Lloyd's library. In 1733 he purchased a Bible from his master for seven shillings and six pence, an indication of the depth of his religious commitment, his thriftiness, and the nature of his master's benevolence. Since he was well-read in the Bible and considered an exemplary slave, and since there were black and Indian churches on Long Island and in Connecticut during this era, it is highly possible that Hammon was a slave exhorter. In 1760 he became the first black American to publish a poem in the colonies. Apparently this distinction and the prestige it brought his owner contributed to the poet not being freed upon the elder Lloyd's death in 1763. Instead, he was inherited by Joseph, one of four sons. After Joseph's death during the Revolutionary War, the family retainer was passed on to John Lloyd Jr., a grandson (S. Kaplan 171–78). With the British takeover of Long Island, the patriotic Lloyd family took their talented, faithful servant with them to Hartford, Connecticut, where Hammon is believed to have died a free man between 1790 and 1806, since slavery was abolished in the state in 1784 and the Revolutionary War ended in 1783 (Wegelin 15).

Hammon's first broadside poem was titled *An Evening Thought. Salvation by Christ, with Penetential Cries: Composed by Jupiter Hammon, a Negro Belonging to Mr. Lloyd of Queen's Village, on Long Island, the 25th of December, 1760*. Lacking the originality, ironic tension, graphic imagery, and call-and-response pattern of black American spirituals, the poem reveals Hammon's personal resignation to slavery and the inspiration of the Psalms and Methodist hymnals:

> Lord, hear our penitential Cry:
> Salvation from above;
> It is the Lord that doth supply,
> With his redeeming Love. (29)

The repetition of "Salvation" in twenty-three of the poem's eighty-eight lines does not significantly elevate the prosaic quality of the verse.

The next broadside was *An Address to Miss Phillis Wheatley, Ethiopian Poetess, in Boston, Who Came from Africa at Eight Years of Age, and Soon Became Acquainted with the Gospel of Jesus Christ*. Published in Hartford on August 4, 1778, this twenty-one-stanza poem celebrates the salvation of his more famous and youthful contemporary from "heathen" Africa:

> Thou hast left the heathen shore;
> Through mercy of the Lord,
> Among the heathen live no more,
> Come magnify thy God.
> Thou, Phillis, when thou hunger hast,
> Or pantest for thy God,
> Jesus Christ is thy relief
> Thou hast the holy word.

As usual, the poet reminds his reader that ultimate freedom and joy is not earthly but heavenly:

> While thousands muse with earthly toys,
> And rage about the street,
> Dear Phillis, seek for heaven's joy's,
> Where we do hope to meet. (34–35)

Contrary to the poet's view, Phillis Wheatley was more capable of coping with and giving poetic form to the two planes of reality than he. A third poem, *An Essay on the Ten Virgins,* was printed in 1779 and advertised in the *Connecticut Courant* on December 14, 1779, but no copy has been preserved. Hammon's unimaginative use of the meter, rhyme, diction, and stanzaic pattern of the Methodist hymnal, combined with the negative image of Africa and conciliatory tone of these early poems, reveals the poet's limitations and the sociopsychological price he paid for the mere semblance of cultural assimilation.

As his first published sermon indicates, Hammon was under fire from his black "Brethren" and sisters for his otherworldly view of freedom. *A Winter Piece: Being a Serious Exhortation with a Call to the Unconverted: and a Short Contemplation on the Death of Jesus Christ,* published in Hartford in 1782, attempts to defend his ostensible betrayal of his people's struggle for freedom in this life:

> My dear Brethren, as it hath been reported that I had petitioned to the court of Hartford against freedom, I now solemnly declare that I never have said, nor done any thing, neither directly nor indirectly, to promote or to prevent freedom; but my answer hath always been I am a stranger here and I do not care to be concerned or to meddle with public affairs, and by this declaration I hope my friends will be satisfied, and all prejudice removed, Let us all strive to be united together in love, and to become new creatures. (Qtd. in S. Kaplan 174)

The lessons of the Bible and slavery had taught him that for body and soul, black and white, individual and nation, freedom was God's alone to grant:

> Come my dear fellow servants and brothers, Africans by nation, we are all invited to come, Acts x, 34. Then Peter opened his mouth and said, of a truth I perceive that God is no respecter of persons, verse 35. But in every nation he that feareth him is accepted of him. My Brethren, many of us are seeking a temporal freedom, and I wish you may obtain it; remember that all power in heaven and earth belongs to God; if we are slaves it is by the permission of God, if we are free it must be by the power of the most high God. Stand still and see the salvation of God, cannot that same power that divided the waters from the waters for the children of Israel to pass through, make way for your freedom. (Qtd. in S. Kaplan 175)

Hammon's reference to himself and his people as "Africans by nation" reflects his awareness of the duality of his identity, a duality he unfortunately sought to transcend rather than synthesize through religiosity. Appended to the sermon is the seventeen quatrain "Poem for Children with Thoughts of Death" as further testimony to the poet's piety.

The sermon and poem, believed to have been written soon after *A Winter Piece*, contain references to "the Present War." In *An Evening's Improvement. Shewing the Necessity of Beholding the Lamb of God*, Hammon is parodoxical in his passive providential philosophy of life. While expressing a jeremiadic belief in an avenging God for "our sins," including the national sin of slavery:

> And now my brethren, I am to remind you of a most melancholy scene of Providence; it hath pleased the most high God, in his wise providence, to permit a cruel and unnatural war to be commenced. [. . .] Have we not great cause to think this is the just deserving of our sins. [. . .] Here we see that we ought to pray, that God may hasten the time when the people shall beat their swords into a ploughshares and their spears into pruning-hooks, and nations shall learn war no more. (Qtd. in S. Kaplan 175–76)

And in the second half of "A Dialogue Intitled the Kind Master and the Dutiful Servant," the two-page poem concluding the sermon, the poet piously stands above the Revolutionary War and prays for peace:

> Servant
> Dear Master, now it is a time,
> A time for great distress;
> We'll follow after things divine,
> And pray for happiness.
> Master
> Then will the happy day appear,
> That virtue shall increase;
> Lay up the sword and drop the spear,
> And Nations seek for peace. (44)

Banal, bloodless, and commonplace, these lines on Christian virtue tell us as much about the otherworldly theology that whites imposed on colonial blacks as they do about Hammon's pacifist identity and conservative poetry and prose.

The most decisive evidence of the poet-preacher's exploitation by those who found his religious convictions a model for African American character and behavior is found in Hammon's final discourse, *An Address to the Negroes of the State of New York.* Dedicated to the African Society of New York in 1786, the *Address* was published two years after slavery was outlawed in the state and a year before it became the eleventh state to ratify the Constitution. Since Hammon was seventy-six at the time, he sincerely intended this discourse to be the "last [. . .] dying advice, of an old man." With an unrelenting faith in God and white people, whose sinful habits, he believed, did not in God's eyes and his own condone the sins of slaves, Hammon preaches against the sins of disobedience, stealing, lying, swearing, and idleness. Consciousness of the irony of his people's oppression by those who had waged a costly and bloody war to end their own oppression is expressed but quickly suppressed by personal resignation to slavery and otherworldliness:

> Now I acknowledge that liberty is a great thing, and worth seeking for, if we can get it honestly, and by our good conduct prevail on our masters to set us free. Though for my own part I do not wish to be free: yet I should be glad, if others, especially the young negroes were to be free, for many of us who are grown up slaves, and have always had masters to take care of us, should hardly know how to take care of ourselves; and it may be more for our own comfort to remain as we are. [. . .] Getting our liberty in this world is nothing to having the liberty of the children of God. (Robinson 42)

Jupiter Hammon's importance as a poet is essentially historical and sociological, for his blind faith in the benevolence of whites and the kingdom of heaven is a vivid illustration of the ambiguous political role of too many early African American integrationist writers and preachers whose socialized ambivalence was both a blessing and a curse in the struggle of blacks for independence.

2

In contrast to Jupiter Hammon, several eighteenth-century black ministers asserted their right to be free of prejudice and to run their own affairs by breaking off from the established white churches and organizing their own separate institutions. Although the dates and themes of their miscellaneous writings do not fall strictly within the revolutionary era, their struggle for freedom of worship paradoxically has much in common with one of the ultimate goals of the revolution. David George, a slave, started the first black Baptist church among the slaves in the colonies in Silver Bluff, South Carolina, between 1773 and 1775. In 1788 Andrew Bryan, another slave exhorter whose master encouraged his preaching because he believed it had a salutary influence on other slaves, established the First African Baptist Church in Savannah, Georgia. But the most celebrated black church fathers are ex-slaves Richard Allen and Absalom Jones. Dragged from their knees while praying in St. George's Methodist Episcopal Church of Philadelphia, these two ministers and the other blacks attending service "all went out of the church in a body, and they were no more plagued with us in the church." In Reverend Allen's words, "We were determined to seek out for ourselves, the Lord being our helper" (qtd. in S. Kaplan 81, 85). Thus, in 1794 Allen founded the Bethel African Methodist Episcopal Church and fought for many years to protect his church and congregation from the hostility of white Methodist preachers and trustees. During the same year, Jones, who had earlier accepted an Episcopalian pastorate, dedicated the St. Thomas African Episcopal Church of Philadelphia. Less assertive, but no less pious or significant, is Phillis Wheatley.

As the first slave and second woman writer in America to publish a book of poems, Phillis Wheatley achieved literary distinction for her extraordinary development as a black poet on both sides of the Atlantic. To many of her contemporaries her poetry was indisputable evidence of the mental equality of blacks. But Moses Coit Tyler's observation in *The Literary History of the American Revolution* (1897) that "her career belongs rather to the domain of anthropology, or of hagiology, than to that of poetry—whether American or African" is more useful as an example of the tenacity of eighteenth-century racial prejudices and the limitations of nineteenth-century American scholarship than as a reliable assessment of the literary merits of "Afric's muse," as she calls herself in "Hymn to Humanity." Like Jefferson, Tyler believed her poetry "below the dignity of criticism" (1: 186). But as Julian Mason Jr. rightly observes in the authoritative edition of the poet's complete works: "Her poems are certainly as good or better than those of most of the poets usually included and afforded fair treatment in a discussion of American poetry before 1800, and this same evaluation holds true when she is compared with most of the minor English poets of the eighteenth century who wrote in the neoclassical tradition" (xxxi).

A frail, precocious African child of seven, Phillis Wheatley arrived in Boston on a slave ship from Senegambia, the territory known in modern Africa as Senegal and

Gambia, in 1761. She was purchased by John Wheatley, a prosperous tailor and owner of several household slaves, as a special servant for his wife, Susannah Wheatley. The Wheatleys were dedicated to missionary work among Indians and blacks; their home was a well-known meeting place for Boston's cultured society. Once Mrs. Wheatley and her daughter, Mary, discovered Phillis Wheatley's quickness of mind, their humanitarian impulse to provide her with the proper cultivation was irresistible. In a letter to her London publisher in 1772, Mr. Wheatley wrote, "Without any assistance from School Education, and by only what she was taught in the Family, she, in sixteen Months Time from her Arrival, attained the English Language. to which she was an utter stranger before, to such a Degree, as to read any, the most difficult parts of the Sacred Writings, to the great Astonishment of all who heard her" (qtd. in Mason 1). Thanks mainly to Mary Wheatley's teaching, as Benjamin Brawley points out in *The Negro in Literature and Art,* Wheatley soon learned "a little astronomy, some ancient and modern geography, a little ancient history, a fair knowledge of the Bible, and a thoroughly appreciative acquaintance with the most important Latin classics, especially the works of Virgil and Ovid" (17–18). As she developed beyond mere literacy, she took pride in Terence's African heritage, became proficient in grammar, and favored Pope's translations of Homer among the English classics. Mrs. Wheatley's favorite, the young poet was not allowed to associate with the other domestics or do hard work. Her memory of Africa was vague, and her only recollection of her mother was that she poured out water before the rising sun. Gradually her frail health and literary genius earned her privileged treatment as a companion to her mistress and as an adopted member of the family. "I was treated by her more like her child then her servant," Wheatley wrote in 1774 to her African friend, Obour Tanner; "no opportunity was left unimproved of giving me the best of advice; but in terms how tender! how engaging!" (Qtd. in Mason 107).

Eager to write, "she learnt in so short a Time, that in the Year 1765, she wrote a Letter to the Rev. Mr. Occum, the Indian Minister" (qtd. in Mason 1), who later published a hymnal for his people. In 1767, when she was only fourteen, Wheatley wrote her first poem, "To the University of Cambridge, in New England," in blank verse. Bearing witness to the success of Mrs. Wheatley's missionary efforts, the first stanza of the original manuscript reads:

> While an intrinsic ardor bids me write
> The muse cloth promise to assist my pen.
> 'Twas but e'en now I left my native shore
> The sable Land of error's darkest night.

> There, sacred Nine! for you no place was found.
> Parent of mercy, 'twas thy Powerful hand
> Brought me in safety from the dark abode. (63)

Ironically, with the restrained moral fervor of an assimilated young black New England convert, she boldly admonishes the Harvard students:

> Let hateful vice so baneful to the Soul,
> Be still avoided with becoming care;
> Suppress the sable monster in its growth,
> Ye blooming plants of human race, divine
> An Ethiop tells you, tis your greatest foe
> Its transient sweetness turns to endless pain,
> And bring eternal ruin on the Soul. (63–64)

Six years later in the first edition of her work, she significantly revised the poem, cutting it from thirty-two to thirty lines and changing "The sable Land of error's darkest night" to "The land of errors, and *Egyptian* gloom," and "the sable monster" to "the deadly serpent" (Mason 5–6). Unlike Jupiter Hammon, maturity, success, and travel brought increasing artistic and ethnic pride to the young black woman who became a kind of poet laureate for what was then the literary capital of America.

Between 1768 and 1769 the young poet wrote at least three more poems. The first, "To the King's Most Excellent Majesty, 1768," praises King George III for his last favor to the colonies, the repeal of the Stamp Act, and wishes him God's blessings so that he may give further evidence to "his subjects" of his concern for peace and freedom. The second, "On the Death of the Rev. Dr. Sewell, 1769," was the first of several occasional poems celebrating or lamenting the birth or death of Boston's elite. The Reverend Dr. Joseph Sewall (son of Chief Justice Samuel Sewall, who was both presiding judge at the Salem witch trials and the author of the first New England antislavery tract) was pastor for fifty-six years at Boston's famous old South Church where Wheatley became the first of her race to be baptized in 1771. The third poem, "On Being Brought from Africa to America," is the earliest effort of the fifteen-year-old poet to come to grips with the dual nature of her identity. Her shortest poem, it reads:

> 'Twas mercy brought me from my *Pagan* land,
> Taught my benighted soul to understand

> That there's a God, that there's a *Saviour* too:
> Once I redemption neither sought nor knew.
> Some view our sable race with scornful eye,
> "Their colour is a diabolic die."
> Remember, *Christians, Negroes,* black as *Cain,*
> May be refin'd, and join th' angelic train. (7)

As in the original poem to the Harvard students, the poet accepts the social prejudices and religious mythology of the revolutionary period and considers herself fortunate to have been redeemed by Christ and "refin'd" by the Wheatleys. At the same time, the closing couplet boldly and ingeniously reminds Christians who look on her people with "scornful eye" that it is their duty to cultivate the moral and intellectual capacities of "Negroes" so that they, too, may enjoy spiritual if not social equality. Circulated among the Wheatleys and their friends, these poems soon won a local reputation for the young poet. "The Wheatleys had adopted her," writes J. Saunders Redding in *To Make a Poet Black,* "but she had adopted their terrific New England conscience" (9).

From her first appearance in print with the elegy *An Elegaic Poem, on the Death of George Whitefield* (1770) to the London publication of her first edition of *Poems on Various Subjects, Religious and Moral* in 1773, Wheatley became the object of curiosity and admiration. Her poems and her person were used as evidence in the debate over the intellectual equality of blacks. Reprinted in Boston, Newport, New York, Philadelphia, and England, the elegiac broadside, addressed primarily to the Countess of Huntingdon, philanthropist and Whitefield's patron, immediately extended the poet's reputation. The lines "Great Countess, we Americans revere / Thy name, and mingle in thy grief sincere" allude to the Countess of Huntingdon's philanthropic work and the poet's sense of identity as an American. But her silence about the Boston Massacre, especially the death of the fugitive slave Crispus Attucks, which occurred a few blocks from the Wheatley house in the same year as Whitefield's death, is curious. The circumstances of her privileged position in the Wheatley household seem to have compromised the poet's sense of ethnic and national identity.

In Boston, Wheatley was frequently invited to the homes of people in Mrs. Wheatley's social and missionary circle, where she was regarded with "peculiar interest and esteem." Her trip to England with Nathaniel Wheatley in May 1773, we now know from the recent discovery of new letters by the poet, was not merely for reasons of health but also for an introduction to British missionary circles during a politically volatile time. For in April, Parliament passed the Tea Act and sparked yet another chain of events destined to culminate in the revolution. Against this backdrop, Wheatley's new admirer and patron, Selina, Countess of Huntingdon, to whom the poet's first edition was dedicated, introduced her to British society, where her exceptional talent and tact as a conversationalist apparently steered her clear of political subjects and won her praise and presents, including a copy of the 1770 Glasgow folio edition of *Paradise Lost* from the lord mayor of London. Mrs. Wheatley's illness and request for her prevented the poet from accepting an invitation to stay in England for presentation at the court of George III. In October Wheatley, little improved in health but much in reputation, was back in Boston. Before she left London, however, she participated in arrangements for the publication of her first volume of poetry.

The first edition of *Poems on Various Subjects, Religious and Moral* contains Wheatley's best poetry. Critics have noted the influence of English writers on her poetry, especially the debt to Milton for "An Hymn to the Morning" and "An Hymn to the Evening," to Gray for the Whitefield elegy, and to Addison and Watts for "Ode to Neptune" and "Hymn to Humanity." But the greatest influence on the volume of thirty-nine poems was religion and neoclassicism. Her Christian convictions and the influence of the Bible are most clearly seen in the inventive use of biblical narrative in "Goliath of Gath," one of her longest poems, and "Isaiah LXIII." In the tradition of New England colonial writers, she freely embellishes the biblical account of David and Goliath—a convention that became even more distinctively employed in the African American tradition. She casts the poems, however, in the neoclassical mode of iambic pentameter couplets, invocation to the muse, elevated language, classical allusions, and panoramic scope. Here—particularly in her precision of meter, use of heroic couplet, and stilted diction—her models were Alexander Pope and the Latin writers themselves. The mixture of Christian and classical references in *Poems on Various Subjects* impressed some of her contemporaries with her genius and acculturation. Others were more fascinated by her youth, sex, race, or class.

Wheatley was certainly aware of the duality of her identity and reception. Her pride in and exploitation of her African identity is apparent in the reference to Terence in "To Maecenas" and in her self-image in several poems as "Ethiop," "Afric's muse," and "vent'rous Afric." The degree to which she was also conscious of the larger society's Manichaean image of Africa and its descendants is obvious in "On Being Brought from Africa to America," "To the University of Cambridge, in New England," and "To the Right Honourable William, Earl of Dartmouth, His Majesty's

Principal Secretary of State for North America, etc." In the last poem, written in 1772 upon the Earl of Dartmouth's appointment, with the hope of encouraging him to use his new power to support the colonies' struggle for freedom, we see the skillful manner in which the nineteen-year-old slave gives poetic form to her double vision:

> Should you, my lord, while you peruse my song
> Wonder from whence my love of *Freedom* sprung,
> Whence flow these wishes for the common good,
> By feeling hearts alone best understood,
> I, young in life, by seeming cruel fate
> Was snatch'd from Afric's fancy'd happy seat:
> What pangs excruciating must molest,
> What sorrows labour in my parent's breast?
> Steel'd was that soul and by no misery mov'd
> That from a father seiz'd his babe belov'd:
> Such, such my case. And can I then but pray
> Others may never feel tyrannic sway? (34)

Wheatley, as these lines indicate, was more conscious of her African heritage and sophisticated in her craftsmanship than Jupiter Hammon, but her religious indoctrination and unique status in the Wheatley family dictated against the expression of more positive, unequivocal sentiments about her African past.

The poet's visit to England was the high point in her brief career and a test of her piety. In London she was received as a "most surprising genius," but a very important friend of the American missionary movement, John Thornton, believed such praise a worldly snare and cautioned her against pride in her intellectual gifts. Merchant, philanthropist, and Calvinistic Anglican, Thornton and the Countess of Huntingdon, the patron of colonial black writer John Marrant, persuaded him in 1785 to go to Nova Scotia as a missionary. Thornton and the Countess of Huntingdon also supported Eleazer Wheelock's Indian Charity School in New Hampsire. Both philanthropists kept in close contact with the Wheatleys, who disbursed the funds Thornton donated to Indian missionary work, posted him on its progress, and sent their son to him for improvement. Thornton was particularly interested in hearing about the progress of Wheelock's famous pupil, the Monhegan Indian preacher Samson Occom. It was to Occom, of course, that eleven-year-old Phillis wrote her first letter. Occom and Thornton both considered the young poet a potential missionary and encouraged her to become "a Female Preacher to her kindred." But in writing to Thornton in 1774 she respectfully declined this role, considering it "too hazardous" and herself "not auffciently Eligible." Moreover, she did not want to leave her "British & American Friends" and confessed that she was no longer an African but an African American: "How like a Barbarian should I look to the Natives; I can promise that my tongue shall be quiet for a strong reason indeed being an utter stranger to the Language of Anamaboe." In this manner, the poet tactfully responded to Thornton's view that "silent wonder and adoration of the wisdom and goodness of God" becomes faith more than does the ability to "talk excellently of divine things, even so as to raise the admiration of others." In the same letter the poet informs Thornton of Mr. Wheatley's "generous behaviour in granting me my freedom [...] about 3 months before the death of my dear mistress & at her desire, as well as his own humanity" (qtd. in Rawley 673–74).

Mrs. Wheatley's death on March 3, 1774, and Wheatley's personal hardships over the next decade were to test her faith even more. Writing to her friend Obour Tanner on March 21, she expresses the depth of the loss of her best friend: "I have lately met with a great trial in the death of my mistress; let us imagine the loss of a parent, sister or brother, the tenderness of all were united in her" (qtd. in Mason 107). Despite this loss, the poet continues to invoke her muse for occasional poems such as the 1775 encomium "To His Excellency General Washington." Washington was so pleased by the poem that he invited Wheatley to visit him at Cambridge, an invitation she gladly accepted in 1776. In that poem, "Liberty and Peace," and "On the Capture of General Lee," the poet coined the term "Columbia" to refer to America. With the death of Mr. Wheatley on March 12, 1778, the family household broke up, and the next month Wheatley married John Peters. Legend has it that her husband was a respectable but vain black man who tried his hand as a baker, grocer, doctor, and lawyer without much success. The marriage resulted in estrangement from her former white friends and a life of poverty. Yet on October 30, 1779, the *Evening Post and General Advertiser* outlined her "Proposals" for publishing by subscription a new volume of "Poems & Letters on various subjects, dedicated to the Right Hon. Benjamin Franklin Esq: One of the Ambassadors of the United States at the Court of France." Since the treaty ending the war was not signed until 1783, she was unable to secure enough subscribers and the book was not published. Misfortunes began to multiply. Her husband was jailed for debt; two of her children died between 1783 and 1784; and she was reduced to working in a cheap lodging house. On December 5, 1784, Phillis Peters died and was buried with her third child, who died soon after his mother. Her husband disappeared with the unpublished manuscript of her second book. Two years later her first and only book was republished in America (P. Hill et al. 95).

A vivid example of cultural and ethnic divisions during the revolutionary era is the manner in which Wheatley's genius and poetic talents were praised in the beginning by General Washington in 1776 and dismissed at the end by Thomas Jefferson in 1784. In different degrees and under different circumstances, both Washington and Jefferson were Virginia slaveholders who believed that slavery ought to be abolished by law; that blacks were inferior to whites; and that blacks and whites should be separated. Of the two, however, Jefferson seems to have held the stronger convictions. In response to the letter and poem sent to him by the poet, Washington wrote to "Miss Phillis":

> I thank you most sincerely for your polite notice of me in the elegant lines you enclosed; and however undeserving I may be of such encomium and panegyric, the style and manner exhibit a striking proof of your poetical talents; in honor of which, and as a tribute justly due you, I would have published the poem, had I not been apprehensive that, while I only meant to give the world this new instance of your genius, I might have incurred the imputation of vanity. This, and nothing else, determined me not to give it a place in the public prints.
>
> If you ever come to Cambridge, or near head-quarters, I shall be happy to see a person so favored by the Muses, and to who nature has been so liberal and baneficient in her dispensations.

The sincerity of these sentiments take on a different color in the light of a letter written a few weeks earlier to his former secretary in which Washington says, "I recollect nothing else worth giving you the trouble of, unless you can be amused by reading a letter and poem addressed to me by Miss Phillis Wheatley" (qtd. in Mason 17, 88; G. Washington 4: 360–61).

In contrast to Washington's amused benevolence, Jefferson's "suspicion" that "the blacks are inferior to the whites in the endowments both of body and mind" sounds more like a conviction when we read the following remarks in *Notes on the State of Virginia*:

> Misery is often the parent of the most affecting touches in poetry. Among the blacks is misery enough, God knows, but no poetry. Love is

the peculiar oestrum of the poet. Their love is ardent, but it kindles the senses only, not the imagination. Religion, indeed, has produced a Phillis Wheatley; but it could not produce a poet. The compositions published under her name are below the dignity of criticism. The heroes of the *Dunciad* are to her, as Hercules to the author of that poem. (140)

No African American writer during the revolutionary period was more integrated in her society than Wheatley; yet, when she was not the object of paternalistic indulgence from admirers, she was the object of intellectual derision from detractors. In either case, the genius and piety that inform her double consciousness and love of liberty commanded the attention of the age and the ages to follow.

3

Five years after Phillis Wheatley's death in 1784, Olaudah Equiano published in London *The Interesting Narrative of the Life of Olaudah Equiano, or Gustavus Vassa, the African, Written by Himself* and became the new celebrated black writer of the period. While Wheatley's memories of Africa were vague and essentially religious, those of Equiano are probably the earliest, most detailed first-person ethnographic description of the Middle Passage, the nature of freedom and bondage in Africa, the Caribbean, and the colonial experience in America from a black perspective. Although it can be read as a spiritual memoir or a travel book, literary critics generally consider the *Narrative* to be the first major slave or liberation narrative, a genre that became popular during the Abolition movement of the nineteenth century and remains a literary testament to the will of an oppressed people to be free. Completed in 1788 and published in 1789, it was first published in America in 1791 and appeared in its eighth edition in London in 1794. Although questions were raised as early as 1792 about the facts of Equiano's African identity, the authority and authenticity of the date and place of Equiano's birth in Africa is more provocatively challenged in contemporary literary critic Vincent Carretta's "Olaudah Equiano or Gustavus Vassa? New Light on an Eighteenth-Century Question of Identity." So far, however, Carretta's argument that Equiano was born in South Carolina rather than Africa is not supported by most critics.

Neither a black American nor a black Englishman, Equiano was born in 1745, spent his early childhood in Benin, now a part of southern Nigeria, and his mature years in antislavery work in England as an Anglophone acculturated African. But, as Arna Bontemps notes in *Great Slave Narratives*, his slavery in Virginia and years in the service of a Philadelphia Quaker merchant, "who saw to his education [. . .] and put him to work on small trading vessels in the West Indies as well as on plantations" (1), were the years that probably shaped his early consciousness and provided the frame of reference for his *Narrative*. Bibliophiles and students of American cultural and literary history generally consider Equiano's *Narrative* the most influential of the eighteenth-century black autobiographies. Two other historically significant but less expansive and personal narratives by native-born black Americans are Briton Hammon's fourteen-page memoir *A Narrative of the Uncommon Sufferings and Surprising Deliverance of Briton Hammon, a Negro Man*, published in Boston in 1760, and ordained evangelist John Marrant's more dramtic *A Narrative of the Lord's Wonderful Dealings with J. Marrant . . . Taken Down from His Own Relation. Arranged and Corrected, and Published by the Reverend Mr. Aldridge*, with the sponsorship of his abolitionist patron the Countess of Huntingdon in London in 1785.

Living in the fertile province of "Essaka," some distance from the capital of Benin and the sea, Equiano "had never heard of white men or Europeans, nor of the sea; and our subjection to the king of Benin was little more than nominal, for every transaction of the government [. . .] was conducted by the chief of elders." His father was an elder who with other "chief men, decided disputes and punished crimes." In most cases, the trial was short and "the law of retaliation prevailed." The youngest and favorite of seven children, Equiano lived for his first eleven years in a collective, agrarian, religious society whose basic modes of expression were oral. "We are almost a nation of dancers, musicians and poets," he says. "Thus every great event such as a triumphant return from battle or other cause of public rejoicing is celebrated in public dances, which are accompanied with songs and music suited to the occasion" (5, 7; the 1969 edition contributed to the resurgence of interest in Equiano's *Narrative* during the Black Studies movement). To improve the blessing of an uncommonly rich and fruitful land, agriculture was his people's chief industry; "and everyone, even the children and women are engaged in it. [. . .] Everyone contributes something to the common stock; and, as we are unacquainted with idleness, we have no beggars." As for religion, Equiano—revealing his European acculturation by assuming a third-person voice—writes:

> The natives believe that there is one Creator of all things, and that he lives in the sun, and is girted round with a belt; that he may never eat or drink, but, according to some, he smokes a pipe, which is our own

> favorite luxury. They believe he governs events, especially our deaths or captivity; but, as for the doctrine of eternity, I do not remember to have ever heard of it; some, however, believe in the transmigration of souls in a certain degree. Those spirits which were not transmigrated, such as their dear friends or relations, they believe always attend them, and guard them from the bad spirits of their foes. For this reason they always, before eating as I have observed, put some small portion of the meat, and pour some of their drink, on the ground for them; and they often make oblations of the blood of beasts or fowls at their graves. (12–13)

In contrast to Phillis Wheatley, Christianity altered but by no means destroyed Equiano's respect for the holistic culture and tribal religion of his people and their reverence for priests, magicians, and wise men.

Despite obvious differences in color and culture between Europeans and Africans, Equiano does not accept the absurd correlations between the color of one's skin and the content of one's mind that characterizes Thomas Jefferson's *Notes on the State of Virginia*. Equiano asks,

> Are there not causes enough to which the apparent inferiority of an African may be ascribed, without limiting the goodness of God, and supposing he forebore to stamp understanding on certainly his own image, because "carved in ebony?" Might it not naturally be ascribed to their situation [. . .]? Does not slavery itself depress the mind, and extinguish all its fire and every noble sentiment [. . .]? Let the polished and haughty European recollect that his ancestors were once, like the Africans, uncivilized, and even barbarous. Did Nature make *them* inferior to their sons? and should *they too* have been made slaves? (17–18)

In short, inferiority to an acculturated yet proud African writer of the eighteenth century was not an innate, racial constant for nonwhites but the result of different historical and social circumstances.

Regarding slavery in Africa, he confesses that sometimes his nation sold slaves to traders, "but they were only prisoners of war, or such among us as had been convicted of kidnapping, or adultery, and some other crimes which we esteemed heinous." Although his nation and family kept slaves, the difference between the system of slavery in Africa and the New World was crucial:

> With us, they do no more work than other members of the community, even their master; their food, clothing, and lodging were nearly the same as theirs (except that they were not permitted to eat with those who were free-born); and there was scarce any other difference between them, than a superior degree of importance which the head of a family possesses in our state, and that authority which, as such, he exercises over every part of his household. Some of these slaves have even slaves under them as their own property, and for their own use. (12)

When he was eleven, Olaudah Equiano and his sister were kidnapped by native traders, sold to different African nations, and learned their diverse cultures, especially a few different languages. "The languages of different nations did not totally differ, nor were they so copious as those of the Europeans, particularly the English. They were therefore, easily learned; and while I was journeying thus through Africa, I acquired two or three different tongues" (23). During his manhood he also saw firsthand the difference in slavery in Africa, America, and the Caribbean.

After the wonder of seeing the sea for the first time and the mysterious movement of slave ships, as well as the terrors of the Middle Passage and the dread that "we should be eaten by these ugly men," the narrator was sold to a Virginia planter. He received his most indelible impression of the treatment of slaves in Virginia when he was called to his master's house to fan him and saw a black woman cooking with an iron muzzle locked on her head so that she could neither speak, eat, nor drink. Equiano was sold after "some time" to the captain of a merchant ship and lieutenant in the Royal Navy, who renamed him Gustavus Vassa, which he used more frequently than his African name, and took him to England. In two or three years he not only spoke English and felt "quite easy with these new countrymen, but relished their society and manners. I no longer looked upon them as spirits, but as men superior to us; and therefore I had the stronger desire to resemble them, to imbibe their spirit, and imitate their manners" (32, 48). The next step in adopting his new culture was to persuade his mistress in 1759 to have him baptized. He did not become "a first-rate Christian" and missionary, however, until much later after he had searched in vain for the key to salvation among the Quakers, the Roman Catholics, the Jews, and the Turks. He ultimately found the key in Methodism and sought unsuccessfully to be ordained for missionary work "among his countrymen" in Africa (74, 76, 90).

In 1763 he was sold to Robert King, a Quaker merchant in the West Indies. While working on his master's boats, Equiano witnessed the general practice of white men brutally raping female slaves, including "females not ten years old." He also observed how the system of absentee landlords left many island estates in the hands of managerial incompetents and human butchers. As in America, the Caribbean had its instruments of torture. "The iron muzzle, thumb-screws, &c., are so well known as not to need a description, and were sometimes applied for the slightest faults." The inhumanity of slavery made him "determined to make every exertion to obtain my freedom and to return to Old England" (76, 90).

In 1766 while the colonists were stiffening their resistance to the Stamp Act, Equiano finally accumulated enough money by trading goods to buy his freedom from King but agreed to continue working for him as a free "able-bodied sailor at thirty-six shillings per month." In this capacity he made several trips to America and experienced the precarious existence of a free black in the colonies. In Savannah, Georgia, for instance, he was severely beaten one night and left for dead by white men. The next morning he was carted off to jail. A similar fate occurred to a free black carpenter he knew "who, for asking a gentleman that he worked for for the money he had earned, was put into gaol; and afterwards this oppressed man was sent from Georgia, with false accusations, of an intention to set the gentleman's house on fire, and run away with his slaves" (104, 106). On another occasion only his intelligence, proficiency in English, and independent spirit prevented his kidnapping by "white ruffians." As a free, acculturated black (he became a hairdresser, played the French horn, and went to night school), Equiano was a restless man who continued to respond to the call of the sea and, as in travel books of the era, different cultures: Madeira, Jamaica, Barbados, Smyrna, Genoa, Portugal, Spain, Honduras, and Nicaragua. In the 1780s he became London's most celebrated black abolitionist, culminating his fight against oppression with the first publication of the *Narrative* in 1789, the same year that George Washington became the first president of the United States. Until his death on April 3, 1797, Olaudah Equiano's spiritual vision of himself and the world was that of a Anglo-African Christian convert.

4

In the beginning of *A History of American Literature,* Moses Coit Tyler writes from a Eurocentric approach that omits African American writers such as Phillis Wheatley, Frederick Douglass, and Frances Watkins Harper: "The American people, starting into life in the early part of the seventeenth century, have been busy ever since in recording their intellectual history in laws, manners, institutions, in battles with man and beast and nature, in highways, excavations, edifices, in pictures, in statues, in written words. It is in written words that this people, from the very beginning, have made the most confidential and explicit record of their minds" (5). As Howard Mumford Jones acknowledges in his foreword, "Tyler was emphatically the child of his age. [. . .] His is an Anglo-Saxon history" (vii). In contrast, as descendants of Africa and bearers of the legacy of an oral tradition, black revolutionary era acculturated slave and servant petitioners for freedom, Jupiter Hammon, Phillis Wheatley, and Olaudah Equiano were more attuned to the power of the spoken word, of British literature, and of the profound belief in man as a child of God. Confronted by the paradox of their situation as slaves in a largely white Anglo-Saxon Protestant society that had waged a war to realize its belief in the equality and inalienable rights of man, colonial African American writers, with the exception of Hammon, were more interested in struggling for physical and spiritual freedom than political and economic independence. Their introduction to the written word was primarily to make them more efficient servants, yet they used their acquired knowledge of reading and writing to solicit the good will of the larger white society. Since it was the Bible that served as the principal tool of cultural adaptation and the Protestant church that allowed marginal social assimilation, the most striking quality of the writings of African Americans between 1764 and 1789 is their Christian piety, faith in the philosophy of equal rights endowed by the Creator as expressed in the Declaration of Independence, and dual vision of the writers themselves as African Americans.

In the colonial and revolutionary era African American writers' efforts to reconcile their dual identity and attain recognition of their freedom and human rights, they did not, as many black writers of the 1960s sought to do, voluntarily seek to reject either aspect of their identity. In the words of Du Bois, "He would not Africanize America, for America has too much to teach the world and Africa. He would not bleach his Negro soul in a flood of white Americanism, for he knows that Negro blood has a message for the world." He wanted simply "to make it possible for a man to be both a Negro and an American, without being cursed and spit upon by his fellows, without having the doors of Opportunity closed roughly in his face" (17). Of early white American writings, Tyler says, "Literature as a fine art, literature as the voice and the ministress of aesthetic delight, they had perhaps little skill in and little regard for; but literature as an instrument of humane and immediate utility, they honored, and at this wrought with all the earnestness that was born in their blood" (8). Because of their resistance to racialized slavery and segregation, no less is true of the writings of early black Americans.

III

The Image of Africa in the Afro-American Novel

Two of the extraordinary highlights of my career were invitations from Professor Michel Fabre, the late eminent French critic of African American literature and author of the definitive biography of Richard Wright, to lecture at the Sorbonne in 1975 and 1981. It was while I was a visiting professor at the University of Freiburg that I received the first invitation in 1975 to present my lecture "Oral Culture, Afro-American Folklore, and the Function of the Literary Artist" to his graduate students and colleagues. After a passionate and provocative question and answer session, which included his African American student Melvin Dixon, the late talented poet and critic, my wife and I were wined and dined by our generous and gracious hosts, Professors Michel and Genevieve Fabre. The invitation in 1981 to participate in the hugely successful, grandly promoted, and well-attended international conference "Images of Africa in the New World," jointly sponsored by the Centre d'Etudes Afro-Américaines et du Tiers Monde Anglophone (Université Paris III) and the Centre d'Etudes et de Recherches sur les Civilisations, Langues et Littératures d'Espression Française (Université Paris XII) was the genesis of my essay "Images of Africa in the Afro-American Novel." Although several papers presented in the English-speaking section of the conference were not published in the first issue of Commonwealth: Essays and Studies *because of limited space and finances, it was an honor to have my essay included with those by Pierre Denain, Lilliane Blary, Michel Fabre, Steven Rubin, Susan Willis, and Françoise Pfaff.*

"CONRAD," SAYS CHINUA ACHEBE, "WAS A BLOODY RACIST." NEITHER AS INJUDICIOUS nor as inexplicable as it may seem on the surface, Achebe's indictment was occasioned by Joseph Conrad's use of Africa as the psychological and moral antithesis of Europe, of his dehumanization of the African in a novel that critic Albert Guerard considers "among the half-dozen greatest short novels in the English language." For Achebe, the primary question that *Heart of Darkness* raises is "whether a novel which celebrates this dehumanization, which depersonalizes a portion of the human race, can be called a great work of art" (32, 38). Let me leave this question for you to consider for the moment, while I turn from Conrad and the modern British novel to a reviewer's comment on a contemporary American novel by Philip Caputo called *Horn of Africa,* a novel that is already a Book-of-the-Month Club Special Fiction Alternate and Playboy Book Club Main Selection. Joseph Conrad, writes a reviewer in the *Boston Globe,* "is the only possible literary comparison to Caputo. [. . .] Every act is either symbolic or diabolical. There are no 'human' relationships because this is not a book about 'humanity,' unless you agree with Caputo that humanity is the equivalent of insanity, hatred, blood-letting, terror, cowardice" (Manning 1). Like the images in the novels of Conrad, Graham Greene, and Caputo, those in Paul Theroux's *Girl at Play,* John Updike's *The Coup,* and William Stevenson's *The Ghosts of Africa* are white images of African culture and character that tell us more about the fantasies and values of the West and the authors than they do about Africa.

The topic of my remarks today, however, is not so much the white image of Africa in the modern British and contemporary American novel as it is the black image of Africa in the Afro-American novel. My thesis is that the depiction of Africa in the Afro-American novel reveals more about the struggle for racial equality and personal identity by blacks in the United States and about the moral and political consciousness of the authors than it does about the complex reality of Africa itself. By Afro-American novel I mean any extended prose narrative written by an American of African descent and hybrid cultural identity that deals with the tragic-comic experience of black Americans. In developing this thesis I will begin with an outline of white images of Africa in Western culture, followed by brief surveys of images of Africa in the early and pre–World War II Afro-American novel, and conclude with images in the novels of Richard Wright, John A. Williams, William M. Kelley, and Frank Yerby.

White Images of Africa in Western Culture

By and large, Afro-Americans did not acquire their knowledge about Africa through direct experience; rather, it was transmitted to them through the eyes and mind of the dominant white social group, which, in satisfying its own psychological, moral, and social needs, spawned many negative stereotypes of African character and culture. As the studies of Winthrop Jordan, David Brion Davis, George M. Fredrickson, and Thomas Gossett reveal, white images of Africa date back to antiquity, but the most pernicious were developed during the period of European expansion and reinforced in the eighteenth and nineteenth centuries by Europeans and Anglo-Saxons seeking to justify their notions of slavery based on racial and cultural superiority.[1] These stereotypes were rooted in the view of whites that blacks were naturally inferior because they were different in biological appearance and cultural lifestyle, differences that were considered in early anthropology as deviations from the Western norm (Jordan 216–65, 343). Christianity and the Bible reinforced Western symbolism that associated the color white with everything good, pure, and beautiful and the color black with everything bad, evil, and ugly. When the skin color of Africans was directly linked to their non-Christian religious customs, the die of antiblack racism was cast.

From the Bible, then, came the image of Africans and their descendants as the creatures of Satan, the cursed children of Ham, and the bearers of the curse of Cain. From Montaigne's "Of Cannibals" (1580), Dryden's *The Conquest of Granada* (1671), Aphra Behn's *Oroonoko* (1688), and Rousseau's *Emile* (1672) came the image of Africans as Noble Savages, the embodiment of the theory that men living in harmony with the laws of nature and their own instincts are superior to other men and that whatever evils these natural men develop is the result of civilization. Paradoxically, this benign myth of the Noble Savage was complemented by the more tenacious and malign myth of Africans as savages and apes. "It is scarcely surprising," Jordan states with obvious irony, "that civilized Englishmen should have taken an interest in reports about cosmetic mutilation, polygamy, infanticide, ritual murder and the like—of course *English* men did not really *do* any of these things themselves" (24). Also, given the traditional speculations about anatomical and sexual affinities between apes and men and the tragic coincidence that Englishmen came in contact with apes and Africans at the same time and in the same place, "it was virtually inevitable," says Jordan, "that Englishmen should discern similarity between the man-like beasts and the beastlike men of Africa" (30). These views were embedded in the sixteenth-century concept of the universe as "The Great Chain of Being" and reinforced by eighteenth-century pseudoscientific studies that divided mankind into hierarchical systems of ethnic groups with Europeans at the top and Africans on the bottom of the chain. Caught in this chain of ideological and social forces, Africa and her progeny fell victim to the myth of an ignoble past and were cast by Europeans and Anglo-Americans alike as archetypal scapegoats on a Manichaean world stage on which they represented evil heathens and savages who were natural slaves.

I will not rehearse here the many indictments of antebellum and postbellum American literature by black critics and literary historians for its creation of a gallery of Buffoons, Sambos, Uncle Toms, Mammies, and Babos, for the following understatement by Sterling A. Brown, author of the groundbreaking 1933 article "Negro Character as Seen by White Authors," aptly sums up the history of the image of blacks in American fiction: "The treatment of the Negro in American fiction, since it parallels his treatment in American life, has naturally been noted for injustice. Like other oppressed and exploited minorities, the Negro has been interpreted in a way to justify his exploiters. [. . .] The African [. . .] is now receiving substantially the same treatment as the American Negro" (1). From this brief outline of white images of Africa and her sons and daughters in Western culture it can be reasonably inferred that the predominant image transmitted to black Americans of their motherland by the dominant culture was extremely negative. And since their African and slave past was the primary basis for their status and stigma as a discriminated minority, whether they accepted or rejected these demeaning white images, Afro-Americans have historically responded with ambivalence to Africa. Marion Berghahn's *Images of Africa in Black American Literature* lucidly and persuasively illustrates these attitudes in the general literature, especially the poetry, through the 1950s. So I will focus on the Afro-American novel to discover whether and how this ambivalence is expressed in that tradition.

Early Images of Africa in the Afro-American Novel

The attitudes of Afro-American novelists toward Africa are most apparent in their choice of narrative setting, use of color symbolism, delineation of character, and handling of point of view. It is instructive that in the history of the Afro-American novel only three are set in Africa itself: Henry Downing's *The American Cavalryman* (1917), George Schuyler's *Slaves Today* (1931), and Frank Yerby's *The Dahomean* (1971). Before taking a closer look at the pre–World War II novels of Downing and Schuyler, deferring for the moment an analysis of Yerby's novel, let me briefly examine how the use of color symbolism and characterization reveal the mixed attitudes of nineteenth-century black novelists toward Africa. In reacting to the grotesque appearance and manners of white stereotypes of blacks and seeking to project their own images of black American identity, both its ugliness and beauty, early black novelists were guided by their struggle for freedom and equality as an ethnic group and as individual artists. Social conditions and cultural exigencies compelled most of them to attempt a synthesis of the contrary narrative tendencies toward social realism and romance. "In giving this little romance expression in print," Pauline Hopkins writes in the preface to *Contending Forces*, "I am not actuated by a desire for notoriety or for profit, but to do all that I can in a humble way to raise the stigma of degradation from my race" (3–4). Achieving this objective involved adopting, rejecting, or qualifying the black/white symbolism of abolitionist literature, the Bible, and popular fiction of the period. Thus while one novelist wrote, "Surely the Negro race must be productive of some valuable specimens, if only from the infusion which amalgamation with a superior race must eventually bring" (Hopkins 87), another ended his novel with the ominous line, "Woe be unto those devils of whites, I say" (Delany 313). These novelists reflect the identity conflict caused by the myth of white supremacy and the rituals and color symbolism that justified and perpetuated it. In many cases white and black characters were idealized, but in the more realistic novels the attitude of the author was ambivalent, and frequently irony was at work.

For example, Martin Delany, a black nationalist and abolitionist whose advocacy late in his career of the emigration of blacks to Central America or Africa culminated in his leading an exploration party up the Niger River in 1859, clearly transvaluated traditional Western color symbolism in his novel *Blake*. The beauty and strength of blackness are affirmed in the characterization of servants Aikey and Sampson, while the discrimination against blacks by mulattoes in the Brown Fellowship Society is condemned. More important, a radical consciousness that foreshadows black nationalist sentiments in the United States during the 1960s is apparent in Delany's portrayal of Blake as the archetypal "messenger of light and destruction," the daring black mastermind of an underground organization that plans to liberate slaves in the United States and Cuba. It is also evident in the epithets the protagonist employs for whites—"candle face," "devils," "white oppressor," and "alabasters"—as well as in the depiction of two Africans: Abyssa, a captive Muslim woman trader from the Sudan who becomes a pious Christian convert, and Mendi, a captive Mendi prince who, like Cinque of the *Amistad* revolt in 1839, defies his captors, frees himself, and leads an abortive slave rebellion. Among the psychological and political advantages that Blake and Placido, the rebel Cuban poet and coleader of the planned revolution, identify for mulattoes to affirm their African heritage are the eventual emergence of a wealthy, powerful new Africa and the political acceptance of African people among the great nations of the world. For Blake and Placido, as for Delany, the attainment of black independence in the Americas and Africa would mean not only the end of white control over the land and lives of nonwhites but also the dawn of a new era of peace and prosperity. Delany's romantic vision was not to become an African reality, as we now know, until after European imperialism, with the support of the United States, reached its peak with the Berlin Conference in 1884 in which the delegates agreed that the Congo should be the personal property of King Leopold II and began its decline in the 1960s (Conrad 86–98; Twain 77–79).

Images of Africa in the Pre–World War II Novel

Turning from Delany and the nineteenth century to the twentieth-century novels of Downing and Schuyler, we discover that both are set in modern Liberia. Both reject direct correlations of evil and good with skin color, both strive for realism in characterization, and both are critical of the elitism of Americo-Liberians and the exploitation of the indigenous native populations by the ruling class. However, whereas Downing's *The American Cavalryman* is a melodramatic love story, Schuyler's *Slaves Today* is a satire; and whereas Downing, a former U.S. consul in Luanda, Angola, based his romance on the career of Major Charles Young, a black West Pointer (Schuyler, *Slaves Today* 143), Schuyler, who in 1931 spent three months in West Africa researching his narrative, based his novel on the scandalous contract labor system in which the Liberian government sent thousands of tribesmen on two-year contracts to Fernando Pocacao plantation (C. Wilson 115–27).

Downing's ambivalence toward Liberia is evident in his depiction of characters. The African characters are sympathetically yet condescendingly represented as superstitious savages. Lodango, the paramount chief of the Imbunda, is referred to by the undramatized omniscient narrator as a "savage" and "barbarian." He is described as a "perfectly proportioned bronze statue," and one of the female servants thinks of him as "a perfect specimen of his sex—eloquent, brave, cunning, persuasive, and cruel" (30, 35). Seeing cultural differences through ethnocentric eyes, Downing, the implied author, tacitly imposes negative value judgments on the sketchy descriptions he provides of several "savage rites," including cicatrization and the "sassawood" ordeal in the sacrifice grove. After alluding to "great mounds of human skulls, bleached white," along the sides of the grave, Downing writes with wry humor, "A witch-doctor, grotesquely decorated with fetishes and charms and carrying two long feathertipped wands, was doing divers terpsichorean gymnastics—cake-walking, turkey-trotting, sugar-dipping, Halleluiah-jumping—up and down the path in most Wonderful fashion" (281). In contrast to this condescending image of incongruity and anomaly, the author intrudes early in the narrative to explain that "no attempt will be made to write the language as it was brokenly spoken by Lupelta, *or* by any other person, civilized or savage, who appears in these pages, though there are certain peculiarities of speech common among the narratives which must be retained" (27). Even though the most frequent peculiarity of speech that punctuates the dialogue is the exclamation "Wow," the natives in *The American Cavalryman,* unlike those in *Heart of Darkness,* are nevertheless humanized by their power of speech.

Downing's protagonist, Captain Paul Dale, is represented as a fair-skinned West Point graduate and American cavalry officer who rescues and falls in love with Lupelta, who was raised in the bush as a native after being kidnapped as a child from her father, a former trade agent who passes for white and has become an influential New York banker. Captain Dale's self-serving expansionist view of Liberians is that "because of their ignorance, they have failed to use opportunity wisely. One should not expect children to perform duties such as experienced persons would have found it exceedingly difficult to accomplish. Liberia's present misfortunes are the outcome of the false training of a ruling class lacking in mental and moral virility. The infusion of new life into the country would set things right" (151). Acting on this conviction at the end of the novel, Dale marries the president of Liberia's stepdaughter because Lupelta, through an incredible coincidence of plot, is ironically considered to be white. Granted an extended leave from the military, he plans to return to Liberia "to develop the agricultural resources" of the country and to help save it "from being absorbed by some European power" (306).

The image of Liberia in Schuyler's *Slaves Today* is more ironic and sympathetic than in Downing's *The American Cavalryman.* The ironic situation of the novel is that although their forefathers had come to Africa "to found a haven for the oppressed of the black race [. . .] their descendants were now guilty of the same cruelties from which they had fled. The Americo-Liberians were to rule; the natives to obey" (100–101). Consistent with his purpose of arousing "enlightened world opinion against this brutalizing of the native population in a Negro republic," Schuyler, a political conservative, acerbic journalist, and racial gadfly, shares these characteristics with the implied author, who provides ironic descriptions of the Americo-Liberians and sympathetic portrayals of the indigenous peoples, whom the omniscient narrator refers to by their tribal names of Gola, Bassa, Kpwessis, Grebo, and Vai or as natives and aborigines. The implied author not only respects the aborigines as people but also expresses sympathy toward their culture, outlining, for instance, the social advantages of polygamy for the natives. In contrast, he is critical and occasionally satirical in his treatment of the ruling class.

Sidney Cooper Johnson, the president of Liberia and a lawyer by training, is described as having "won international fame for saying nothing adroitly" (11). Clearly "not of the material of his pioneer grandparents," he believed that "a ruling class [...] must be supported in leisure by those whom it ruled" and used his office to protect the power and privilege of the Liberian aristocracy and his conservative political party. Commissioner David Jackson, one of his most unscrupulous appointees, used the power of his office to levy exorbitant taxes on the native villages, to take their wives and daughters as concubines, to abuse and kill resisting village leaders, and to kidnap their men for forced domestic and foreign labor. Ironically, Commissioner Jackson and Captain Burns, Schuyler stresses, "were but slightly less dark than the natives over whom they ruled but they felt no kinship with the aborigines for that reason. It was no more difficult for them to oppress and exploit fellow black men than it usually is for powerful whites to do the same thing to fellow white men. Color did not enter here—it was class that counted" (100).

Between the publication of *The American Cavalryman* in 1917 and *Slaves Today* in 1931, the United States experienced the throes of the turbulent twenties, including the resurgence of the Ku Klux Klan. Profoundly disillusioned with American values after World War I, especially with the disparity between industrial wealth and spiritual poverty, many white intellectuals and artists turned for salvation to promoting homegrown urban varieties of the Noble Savage. Carl Van Vechten, a white critic, novelist, and patron of black artists, played a major role in promoting a primitive image of Harlem and blacks in his controversial yet commercially successful *Nigger Heaven* (1926). A transplanted Jamaican and social radical, Claude McKay was ostensibly influenced by Van Vechten's representation of cultural primitivism and sensationalism in his first novel, *Home to Harlem* (1928), but moved beyond it in *Banjo* (1929), his second novel, to reject white European civilization and embrace Africa. Ray, the black protagonist whose education, sensibility, and dreams foster ethnic and cultural ambivalence, feels emotionally and spiritually close to Africans he sees and hears in the old part of Marseilles:

> The Africans gave him a positive feeling of wholesome contact with racial roots. They made him feel that he was not merely an unfortunate accident of birth, but that he belonged definitely to a race weighed, tested and poised in the universal scheme. They inspired him with confidence in them. Short of extermination by the Europeans, they were a safe people, protected by their own indigenous culture. Even though they stood bewildered before the imposing bigness of white things, apparently unaware of the invaluable worth of their own, they

were naturally defended by the richness of their fundamental racial values. He did not feel that confidence about Aframericans who, long-deracinated, were still rootless among phantoms and pale shadows and enfeebled by self-effacement before condescending patronage, social negativism, and miscegenation. (320)

Also ambivalent toward his African characters was Rudolph Fisher, the talented physician who was one of the most witty and admired of the Harlem Renaissance writers. In his detective novel *The Conjure-Man Dies* (1932), he represents two idealized modern Africans, N'gana Frimbo and his tribal servant, N'oga Frimbo. N'gana is an African king, a Harvard graduate, a student of philosophy, and a popular Harlem psychic. Ironically, while the average Harlemite believes Frimbo is a "caster of spells," the erudite Frimbo rejects these beliefs as superstitious nonsense. Characterized by contradictions that suggest the ambivalence of the authors about their ascribed and achieved identities, the image of Africa in pre–World War II Afro-American novels thus reflects the efforts of black Americans to define their own personal and ethnic identity by coming to terms with their historical and cultural experiences.

Images of Africa in the Post–World War II Novel

Since World War II, the winds of social change have blown through America and Africa with hurricane force, whirling from the integration movement of the 1940s and 1950s to the Black Power movement of the 1960s, and from colonialism to independence and neocolonialism for most of Africa, beginning with Ghana in 1957. In the United States the violent resistance of whites to the Supreme Court school desegregation decision in 1954 and to acknowledging the civil rights of blacks, as well as the liberation of African nations and Cuba in the 1960s, awakened the dormant political nationalism of many black Americans. Stokely Carmichael and other Black Power advocates redefined the liberation struggle of black America as part of the larger global struggle of oppressed Third World people against Western imperialism, revealing both continuity and change in attitudes expressed in the nineteenth century by Delany. Frustrated by the snail's pace of integration efforts and the tactics of passive resistance, they revived indigenous theories of the colonial relationship of blacks to the dominant social group in the United States. Contending with political nationalism in the struggle for black liberation during the period was cultural nationalism. Black was beautiful, and Africa was in vogue. The cry of "We are an African people" was heard from the political platform and the printed page. African art, clothing, names, hairstyles, and foods were the rage, and black intellectuals and artists were going on safari to the motherland in search of their roots. The image of Africa in the novels of Richard Wright, John A. Williams, William Melvin Kelley, and Frank Yerby are representative of this eventful period of identity reformation.

Although Africa and Africans do not play a major role in the novels of Richard Wright, a social radical and the self-exiled father of the modern Afro-American novel, and John A. Williams, a longtime journalist, astute critic of American racism, and grossly underrated novelist, their attitudes toward the continent and its politicians in *The Long Dream* (1958) and *The Man Who Cried I Am* (1967) are decidedly negative when not ambivalent. In *The Long Dream,* as in all of his novels and short stories, Wright arguably accepts conventional white/black binary symbolism and the negative white image of Africa (Berghahn 154–67). For example, in a long discussion about Africa with his friends, especially Sam, whose father is a Garveyite, Fish, the protagonist, becomes so consumed by anger and self-hatred at being forced to confront his historical relationship to Africa and his blackness that he attacks Sam and later spits at his own face in the mirror, whispering venomously, "Nigger" (Wright 29–34).

In *The Man Who Cried I Am* Williams represents Jaja Enzkwu, a Nigerian diplomat, as an "eagle-faced, hot-eyed Jaja with his sweating pussy-probing fingers and perfumed agbadas" (299). It is Jaja, the Machiavellian African politician with dreams of empire building, who discovers the existence of Alliance Blanc, the confederacy of white Europeans and Americans that plans to subvert potential African unity and terminate the minority threat in the United States. "Any half-way good looking white woman can make a fool of him," writes Harry Ames, "but he doesn't trust a gathering of more than a single white man" (303). Harry Ames, the implied author's fictional treatment of Richard Wright and a major character in the novel, is trapped by his "contempt for everything African." This attitude explains in part why Jaja gave him the key to the safe-deposit box containing the secret information about the alliance, knowing that if he were killed by agents, Harry probably would also be killed. Although neither Max Reddick, the protagonist, nor apparently the implied author share Harry's hatred, they do share his negative image of Jaja, who in pursuit of his objective of ruling all of Africa one day had offered to turn over the secret papers to the Americans if they gave him Nigeria. Instead, they killed him, Harry, Max, and every other black who discovered the existence of the alliance and the King Alfred Plan.

The image of Africa in William Kelley's *A Different Drummer* (1962) and *Dunfords Travels Everywheres* (1969) is mythopoeic and evocative of complex racial memories. In *Dunfords Travels Everywheres,* Kelley, a born-again black cultural nationalist and awesomely talented novelist, constructs an implied author who imaginatively appropriates the characters, structure, and language of Joyce's *Finnegan's Wake* to represent a complex belief and linguistic system that illuminates why Afro-Americans should not subscribe to racial stereotypes about integration nor sacrifice their historical and psychological kinship to Africa and one another for integration with Euro-Americans. The implied author also adapts the poetic and prose *Eddas*—the mythology, ethical conceptions, and heroic lore of the Norse—to contrast with his reconstruction of African mythology and to "telve int'dRelationship betwine weSelf n d'cold Glareys o'Stunangle" (89). Allusions to the treachery and fratricide of Odin, the father of the gods, and Balder, his son and the most beloved god, who is killed with mistletoe by his brother Hoder in a plot devised by Loki, Odin's foster-brother, link the fall or assassination of a beloved American president to the prophecy of the "Iklander."[2] Innovatively and boldly creating a new language system, Kelley writes, "The misaltoetumble of the leader of La Colon y de la Thour Yndia. Company, Prestodent Eurchill Balderman, preachful as expected, Loki to fry" (49). The northern origins and chilling, life-destroying values of Odin and his descendants are symbolically contrasted with the equatorial origins and passionate, life-giving values of Africa and its descendants. Africans and their descendants, says the protagonist's dramatized alter ego, should beware that their physical and creative energies not be used for fuel to warm the descendants of "W. Oten Chiltman." Their legends and lives glorify death and destruction "almost since the bin of bawn," the implied author rhapsodies stylistically, "he lobbed them to lobe a heart for the frigg of it, unrevel a ball for the yarn of it, barn, a burn for the beef of it, but a hut for the strut of it, incise a shoe for the sock of it, heat a sheet for the wick of it. That and alotoflikkyr and Heshappy, Mr. Chityle" (54). Unfortunately, readers who resist trends toward modernist experiments with structure and style in the novel will probably find that it takes too much time and effort to understand Kelley's irony, parody, multileveled puns, and varieties of repetition will not adequately appreciate the richness of his comic imagination and fabulation in celebrating an idealized yet positive image of Africa.

Kelley is more realistic and therefore more accessible, but no less impressive, in his fabulation in *A Different Drummer,* which has a double plot and dual protagonists. The first plot concerns the moral awakening and personal revolt of Tucker Caliban against the control of whites over his life, and the second focuses on the education of whites, especially young Harry Leland and Dewey Willson III, about the nature of antiblack racism and the meaning of courage and self-reliance. Affirming the principle of self-reliance, Kelley imaginatively interweaves the Afro-American residual oral forms of legend and myth in *A Different Drummer* to create an implied author whose transcendental vision of man has historic and mythic dimensions. The legend of the revolutionary heroism of Tucker Caliban's African ancestor and the myth of his blood as the explanation for Tucker's personal courage contrast with the failure of courage of the Willsons, whose name is symbolically ironic, and society in general to affirm the natural rights of man.

Kelley features the world-weary Mr. Harper to pass on to us the local legend of Tucker's great-great-grandfather and the continuity of his blood through his infant son down to Tucker himself. An enlightened white effete who claims to believe in genetics and not in superstition, while simultaneously enjoying his role as oral historian and social analyst, Mr. Harper and the implied author, himself, disarm us by admitting that his story is not "all truth." Consistent with his modernist vision and imaginative literary adaptation of myth and tall tales, Kelley, in sympathy with the implied author, justifies half lies and the exaggeration of facts as improving on the truth and the appeal of the story. In describing, for example, the nameless African chief's attack on the slave auctioneer before escaping from De Witt Willson, who had paid a thousand dollars for him, Mr. Harper delights in the hyperbole of the tall tale. "Some folks swear, though not all," he tells us, "that, using his chains, he sliced his head off—derby and all—and that the head sailed like a cannonball through the air a quarter mile, bounced another quarter mile and still had up enough steam to cripple a horse some fellow was riding into New Marsails" (24). After freeing himself, the African subsequently liberates other slaves in the area, beginning with De Witt Willson's, until he is betrayed by one of his men and shot by Willson before he could take his baby son with him in death. The reader, like the listening men on the porch in the novel, is skeptical of Mr. Harper's story. But the implied author reinforces its validity and Mr. Harper's reliability through the support of the storeowner Mr. Thompson, who tells the skeptics on the porch and the reader, "If that's what Mister Harper says, it's got to be part of the answer anyways" (33). In other words, recurring images of Africa and Africans in the minds of Afro-American residual oral forms of fictional characters and of implied authors reveal deeply held beliefs of not only individuals but also of a race, a class, and even a nation.

Unquestionably, the most realistic and fascinating images of Africa and Africans are found in Frank Yerby's historical novel, *The Dahomean*. It is the only contemporary Afro-American novel set in Africa. Based principally on Melville Herskovits's highly respected two-volume anthropological study, *Dahomey: An Ancient West African Kingdom,* the novel seeks, as a note to the reader states, to entertain and "to correct, so far as it is possible, the Anglo-Saxon reader's historical perspective" (5). For Yerby, a self-exiled debunker of historical myths, "myths solve nothing, arrange nothing" (6);[3] thus, unlike Kelley and Conrad, he attempts to give us historical truth, no matter how unsettling it is to racists, liberals, black nationalists, and, presumably, Africans themselves.

Introduced by a brief prologue and divided into two major parts, the first showing the ritualistic passage into manhood of the protagonist and the second the precipitous rise and fall of his fortunes among his people, *The Dahomean* opens and closes in Virginia. But its major setting is Dahomey in the late 1830s during the actual reign of His Royal Majesty Gezo, the ninth king of Dahomey (Yerby 14, 133).[4] The king tells the story in retrospective narrative seven months after the murder of his family and his sale to Europeans by black slavers. It is the story of Nyasanu Dosu Agausu Hwesu Gbokau Kesu, son of Gbenu, a great chief, and himself lately governor of the province of Alladah in Dahomey, husband of six wives, one of them the daughter of the king.

As the novel unfolds with the frequent use of Fau words and the occasional use of metaphorical language, all contributing to its verisimilitude, we quickly discover that Yerby is sympathetic toward Africa yet critical of those customs he feels violate a respect for human life, dignity, and freedom, imaginatively but not always convincingly using the Dahomean characters themselves to express the criticisms. Initially, it is Gbenu, a village chief and Nyasanu's father, who educates his son and the reader to Yerby's critique of the evils of Dahomean culture, particularly the tyranny, extravagance, and human sacrifices of the royal family. But Gbenu's voice is melodramatically close to the implied author's social message: "From birth to death we are taxed, taxed, taxed, my son—so that the princesses and princes may live in licentious idleness—that is, if even our lives are not required of us for some small fault, or because the king needs a certain kind of worker—a *blacksmith* say, to be sent to the ancestors to make *ase* or hoes for the royal dead!" (31). The only escape from the tyranny of Dahomean life, says Gbenu in didactic fidelity to the thematic and structural design of the novel, is "to be sold as slave to the *furtoo*—those hideous creatures who come in huge canoes from across the sea—and who have no skins" (32).

Kpadunu, Nyasanu's best friend, is also critical of the moral corruption of the royal family, especially their slave trading: "We attack the Maxi, *xauntau daxo mine,* so that Dada Gezo can procure a supply of slaves to sell for gold, iron, and gun powder to the *furtoo,* those hideous skinless people from beyond the sea. Thus he adds to the great wealth he has already gained by taxing us nearly to death and enables himself to support his many wives and those puffed-up idlers and eternally rutting she-jackals he *thinks* are his sons and daughters in lascivious idleness" (55). In addition, he is ambivalent about the magic of diviners, priest, and sorcerers, his own guild: "I don't believe in it, and I do. The feelings I have alternate—according to the mood I'm in, I suppose. Most of it—nearly all of it—*is* fakery, Brother" (153). Since the diviners correctly predicted that Kpadunu would not survive the war campaign for slaves and that Nyasanu's life would end in Dahomey to begin anew in a far off land, Yerby's ambivalence about magic is also apparent.

It is the implied author's emotional and moral identification with his protagonist, however, that most clearly reveals his ambivalence toward Dahomean culture. After having Nyasanu, whose name means "man among men," sympathetically explain early in the novel the religious, economic, and social reasons for polygamy, all of which are related to the importance of having many children, the implied author later has him mentally reject the custom. And then, using the occasion of the jealousy of Nyasanu's principal wife at his imminent marriage to a princess, the implied author editorializes about the custom:

> For the strict truth of the matter was that most West African women, in their heart of hearts, hated it. Even Dahomean custom, rigid enough on most questions of morals, provided two outlets for female rebellion against becoming the ninth, the twentieth, or the fortieth wife of some grizzled old chief their fathers had engaged them to out of policy; *asidjosi*, in which the girl in question ran off with the younger, handsomer, simpler man, with fewer wives or none, whom she preferred, whereupon the lover made the relationship legal by paying back the rejected official suitor's gifts and work; and *xadudo* which was exactly the same thing except that nothing was paid back, and the marriage rites never performed so that the couple went on living in sin, as it were. (339–40)

More sensational than the custom of polygamy, however, were the atrocities and sadism of war and the custom of human sacrifices. For brave yet sensitive souls like Nyasanu,

> the tyranny of the Dahomean kings was a soul-crushing thing. How many lives did the king take each year in his monstrous "customs"? More than thirty or forty, surely. And if rumors had it right as rumor often did,

the king sent a man and a woman of his household *every* morning to the ancestors to thank them for allowing him to see a new day. Which meant, since the year had three-hundred-sixty-odd days, that Gezo sacrificed over seven hundred human beings a year simply to bid the ancestors good morning! (55)

In demythologizing the disingenuous myths about Africa, Yerby thus points to the absolute power of the king as the greatest evil of Dahomean life and to the moral sensitivity of Gbenu, Kpadunu and Nyasanu as the most redeeming trait in the Dahomean man.

In retrospect, then, the image of Africa in the Afro-American novel reveals changes and continuities in the social arena and tensions in the Afro-American novelist's self-image as he struggles to become his own mythmaker and to come to terms with the historical truth of his African past in defining his personal and ethnic identity in relation to the world. Because their struggle to define themselves in life and art is waged in a social arena that promotes the Eurocentric myth of white supremacy, a struggle that has resulted in their socialized ambivalence and double consciousness, Afro-American novelists have responded with mixed emotions to the question, What is Africa to me? Unlike most Afro-American poets and white American novelists, most black American novelists avoid directly treating the question of African heritage. In the history of the Afro-American novel, only Downing, Schuyler, and Yerby actually use Africa as a setting. Although Delany imaginatively displaced the Satanic image with the Messenger of Light and Destruction, neither modern nor contemporary novelists, despite the Black Power movement of the 1960s, have broken completely free from white images and stereotypes of the African as Noble Savage and Barbarian. Finally, traditional black and white oppositional symbolism is usually transvaluated, with Richard Wright as the most important modern exception, and the criticism of Africa is primarily focused on radical cultural differences that, even when viewed sympathetically, the novelists ironically consider undesirable in modern man when assessed through the prism of traditional Afro-American cultural standards.

In closing, let us return to the question I posed by Achebe at the beginning of these remarks: Can a novel that celebrates the dehumanization of a portion of the human race in the manner of Conrad's *Heart of Darkness* be called a great work of art? Of course, on the face of it this question is aesthetically problematic, especially for the psychological experimentation of the modernist novel. But if we assume with Harry Levin that a classic or great literary work of art is a text that gains a place for itself in our culture by its "precision of style, formality of structure, and, above all, concern for the basic principles that animate and regulate human behavior" (viii), then *Heart of Darkness,* although illuminating and important, as an experimental modern novel, is, as Achebe declares, not a great work of art. However, whereas only Yerby provides a documented, reliable account of West Africa, it seems reasonable to conclude that whether realistic or modernistic, the image of Africa in the Afro-American novel, as in the British and American novels, generally tells us more about the fantasies and values of the West and the author than it does about Africa.

Notes

1. Jordan, *White over Black*; David Brion Davis, *The Problem of Slavery in Western Culture* (Ithaca: Cornell UP, 1966); George W. Frederickson, *The Black Image in the White Mind: The Debate on Afro-American Character and Destiny, 1817–1914* (New York: Harper Torchbooks, 1972); and Thomas E. Gossett, *Race: The History of an Idea in America* (New York: Schocken, 1965).

2. See E. O. G. Turville-Petrie, *Myth and Religion of the North* (New York: Holt, 1964); *The Poetic Edda,* trans. Lee M. Hollander, 2nd rev. ed. (Austin: U of Texas P, 1964); *The Prose Edda of Snorri Sturluson: Tales from Norse Mythology,* trans. Jean I. Young (Berkeley: U of California P, 1973); and Edith Hamilton, *Mythology* (New York: Mentor, 1969) 300–15.

3. See also Darwin T. Turner, "Frank Yerby as Debunker," *The Black Novelist,* ed. Robert Hemenway (Columbus: Merrill, 1970) 64–71.

4. Yerby states that Gezo was the tenth king, but the chronology of kings in Herskovits indicates that he was the ninth. See Melville J. Herskovits, *Dahomey: An Ancient West African Kingdom,* vol. 1 (New York: Augustin, 1938) 12–14.

IV

Jean Toomer's "Blue Meridian": The Poet as Prophet of a New Order of Man

This essay actually had its origins in research at Fisk University in 1969 on Jean Toomer for my doctoral dissertation, "The Afro-American Novel and Its

Tradition." Arna Bontemps, the celebrated Harlem Renaissance poet and retired Fisk University librarian, whom I interviewed with three of my graduate students while I was on the faculty at the University of Massachusetts and he was on the staff of the Beinecke Library at Yale University, graciously provided me with a letter of introduction to Dr. Jessie Carney Smith, the dean of Fisk Library. Because I also wanted to interview Toomer's widow, Mrs. Marjorie Content, he surprisingly provided me with both her telephone number and address. What luck! He told me that she had called him before his retirement from Fisk in 1964 about the acquisition of Toomer's papers. So with Bontemps's and Smith's kind interventions and the gracious assistance of Ann Shockley, the head of special collections, I, like Professor Darwin Turner and other early Toomer scholars, was granted access to the uncataloged boxes of the recently acquired treasure trove of Jean Toomer manuscripts, letters, and notes. During my research I was again surprised to discover that some of Toomer's papers were in the Amistad Collection of the American Missionary Association, which at that time was also on the Fisk campus but was in litigation over ownership of the Toomer papers with the Fisk administrators. My Toomer research was therefore much more exciting, fruitful, and productive than I had imagined it would be. In addition to highly valuable information and insights for my dissertation, it resulted in three publications and an unpublished monograph for Broadside Press. The publications include "A Key to the Poems in Cane" (1971), "Cane: A Portrait of the Black Artist as High Priest of Soul" (1974), and "Jean Toomer's 'Blue Meridian': The Poet as Prophet of a New Order of Man" (1980).

IT MAY COME AS A SURPRISE TO MANY OF HIS NEW ADMIRERS, BUT JEAN TOOMER viewed himself as a cultural aristocrat, not a cultural nationalist. Recalling how the discovery of Goethe's *Wilhelm Meister* helped him to pull together the scattered pieces of his life, he wrote in 1918:

> I was lifted into and shown my real world. It was the world of the aristocrat—but not the social aristocrat; the aristocrat of culture, of spirit and character, of ideas, of true nobility. And for the first time in years and years I breathed the air of my land. [. . .] I resolved to devote myself to the making of myself such a person as I caught glimpses of in the pages

of *Wilhelm Meister*. For my specialized work, I would write. (Toomer, "Outline" 37)

More like the avant-garde of the lost generation than the vanguard of the Harlem Renaissance, Toomer was deeply involved in creating a synthesis of new forms and themes. In the wake of World War I he completely devoted himself to the task of learning the craft of writing. During this period he confessed to being strongly influenced by two approaches to literature. First, he was attracted to those American writers and works that used regional materials in a poetic manner, especially Walt Whitman, Robert Frost, and Sherwood Anderson (Toomer, "Outline" 43–55). Second, he was impressed by the imagists. "Their insistence on fresh vision and on the perfect clean economical line," he wrote, "was just what I had been looking for. I began feeling that I had in my hands the tools for my creation" (Toomer, "Outline" 55). The artistic fusion in *Cane* (1923) of symbols of the black American's African and southern experience and the Afro-American tradition of music bears witness to this influence and establishes the book as a landmark in modern American literature.

Following the publication of *Cane*, Toomer, convinced by personal experience and extensive reading that "the parts of man—his mind, emotions, and body—were radically out of harmony with each other" ("On Being American" 48), discovered the method for unifying these three centers of being in the teachings of George Ivanovitch Gurdjieff, the "rascal sage." A synthesis of Western science and Eastern mysticism, Gurdjieff's system was a rigorous discipline that taught self-development and cosmic consciousness through self-awareness, sacred exercises, temple dances, and various psychic feats. In 1934 Toomer began making annual retreats to the Institute for the Harmonious Development of Man, Gurdjieff's headquarters in Fontainebleau-Avon, France. He returned as a Gurdjieffian prophet to spread the gospel in Harlem—where his sessions included such talented artists as Aaron Douglass, Wallace Thurman, Harold Jackman, Nella Larsen, and Dorothy Peterson—and in Chicago. He also continued writing voluminously, but most of these writings, which repudiate racial classifications and celebrate a Gurdjieffian vision of life, were rejected by publishers.

The most significant exception is "Blue Meridian," a long Whitmanesque poem. "Blue Meridian" is the poetic zenith of Toomer's quest for identity. It represents the resolution of a long process of agonizing emotional and intellectual turmoil over the problems of race and aesthetics as viewed through the prism of his own personal crisis. Toomer began grappling with the question of race in high school and began the first draft of the poem, then titled "The First American," in the early

1920s. Completed in 1930, a section of the poem appeared as "Brown River, Smile" the following year in *The Adelphi*. But the entire poem was not published until 1936, when it appeared in Alfred Kreymborg, Lewis Mumford, and Paul Rosenfeld's *The New Caravan*.

Toomer the poet/prophet sings exultantly of a new world order in "Blue Meridian." Neither black nor white, Eastern nor Western, the new order of man is "the blue man, the purple man"; the new people are the "race called the Americans," and the new society is America, "spiritualized by each new American." Through evolution the regenerated American is also the harmoniously developed, universal man, free of definitions and classifications that restrict or confine the vitality of his being. For Toomer, as for Whitman, America was, in Whitman's exuberant words, "the greatest poem," "a teeming nation of nations," and "the race of races" (1667–68).

"Art," writes Toomer, "is a means of communicating high-rate vibrations," and the artist is he "who can combine opposing forms and forces in significant unity" (*Essentials* iv). Toomer splendidly fulfills both the letter and spirit of these definitions in "Blue Meridian." As in *Cane*, the chief symbol in "Blue Meridian" is implicit in its title. In the context of the poem, the meridian, which generally denotes the highest point of prosperity, splendor, and power, symbolizes the spirit of mankind. On the geographical and astronomical planes it also represents the imaginary circles that connect both geophysical poles and the circle passing through the celestial poles (*Webster's* 13). Other important symbols relating to the spiritual power of the new American include the Mississippi River, a pod, a grain of wheat, a waterwheel, crocks (i.e., earthenware receptacles), and the cross. The title of the poem thus generates a series of symbols that reinforce the themes of potential wholeness, evolution, and cosmic consciousness. So intricate is the symbolic pattern that the color progression of the meridian from black to white to blue corresponds to the movement of the poem through different stages of man's historical and organic development to a higher form.

Retracing the stages of man's development and the process by which the new American was born, Toomer invokes the primeval forces of life waiting to energize select men to a higher form of being. In the first section of the poem primal darkness is upon the face of the deep:

>   Black Meridian, black light,
>   Dynamic atom-aggregate,
>   Lay sleeping on an inland lake. (633)

In order to elevate himself man must let the "Big Light" in to awaken his dormant potential. Neither Christian nor mystical in the traditional sense, the genesis is an eclectic yet harmonious blend of Darwinian evolution and Gurdjieffian mysticism. The poet invokes the "Radiant Incorporal, / The I of earth of mankind" to crash through confining barriers, across the continent, and spiral on into the cosmos through the use of alliteration, anaphora, and Darwinian evolutionary signs:

> Beyond plants are animals,
> Beyond animals is man,
> Beyond man is the universe. (633)

At this stage the Mississippi River, sister of the Ganges and main artery of the Western world, has the potential to become a sacred river, which is realized in the White Meridian section of the poem. Similarly, each form that appears in the first section, the Black Meridian stage, contains the seed for its future growth. For, since Adam, man has been in a state of becoming, ready to unite parts and reconcile opposites into a moving whole of total body and soul:

> Men of the East, men of the West
> Men in life, men in death,
> Americans and all countrymen—
> Growth is by admixture from less to more,
> Preserving the great granary intact,
> Through cycles of death and life,
> Each stage a pod,
> Perpetuating and perfecting
> An essence identical in all,
> Obeying the same laws, unto the same goal,
> The far-distant objective,
> By ways both down and up,
> Down years ago, now struggling up. (633)

The poet is firm in the conviction that the capacity for growth is common to all men and has always been present in America. Past generations, however, have not fully realized their human potential and, by extension, the promise of the nation and the universe.

Toomer's purpose, then, is not the glorification of the common man but the celebration of "A million million men, or twelve men," the result of a long process of natural selection and self-realization. Elitist in nature, Toomer's view of modern man in "Blue Meridian" is essentially Gurdjieffian. Comparing man to an acorn, Gurdjieff says: "Nature make many acorns, but possibility to become tree exist for only few acorns. Same with man—many men born, but only few grow. People think this waste, think Nature waste. Not so. Rest become fertilizer, go back into earth and create possibility for more acorns, more men, once in while more tree—more real man. Nature always give—but only give possibility. To become real oak, or real man, must make effort" (qtd. in Peters 42). For both Gurdjieff and Toomer, the real man, the new man, must manifest understanding, conscience, and ability. Defective men—those who lack or fail to acquire these three attributes—become the fertilizer for perpetuating the promise of eternally awake souls.

Included among the defectives in "Blue Meridian" are old gods and old races. The old gods, "led by an inverted Christ, / A shaved Moses, a blanched Lemur, / And a moulting Thunderbird," have failed to transform the soul of man. All that remains of their existence is "Their dust and seed falling down / To fertilize the seven regions of America." The waves of old peoples have similarly failed. The European races, "displaced by machines" and "Baptized by finance," could not rise above materialism; the African races—moaning "O Lord, Lord, / This bale will break me— / But we must keep the watermelon"—were weighted down by racism and a negative self-image; and the red race, whose organic relationship with nature was ruptured when its members were "serpentine" into reservations and towns, was annihilated by an alien culture. These were the early inhabitants of the New World, great races of nondescript persons waiting to be fused into the first Americans:

> Drawing, in waves of inhabitation,
> All the peoples of the earth,
> Later to weed out, organize, assimilate,
> Gathered by the snatch of accident,
> Selected with the speed of fate,
> The alien and the belonging,
> All belonging now,
> Not yet made one and aged. (637)

The creation of the new man is a long evolutionary process engineered by nature. This is the myth of America as told by a twentieth-century Gurdjieffian poet/priest.

In the past America did not fulfill its promise because each American did not lift himself "To matter uniquely man." Out of a past blind to the transcendent value of understanding, conscience, and ability—words the poet would give his life "to see inscribed / Upon the arch of our consciousness"—comes the hell of the Depression. The vital material and spiritual forces of mankind have gone wrong:

> An airplane, with broken wing, In a tail spin,
> Descends with terrifying speed—
> "Don't put me on the spot!"—
> From beings to no-things,
> From human beings to grotesques,
> From men and women to manikins,
> From forms and chaoses—
> *Crash!* (640)

The eagle, majestic symbol of American extremes of production and destruction, has degenerated into a one-winged plane of death. And the heroic daring of a Lindberg—"Flight symbol of the alone to the Alone"—is displaced in newspaper headlines by the unheroic exploits of Al Capone. Because man is responsible for his own downfall and spiritual blight, he must follow the poet's example and assume the responsibility for his own regeneration.

In the second section of the poem Toomer lustily calls forth the new American and shows him the highway to love and "unstreaked dignity." This stage opens with a heavenly white light, as the symbol of hope and emerging consciousness:

> White Meridian, white light,
> Dynamic atom-aggregate,
> Lay waking on an inland lake. (642)

The poet exhorts modern man to break from a moneyed and machined death, urging him to move on to a new level of consciousness:

> Walk from it, Wake from it,
> From the terrible mistake

> That we who have power are less than we should be.
> Join that staff whose left hand is
> Demolishing defectives,
> Whose right is setting up a mill
> And a wheel therein, its rim of power,
> Its spokes of knowledge, its hub of conscience—
> And in that same heart We will hold all life. (643)

Breaking free from his islandized condition and fixing his sight on universal man, Toomer, like Whitman, becomes the creator deploring a litany of injunctive anaphora to call into being a new world order:

> Unease the races, Open this pod,
> Free man from this shrinkage,
> Not from the reality itself,
> But from the unbecoming and enslaving behavior
> Associated with our prejudices and preferences.
> Eliminate these;
> I am, we are, simply of the human race.
>
> Uncease the nations,
> Open this pod,
> Keep the real but destroy the false;
> We are of the human nation.
>
> Uncease the regions—
> Occidental, Oriental, North, South—
> We are of Earth.
>
> Free the sexes,
> I am neither male nor female nor in-between;
> I am of sex, with male differentiations.
> Open the classes;
> I am, we are, simply of the human class.
>
> Expand the fields—
> Those definitions which fix fractions and lose wholes—

> I am of the field of being,
> We are beings.
>
> Uncease the religions;
> I am religious.
> Uncease, unpod whatever impedes, until,
> Having realized pure consciousness of being,
> Sensing, feeling and understanding
> That we are beings
> Co-existing with others in an inhabited universe,
> We will be free to use rightly with reason
> Our own and other human functions. (644–45)

Unlike Whitman's bombast and the unqualified democratic strain of his America, Toomer's social imperatives and the expansive mood of his first-person pronouns affirm a Gurdjieffian world of beings who have realized the value of intelligence, conscience, and ability.

But were it not for his imaginative use of concrete symbols, readers would surely be lost in a sea of abstractions. In this section of the poem a waterwheel becomes the agent for invigorating the soul. But first the poet acknowledges the regenerative influence of a special woman in his life, probably Margaret Naumberg:

> Much that I am I owe to her,
> For she was going where I was going,
> Except that on the way we parted.
> She, individualized and beautiful,
> Remarkable beyond most,
> Followed, at one turn, her picture of herself— (647)

The poet does not follow for fear he might lose himself and betray "the task of man." Instead he responds to the music of "sacred and profane extremes" and the song of himself:

> And some rare times
> I hear myself, the unrecorded,
> Sing the flow of I,
> The notes and language not of this experience,
> Sing I am,

> As the flow of I pauses,
> Then passes through my water-wheel—
> And these radiant realities, the living others,
> The people identical in being. (648)

After invoking the waterwheel, "its rim of power, / Its spokes of knowledge, its hub of conscience," to transform their lives, the poet and his nameless female companion experience the White Meridian:

> Sun upon clean water is the radiance of creation
> And once, far out in the vast spread,
> Our eyes beheld a sacrament;
> Her face was marvelously bright,
> My brain was fiery with internal stars,
> I felt certain I had brought
> The gods to earth and men to heaven;
> I blessed her, drawing with the fingers
> Of my spirit the figure of the cross;
> I said to her—
> "All my senses will remember you as sweet,
> Your essence is my wonder." (648)

This mystical experience marks the spiritual rebirth of the poet.

The poem now approaches its final stage, the Blue Meridian, with the poet heralding the dawn of a new people, the synthesis of contrasting and conflicting forces:

> A strong yes, a strong no,
> With these we move and make drama,
> Yet say nothing of the goal.
> Black is black, white is white,
> East is east, west is west,
> Is truth for the brain of contrasts;
> Yet here the high way of the third,
> The blue man, the purple man
> Foretold by ancient minds who knew,
> Not the place, not the name,

> But the resultant of yes and no
> Struggling for birth through ages. (651)

Earlier lines and images of the poem reappear in transfiguration, spiritualized by the regeneration of the poet, "America among Americans, / Man at large among men." While the Mississippi River fulfills its sacred potential, a fusion of Christian and Gurdjieffian symbols reflect the crowning achievement of an unbroken chain of millions of ancestors:

> Mankind is a cross,
> Joined as a cross irrevocably—
> The solid stream sourcing in the remote past,
> Ending in far off distant years,
> Is the perpendicular;
> The planetary wash of those now living
> Forms the transverse bar. (652)

For Toomer, America was the majestic base "Of cathedral people," a people who were genuinely interracial and capable of cosmic consciousness. Thus, as the streams of humanity merge, as the forces of nature are reconciled and all divisions harmoniously resolved, the poem reaches its final stage:

> Blue Meridian, banded light,
> Dynamic atom-aggregate,
> Awakes upon the earth;
> In his left hand he holds elevated rock
> In his right hand he holds lifted branches,
> He dances the dance of the Blue Meridian
> And dervishes with the seven regions of America. (653)

At the end of *Cane,* the apparent analog for the Black Meridian section of the poem, Toomer left us with only the promise of self-realization. In "Blue Meridian" the poet moved beyond race to become the prophet of a new order of man known as the American. But rather than a betrayal of race for cheap chauvinism, Toomer's poetic resolution of his private and public quest for identity and fulfillment represents a genuine effort to cast off all classifications that enslave human beings and inhibit the free play of intelligence and goodwill in the world.

Disillusioned by Gurdjieff's charges of mishandling funds and by his scandalous conduct during a trip to America, Toomer broke with his spiritual master in 1932, but even after becoming a Quaker confessed that most of his main ideas were inspired by Gurdjieff. Around 1940, the poet/priest's health began breaking down from an acute case of insomnia, alcoholism, and arthritis. After a kidney operation and Jungian psychoanalysis, Toomer spent his final years in a Philadelphia nursing home, where he died on March 30, 1967.

V

The Legacy of James Baldwin: The Artist as Redemptive Lover and Righteous Witness

On December 1, 1987, James Baldwin died in southern France. On December 8, Toni Morrison, Maya Angelou, and Amiri Baraka paid tribute to Baldwin at his funeral in the Cathedral of St. John the Divine in New York City. And on December 22, I received a commission from the World & I, *the thick, glossy, cosmopolitan Washington Times Corporation publication, to write the following feature article for inclusion with four critical commentaries on James Baldwin's work for the Book World section of the magazine, which also included "My Dungeon Shook: Letter to My Nephew on the One Hundredth Anniversary of the Emancipation" from* The Fire Next Time. *Like Baldwin, whom family, friends, and colleagues called Jimmy, I was raised in New York City and graduated from the predominantly white, significantly Jewish De Witt Clinton High School in the Bronx. I first met Jimmy in 1962 at Howard University while I was a graduate student attending his guest lecture. We developed a collegial relationship in 1983–84 after he was recruited to Happy Valley as Five College Professor of Literature and based in the Department of English at the University of Massachusetts, Amherst, where I taught for twenty-four years. Because students, faculty, and administrators gave him little privacy or peace while he was completing books on the Atlanta children murders and on the three martyrs Martin Luther King Jr., Malcolm X, and Medgar Evers, we did not spend much time together. But on a visit with his two assistants to my home one evening, this extraordinary black man of letters and expatriate on a return visit to the United States from France exchanged tales with me and my wife, Carrie, about De Witt Clinton High School while enjoying an awesome continen-*

tal meal of my wife's coq au vin, complemented with a 1984 Maison Nicolas Merlot Réserve, topped off by a couple of generous glasses of Red Label Scotch, Jimmy's favorite medicinal drink. My tribute to Jimmy came out in the World & I *during the national controversy over the posthumous attack by Julius Lester, a former colleague in the W. E. B. Du Bois Department of African American Studies and recent convert to Judaism, fallaciously accusing Jimmy in Lovesong: Becoming a Jew (1988) of anti-Semitic remarks in a 1984 class lecture titled "Blacks and Jews." "The Legacy of James Baldwin" closes with a provocative comparison of Jimmy's role and reception as a righteous writer-as-witness to that of Elie Wiesel, the celebrated Jewish survivor of Nazi death camps.*

"SOCIETIES NEVER KNOW IT, BUT THE WAR OF AN ARTIST WITH HIS SOCIETY IS A lover's war, and he does, at his best, what lovers do, which is to reveal the beloved to himself and, with that revelation, to make freedom real" (*Price of the Ticket* 318). James Baldwin, my colleague at the University of Massachusetts since 1983, wrote in 1962. Two years earlier, when I first met him while he was talking to Howard University students in Founders' Library, I was immediately struck by the awesome contrast of so powerful a spiritual force emanating from so small and fragile a physical form. His big, extraordinary eyes flashed fiercely above a wide, warm, infectious smile that evoked memories of the stark, prominent features of a black African mask. His soul seemed to burn with the passion of his eloquent yet unrequited love for his countrymen, while freezing at the terrible evil of their willful innocence and dehumanizing racism. In his writings, as in his talks, which are stylistically more like sermonettes than lectures, the powerful truth of his mixed emotions about the price of a ticket for the journey from darkness to light is a liberating force for those who truly hear it and accept the burden and blessing of the common humanity that it affirms. "The very time I thought I was lost," Baldwin wrote in an open letter to his nephew in commemoration of the centennial anniversary of the Emancipation Proclamation, "my dungeon shook and my chains fell off. You know, and I know that the country is celebrating one hundred years of freedom one hundred years too soon. We cannot be free until they are free" (*Price of the Ticket* 336).

As novelist, essayist, dramatist, and poet, what is the legacy of this Manchild of the Promised Land, of this artist of redemptive love, of this modern black American writer-as-witness called James Arthur Baldwin? Who, finally and inexorably, are the beneficiaries of the tragic yet sublime redemptive love that we find in his twenty-two books, which include *Go Tell It on the Mountain* (1953), *Notes of a Native Son* (1955), *Nobody Knows My Name* (1961), *The Fire Next Time* (1963), *Blues for Mr. Charlie* (1964), and *Jimmy's Blues* (1985)? In reflecting, at this time and in this place, on these questions, we can most meaningfully understand and appreciate Baldwin's artistic authority, authenticity, agency, righteous indignation, and place in literature by listening more to his voice than to mine.

Manchild of the Promised Land

"Know whence you came," Baldwin implored his nephew and us one year before the most memorable civil rights march on Washington in modern American history. "If you know whence you came, there is really no limit to where you can go" (*Price of the Ticket* 335). Descended from African ancestors, the grandson of a slave, and the stepson of an Old Testament evangelist, James Baldwin was born August 2, 1924, in the womb of Harlem, the much-heralded Promised Land of the North for many southern blacks who, in search of freedom and wholeness, more often than not found it to be merely another Babylon. He was raised in the bosom of the black Pentecostal church under the stern eye of his stepfather, David, an outrageously demanding, protective, and paranoid Old Testament minister.

Passing on to his nephew the hard-learned lessons and bittersweet truths of his own youth in the Promised Land, Baldwin writes:

> Now, my dear namesake, these innocent and well-meaning people, your countrymen, have caused you to be born under conditions not very far removed from those described for us by Charles Dickens in the London of more than a hundred years ago. [. . .] This innocent country set you down in a ghetto in which, in fact, it intended that you should perish. [. . .] You were born where you were born and faced the future that you faced because you were black and *for no other reason*. The limits of your ambition were, thus, expected to be set forever. (*Price of the Ticket* 334–35)

Since the contradictory sanctioning of freedom and slavery in the U.S. Constitution in 1787 and the institutionalization of the myth of America as the new biblical Garden of Eden, the cardinal Christian principle of love and the constitutional guarantees of unalienable human rights, Baldwin reminds us, were being perverted on a grand scale by the children of God and the citizens of the American Republic.

"The idea of white supremacy," Baldwin writes with righteous indignation in "Stranger in the Village,"

> rests simply on the fact that white men are the creators of civilization (the present civilization, which is the only one that matters; all previous civilizations are simply "contributions" to our own) and are therefore civilization's guardians and defenders. Thus it was impossible for Americans to accept the black man as one of themselves, for to do so was to jeopardize their status as white men. But not to accept him was to deny his human reality, his human weight and complexity, and the strain of denying the overwhelmingly undeniable forced Americans into rationalizations so fantastic that they approached the pathological. [. . .] People who shut their eyes to reality simply invite their own destruction, and anyone who insists on remaining in a state of innocence long after that innocence is dead turns himself into a monster. (*Price of the Ticket* 88–89)

Driven by the wrath of his stepfather's fundamentalist zeal and by the menacing power of whites and powerlessness of blacks, young James fled for refuge to the black Pentecostal church, with its neo-Calvinist doctrine of original sin and carnality, and was called to preach at fourteen. But in his ministry he discovered "that there was no love in the church. It was a mask for hatred and self-hatred and despair. The transfiguring power of the Holy Ghost ended when the service ended, and salvation stopped at the church door." He continues this lament in "Down at the Cross":

> When we were told to love everybody, I had thought that that meant *everybody*. But no. It applied only to those who believed as we did, and it did not apply to white people at all. [. . .] But what was the point, the purpose, of *my* salvation if it did not permit me to behave with love toward others, no matter how they behaved toward me? What others did was their responsibility, for which they would answer when the judgment trumpet sounded. But what I did was *my* responsibility, and I would have to answer, too. (*Price of the Ticket* 348–49)

In time Baldwin grew to hate the tyranny and duplicity of the church and whites as much as the tyranny and complicity of his stepfather and other blacks, leaving the church at seventeen and his stepfather's house the following year. The dialectic tension in Baldwin's voice, as in his life, between hatred and love, rejection and acceptance, Afrocentric and Eurocentric influences, his racial identity and his national identity—the distinctive characteristic of Afro-American culture and character that Du Bois poetically described as double consciousness, that Melville J. Herskovits anthropologically classified as socialized ambivalence, and that Ralph Ellison aesthetically encoded as double vision—is thus both the product and process of his historical experience and bicultural identity as an American of African and slave ancestry.[1] The complexity of this tension is intensified and extended in Baldwin's case by his acknowledged homosexuality.

In 1948 Baldwin fled from the racial and sexual oppression of America to France. Tormented by his experience with the perversion of the Christian principles of Faith, Hope, and Charity into Blindness, Loneliness, and Terror by many blacks, as well as most whites, he nevertheless confesses: "There was in the life I fled a zest and joy and a capacity for facing and surviving disaster that are very moving and very rare. Perhaps we were, all of us—pimps, whores, racketeers, church members, and children—bound together by the nature of our oppression, the specific and peculiar complex of risks we had to run; if so, within these limits we sometimes achieved with each other a freedom that was close to love" (*Price of the Ticket* 349). Returning from France in 1957 and counseling his nephew not to be afraid during the civil rights demonstrations of the early 1960s, Baldwin concludes his letter with compassion:

> I said that it was intended that you should perish in the ghetto, perish by never being allowed to go behind the white man's definitions, by never being allowed to spell your proper name. You have, and many of us have, defeated this intention; and, by a terrible law, a terrible paradox, those innocents who believed that your imprisonment made them safe are losing their grasp of reality. But these men are your brothers—your lost, younger brothers. And if the word *integration* means anything, this is what it means: that we, with love, shall force our brothers to see themselves as they are, to cease fleeing from reality and begin to change it. For this is your home, my friend, do not be driven from it; great men have done great things here, and will again, and we can make America what America must become. (*Price of the Ticket* 336)

A year after the first appearance in white magazines of the plea and warning of "My Dungeon Shook" and "Down at the Cross," the essays were published in *The Fire Next Time*. Also in 1963, a million or so people marched on Washington, were inspired by the now classic "I Have a Dream" speech of the drum major of the civil rights crusade, the Reverend Dr. Martin Luther King Jr., and successfully lobbied for the Civil Rights Act of 1964. All of us are thus the beneficiaries of Baldwin's brotherly love and righteous indictment of the racial, economic, and sexual oppression committed by the willfully innocent.

Artist of Redemptive Love

"For me," Baldwin told his first biographer, "writing was an act of love. It was an attempt—not to get the world's attention—it was an attempt to be loved. It seemed the only way to save myself and to save my family. It came out of despair. And it seemed the only way to another world" (qtd. in Eckman 46). For Baldwin love, which was more like agape than philos or eros, generally signified a state of being or grace, not mere physical intimacy. Driven by a Christian fundamentalist sense of outraged divine justice that was reified by the religious tyranny of his stepfather and by the social oppression of whites, Baldwin began developing his sensibility as an artist of redemptive love at eight, as his mother recalls (Eckman 41), with the discovery of Harriet Beecher Stowe's *Uncle Tom's Cabin*. The book's themes of the sin of slavery and the salvation of Christian love probably explain why he considered it the paradigmatic protest novel. He began writing songs and plays in elementary school, attracting the attention of a white teacher who introduced him to his first Broadway play and a world beyond Harlem and his stepfather's religiosity. After publishing his first story in a church newspaper when he was about twelve, he served as an editor of his junior high school magazine and studied French with Countee Cullen, a major poet of the Harlem Renaissance period of the mid-1920s, who not only frequently spent his summers in France but also was the faculty adviser to the literary club in which Baldwin was a prominent member. He later became an editor of the *Magpie* at DeWitt Clinton High School, where Cullen had achieved distinction a generation earlier as an honor student, poet, and associate editor of the same literary magazine (Eckman 49–50).

Torn between the call of the flesh and the cry of the soul, encouraged for his intelligence by teachers, and both admired and attacked by classmates—who occasionally called him "Froggy" and "Popeyes"—young Baldwin sought sanctuary in the library as much as in the storefront church, painfully developing his frustrated feelings of love, hatred, fear, and loneliness into plays, poetry, and short stories (Eckman 48, 81). Reflecting on the influences on his early writing style in "Autobiographical Notes," Baldwin wrote, "The King James Bible, the rhetoric of the storefront church, something ironic and violent and perpetually understated in Negro speech—and something of Dickens' love for bravura—have something to do with me today. [. . .] But finally, I suppose, the most difficult (and most rewarding) thing in my life has been the fact that I was born a Negro and was forced, therefore, to effect some kind of truce with this reality" (*Notes of a Native Son* 5).

While in high school, he discovered Richard Wright and adopted him as a literary father. "In *Uncle Tom's Children*, in *Native Son*, and above all, in *Black Boy*, I found expressed, for the first time in my life, the sorrow, the rage, and the murderous bitterness which was eating up my life and the lives of those around me," he confessed in "Alas Poor Richard." Wright's "work was an immense liberation and revelation for me. He became my ally and my witness, and alas! my father" (*Price of the Ticket* 274).

In turning from sacred to secular love, from the pulpit to the pen, from Harlem to Greenwich Village and Paris to bear witness to the bittersweet truth of his vision of the Republic, Baldwin felt compelled to sacrifice his literary father on the altar of faith in himself. Although Saul Levitas of the *New Leader*, Randall Jarrell of the *Nation*, Elliott Cohen and Robert Warshow of *Commentary*, and Philip Rahv of *Partisan Review* published his first commercial book reviews and essays, Wright gave him encouragement in the early stages of *Go Tell It on the Mountain*, helped him to win a Eugene F. Saxton Fellowship, and tolerated him as a devoted fan. But as in his relationship with his stepfather, Baldwin was awed by Wright's personality and intimidated by his artistic achievement. With the apparent Brutus thrust of early essays in *Notes of a Native Son* and *Nobody Knows My Name*, essays that he has subsequently explained as attempts to clarify something to himself rather than as attacks on Wright (Lester 22), he therefore not only killed the relationship between Wright and himself but also implied by contrasting *Native Son* with *Uncle Tom's Cabin* as protest novels that his own novels would provide a more truthful, comprehensive, aesthetically satisfying reconstruction of the richness and vitality of Afro-American culture and character.

Actually, the way of life to which Baldwin bears witness in his novels is characterized by a biblical imagination and rhetoric that in its eschatological emphasis on guilt, suffering, and love is almost as bleak as that in *Native Son*. In Go *Tell It on the Mountain*, members of the Grimes family are frustrated in their efforts to realize their potential for loving one another and life by the religiosity of the storefront Pentecostal church. In *Giovanni's Room* (1956), the subject of black culture is displaced by a sympathetic treatment of the terrifying quest for love by David, a white bisexual American, and the social problems of white homosexuals in France. In *Another Country* (1962), a tortuous and passionate series of racial and sexual encounters between whites and blacks, homosexuals and heterosexuals, northerners and southerners, and Europeans and Americans drives New York jazz musician Rufus Scott to suicide but becomes the rite of passage to self-understanding for his jazz-singing sister Ida and the social rebels of modern America who rather desperately and radically affirm bisexuality as the highest form of love and freedom. In *Tell Me How Long the Train's Been Gone* (1968), Leo Proudhammer struggles with such private and public anxieties as racism, a heart condition, a white mistress, a militant black lover, and armed black resistance as he claws his way to the top of the mountain of success as a black actor. In *If Beale Street Could Talk* (1974), Tish and Fonny, the blues-singing protagonists, are able to endure and transcend the agony of harassment in the inner city and prison through love (heterosexual and familial) and art (black music and sculpture). And in *Just Above My Head* (1979), Hall Montana, the first-person narrator-witness and older brother of the gospel-singing gay protagonist, testifies about the agonizing realities of human suffering and the ecstatic possibilities of love in the lives of those touched by his brother's journey on the gospel road.

As intriguing as the truth and beauty of these novels are, only *Go Tell It on the Mountain*, *If Beale Street Could Talk*, and *Just Above My Head* arguably illuminate the anxieties and ambivalences of the shared experience of black Americans (Bell, *Afro-American Novel* 219–33). But like Wright, Baldwin focuses sharply on a single dimension of black culture. His emphasis is not political and existential rebellion, however, but spiritual and sexual reconciliation, not the terrifying realities of hatred, but the liberating possibilities of love. In contrast to Wright's unrelenting naturalistic vision and narrative drive, Baldwin's short stories and novels are memorable primarily for the soul-stirring eloquence and resonance of their eschatological vision, biblical rhetoric, and black modalities of music as their major characters bear witness to the depths of our suffering and the heights of our salvation through love.

Modern Black Writer as Righteous Witness

Because of his eloquent advocacy of civil rights and consistent indictment of the evils of white America, as he stressed the moral imperatives of black nationalism in his writings, Baldwin is considered by many readers to be a controversial polemicist for blacks and by some a strident Old Testament–style prophet like Jeremiah and Isaiah.[2] But by word and deed, Baldwin most clearly and humbly defines himself as a witness. "I have never seen myself as a spokesman," he told an interviewer for the *New York Times Book Review* in 1984. "I am a witness. In the church in which I was raised you were supposed to bear witness to the truth. Now, later on, you wonder what in the world the truth is, but you do know what a lie is." In other words, he says, "[I am] witness to whence I came, where I am. Witness to what I've seen and the possibilities that I think I see" (Lester 22).

Although in his early essays the distinction between the private and public voice was often misread because of his ambiguous use of the first-person plural pronoun "we" rather than the singular "I," sometimes stressing his American national and other times his black ethnic identity, he declares that he never assumed that he was speaking for others: "What I tried to do, or to interpret and make clear was that what the Republic was doing to that woman [Fannie Lou Hamer, the Mississippi civil rights organizer], it was also doing to itself. No society can smash the social contract and be exempt from the consequences, and the consequences are chaos for everybody in the society" (Lester 22). Baldwin's message is clear: We must learn from the lessons of our ancestors, especially the national sin of slavery, and accept our personal and social responsibility for experiences, especially the ideology and practice of racial and cultural supremacy, that perpetuate social injustice and inequality. We must do this if we are to affirm our moral nature through atonement (e.g., by vigorously enforcing affirmative action statutes) and if we are to create a better, more just world for our children.

When asked by the *Times* interviewer about the validity and viability of his interpretation of the role of the writer as witness, Baldwin responded:

> In one way or another, one is very much a prisoner of his time. But I know what I've seen and what I've seen makes me know I have to say, *I know*. I won't say I believe, because I know that we can be better than we are. That's the sum total of my wisdom in all these years. We can also be infinitely worse, but I know that the world we live in now is not necessarily the best world we can make. I can't be entirely wrong. There're two things we have to do—love each other and raise our children. We have to do that! The alternative, for me, would be suicide. (Lester 22)

Writers, critics, and academicians from Ralph Ellison, Maya Angelou, and Toni Morrison to Benjamin DeMott, Henry Louis Gates Jr., and Trudier Harris have praised Baldwin as one of America's most gifted writers (the peer as an essayist,

I believe, of Thoreau and Emerson). But the only white writers whom Baldwin spontaneously and unqualifiedly identifies as witnesses are Dostoyevsky, Dickens, James, and Proust.[3] Aware of the "trick bag" that the interviewer was putting him in by insisting on names of white writers of his own post-Holocaust, post-Hiroshima generation, Baldwin explains with candor:

> Generally, most white American writers think of themselves as *white*. To be a white American is to have a very peculiar inheritance. All white American writers came from someplace else, even if they were born here. My past after all, stretches back to Africa by way of Europe. But most white American writers seem to have cut off their heritage at Ellis Island. Their testimony, for me, does not include enough. [. . .] One could say that they reveal their heritage in unconscious ways . [. . .] My experience is larger, and my comment says more about me than them. I think, too, that the effort on the part of the Republic to avoid the presence of black people reflects itself in American literature fatally, to the detriment of that literature. (Lester 23)

Although Baldwin overlooks Twain and Faulkner, who both bear witness in their most important novels to the terrible price we pay for the dehumanization of others, neither writer was his contemporary nor provoked as great a degree of ambivalence from white readers about the moral challenge of his art and his place in American literature.

The degree to which Baldwin's messianic love for and faith in the American Republic is unrequited can be illustrated by a comparison with the reception accorded Elie Wiesel, the celebrated Jewish survivor of Nazi death camps and writer in French who also interprets his role as bearing witness to the guilt, suffering, and possibilities of love in a post-Holocaust, post-Hiroshima world.[4] Both writers were educated as children in the traditions of the most doctrinaire and mystical religious sects of their ethnic groups, Baldwin in Pentecostalism and Wiesel in Hasidism. Both were estranged as teenagers from God and man by the genocidal atrocities of the guardians of civilized culture, Baldwin by white Americans and Wiesel by Nazi Germans. Both drew on the rhetoric and legends of the principal texts of their respective cultural traditions for the passion and purpose of their books, Baldwin from Afro-American folklore and the King James Bible and Wiesel from the Jewish Torah, the Talmud, and kabbalah. And both bear witness to the innermost circle of hell in their journeys from silence to speech, from darkness to light, as they remind children of this generation of their responsibility to acknowledge and atone for the sins of their grandfathers as well as their own—Baldwin invokes the spirits of the many thousands lynched with impunity in predominately white American communities and the enslaved millions of African descent in the New World, and Wiesel invokes the spirits of the millions of Jews who were marched to the ovens in such concentration camps as Auschwitz and Buchenwald.

In telling and retelling their cosmic tale of the dance of life and death performed to the symphony of racial and cultural supremacy, each author spotlights the systematic dehumanization and destruction of his own people as the most heinous act of civilized man. But Wiesel, Andrew Mellon Professor of Humanities at Boston University since 1976 and chairman of the United States Holocaust Memorial Council, is generally more stark and tormented in his writings than Baldwin. Even though Wiesel's *A Beggar in Jerusalem* won France's Prix Medici in 1969, neither it nor novels like *Dawn, The Accident, The Testament, The Town Beyond the Wall,* and *The Gates of the Forest* are arguably more aesthetically satisfying in style or structure, especially for black American readers, than Baldwin's *Go Tell It on the Mountain,* which, like *Night,* Wiesel's concentration camp memoir, is a literary classic. Unlike Wiesel, who in 1985 received the highest U.S. civilian award, the Congressional Gold Medal of Achievement, and in 1986, the Nobel Peace Prize, Baldwin's highest honors before his death on December 1, 1987, were the George Polk Memorial Award for *The Fire Next Time* in 1963 and the French government's Commander of the Legion of Honor in 1986.

What, then, is the legacy of James Arthur Baldwin: Manchild of the Promised Land, artist of redemptive love, and modern gay black American writer as righteous witness? And who are his beneficiaries? The legacy of his life in the wilderness and literary labors is the simple but ineluctable truth that love is redemptive. Although this truth resonates throughout his work, it is reduced to the following powerful social proposition at the end of "Fifth Avenue Uptown": "It is a terrible, an inexorable, law that one cannot deny the humanity of another without diminishing one's own: In the face of one's victim, one sees oneself" (*Price of the Ticket* 213). In the introduction to his collected nonfiction, *The Price of the Ticket* (1985), Baldwin best sums up the mission of his life and the message of his body of literature: "In the church I come from—which is not at all the same church to which white Americans belong—we were counselled, from time to time, to do our first works over. [. . .] To do your first works over means to reexamine everything. Go back to where you started, or as far back as you can, examine all of it, travel your road again and tell the truth about it. Sing or shout or testify or keep it to yourself: but *know whence you came*" (xix). Children born and yet to be born of God and woman as well as black and white partners in the American social contract of constitutional democracy are the beneficiaries of Baldwin's testimony and legacy of indomitable Faith, Hope, and Charity, if only we will read, hear, and heed his voice before we, too, are called to meet our ancestors and our God.

Notes

1. Unlike the generalized ambivalence of all hyphenated ethnic Americans, the double consciousness of black Americans is the historical product of slavery and racial segregation and the anthropological processes of cultural retention, reinterpretation, and syncretism. For a valuable discussion of the vital importance of these tropes and processes to Afro-American culture and character, see Bell, *Afro-American Novel* xv–xvi, 3–20, and 345–46n6. For double consciousness, see Du Bois, "Strivings" 194–98 and "Of Our Spiritual Strivings," *The Souls of Black Folk* (1903; Greenwich: Crest, 1965) 16–17. For socialized ambivalence, see Herskovits, *Life* 295–96 and Norman E. Whitten Jr. and John F. Szwed, ed., introduction, *Afro-American Anthropology: Contemporary Perspectives* (New York: Free Press, 1970) 26–27. For double vision, see Ellison, "The World and the Jug," *New Leader* 46 (December 9, 1963): 22–26; and *Shadow and Act* 137.

2. See, for example, Harold Bloom, ed., *James Baldwin: Modern Critical Views* (New York: Chelsea, 1986).

3. See Lee A. Daniels, "James Baldwin, Eloquent Essayist in Behalf of Civil Rights, Is Dead," *New York Times* 2 Dec. 1987: D27; "James Baldwin: His Voice Remembered," *New York Times Book Review* 20 Dec. 1987: 1, 27, 29; Louis H. Pratt, *James Baldwin* (Boston: Twayne, 1978); Kenneth Kinnamon, ed., *James Baldwin: A Collection of Critical Essays* (Englewood Cliffs, NJ: Prentice-Hall, 1974); Therman B. O'Daniel, ed., *James Baldwin: A Critical Evaluation* (Washington, DC: Howard UP, 1977); and Trudier Harris, *Black Women in the Fiction of James Baldwin* (Knoxville: U of Tennessee P, 1986).

4. See Samuel G. Freedman, "Bearing Witness: The Life and Work of Elie Wiesel," *New York Times Magazine* 23 Oct. 1983: 32–36, 40, 65–69.

3

Modern and Contemporary African American Vernacular and Literary Voices

I

The Blues Voices in John Edgar Wideman's *Two Cities*

An invitation from the editors of the American Book Review *for a review of John Edgar Wideman's* Two Cities *was the primary occasion for "The Blues Voices in John Edgar Wideman's* Two Cities.*" Because the editors were receptive to my writing style of long, interdisciplinary critical articles, and because I was preparing a reevaluation of Wideman's novels for revision and update of my 1987 study of the African American novel, I was delighted to accept the invitation. As readers will discover, this article reveals my efforts to develop a more distinctive blues voice in my own style and structure of critical writing.*

IF TROUBLE WAS MONEY, TO BORROW A LINE FROM BLUESMAN ALBERT COLLINS, the black folks in John Edgar Wideman's latest novel would be millionaires. *Two Cities* is a compelling culmination of the theme of contemporary black urban male double consciousness developed in Wideman's thirteen previous critically acclaimed books. It interweaves a legendary political tragedy of Philadelphia with a blues love story of Pittsburgh. It is a novel that thematically and stylistically explores the boundaries and bridges that paradoxically separate and connect fact and fiction, past and present, places and people, black and white, men and women, young and old. It is an experimental novel that linguistically celebrates the resourcefulness and resiliency of the African American blues voice. That voice, in the words of Ralph Ellison, keeps "the painful details and episodes of a brutal experience alive in one's aching consciousness, to finger its jagged grain, and to transcend it, not by the consolation of philosophy but by squeezing from it a near-tragic, near-comic lyricism" (*Shadow and Act* 78). Like the Homewood trilogy, *Two Cities* is grounded in the authority and authenticity of the sights and sounds of Wideman's remembrances of his youth in the Homewood neighborhood of Pittsburgh. Wideman artistically transforms the memories of his "hood" into the agony and ecstasy, the desperation and hope of personal and communal love and loss. He achieves this through the alchemy of his literary imagination, political ideology, and the African American vernacular tradition that he shares with his narrators, characters, and primary audience.

Similar to *Philadelphia Fire*, *Two Cities* is a meditation and lamentation on African American history and communities, especially the 1985 incendiary deaths of at least eleven black MOVE members, including children, in their fortified home and headquarters. Despite black neighbors' protests of this quasi-military assault with machine guns, antitank weapons, explosives, and a helicopter-dropped bomb, the Osage (middle-class) neighborhood that Wideman also at one time called home was destroyed by fire. Ironically, this tragic, destructive assault was executed by predominantly white policemen under the orders of a liberal black politician, Mayor Wilson Goode. The novel also invokes the spirit of John Africa, the radical Afrocentric leader of MOVE, a back-to-nature, black primitivist sociocultural organization, to represent Wideman's vision of the conflicting passions and purposes of contemporary black urban America. Wideman also uses John Africa as a symbol to challenge the implied author, main narrator, and audience to acknowledge the perversities and paradoxes that separate and connect time, place, and people in contemporary urban America.

Wideman's tale of two cities is, as the book jacket notes, essentially a "redemptive, healing love story" between Robert Jones and Kassima, a young black reclusive widow and mother in mourning for the deaths of her husband, from AIDS in prison, and two sons, from gang violence in the streets of Pittsburgh. After the loss of her husband and sons within the brief period of ten months had driven her into months of emotional and physical withdrawal, Kassima yields one night to her sexual urge for a man. She goes to Edgar's bar and is picked up by Jones for a one-night stand. Having prayed "for a tallish, not too much belly, brown-skinned, slow-smiling man with big hands and clean, neat fingernails [. . .] who wouldn't argue about wearing a johnny," Kassima not only found her a "nice man" but she and Jones also had "a balling good time and started seeing each other regular" (50). Jones is a fifty-year-old former family man whose one-night stand turns into a crying, singing day of ecstatic lovemaking, redemptive homecoming to the neighborhood of his youth, and spiritual healing for him and Kassima.

But this love affair is cut short by Kassima's retreat behind her personal barrier, fearing another loss of a loved one when Jones is threatened with a gun while playing schoolyard basketball. "When I saw you almost killed in the park, knew I couldn't go down that road again," she tells him on the phone. "Starting over, I mean. Giving everything, losing it, then starting over with nothing. Not a goddamn thing. Nothing. Huh-uh. Had to be something of me wouldn't die if I lost you. Wasn't even about you. Loved you then and love you now. It's about me. About having something left I can count on if there's no you" (130–31). Jones's and Kassima's voices of redemptive and healing love are framed by the blues voice of Mr. Mallory, an eccentric college drop-out, self-educated old photographer, and bagman who has migrated from Philadelphia to Pittsburgh to record the continuities and discontinuities in the lives of black families and neighborhoods. A boarder in Kassima's old house on Cassina Way, where Jones apparently developed his manhood under women, he is a bridge between the legendary past of his friend John Africa and the redemptive love of Jones and Kassima.

Although Kassima distances herself from "folks who are Bible crazy, church crazy," it is by reading the Bible, especially the book of Lamentations, that she finds the story of transcending grief that becomes her song of redemption. As she fingers the jagged grain of her aching experiences and bridges the barrier that separates her from Jones, she reflects to herself: "Found my story. My song. Got so tangled up in it, scared me for a while. [. . .] Why did evil prosper round here and children die. Got through the worst finally and started stepping out a little, listening to the part of me wanted to live, wanted to be a live woman again. Got through wanting to die and one of the things made it through with me the Book of Lamentations, this story about people beat down so low they got to pray for a reason to pray" (54).

It is Mallory's code-switching voice between African American Vernacular English (AAVE) and Standard American English (SAE), however, that establishes the moral and political authority and authenticity that becomes the linguistic norm. This code-switching voice opens and closes the retrospective, discontinuous, fragmented narrative of mainly flashbacks, reveries, and interior monologues. "Everything connects; nothing connects. Two simple truths and each made perfect sense on its own but together they mystified him," the third-person omniscient narrator states as he reveals the paradox of how the more things change the more they remain the same. "Once upon a time he'd stood on the Spring Garden Street Bridge with John Africa. Today he's in another city, alone in a room on Cassina Way. Then and now. Two cities. He thinks he understands each in its turn, but now. No words for what separates and connects these moments. He couldn't understand, could only witness" (6–7). Mallory thus prowls the streets with a camera and a shopping bag, bearing witness to the truth of the impact of the fiery death of John Africa and the MOVE members on the present. But he is "always muddling somewhere in between, becoming a stranger to himself, a taint man sure enough" (7).

In the middle of the book, when he dies in Kassima's bed and leaves her the legacy of a box of his pictures that nobody has seen and that she has promised to burn, Murray's death becomes the bridge that once again connects Jones and Kassima, who calls the lover she has shut out of her life for help in understanding Murray's death and photographs. Like Jones as a young man, Murray walked out on his wife and children. But after Kassima shows compassion during his fatal illness, he not only expresses regrets for deserting his family but also begins flirting and talking with her about his travels and picture taking. "My pictures are pretty postcards with the world arranged nice and neat," he says in an imaginary letter to a painter. "But I don't want to hide the damage. I want to enter the wound, cut through layer by layer like a surgeon, expose what lies beneath the skin" (118–19). Furthermore, during his rapidly declining health, Mallory begins relating to Kassima as his orphan daughter and praising her for transcending bitterness over her tragic personal losses. In the closing pages of *Two Cities* Mallory explains to the ghost of John Africa, "I'm the best blues singer in the known universe. As long as I don't open my mouth. [. . .] My blues-singing can't be out loud. Has to play inside my mind. Where it's perfect. [. . .] I tell myself I want to be a photographer, to take pictures, but the way I go at it is like singing the blues inside my head. Act like I'm the camera, not a photographer" (216–17).

For Wideman, the question of the relationship of the blues and the African American vernacular tradition to SAE is fundamental to the construction of an authentic African American literary and cultural identity. In addition to the implied author's bilingual fluency in code-switching and fidelity to the grammar, idioms, vocabulary, pronunciation, and rhythm of African American speech in *Two Cities,* Wideman's shift between the general literary and the African American vernacular tradition is subtly subversive in challenging the traditional dominance of SAE. In the Greek myth of Medusa, the female monster whose severed head, which was the ultimate penalty for her sexual violation of the temple of Athena, would turn those who looked at it to stone, and the folk legends of the murders of Emmett Till and John Africa for their alleged sexual violations are interwoven with allusions to soul food, folktales, superstitions, and lyrics from gospel, blues, and jazz music.

Based on Wideman's affirmation of his black voice in fiction in critical articles as well as in his other fiction, he is sociolinguistically and aesthetically sympathetic with Mallory's privileging of his first language of AAVE in his art even though it is demeaned by institutional authorities as "a minstrel tongue" and even though he speaks more than one language. "For a long time I was confused," Mallory confesses, "didn't know better than to believe what others said about my way of speaking. I had to teach myself to remember the love and power of the language spoken by the people who taught me to feel, to live in a body. That language is what I want my pictures to speak" (128). Moreover, it is the authority of Wideman's virtuoso use of the African American vernacular tradition, especially black religion, speech, and music, that authenticates the resiliency and resourcefulness of the characters and culture of Homewood and other black communities in *Two Cities*.

But the moral and political authority of Wideman's performance in the novel is seriously flawed for many readers by two key elements involving Mallory. The first is his celebration of the controversial John Africa not only as a friend but also symbolically as a legendary black freedom fighter and martyred leader. The second is the ominous defiling of Mallory's corpse by black gang members at the close of the novel. According to Hizkias Assefa and Paul Wahrhaftig's *Extremist Groups and Conflict Resolution*, John Africa, who was born Vincent Leophart and called Dog Man because he generally had a pack of stray dogs trailing behind him as he walked, founded MOVE or the Movement as "a radical, activist, counterculture organization" of about fifty white and black members at its peak around 1968 in West Philadelphia. The founder and philosophical leader of the group that many whites and blacks, including neighbors in the Powelton Village and Osage Avenue sections, called a cult, John Africa was, according to his followers, an antimachine, sensitive, friendly advocate of natural over man-made laws. But his extreme cultural primitivist and quasi-religious philosophy encouraged behavior among his followers that alienated his black middle-class neighbors on Osage Avenue and white authorities, culminating in two tragic, violent confrontations that resulted in loss of life in 1978 and 1985. The confrontations with black neighbors and white authorities in 1985 were primarily ignited by violations of health laws and safety issues. These laws and issues included outdoor toilets in the backyard, trash and garbage accumulating and rotting in and around the house, and half-naked children rummaging in trash cans for food. Other transgressions of social and cultural conventions included collecting and feeding raw meat to stray dogs, fencing off the alley behind the house for a dog run, threatening neighbors with arms and hazardous fortifications, and haranguing neighbors with obscenities by bullhorn around the clock for the release of imprisoned MOVE members. For many readers, the uncompromising subversive beliefs, values, and behavior of John Africa and MOVE make them highly problematic moral and political authorities for the central norms of the novel.

Second, although Mallory, Jones, and the implied author express compassion, anger, and responsibility for both the "young men killed and crippled in the streets" and their killers, neither the feeling nor the respect is mutual for the fratricidal gang members in the final episode of the novel. After raiding the funeral parlor, dumping the caskets of the dead member of the Reds gang and Mallory in the street, and repeatedly shooting the dead boy, some of the rampaging Blues gang "spit and peed" on the dead body of the Reds member. Even though the gang members allowed the angry, yelling, preaching Kassima to dump the box of his pictures on Mallory's naked, defiled body, the ray of hope for the future implicit in the revelation of her courage and pregnancy in this final episode is overshadowed by the ominous hatred and violence of the black youth.

Nevertheless, as in *Philadelphia Fire*, *Two Cities* passionately and artistically challenges readers to acknowledge the perversities and paradoxes of the life and death of John Africa, MOVE, and young black men in contemporary urban America. *Two Cities* also reinforces Wideman's reputation as one of the most ingenious experimental writers to validate and valorize the richness of the African American vernacular tradition, especially black speech and music, in exploring the tensions of contemporary urban African American and black male identity. To the *Washington Post* reporter David Streitfeld, Wideman succinctly stated his artistic purpose: "My novels [...] attempt to exploit the inherent tension between what is fictional and what is factual, and to illuminate how unsteady and unpredictable the relationship is" (x15). Bluesman Buddy Guy would probably say that among other things, Wideman's blues voice is telling black male readers: "Sometimes you have to cry; sometimes you have to lie. But you can make it if you try."

II

Clarence Major's Homecoming Voice in *Such Was the Season*

The inspiration for this article on Such Was the Season *came from my interest in discovering whether the apparent experiments with postmodernism by such African American novelists as Ishmael Reed, Clarence Major, and Percival*

Everett were commercially successful with black readers. Relying primarily on a self-contradictory and self-undermining style and structure, postmodernism subverts the traditional grounds for the stability and universality of truth and reality. It repudiates the unifying ability of master narratives like myths and the ability to represent truth through mimetic art. And it argues that the meaning of literature derives from the indeterminacy of its language. This type of literary aesthetic has considerable success with many academic critics and the white cultural elite. But does it have mass commercial appeal, especially with black readers and African American novelists? In his collection of essays, The Dark and Feeling, Clarence Major, echoing Ishmael Reed, argues that "the novel not deliberately aimed at bringing about human freedom for black people has liberated as many minds as has the propaganda track, if not more. This does not mean that a wholly human novel by a black writer necessarily becomes assimilable for just anybody. It does mean, though, that a work that takes long root in its author's experience—race being a part of that experience—not only makes sense anywhere in any language but also is likely either to raise hell or to lower heaven." With the ostensible motivation of wider commercial success, especially among black readers, Such Was the Season, *however, is a more conventional and successful modernist neorealistic novel in its style and structure.*

"Unlike his previous fiction, which was unstintingly experimental, *Such Was the Season* is an old-fashioned, straight-ahead narrative crammed with action, a dramatic storyline and meaty characterization," writes novelist Al Young (19). This is the consensus of reviewers of Clarence Major's fifth novel. However, although more conventional and accessible on the surface for readers than his other novels, *Such Was the Season* is actually an exploration on its lower frequencies of the double consciousness of the implied author as well as of Dr. Adam North, whom the narrator/protagonist calls Juneboy, as both return to their southern black vernacular roots. Rather than "contagious affection" for his characters, especially Annie Eliza Sommer-Hicks, the black matriarchal narrator/protagonist, Major's homecoming voice is characterized by social and cultural ambivalence.

Set in the post–Black Power and post–Black Arts era in a black bourgeois community of Atlanta, Georgia, in the 1970s, the narrative structure of *Such Was the Season* is indeed rather conventional. Annie Eliza retrospectively tells us about her "killer-diller" week. During the exciting week, Juneboy, her estranged nephew, returns as Dr. Adam North to Atlanta from racially and culturally contrasting Yale and Howard Universities to lecture at similarly contrasting Spelman and Emory on his sickle cell research and to stay with her and his southern family. Renee, Annie Eliza's materialistic, feminist daughter-in-law, announces her candidacy for the state senate at a large dinner party. In addition, Senator Dale Cooper, Renee's political opponent and the incumbent, becomes mysteriously sick with a rare sickle cell disease and is nearly assassinated. The Reverend Dr. Jeremiah Hicks, Renee's husband and Annie Eliza's hustler/minister son, is involved in a local tomato industry scandal and nearly killed by an abused lover. The excitement continues when DeSoto Hicks, Annie Eliza's police sergeant son, hosts the family at the policeman's ball; and Annie Eliza aids Juneboy in his quest to reconcile himself to his southern past and family, especially his murdered father, Scoop, a numbers runner for the local illicit lottery game and surrogate father to Jeremiah. Annie Eliza is a sassy, elderly, pre–Black Power representative of a southern woman of her racial, ethnic, and regional vernacular culture and class. But the implied author and Juneboy are respectfully ambivalent about her beliefs, values, and behavior. She is a septuagenarian whose own self-contradictoriness is apparent in her ambivalent reference to Renee as a "nigger" (19), her feeling like a "pickaninny" in the company of some whites, her confession of telling a "pickaninny" joke to her favorite white employer (152), and her disapproval of interracial romance even on television, which she watches compulsively. She also has for many years worn a "blond but kinda red" wig, which may have once looked "real natural" on her, but, as her sister Esther told her bluntly two years earlier, now makes her "look like one of these here street hussies." Defiantly, she says, "I wore my wig all over Chicago, strutting my stuff just as pretty as I pleased" (17).

Is this behavior consistent with Annie Eliza's self-identification as "just a plain down-to-earth common sense person" (16)? Is she more folksy than folk? To be folksy is to be a stereotypical rather than a typical or individual member of the common people. To act folksy is to exploit the surface, distorting appearances of reality rather than exploring deeper, complicating significations of reality. The informality of folksiness distorts and demeans the ways of black folk for personal survival or self-aggrandizement by reinforcing the mythic racial and cultural sense of superiority of white people. What then is the implied author revealing about the ironies and paradoxes of Annie Eliza's double consciousness as an elderly southern black woman of the 1970s? How are readers encouraged to respond to her voice and worldview, which make little or no fixed distinctions between fact and fiction?

The illusory character of reality and the reality of illusoriness are dramatized and symbolized by the manner in which television informs Annie Eliza's consciousness and language. The rhythms of her everyday life, like the rhythms of her southern black vernacular speech, are punctuated by the integration of the technology of television with the traditional morality—the passions, prejudices, and pride—of hardworking, churchgoing, home-owning lower-middle-class southern Negro housewives of the 1940s and 1950s who helped to support their families by child-rearing, cooking, ironing, washing, and cleaning for white folks. Her vibrant, idiomatic dialect illuminates her uncolleged, opinionated, independent, protective, provincial, pragmatic, politically conservative character.

This is particularly true of the sound and sense of her sayings, slang, and sentences that express, for example, her anxiety about her arthritis, stomach pains, and sex life while she watches the soap opera romance of Luke and Laura on *General Hospital*:

> "My body was talking to me something powerful," she says. "I sho wont having no labor pains. Specially since I hadn't been nowhere near no man in that respect in many, many years. I ain't had no use for all the bother that goes with being like that with mens. Oh, I tried it one time after Bibb's death, but it didn't work. Just one time. It wont worth it, child. I might as well had a been shelling peas or shucking corn." (12–13)

The multiple negations and inherent variability in the use of past and present verb tenses, as well as the familiar direct-address term "child," which implies an intended primary audience of her racial, generational, and gender peers, seem appropriate for the speaker's socioeconomic class, age, race, region, and sex.

Later, at Renee's dinner party, the mayor

> ast Juneboy what he did and Juneboy told him nicely bout the research he was spose to be doing, he said, into sickle cell anemia. The mayor sounded real interested and ask Juneboy all about it and Juneboy talked up a storm like he knowed everything in the world bout this Negro disease. He used big words too, words like hemoglobin. Juneboy told the mayor some organization done gave him a grant, which is money, and

> Juneboy let the mayor know that he was spending a year spending his money from the grant peoples at Howard University Hospital. (21)

The only dialectal rules observed here are those of the pronunciation of "ask," the regularizing of the irregular past form of "know," the loss of the initial unstressed syllable in "about," and the completive aspect "done gave." Conspicuously absent in Annie Eliza's speech is the usual reduction in southern African American Vernacular English (AAVE) of "-ing" suffixes as in "singing" to "singin" and only infrequent uses of the uninflected form of the verb "to be" in a position in which a Standard American English (SAE) speaker would use an inflected form. But the rhythm, inherent variability, and peripatetic style of the literary idiolect seem authentic enough.

As Renee talks about her hospitalized, mentally ill mother, Betsy, Annie Eliza's vernacular reflections on Betsy and the blues tradition further illuminate the color, class, sexual, and cultural conflicts of her personal identity:

> For some reason when I think of Betsy I see her in that bright pink dress she had when she and Bob was together in that awful place we saw them once. Place called Tiny's Little Red Rooster in Marietta on a dirt road out where some colored shacks stood by a cornfield. Bibb and me went there not knowing what to spect. There was this old sinner man singing nasty songs bout what he was gon do to some gal when he catch her. He said stuff that no child of God could stand to hear: real ugly filth—stuff bout how big his thang is and what he plan to do with it. All kinda filth came outta his mouth. He talked about going up side the woman's head if she spent his money. He sang another song bout how some gal broke his heart but that old nigger never had no heart to break if you ast me. (35–36)

For Annie Eliza, as for many southern black churchgoing women of her generation and lower-middle-class status, the blues was the music of sin and sinners rather than a distinctive secular form of cultural affirmation of the physical and spiritual resiliency of ordinary black people.

Equally revealing of Annie Eliza's character and the moral, intellectual, and cultural ambivalence fostered by the implied author's double consciousness is the pride of the narrator/protagonist in the material success of her sons, Jeremiah and DeSoto. Worried "bout Juneboy's pearance" at Renee's big dinner party, she says:

"You see, I didn't want him to embarrass our side of the family. Esther's children never had the privileges my boys had. They didn't have a proper father. I mean, they were sorta raised here and there first by Momma and they no-good father and his crazy sisters. Then Esther took them up to Chicago but she had to work all the time. They didn't come up with good strict home training. That's the only way children learn good manners" (18). Ambivalent about the upper-middle-class arrogance of Jeremiah's wife, Renee, Annie Eliza tells Juneboy and readers that "she just one of them nigger gals spoiled something you wouldn't believe, and, child, so full of herself she can't smell her own stink. And all just cause she comes from the Wright family. You know the Wrights is one of the biggest and richest Negro family in politics in Atlanta" (19).

Expecting Juneboy to be as impressed as she is by the driveway "full of Cadillacs and Mercedes-Benzes" and the musical doorbells of Jeremiah and Renee's home, Annie Eliza wryly comments on his disappointing response: "Wouldn't you know it, the poor boy was so unused to such class he just didn't pay no tention to it the way polite people with right kind of background would have. I could hear them bells in there making all that sweet music and I just gave praise to the Lord that at least one of my boys had made it big in this world" (19–20). This is more than mere verbal irony. (The night before, Annie Eliza had suspected that Juneboy was trying to impress them with his stories about his travel experience in Poland!) Similar to Jeremiah's youthful, illicit gambling as a numbers runner to pay for his college education, his embezzlement of Scoop's bank accounts to build his church, and his involvement in the tomato industry scandal, the dramatic irony here invites the reader to share the mixed emotions of the implied author and Juneboy for the simplicity and sincerity of Annie Eliza's residual folk beliefs and values. But the reader also shares their ambivalence about the prejudices, provincialism, and paradoxes of her beliefs and values.

Atlanta-born Major, who tells interviewers that he remembers the mature vernacular voices of the women in his family and who has published a revised, expanded edition of his 1970s dictionary of African American slang, succeeds in capturing the literary idiolect of the time, place, class, sex, and individuality of Annie Eliza. The pronunciation, vocabulary, and grammar seem authentic and authoritative for the individualized vernacular speech of a southern black woman who claims to have changed the diapers of her sixty-three-year-old sister, Esther. Raised in a segregated black urban Georgia speech community at the turn of the century, she has lived in East Point for thirty-six years, since her dead husband, Bibb, bought the house in 1947 with his veteran's benefits. Although not as important in the literary reconstruction of spoken dialect as grammar, such lexical and slang items as "killer-diller," "killer," "hussie," "no-count," "doodly-squat," and "hootchie-kootchie man" were popular during that era. Annie Eliza tried for a while during the 1960s to adopt "Blacks" instead of "Negroes" as her preferred post–civil rights term of racial identification, but it just didn't feel right to her generation and tongue. "You called somebody black back in the thirties and forties when I was coming up," she explains, "you insulted them something terrible" (22).

The most striking aspect of the state of mind of the implied author and Juneboy is manifested in the pride that Annie Eliza expresses in her Cherokee heritage and the first family homecoming. As she recalls, homecoming

> use to be a big thing, a custom in our family. Nowadays only time folks get together is [. . .] when somebody dies or somebody marries or has a baby. But we Sommers use to all go down to Monroe to see Momma and Poppa when they was still living. We did it in the spring, in the first week of May. [. . .] At them homecomings everybody was feeling real good. We all helped Momma cook up a lot of fried chicken and made potato salad and we ate watermelon and drank lots of ice tea. Sometimes the men folk would sneak off and drink whiskey but we womens just pretended we didn't know. We singed a lot of happy songs too. (3)

At the first homecoming, her African American and Cherokee father, Olaudah Equiano Sommer, "talked Indian" and "told us a story bout his father, a important man in the Cherokee Nation, who helped collect money to send colored families to Liberia. You see, back then a lot of Negroes still wanted to go back to Africa." At other homecomings her father would tell stories about "how his father made good luck come to the tribe. [. . .] So homecoming was a time of happiness, story-telling, a time when we all come together and membered we was family and tried to love each other, even if we didn't always do it so well" (4–5). In *Such Was the Season* both Major and Juneboy are returning after many years to the South for their homecoming.

Like Annie Eliza and Juneboy, Major, as he reveals on the back cover of his book of poems *Some Observations of a Stranger at Zuni in the Latter Part of the Century* and in his autobiographical essay "Licking Stamps, Taking Chances," has memories of stories told by his maternal grandmother of her Cherokee ancestry. Similar to most of his central male characters, Major has much in common with Juneboy. Both were born in Atlanta and left the South at eighteen with their divorced mothers; both were first married to black women with whom they fathered two sons and from whom they were divorced at a young age; and both currently have intimate commitments to white women. In addition, both have advanced college degrees and teach at predominantly white universities; both have traveled in Europe, including Poland, as professors; and both returned briefly to the South on lecture trips and stayed with relatives after thirty or more years absence. As black intellectuals and professionals, both also have mixed emotions and success in reconciling the tensions of their biracial, bicultural identities in returning to their southern vernacular roots.

Early in the novel, Juneboy confesses poignantly to Annie Eliza,

> "You know, I've come here because of the lecture they asked me to give at the university, but I have another reason for returning to the South, especially to Atlanta. I have been suffering spiritually, longing for something I think I lost a long time ago. Aunt Annie Eliza, as old as I am, I should have resolved so many questions that I haven't managed to. Who am I? Where did I come from? My first questions, and they are still unanswered. I've been running from my early self, and now I want to stop. Somehow, I am hoping that I can get back in touch with that little boy I was, looking up into my mother's and father's faces and discovering the world. I tried to become a different person and I guess I succeeded. But now I need to find that earlier self and connect it with the new self that I am now." (7–8)

Juneboy's quest, in other words, is similar to that of the quasi-autobiographical male protagonists in most of Major's and much of Jean Toomer's fiction.

Juneboy's mixed emotions about his homecoming are apparent in the failure of his Spelman lecture and the failure to find his father's grave. "It was like trying to make an egg stand on its end," he tells his aunt. "The time of year, the season, was wrong. I worked at it, I worked hard at it, Aunt Annie Eliza. I told them what I dream of discovering and they listened as well as any audience can, but I felt sq[ua]re, in the end, that I had not reached them, they had not understood. Not a single face in the audience gave off that certain light of recognition" (7). The allusion here to the book's title, borrowed from Jean Toomer's poem "November Cotton Flower," gives resonance to the thematic and stylistic irony of homecoming as a ritual of reintegration and regeneration even in an unfavorable climate. Annie Eliza ashamedly concludes that "maybe Juneboy didn't know as much as he thought he did" (7).

But the frustration and estrangement voiced here about the distance between himself and the black intellectuals at Spelman seem more regional, cultural, emotional, and psychological than intellectual.

Juneboy's efforts to visit the grave site of his hustling yet compassionate father, Scoop, in order to reconcile himself with his father's memory proves unsuccessful. Annie Eliza considers Scoop "a no-count person," although he became her son Jeremiah's surrogate father while alive and his economic sponsor after death. She drives Juneboy eighty miles north past Athens to the town of Lexington, where Scoop was buried after being killed in a gunfight in a gambling dispute with a white man. On the way, Juneboy asks his aunt to stop in Monroe so that he can see his grandparents' old home and the family graves, where he takes pictures.

When they finally arrive in Lexington, they are surprised to discover that the "colored cemetery" where Scoop was buried is now under the concrete parking lot of a housing project. "In a way," says Juneboy with mixed emotions, "it's a fitting burial for Scoop. It's like he has lent his flesh and spirit to the continuation of the culture. The little kids playing in those parking lots are the ongoing spirits of all those silent souls down beneath the concrete. Scoop's spirit reaches up through the hard surface and spreads like the branches of a summer tree" (60). Although he is unsuccessful in paying his respects to his dead father, Juneboy feels that the week he has spent with his family has been good for him. "This is to say thank you, Aunt Annie Eliza, Donna Mae, Whitney, DeSoto, Buckle, for your hospitality," he says in a dinner toast the evening before leaving the South. "But you've given me more without knowing it. Through you I've rediscovered who I am and now I can go on from here. I love you all very much" (199).

"I started *Such Was the Season* after I had taken a trip to Atlanta," Major told interviewers Larry McCaffery and Jerzy Kutnik, "and to some extent Juneboy is based on some of my experiences on that trip. But [. . .] correlations start to break down very quickly once narrative and aesthetic demands and all sorts of other things start to operate on these 'facts'" (126). The book was originally titled *Juneboy*, but by the time Major got to the creation of Annie Eliza he found that this was the first novel in which he was not the model for the main character. Major says, "I felt more secure with the woman's voice I was using in *Such Was the Season*. I didn't have to think about inventing that voice because I'd grown up hearing it, I knew its rhythms from the way my relatives in the South speak. It was already there, so all I had to do was just sit at the computer and correct the voice by ear, the way you would write music. If the rhythm was wrong or the pitch off, I knew it instinctively because I'd lived with that voice all my life" (127). As a result, Juneboy is "presented through this folksy, down-to-earth woman's point-of-view," and Major's "own presence is so diminished in Juneboy's identity that he is at best a catalyst rather than a true persona" (125, 126). However, as I have attempted to demonstrate, Annie Eliza's compelling voice in Clarence Major's homecoming in *Such Was the Season* is more folk than folksy, yet it evokes mixed emotions from the implied author, Juneboy, and this reader.

III

Charles Johnson's Philosophical Fiction: Slave Revolt in the Quest for Unity of Being in *Middle Passage*

"Charles Johnson's Philosophical Fiction: Slave Revolt in the Quest for Unity of Being in Middle Passage*" is among my most memorable writing invitations as an African American scholar activist in the Black Studies movement. The editors of the* World & I, *a publication of the Washington Times Corporation, invited me to write two articles for them in 1991. The first, "Keeping the Faith: White Civil Rights and Black Affirmative Action," was a featured article in the Point/Counterpoint section of* Currents in Modern Thought *to celebrate the bicentennial anniversary of the adoption of the Bill of Rights in 1791. This article was so provocative that Morton A. Kaplan, the editor and publisher, wrote an additional opening editorial, "The Tribalization of America," attacking me for what he called my "eloquent case for group rights," which he found "unacceptable in principle and ultimately self-defeating in practice" (14). The second was the review "Slave Mutiny with a Difference" of Charles Johnson's National Book Award–winning third novel,* Middle Passage. *"Charles Johnson's Philosophical Fiction" is a revision that reveals how the novel is a response in part to the vision and form of Melville's* Billy Budd, Moby Dick, *and "Benito Cereno." Its thesis is that the characters, structure, and style of the slave revolt in* Middle Passage *most strikingly mark it as a contemporary rewrite of Frederick Douglass's* Heroic Slave *and Herman Melville's "Benito Cereno."*

Middle Passage, as Thomas Keneally noted in the *New York Times Book Review*, "is a novel in the honorable tradition of *Billy Budd* and *Moby Dick*" (8). Intertextually, Charles Johnson's National Book Award–winning third novel is also in the honorable tradition of accounts of actual slave mutinies, especially those aboard the *Amistad* in 1839 and the *Creole* in 1841. Its ancestral roots may be found in pioneering slave narratives like Olaudah Equiano's *Interesting Narrative of the Life of Olaudah Equiano, or Gustavus Vassa, the African, Written by Himself* (1789) and *The Heroic Slave* (1853) by Frederick Douglass. Based on the successful mutiny of Madison Washington and 134 slaves who were being shipped from Hampton, Virginia, to New Orleans aboard the *Creole*, *The Heroic Slave* is the first novella in African American literature. Cultural dualism and pluralism, then, are the major narrative and ideological impulses that inform the quest for unity of being in the content and form of Johnson's African American philosophical fiction.

After "six bad, apprentice novels" influenced by the Black Arts movement of the late 1960s, Johnson published his first novel, *Faith and the Good Thing* (1974). It is the highly praised black and white folktale, allegory, and myth of Faith Cross, "a brown-sugared soul sister seeking the Good Thing" (15). *Oxherding Tale* (1982), his second novel, is a wry, philosophical first-person neo–slave narrative. In his quest for liberation and the Good Thing (selfhood), its half-white protagonist, Andrew Hawkins, embodies the tensions between the Eastern and Western philosophies of Zen and phenomenology, as well as between black and white racial and cultural traditions. *The Sorcerer's Apprentice* (1986), a collection of eight magical tales of cultural and spiritual transformation with bookend stories about the descendants of Allmuseri sorcerers, owes much of its captivating power of craftsmanship (but not its power of conjuration) to Johnson's mentor, the late novelist and critic John Gardner. In all of his philosophical fiction, Johnson explores the phenomenological foundation or aboriginal faith of his central characters; through detailed descriptions, metaphors, and similes, he encourages the reader's indirect experience or intuition of other lives.

In *Being and Race* (1988), a slender yet important critical survey of black writing since 1970, Johnson reveals the common history of the dual racial and cultural perspectives of his intellectual and aesthetic principles. "Beginning first as a religion *imposed* upon slaves to keep them in line," he argues,

> the black church became, not merely the means through which Western thoughts from Plotinus to Buber entered indirectly into the lived experi-

ence of black people, but a common, spiritual, social, economic, and political experience [...]. Christianity will remain the religion of the Black folk, but Cultural Nationalism will continue to intoxicate a smaller group within it, being tied to what DuBois once called the ancient "battle of the color-line," and the dualistic style of thought that seems, sadly, to be our racial destiny. (84)

Rather than different worlds, we discover, when we look deeply enough, multiple perspectives of a single, commonly shared world.

In developing his phenomenological world vision in *Being and Race,* Johnson, on one hand, invokes the names of such philosophers as Plato, Socrates, Heidegger, Husserl, Bergson, and Merleau-Ponty. On the other hand, he invokes the names of such writers as André Malraux, John Gardner, Richard Wright, Ralph Ellison, James Baldwin, and John A. Williams. For Johnson, "writers begin their lifelong odyssey in art with expression or experience *interpreted* by others, not with, as popular wisdom sometimes has it, an ensemble of events that already mean something" (4). Like many readers, Johnson believes that Richard Wright's *Native Son* (1940) marks a watershed in black fiction. *Native Son* "remains one of our most phenomenologically successful novels," Johnson contends, because of its "construction of a consistent, coherent, and complete racial universe—Southside Chicago—that is fully shaped by a sensitive if seared black subjectivity" (13). Even more than with his meticulous attention to sociological details, says Johnson, "Wright reminds us through his method here—eidetic description, or presenting things in their lived essence (meaning) for a historical subject—that the world we live in is, first and foremost, one shaped by the mind" (14). Responding to *Native Son,* Ellison's *Invisible Man,* according to Johnson, is "something of the modern Ur-text for black fiction" (15). Like Melville's *Billy Budd, Moby Dick,* and "Benito Cereno," the vision and form of these fictions are calls to which Johnson and other writers are challenged to respond.

The Narrative of Slave Revolt

The characters, structure, and style of the slave revolt in *Middle Passage* most strikingly mark it as a contemporary rewrite of Douglass's *The Heroic Slave* and Melville's "Benito Cereno." Babo, Francesco, and Atufal, Melville's African mutineers, reappear as self-liberators in Johnson's narrative of the psychological effects of slavery and oppression on human beings—especially the newly freed Illinois bondman Rutherford

Calhoun, slave ship captain Ebenezer Falcon, and the legendary Allmuseri people. In contrast to Madison Washington, Douglass's heroic, humanistic, married orator and slave protagonist, Rutherford is an unheroic, free, philosophizing petty thief and parasitic narrator-protagonist. In 1830 he becomes a cook's helper on a New Orleans slave clipper to escape a mobster's enforcer and a shotgun marriage to a dark yet naive, transplanted, cat-loving Boston schoolteacher.

Falcon, the dwarfish philosopher-buccaneer captain of the *Republic,* bound for the Guinea coast to transport peace-loving, highly prized Allmuseri captives and their deity back to New Orleans, is the demonic antithesis of Melville's Captains Benito Cereno and Amaso Delano. "He was the Devil," Rutherford discovers near the end of his voyage. "Who else could enslave gods and men alike?" (120). As First Mate Cringle reinforces in his explicit allusion to Delano in a self-sacrificial speech to his starving crew, all of these white slave traders tragically blind themselves to the common humanity, intelligence, and resolve for freedom of blacks.

The infamous, erudite, multilingual Captain Falcon, "empire builder, explorer, and imperialist," plundered the religious shrines of the Hottentots, Tibetans, and Allmuseri in his missionary and profiteering zeal "to Americanize the entire planet" (29, 30). In one of several prolix philosophical conversations with the protagonist, Falcon expounds pompously on dualism as "a bloody structure of the mind. Subject and object, perceiver and perceived, self and other. [...] We cannot *think* without them. [...] They are signs of a transcendental Fault, a deep crack in consciousness itself. [...] Slavery, if you think this through [...] is the social correlate of a deeper, ontic wound" (98).

After the mutiny of the polyglot crew is preempted by the revolt of the captive Allmuseri, who ironically prohibit the speaking of English by the survivors, Captain Falcon's dying charge to Rutherford, his "eyes and ears" (57), is to write the truth of their voyage in the ship's log. "Not just Mr. Cringle's side [...] or the story the mutineers will spin," he says, "but things *I* told you when we met alone in secret." Rutherford, who has learned to speak the language of the Allmuseri, promises himself "that even though I'd tell the story [...] it would be, first and foremost, as I saw it since my escape from New Orleans" (146).

The frequent literary and linguistic allusions (e.g., "as the hag in the Wife of Bath's Tale had loved her fickle knight" [17]), anachronisms ("she and her sisters had no one to teach them to think like independent, menless Modern Women" [18]), and anomalies ("He was [...] the very Ur-type of Gangster" [13]) result from filtering the narrative of the slave revolt through Rutherford's educated bicultural consciousness. Before manumitting Rutherford, his biblical scholar master, the Reverend Peleg Chandler, educated him to be a preacher. The reverend not only taught him to read, write, count, and play the piano but also instructed him in "disquisitions on Neoplatonism, the evils of nominalism, the genius of Aquinas and the work of such seers as Jakob Böhme." But after seeing his brother, who is "shackled to subservience," decline to accept their master's deathbed reward of personal wealth, Rutherford rejects the life of a "gentleman of color" to become "a lecher for perception and the nerve-knocking thrill" (3).

Such poetic similes as "[the] wind off the water was like a fist of fresh air" (4) evoke the reader's sense of wonder at commonplace experience. But figures of speech and tropes that yoke the commonplace to disparate Eastern and Western religions (as in "an evening sky as blue as the skin of heathen Lord Krishna" and in "She was [. . .] as out of place in New Orleans as Saint Teresa would be at an orgy with de Sade" [5]) suggest more about the synthesized cultural dualism and wit of Charles Johnson than they do about Rutherford Calhoun. But for discerning readers, these figures of speech do not consistently and coherently conjure up the sense of a unity of being.

Slavery's Impact on Culture and Character

Rutherford's discovery of the relativity of historical truth, of the horrific impact of the transatlantic slave trade on the culture and character of all aboard the *Republic,* a parody of Plato's ideal society and an ironic symbol of American social and cultural diversity, transforms or destroys his life and the lives of others, especially the Allmuseri. The sobering truth of his ironic role in enslaving his African ancestors does not begin to dawn on him until he is warned of the danger of Arab traders' stealing him off the ship and selling him back into slavery with the Allmuseri. Physically, the Allmuseri "seemed a synthesis of several tribes, as if longevity in this land had made them a biological repository of Egyptian and sub-Saharan eccentricities or—in the Hegelian equation—a clan distilled from the essence of everything that came earlier. Put another way, they might have been the Ur-tribe of humanity itself" (61). According to their oral history, they were once a seafaring people who had sailed to India and Central America, developed an elegant fighting art similar to the Brazilian capoeira, spoke a gnomic language "that dovetailed articles into nouns, nouns into verbs," and wrote in pictograms (77). "Eating no meat, they were easy to feed. Disliking property, they were simple to clothe. Able to heal themselves, they required no medication. They seldom fought. They could not steal. They fell *sick,* it was said, if they wronged anyone" (78).

Like Equiano, the Allmuseri panicked at the sight of "the great ship and squalid pit that would house them sardined belly-to-buttocks in the orlop, with its dead air and razor teethed bilge rats" (65). Like him, they thought the white sailors were barbarians shipping them to America to be eaten. Cannibalism, as Johnson dramatizes it with detailed relish, in the parodic eating of First Mate Cringle's body by Rutherford and the crew, was not uncommon for men at sea. Cringle's New England gentility, innocence, and sacrifice parody the Christ-figure characters of Billy Budd and Amasa Delano. In the Allmuseri mythology, "Europeans had once been members of their tribe—rulers even, for a time—but fell into what was for these people the blackest of sins. The failure to experience the unity of Being everywhere was the Allmuseri vision of Hell. [. . .] That was where we were taking them—into the madness of multiplicity—and the thought of it drove them wild" (65). Until he sees the stolen Allmuseri god stored in a crate in the ship's hold, Rutherford also fails to experience the unity of being.

Transformed by his participation in the brutal, dehumanizing enslavement of a people in whom, unlike the ethnically diverse white sailors, he ironically sees himself, his guilty past, and his ominous future, Rutherford sits with his hair turning white as he asks himself, "How could I feel whole after seeing it? How could I tell my children of it without placing a curse on them forever? How could I even dare to *have* children in a world so senseless?" (67). As he helps to throw overboard the rotting corpse of an African man about his own age of twenty-three, there is little discernible ethical distance between the implied author and Rutherford. And there is even less intellectual distance between them when Rutherford discovers that rather than pure essence the lives and culture of the Allmuseri were "process and Heraclitean change, like any men, not fixed but evolving and as vulnerable to metamorphosis as the body of the boy we'd thrown overboard" (124). This philosophy is dramatically and psychologically reinforced as Rutherford realizes that the horrors of slavery on board the *Republic* have reshaped the souls as well as the bodies of the Africans, so that they were "no longer Africans, yet not Americans either" (125).

When Rutherford descends into the hold to feed the omnipotent Allmuseri deity, who is believed to sustain everything in the universe and to assume the image of all things, the god appears to him as his fugitive-slave father, Riley Calhoun, whom Rutherford hates for abandoning him in slavery. In "a seriality of images" the god reconciles him to his father by delivering "the *complete* content of the antecedent universe to which my father, as a single thread, belonged. [. . .] He seemed everywhere, his presence, and that of countless others, in me as well as the chamber, which had subtly changed. Suddenly I knew the god's name: Rutherford" (169,

171). Many readers will not share this epiphany even though as one of few survivors of the mutiny and storm-wrecked ship, Rutherford becomes a changed man. He returns to New Orleans and his Boston schoolteacher with Baleka, the Allmuseri girl with whom he has bonded as surrogate father. As the novel ends, Rutherford testifies, "The voyage had irreversibly changed my seeing, made of me a cultural mongrel, and transformed the world into a fleeting shadow play I felt no need to possess or dominate, only appreciate in the ever extended present" (187). Like the slave narrators and Ellison's *Invisible Man*, Charles Johnson's protagonist comes to terms with the cultural dualism of his past by writing it down. But after this fleeting consciousness of personal and cosmic wholeness, the absence of closure at the end of *Middle Passage* suggests that the quest for unity of being remains open.

IV

Trey Ellis's Voice of the New Black Aesthetic in *Platitudes*

Based on my critical study The Contemporary African American Novel *and delivered as a lecture at Peking University (BEIDA), the most prestigious university in China, during my spring 2004 Fulbright Lectureship in the People's Republic of China (PRC), "Trey Ellis's Voice of the New Black Aesthetic in* Platitudes*" was a major achievement in fulfilling the two basic goals of my Fulbright award. The first was to promote distribution of the Mandarin translation in 2000 of my book,* The Afro-American Novel and Its Tradition *and a bilingual edition of the 2004 publication of its English sequel,* The Contemporary African American Novel: Its Folk Roots and Modern Literary Branches. *The second was to promote the development of African American Studies in Beijing and Sichuan Province by teaching at the Beijing Foreign Studies University (BEWAI), the most highly respected language institution in China, lecturing at various universities, especially the Southwest University of Science and Technology (SWUST) in Mianyang and BEIDA, and by spreading the news about the blues (the roots of jazz, rhythm and blues, and rock and roll) everywhere I lectured.*

It is my understanding from my students and Deputy Dean Li Youwen that the following two postgraduate courses that I taught in African American

Studies were the first to be offered in the curricula of the American Literature Center and American Studies Center in the School of English and International Studies (SEIS) at BEIWAI: "The Political Economy and Globalization of African American Culture from the Blues to Hip Hop" and "The African American Literary Tradition." In addition, at least six students were referred to me by professors for consultation in writing theses and dissertations on the following authors and topics: Maxine Kingston, William Faulkner, Toni Morrison, Zora Neale Hurston, Harriet Jacobs, Clarence Major, double consciousness, narratology, and contemporary critical theory.

Of the twelve lecture invitations that I received, I accepted the following six: (1) "The African American Literary Tradition," School of Foreign Languages and Culture (SFLC), SWUST, March 4, 2004; (2) "Teaching African American Literature: Theory and Practice," SFLC, SWUST, March 4, 2004; (3) "The 100th Anniversary of African American Blues Music," the Third English Culture Festival, SEIS, BEWAI, April 23, 2004; (4) "The 100th Anniversary of African American Blues Music," BEIDA, May 21, 2004; (5) "'The Negro' as Metonym, Metaphor, and Marginal Man in Go Down, Moses," at "The Third International Conference on William Faulkner," at the Sichuan International Studies University (SISU), Chongqing, China, May 28–30, 2004; and (6) "The Contemporary African American Novel: Trey Ellis's Platitudes and the New Black Aesthetic," BEIDA, June 9, 2004. I also accepted the unexpected honor of an invitation from the Beijing Youth Daily newspaper, which has a paid subscription of over 600,000 readers, to write two essays on the blues that were published bilingually.

Although the postgraduate students and faculty at BEIDA were intellectually intrigued by my Trey Ellis and New Black Aesthetic lecture, they were understandably reticent about the government's censorship of discussions of the Tiananmen Square student revolt of 1989. They were less reticent, however, about the devastating destruction by students during the Cultural Revolution of 1967 of Western influences on printed materials as well as on faculty and administrators at BEIDA.

THE NATIONAL CENSUS OF 2000 PREDICTED THE GROWING POTENTIAL POWER shift in the demographics of the United States to immigrants and native-born people generally called Latinos (i.e., citizens and noncitizens from North, Central, and South American nations of Spanish and various racial and ethnic mixtures) as the largest ethnic political coalition in the nation. Internationally, the cataclysmic ethnic conflicts, migrations, drug wars, or genocidal wars in the former Union of Soviet Socialist Republics, the Congo, and the former Yugoslavia, as well as in Colombia, South Africa, India, Sri Lanka, and Burundi are tragic contemporary developments. They reveal that the struggle of technologically and economically poor menial laborers and blue-collar working-class peoples to reconcile the tension between their national or political and ethnic or cultural identities is a major disruptive problem in the emerging new world order. These demographic shifts and cataclysmic global events explain in part the recent popularity of discourses on multiculturalism, as well as of the stylistic and structural experimentation in narratives with magical realism and postmodernism. These developments have fostered a corresponding shift in power and popularity in the academy away from African American Studies, vernacular theories of art, and neorealism to Postcolonial and Cultural Studies, as well as to postmodern theories and practices of art and literature. In their belated search in the 1980s and 1990s for a pan-American comparative theory and methodology for American Studies, most critics have neglected to acknowledge the legacy of a similar search in the 1960s and 1970s for a pan-African movement in Black Studies and an African Americentric as well as an Afrocentric aesthetic in art. This is most apparent in Amiri Baraka's, Gwendolyn Brooks's, and Toni Morrison's momentous transformation of consciousness and cultural productions during the Black Arts movement and Ishmael Reed's culturally specific neo-hoodoo aesthetic and geographically diverse multiculturalism.

The post–Black Arts movement theory of Anglo-Jamaican critic Paul Gilroy about the culture of the Black Diaspora, the transatlantic sites in the Americas to which dispossessed sub-Saharan nonwhite Africans dispersed and migrated, outlines modern themes of identity formation and double consciousness techniques grounded in transcultural black contemporary music that transcend specific nationalities and ethnicities to produce a shared hybrid black Atlantic culture. In contrast to Gilroy's affirmation of double consciousness in his modern cultural theory, white American proponents of cultural hybridity and multiculturalism such as Myra Jehlen, Amy Kaplan, Frederick Crews, and Gregory S. Jay reject Du Bois's trope of double consciousness and displace Frederick Jackson Turner's theory of the frontier as the most significant defining space for the development of white American ethnicities, politics, economics, and culture.[1] They have also challenged Du Bois's African American theory and trope of double consciousness for its alleged racial binarism and male chauvinism with theories and tropes of transcultural border crossing and multiple consciousness, especially as represented in Gloria Anzaldúa's autobiographical celebration of cultural hybridity in *Borderlands/La Frontera: The New Mestiza* (1987). Many academic critics argue that this theoretical shift from conflicting white Americentric monoculturalism and cultural pluralism to American diasporic multiculturalism represents the most democratic and liberating contemporary American and global identity formations. In many modern and contemporary African American novels, however, native-born biracial, bicultural Americans of black African descent are ironically and paradoxically relegated to the margins of the dominant postindustrial, neocolonial social order of the United States as expendable cheap laborers yet inexpendable consumers, who are represented as either invisible men and women or outsiders.

In the quest for a better life and a more just social order, each generation has developed a new aesthetic to meet the challenge of survival and fulfillment in an ever-changing world of difference and diversity. Code-switching and code-mixing language in her book "from English to Castilian Spanish to the North Mexican dialect to Tex-Mex to a sprinkling of Nahuatl to a mixture of all of these," Anzaldúa, for example, describes herself as a bicultural subject: "I am a border woman. I grew up between two cultures, the Mexican (with a heavy Indian influence) and the Anglo (as a member of a colonized people in our own territory). I have been straddling that *tejas*-Mexican border, and others, all my life. It's not a comfortable territory to live in, this place of contradictions. Hatred, anger and exploitation are the prominent features of this landscape" (preface). Because Anzaldúa speaks in her text from and for multiple subject positions, including the lesbian, postcolonial theorist Homi Bhabha and Americanist Cyrus R. K. Patell argue that her hybridity creates a new "Third Space of enunciation" and provides a solution to the assumed binarism of double consciousness and the hyphenated American (Bhabha 37; Patell 177). As this essay demonstrates, however, African Americans were, to borrow a postmodern phrase, always already marginal people of mixed biological and cultural heritage, writing bidialectally from the distinctive social and linguistic position of paradoxically being at both the margins and center of modern American society.

The shifting cyclical pattern of residual, emerging, and dominant aesthetic movements in literature continues among some artists and cultural workers in the twenty-first century as a New Black Aesthetic (NBA) that stresses racial, class, gender, and sexually transgressive hybridity and multiculturalism. It emerged in response to the residual African Americentric aesthetic of the slave narratives, including neo–slave narratives, and the neo-hoodoo aesthetic that informs novels at different levels from Reed's *Mumbo Jumbo* to Arthur Flowers's Vietnam War novel

De Mojo Blues (1985), as well as to the dominant Afrocentric Black Arts vernacular aesthetic of the 1970s and the Black Womanist political and aesthetic movement of the early 1980s. The most recent movement for an NBA began in the late 1980s with a new generation that novelist Trey Ellis calls "cultural mulattoes," "blacks who grew up in white neighborhoods" but "now live in black neighborhoods" ("Response to NBA" 250–51) and "alienated (junior) intellectuals [. . .] educated by a multi-racial mix of cultures" ("New Black Aesthetic" 234–35). Many were influenced by the African Americentric tropes, transcultural characters, and avant-garde styles of novelists like Ishmael Reed, Clarence Major, John Edgar Wideman, and Toni Morrison, as well as nonblack writers like Twain, Joyce, and Faulkner.

Assuming that African American literature is fundamentally a socially symbolic linguistic construct, I find that the aesthetics of Charles Johnson, Nathaniel Mackey, Trey Ellis, Paul Beatty, Darius James, Percival Everett, and Colson Whitehead seek in different ways to displace rather than complement and expand African American populist, proletarian, and vernacular tropes of core black personal and collective identity with African American urban middle-class satirical tropes that privilege individualism and indeterminate multiculturalism and sexuality. Even so, the five residual oral forms—oratory (including everyday speech acts), myth/ritual performance, legend, tale, and song—as well as satire, irony, and paradox continue to inform the authenticity of the complex dualism and cultural ambivalence of the most engaging contemporary novels and novelists, including those in the NBA movement. Although represented with a parodic and satiric difference, the legendary black ancestor and elder, gifted and often rebellious orator, musician, artist, spiritual leader, and messianic figure are equally enduring symbols and tropes. Contemporary African American novelists deploy these characters and symbols to reconstruct imaginatively our tragicomic struggle as individuals and as a people for authority, authenticity, and agency. Nevertheless, many contemporary antiessentialist critics and readers who seek to move beyond the label of racial provincialism seem obsessed with validating and valorizing transcultural literary relationships while neglecting or rejecting an acknowledgment of the core vernacular roots of intracultural relationships and identities in the African American narrative tradition.

For example, at a 1999 academic conference in Pennsylvania titled "Afro-American Literature at the End of the Twentieth Century," a distinguished African American literary critic reproachfully questioned why all the books under examination were by black Americans. On the one hand, the question was an implied criticism of both the ostensible academic and literary provincialism of the conference program for focusing primarily on the intertextuality among black texts and the apparent anachronism of Afrocentric African American Studies programs in general. On the other hand, it was a call for more ethnic and racial diversity in examining our national identities as Americans. Even though Jewish, Chicano, Puerto Rican, and Asian Studies programs and conference organizers are rarely if ever criticized for racial and ethnic separatism or for generally not including a significant number of African American students, faculty, and books in their courses, neither the criticism nor the call was a new issue in fostering intraracial disunity and defensiveness among African Americans. Regrettably, contemporary proponents of pluralism and multiculturalism frequently neglect or ignore the fact that, in coalition with progressive whites, the struggles of African Americans for civil rights and self-determination have historically expanded and extended the power not only of other minority groups and women in the United States but also of all national and, indirectly, many international liberation groups.

How, then, does this assumed new hybridity relate to the lived and imagined literary identities of such different biracial and bicultural African American novelists as Jean Toomer, Langston Hughes, Rudolph Fisher, Zora Neale Hurston, Ralph Ellison, John Oliver Killens, William Melvin Kelley, Ishmael Reed, Toni Morrison, Charles Johnson, Gloria Naylor, Nathaniel Mackey, Trey Ellis, Paul Beatty, Darius James, Percival Everett, and Colson Whitehead? Like such writers as Van Wyck Brooks and Waldo Frank in their quest for a new mythic American, Toomer celebrated himself in modern literature and life as an essentialist, a poetic realist, and a New American, rather than a New Negro, in the 1920s. As demonstrated earlier in this essay, these novelists construct the double consciousness of their imagined characters and their own social and literary identities in narratives with code-switching and a hybridized language from what Bhabha calls a "Third Space" or from what black critics of my generation call desegregated, predominantly white suburban areas.

In the novel, according to Mikhail Bakhtin, hybridization is "a mixture of two social languages within the limits of a single utterance, an encounter, within the arena of an utterance, between two different linguistic consciousnesses, separated from one another by an epoch, by social differentiation or by some other factor" (358). The hybridized language and identities in pre–Black Arts movement African American novels were compelling constructions of the imagined communities in which the struggle for authenticity, authority, and agency by the authors and their characters unfolded. This exploration of hybridized language and identity continues with a difference in the struggle for authenticity, authority, and agency in the post–Black Arts movement narratives by such novelists as Johnson, Mackey, Ellis, Beatty, James, Everett, and Whitehead. Because of his provocative work on this new direction in the contemporary African American novel, I will focus on Trey Ellis's theory of an NBA and his narrative practice of this theory in *Platitudes*.

On October 14, 1962, William Arthur Ellis III, novelist and screenwriter whose pen name is Trey Ellis, was born in Washington, D.C., to William A. Ellis, a psychiatrist, and Pamela Fern Ellis, a psychologist. While his mother and father attended the University of Michigan and Yale, young Ellis "grew up in the predominantly white, middle and working-class suburbs around Ann Arbor, Michigan, and New Haven, Connecticut." After attending public elementary school in Hamden, Connecticut, he went to private schools in New Haven and graduated in 1980 from Phillips Academy in Andover, Massachusetts. While at Phillips Academy, Ellis studied with the novelist Alexander Theroux. As his second-generation, interracial, elite middle-class acculturation continued at Stanford University, Gilbert Sorrentino, another novelist, guided him in earning a BA in creative writing in 1984. From 1982 to 1983 Ellis worked as a journalist intern for *Newsweek*, and he subsequently contributed articles to such magazines and newspapers as *Playboy*, the *Village Voice*, *Washington Post Book World*, and the *Los Angeles Times*. Traveling widely in Africa, Europe, and Japan, as well as in South and Central America, Ellis became a multilingual cosmopolitan ("New Black Aesthetic" 233–51). He is also the author of several television movies, including *Tuskegee Airmen*, and three novels: *Platitudes* (1988), a metafictional story within a story about the contrasting aesthetics of a black female and a black male writer; *Home Repairs* (1993), a satirical coming-of-age diary of a TV show handyman; and *Right Here, Right Now* (1999), an elaborate parody, with tape recordings as narrative devices, of evangelical cults and motivational speakers that won an American Book Award.

In his three novels and the essays "The New Black Aesthetic" and "Response to NBA Critiques," Ellis boldly defines, defends, and promotes a New Black Aesthetic for his generation. But his NBA is as problematic as the radical black cultural nationalist aesthetic that it seeks to displace. After confessing that he is "a bourgie black boy" who had not lived in a black community other than his family before moving as a freshman "into Ujamaa, Stanford's black dorm," Ellis writes, "Just as a genetic mulatto is a black person of mixed parents who can often get along fine with his white grandparents, a cultural mulatto, educated by a multi-racial mix of cultures, can also navigate easily in the white world. And it is by and large this rapidly growing group of cultural mulattoes that fuels the NBA. We no longer need to deny or suppress any part of our complicated and sometimes contradictory cultural baggage to please either white people or black" ("New Black Aesthetic" 235). Actually, as I demonstrated in *The Afro-American Novel and Its Tradition*, Ellis's advocacy of shifting the thematic, stylistic, and structural focus of African American novels from neorealistic representations of underemployed menial and blue-collar working-class black Americans' traditional vernacular responses to the reality of antiblack racism to the multicultural experiences of the black bourgeoisie is nothing new. The tradition of the African American novel began in the antebellum and postbellum periods by focusing primarily on the lives of mulattoes, especially women, whose phenotype, especially color, was a dominant factor in their class and cultural status, as well as their double consciousness and socialized ambivalence. Also, a major debate between artists and the publishing industry, black and white, during the Harlem Renaissance was about the celebration of the lives of seasonally employed black agrarian folk, the economically uprooted, and the urban, nonwhite, nonunion industrial working class as the authentic African American experience, to the neglect of the transcultural lives and achievements of the black bourgeoisie.

In his 1989 literary manifesto, "The New Black Aesthetic," Ellis argues that Lisa and Kellie Jones, the biracial, bicultural daughters of Amiri Baraka and Hettie Jones, and "many other members of the NBA are the children of Civil Rights workers or black nationalists" and are cultural mulattoes who not only have inherited from their parents a "postliberated aesthetic" but also have chosen to construct a black middle-class identity for themselves (234–35). But the trope of cultural mulattoes is a misnomer. It misguidedly resurrects and reinforces the trope of tragic mulattoes, the pejorative nineteenth-century association of first-generation biologically half-black and half-white persons with the sterility of mules who agonize over being neither white nor black. However, the writers that Ellis identifies as members of the NBA are primarily second- and third-generation progeny of exogamous, often interracial, couples who are college graduates of predominantly white private, elitist academic institutions who raised their children in predominantly white middle-class communities. Anthropologically, then, because the beliefs and values of Ellis's cultural mulattoes were fundamentally shaped by immersion during their formative years in predominantly white middle-class communities, their acculturation and identity formation could be arguably viewed as less authentically black than those of contemporaries who were acculturated in predominantly black communities. Some NBA novelists, however, are also the children or descendants of disaffected black cultural nationalists; of black urban professionals and bourgeois social climbers; or of reactionary black avant-garde artists. How do the ironies, paradoxes, and stark contradictions of the biologically, socially, and culturally mixed backgrounds of this emergent group of artists and writers constitute a new black literary movement and aesthetic that Ellis feels is "separate but better"?

Despite making no suggestion in his initial declaration "that a 'cultural mulatto' has an edge over a black artist more traditionally raised," Ellis claims in his response to critics of his manifesto that "what is new and interesting now [. . .] is that we have a flood of both types." He considers the NBA "an anti-aesthetic that defies definition" and "an attitude of liberalism rather than a restrictive code." Because "today we can be more honest and critical of ourselves than ever before," he argues, "this open-minded far-sightedness may very well produce some of the greatest works of art the world has ever known, because, like Newton, we stand on the shoulders of giants" ("Response to NBA" 251). Rather than a synthesis of the principles, poetics, and politics of the Harlem Renaissance and the Black Arts movements, Ellis's NBA, as he admits, is "fueled by naïve exuberance and [. . . an] unshakable belief that our youthful black power can perfect society and perfect the soul." Although he ascribes a "leftist, neo-Nationalist politic" to the NBA artists who "castigate their buppie contemporaries" ("Response to NBA" 250), moving up from the poverty of the majority of the black working poor to the prosperity of the second- and third-generation black professional middle class and moving out of black ghettoes to predominantly white and racially mixed suburbs seem to be primarily matters of personal choice rather than class privilege and integrationist politics for Ellis. Personal choice and freedom, like lifting yourself up by your own bootstraps or Nike shoelaces even when you can't afford either footwear, are thus the dominant factors in the middle-class values of Ellis's naïve new Talented Tenth and in their African Americentric transcultural identity formations.

Although all of Ellis's novels are semiautobiographical experimental narratives about the transcultural identity formation of young black middle-class men, *Platitudes* is the most compelling thematically, structurally, and stylistically. The novel is primarily a satirical attack on monolithic and stereotypic representations of authentic African American culture and character that argues ironically for transcultural middle-class values as the norm for African American identities. According to critic J. Martin Favor, "Ellis moves in *Platitudes* to create a heteroglossic structure which, in a Bakhtinian sense, allows competing languages of African American identity to 'be juxtaposed to one another, mutually supplement one another, contradict one another and be interrelated dialogically'" ("Ain't Nothin'" 695). While this is certainly a valid way of reading the text, it subordinates an African Americentric reading that privileges its signifying style to a Eurocentric reading of its dialogism. But this type of interpretation fails to address the fallacious assumption of Bakhtin's dialogism that various diverse languages are, or will be, equally and mutually respected epistemological and ontological modes of identity formation in hierarchically constructed heteroglossic communities and texts such as those indigenous to the United States. As students who are criticized for "talking white" discover, phenotypical African Americans who are unfamiliar with African American Vernacular English (AAVE) and speak or write exclusively Standard American English (SAE) are often perceived as culturally white by speakers whose primary speech community is AAVE. Since the dynamics of the interaction between the languages of primary and wider speech communities reveal a struggle for status and power between speakers of standard and nonstandard modes of language, readers, like auditors, should be aware of and attuned to the culturally specific criteria, especially vernacular experiences and voices, by which the proficiency, power, and identity of the speaker and writer—that is, his or her authenticity, authority, and agency—are ascertained and assessed. *Platitudes,* in other words, is most meaningfully read, understood, and appreciated as an African Americentric metafictional and satirical story within a story about the quest in life and literature of black American writers and artists to reconstruct and reconcile with authenticity, authority, and agency the double consciousness and diverse voices of African Americans.

Let me here underscore the layered, complex meanings of authenticity, authority, and agency as they are used in this paper and my new book. The tenth edition of *Merriam-Webster's New Collegiate Dictionary* defines "authentic" as something that is "worthy of acceptance or belief as conforming to fact or reality" (75). In *Sincerity and Authenticity* literary critic Lionel Trilling more narrowly explains authenticity "as a criterion of art and as a quality of the personal life which may be either enhanced or diminished by art" (134). In *Authentic Blackness,* a study of the representation of blackness in the New Negro movement and Harlem Renaissance, critic J. Martin Favor writes that "authenticity derives from uniqueness, but it also fixes that uniqueness to a limited range of possibilities" (153n5). In contrast, philosopher Charles Taylor more directly addresses the complex ethical dimensions of authenticity in *The Ethics of Authenticity:*

> Authenticity (A) involves (i) creation and construction as well as discovery, (ii) originality, and frequently (iii) opposition to the rules of society and even potentially to what we recognize as morality. But it is also true [...] that it (B) requires (i) openness to horizons of significance (for otherwise the creation loses the background that can save it from insignificance) and (ii) a self-definition in dialogue. That these demands may be in tension has to be allowed. But what must be wrong is a simple privileging of one over the other of (A), say, at the expense of (B), or vice versa. (66)

Authenticity is thus conferred from without as well as from within the dialectic process of the rites of passage of one's life. Authenticity also implies both transcending or overcoming restrictive material conditions and transgressing or violating social and moral boundaries. Whether the ultimate reality and liberation are to be achieved through the power of love (agape or eros, heterosexuality or homosexuality) or the power of revolution (peaceful or violent) grounded in the actual or imagined experiences of the authors is a frequent matter of critical concern for readers of the contemporary African American novel and romance.

Although they usually overlap, authority differs from authenticity because it requires the power to influence or command thought, opinion, or behavior. According to social theorist Max Weber, power is "the probability that one actor within a social relationship will be in a position to carry out his own will despite resistance, regardless of the basis on which this probability rests" (152). In "Power as a Social Process," social scientist Marvin E. Olsen reminds us about the three grounds on which legitimate authority often rests: "(a) traditional values, beliefs, norms, and customs, (b) legal prerogatives established through more-or-less rational agreements, and (c) special expertise or knowledge relevant to the situation. To the extent that an actor draws legitimacy from three sources [. . .] his authority is especially strong" (7). Although phenotypically and sociohistorically black writers could claim the authority of their racial and cultural experience with slavery and segregation, the actual authority of the identities of peoples of African descent and their descendants in the United States, as revealed in texts that range from slave petitions and autobiographies to novels by Reed, Morrison, Trey Ellis, and Colson Whitehead, is more complex. The authority of the identities of African Americans emanates not only from the particularity of our historical struggle against slavery, colonization, and antiblack racism in the United States. It also emanates from the language of our individual and collective political agency in the present and future to maintain or change power relationships. The ways that African American novelists and novels use rhetoric, dialectic, and Bakhtinian dialogism, especially the deployment of residually oral forms, illuminate the authority of these strategies in reconciling African American double consciousness. They also illuminate the authority of these strategies in representing the dynamic interdependence of our chromosomes, color, class, geography, culture, consciousness, conscience, commitment, sexuality, and choice in the construction of the core ethnic identities and unity necessary to effect a more just community.

In narratology an agent is the representation of a human being whose speech acts influence events. But as it is used here, agency, to paraphrase Charles Taylor, is the sociocultural and sociopsychological process by which the individual assumes a responsible political position in maintaining or changing the systems of language and power by which he or she constructs and represents a personal and group identity or subjectivity of authenticity and authority (*Human Agency and Language* 3–5). In other words, agency is personal initiative and principled action in effecting social change. The history of the pan-African movement has taught African Americans that the construction of an African diasporic identity of peaceful coexistence is more of a cultural and romantic ideal than, as the unrelenting fratricidal ethnic wars in sub-Saharan Africa indicate, an economic and political reality. For African Americentrics, the construction of a unifying core of shared history and feelings of racial subordination, of resistance, and of triumphant vernacular expressivity has its demographic origins in the Deep South of the United States, especially in the residually oral forms of Gullah culture (e.g., speech, myth, legend, tale, and song) in the coastal regions of Georgia and South Carolina. Varieties of its contemporary perennial life cycle and creative reconstructions occur in urban American centers of native speakers of AAVE and predominantly black inner-city communities of the United States.

As Taylor explains in *Human Agency and Language,* "An individual is constituted by the language and culture which can only be maintained and renewed in the communities he is part of. [...] The community is not simply an aggregation of individuals. [...] The community is also constitutive of the individual, in the sense that the self-interpretations which define him are drawn from the interchange which the community carries on" (8). The sociocultural and sociolinguistic construction of the identities of African Americans begins with the hierarchical power relationship between the nonstandard regional dialects of enslaved Africans and the English dialect standardized for social and cultural reasons by white Americans. Addressing the question of agency in *The Afrocentric Idea,* Molefi Asante, a specialist in speech communications, argues persuasively that "the protest speaker's sensitivity to powerlessness in the society frees him or her to utilize the improvisational mechanisms of African American culture in responding to unpleasant situations."[2] The manner and degree of code-switching by novelists between the pronunciation, vocabulary, and grammar of AAVE, especially its distinctive idioms, sayings, and cultural commonplaces, and SAE in the imaginative construction of the identities of African Americans is therefore one important area of analysis for assessing the agency, as well as the authenticity and authority, of black American novelists, their characters, and their texts.

In *Platitudes* the code-switching, wry humor, parody, and culturally specific tropes memorably and metalinguistically illuminate the authenticity, authority, and agency of Ellis, the implied author, and the major characters, Dewayne Wellington, a black experimental novelist, and Isshee Ayam, a militant womanist novelist, in constructing a distinctively African American vernacular novel. Rather than the conventional frame of a story within a story, the implied author opens *Platitudes* with two realistic, dull fragments of a novel about black characters that Dewayne has difficulties in constructing with gender and vernacular authenticity and authority. So *Platitudes* is actually a composite of three stories satirizing the writing of black aesthetic novels in the 1960s and 1970s. The first is the novel by Trey Ellis with embedded stories by a black male and female writer who respectively privilege middle-class and ordinary working-class values and vernacular voices. The second is the coming-of-age story of sixteen-year-old Earle, a northern and urban materialistic child of the middle class, whose interracially dating black mother and integrationist social life wryly parodies black folk character and culture in code-switching language: "She is neither fat (her breasts don't swell the lace top of the apron she has never owned), nor has she any gold teeth. She cannot sing, nor is she ever called 'Mama' (though that is what she calls her own mother). She does not, not work in public relations and her two-handed backhand is not, not envied by her peers" (4). Earle's mother dates Solomon Levitt, and her son fantasizes about Janey Rosenbloom at "the B'nai B'rith/NAACP dance at the Copa" (4–7). Both Ellis and Dewayne are therefore satirizing not only gender and class issues in black aesthetic novels but also representations of historical social and ethnic relationships, including personal intimacy and political coalitions, between African Americans and Jewish Americans as being socially outdated and narrowly stereotypic rather than authentic.

Advised by a friend in the publishing industry that "black women *sell*," Dewayne begins a second narrative about the urban black northern working-class life of sixteen-year-old Dorothy, who attends a Catholic school for girls and whose mother, Darcelle, is "one of those fundamentalist, tough-as-nails black women who, underneath, are pussycats" and who "can be so street sometimes" (11–13). In response to Dewayne's request for help from readers about which story is more effective, including which characters, witticisms, and grammatical devices he should change for authenticity, Isshee Ayam—a punning parody of African American naming customs, the burning bush episode in the Bible, and the yam episode in Ralph Ellison's *Invisible Man*—provides her authentic versions of Dewayne's stories. She shifts the gender perspective, cultural setting, and characters from a black masculinist urban North to a black womanist rural South. "No," Isshee writes to Dewayne, "we women of color do not need your atavistic brand of representation, thank you" (15). *Platitudes* thus satirizes the chauvinism as well as the vernacular authority and authenticity of black aesthetic male novelists.

Even though satire and parody are at work in the stories by both Dewayne and Isshee, the implied author reveals by the pattern and intensity of his language and imaginative critique less class and aesthetic distance between himself and Dewayne Wellington than between himself and Isshee Ayam. In addition to the names of the writers, the names of Maylene, Nadine, and Lurlene, the sisters; I. Corinthians, the "cardboard-colored" rent collector; Mr. Wyte, the Georgia landlord; and Abe, Moses, and Jesus, the family dogs are parodies of the vernacular representation of African American culture and character that Isshee provides in her rewrite of Dewayne's story in chapter 1. A wryly and sexually exaggerated, even farcical, representation of Earle's Mama as a legendary black matriarch undercuts the intended authenticity of Isshee's chapter: "Yes, from out of those wide Baptist thighs, thighs that shook with the centuries of injustice and degradation, thighs that twitched with the hope of generations yet unplanted, thighs that quivered with the friction of jubilant, bed-thumping, and funky-smelling lovemaking, emerged Earle" (16). In ironic response to Isshee's sassy and sexy African American vernacular reconstruction of the oppressive legacy of slavery absent in Dewayne's story, a literary representation that Ellis is clearly parodying as stereotypic rather than authentic, Dewayne writes, "I'm speechless, Ms. Ayam. How can I thank you for dragging my meager tale back to its roots in Afro-American glory-stories" (19)? Responding "to the tune of John Coltrane's 'My Favorite Things,'" a jazz arrangement of a Rodgers and Hammerstein song, Dewayne and the implied author then seek to validate the authenticity of the urban, middle-class representation of African American culture and character by offering a long, diverse list of "a few of Earle's favorite things." The list ranges widely and randomly from tanks, Janey Rosenbloom, Cream of Wheat, and Slurpees to Christmas, World War II, "not this restaurant, not Lenox Avenue, but a double helping of chicken livers and gravy and grits and rolls" (19–20).

In reconciling the tension between Dewayne and Isshee over who is an authentic literary representation of African American culture and character, the implied author not only ideologically sympathizes with Dewayne but also aesthetically displaces the marginally employed, working-class culture of the majority of African Americans with the white-collar, middle- and upper-class culture of the minority of African Americans. This pattern of reconciliation begins with the exchange of correspondence between Isshee and Dewayne dated December 26 and 31, 1984. Although still critical of Dewayne's "unforgivable penchant for pornography" and "misogynistic belches," Isshee writes on December 26: "I must admit that this latest passage on Dorothy is not altogether without merit. The dialectic between class struggle and cultural assimilation, the mental anguish of rising (???!) from a middle-class Harlem household to the rich, white, New York, controlled-substance-abusing elite is almost interestingly handled" (108–09). She closes her letter by warmly extending "a most merry Kwanzaa and a Happy New Year" to Dewayne and his family.

Equally conciliatory, Dewayne, in turn, writes on December 31: "You are absolutely correct. My prose and my thoughts have changed, tightened, and—if I may be so bold—improved. Isshee—may I call you that—for after just having read and thoroughly enjoyed your *Chillun o' de Lawd, Hog Jowl Junction,* and *My Big Ol' Feets Gon' Stomp Dat Evil Down,* I feel a real intimacy between us" (110). He also closes warmly with "your colleague and fan" (111). Their reconciliation culminates in Isshee's letter of January 20, 1985. As Trey Ellis sustains the satiric and metafictional relationship among the stereotypic or monolithic representations of racial and cultural authenticity in the three versions of *Platitudes,* which is the title of the narratives by Dewayne and Isshee as well as by Ellis, Isshee writes, "After reading your last letter, I feel nothing but shame over my past conduct. I was catty and cruel because I believed you to be yet another misogynistic, insensitive cretin with a penchant for child molesting. I had no idea you were merely another heartbroken human being. [. . .] I believe *Platitudes* is now coming along rather well. The two-completely-different-types-fall-in-love Love Story is a time-honored favorite" (148–49). Isshee is also conciliatory to Dewayne's experimental style, which Ellis, like Dewayne and Isshee, fallaciously assumes is antithetical to African American neorealism. "I have never been a fan of you experimentalists, *per se,* and often find that school a bit too sure of itself and arch, yet I must admit that I sometimes envy your stylistic liberty" (149). Ironic and parodic to the end, *Platitudes,* the insipid yet wryly humorous stories-within-a-story of Earle and Dorothy and of Dewayne and Isshee close in romantic, melodramatic lovemaking scenes.

As critic Favor insightfully observes, "Ellis challenges the notion of a single authenticity by foregrounding the processes of reading and writing, (re)construction and revision" (700). The representation of agency in *Platitudes* is therefore neither leftist nor neo-nationalist. Historically and anthropologically, as a racially and ethnically mixed people acculturated in an antiblack racist society, African Americans have always biologically, culturally, socially, politically, and ideologically manifested different shades and degrees of blackness as authentic. As this essay and *The Contemporary African American Novel,* my most recent critical study, demonstrate, the actual and literary constructions of an authentic African American identity are more complex and complicated than merely a matter of color and class. Since all racial categories are unscientific, even though the dominant group represents itself as the norm, more often than not, when individuals, groups, or organizations are metaphorically and socially called "white," they are actually considered not really black or not black enough, rather than not black at all. Conferred from without and within the rites of passage of one's life or lived experience, authenticity is attained by transcending restrictive material conditions and transgressing social and moral boundaries while both discovering and constructing a usable past and a viable, more just future. This explains, in part, the African American intraracial signifying name of "Oreo" for people who look black but act white, with its multivalent ironic and parodic meanings. For example, in *Our Nig*, an 1859 landmark African American novel, Jim, an African character, proposes marriage to Mag Smith, a white woman who was ostracized and poor because she had a child out of wedlock. "I's black outside, I know, but I's got a white heart inside," says Jim. "Which you rather have, a black heart in a white skin, or a white heart in a black one?" (12). Ellis reconciles the African American double consciousness in his essays and *Platitudes* by displacing rather than complementing urban folk and black working-class culture with the culture of the black bourgeoisie and the NBA of cultural mulattoes.

Notes

1. See Myra Jehlen, Introduction, *Ideology and Classic American Literature*, ed. Sacvan Bercovitch and Myra Jehlen (Cambridge: Cambridge UP, 1986) 1–20; Amy Kaplan, "'Left Alone with America': The Absence of Empire in the Study of American Culture," *Cultures of United States Imperialism*, ed. Amy Kaplan and Donald E. Pease (Durham: Duke UP, 1993) 3–21; Frederick Crews, *The Critics Bear It Away: American Fiction and the Academy* (New York: Random, 1992); and Gregory S. Jay, *American Literature and the Culture Wars* (Ithaca, NY: Cornell UP, 1997).

2. Asante also notes, "That which the speaker expresses by the extreme dimensions of his media of words, tones, fables, myths, legends, and sounds is a sort of word subtlety, intended to subvert the established order by guerrilla rhetoric tactics" (116).

4

Womanist African American Vernacular and Literary Voices

I

Ann Petry's Demythologizing of American Culture and Afro-American Character

"Ann Petry's Demythologizing of American Culture and Afro-American Character" is a revised draft of part of the chapter "Richard Wright and the Triumph of Naturalism" in my critical study The Afro-American Novel and Its Tradition. *Challenging the critical convention of including Ann Petry among a group of black male writers (William Attaway, Carl Offord, Chester Himes, Curtis Lucas, Alden Bland, Willard Motley, William Gardener Smith, and Willard Savoy) influenced by Richard Wright, I wrote it during the post– Black Feminist movement of the early 1980s. It was published in 1985 by Hortense Spillers and Marjorie Pryse in the collection of essays* Conjuring: Black Women, Fiction, and Literary Tradition. *Unlike such critics as Michael Awkward and Calvin Hernton, I do not consider myself a black male feminist. However, because I believe the novels of Ann Petry have been overshadowed and her talent as a modern novelist misrepresented by their frequent comparison to the narrative vision and achievement of Richard Wright, I do consider this essay a modest contribution to this belatedly recognized, important branch of the African American literary tradition.*

THE NOVELS OF ANN PETRY HAVE BEEN OVERSHADOWED AND HER TALENT misrepresented by their frequent comparison to the fiction and achievement of Richard Wright and Chester Himes. Robert Bone, for example, claims that *The*

Street (1946), her first novel, suffers by comparison to Wright's *Native Son* because "it is an attempt to interpret slum life in terms of *Negro* experience, when a larger frame of reference is required." In contrast, he considers *Country Place* (1947), her second novel, "one of the finest [. . .] of the period" because it is "a manifestation not so much of assimilation as of versatility" (180). He does not mention *The Narrows* (1953), the best of her three novels, in either edition of his *Negro Novel in America*. Neither does critic Addison Gayle Jr., who discusses only *The Street* in his book *The Way of the New World* (192–97). For Gayle, Petry is similar to Himes in that she develops characters with some status and education and to Wright in that "both were interested in the effects of environment upon the psychological makeup of characters." Unlike Wright, however, Gayle concludes, "Miss Petry is more interested in the effects of the environment upon her characters than she is in the characters themselves" (192). Whether valid or not, these critical views do not adequately express the complexity and distinctiveness of Ann Petry's aesthetic vision and achievement.

Ann Petry actually moves beyond the naturalistic vision of Wright and Himes in her critical delineation and demythologizing of cultural myths, especially those of the American Dream, the city and small town, and black character. In exploring the black community's place in time and space, its relationship to the American past and future, she effectively debunks the myths of urban success and progress, of rural innocence and virtue, and of pathological black women and men. Embodying the values and beliefs of a community, *myths,* as we are using the term here, are stories people in a particular society tell to organize, explain, and understand the realities and metaphysics of their world. "Myths are not rational," writes James O. Robertson in *American Myth, American Reality,* "at least in the sense that they are not controlled by what we believe to be logic. They are sometimes based on faith, on belief rather than reason, on ideals rather than realities" (xv). Thus myths are a kind of behavioral charter that leads to both negative and positive responses.

Since the "truth" about America and Americans is found in both American myths and American realities, Petry dispassionately explores both in her novels. Like modern social realist and naturalist writers from Sinclair Lewis and Theodore Dreiser to Zora Hurston and Richard Wright, she realizes, moreover, that not all Americans participate in the same myths or use them in the same ways. Race, color, class, sex, and region are the major realities that determine the degree and manner of participation of individuals and communities in our national myths. While, for example, myths of the Founding Fathers such as Benjamin Franklin, who is the colonial paradigm of the successful self-made man, are available to all Americans, black Americans rarely refer to them. "On the other hand," as Robertson states, "many black Americans use the stories and myths of Abraham Lincoln more frequently than other Americans" (18). Despite turn-of-the-century attacks on small-town life such as Sinclair Lewis's *Main Street*, the rural vision of the city by many pre–World War II white American writers is characterized mainly by sin, crime, and violence. At the same time, however, post–World War II younger Americans, especially blacks, dream of the city as a place of opportunity, wealth, and progress. The truth, as Petry reveals in her novels, is actually more complex and paradoxical. So, too, is the socialized ambivalence (the pride and shame of one's identity) and double consciousness (the struggle to reconcile one's dual heritage) of black American character.

The setting and themes of Ann Petry's novels are a natural outgrowth of her intimacy with the black inner-city life of New York and the white small-town life of New England. Born in 1911 in Old Saybrook, Connecticut, Ann Petry grew up in a predominantly white environment and, in the family tradition, graduated in 1934 with a degree in pharmacy from the University of Connecticut. After working in the family drugstores in Old Saybrook and the nearby town of Lyme, she married in 1938 and moved to New York to work and pursue her childhood interests in writing. From 1938 to 1944 she worked as a journalist for two Harlem newspapers: *Amsterdam News* and *People's Voice*. In 1943 her short stories began appearing in the *Crisis* and *Phylon*. The early chapters of *The Street* won her a Houghton Mifflin Literary Fellowship in 1945. In 1948 she returned to Connecticut to raise her family and continue writing. Her publications include four children's books, a collection of short stories, and three novels: *The Street, Country Place,* and *The Narrows*.

The Street is a highly dramatic novel of economic determinism in which the environment is the dominant force against which the characters must struggle to survive. The novel opens symbolically with the November wind and cold and dirt and filth of 116th Street overpowering the hurried Harlem pedestrians, including the apartment-hunting protagonist, Lutie Johnson. It closes with Lutie leaving the city by train after killing the man who assaults her, the snow falling symbolically, "gently obscuring the grime and garbage and the ugliness" of the street. As the plot progresses episodically, we apprehend the street in the same racially segregated and economically exploited sociological manner as the protagonist:

> It was a bad street. [...] It wasn't just this street that she was afraid of or that was bad. It was any street where people were packed together like sardines in a can.
>
> And it wasn't just this city. It was any city where they set up a line and say black folks stay on this side and white folks on this side, so that the black folks were crammed on top of each other—jammed and packed and forced into the smallest possible space until they were completely cut off from light and air.
>
> It was any place where the women had to work to support the families because the men couldn't get jobs and the men got bored and pulled out and the kids were left without proper homes because there was nobody around to put a heart into it. Yes. It was any place where people were so damn poor they didn't have time to do anything but work, and their bodies were the only source of relief from the pressure under which they lived; and where the crowding together made the young girls wise beyond their years. (130)

Poverty and race are inextricably linked to the "Dirty, dark, filthy traps" in which the characters are compelled to live and die.

It was "Streets like 116th Street or being colored, or a combination of both with all it implied" that drove the protagonist's father to drink and the mother to her early grave. It was the same combination of circumstances that "had evidently made the Mrs. Hedges who sat in the street-floor window turn to running a fairly well-kept whorehouse [...] and the superintendent of the building—well, the street had pushed him into basements away from light and air until he was being eaten up by some horrible obsession; and still other streets had turned Min, the woman who lived with him, into a drab drudge so spineless and so limp she was like a soggy dishrag" (40). Lutie Johnson was determined that none of these things would happen to her "because she would fight back and never stop fighting back." But her will to succeed is ineffectual against the relentless economic and racist forces that the narrator and implied author saw as the direct cause of streets like the one on which the protagonist lived. Far from being an accident, we learn through the narrator's probing into Lutie's mind, "They were the North's mob [...] the method the big cities used to keep Negroes in their place" (200).

Unlike Wright's and Himes's protagonists, Lutie Johnson is neither psychologically tormented nor driven by a fear of white people. Raised by her tale-telling, Puritan-minded grandmother, she is a respectable married woman driven by a hunger for the material trappings of middle-class success for herself and her family; she longs for a better life and a place to be somebody. She seeks to satisfy this hunger by naively subscribing to the Protestant ethic and the American Dream as expressed by the Chandlers, the wealthy white New England family for whom she worked for two years as a live-in maid, and as embodied in Benjamin Franklin, with whom she compares herself. Ignoring her own modern, racial, class, and gender social reality—a working-class black woman with an eight-year-old son to support; separated from her unfaithful, unemployed husband; living in Harlem during World War II; struggling to maintain her moral principles and to share equally in the wealth of the nation—she fantasizes "that if Ben Franklin could live on a little bit of money and could prosper, then so could she" (44). After a year with the Chandlers, she finds herself influenced by their material values and belief in the American Dream. They promoted the mythic "belief that anybody could be rich if he wanted to and worked hard enough and figured it out carefully enough. [. . .] These people had wanted only one thing—more and more money—so they got it" (32).

The irony is that Lutie sees, yet fails to act on, the price that the Chandlers pay in spiritual and personal alienation for their material success. In blind pursuit of the American Dream, Lutie loses her family and her hope for happiness, but not her self-respect. When she fails to get the singing job she had counted on to move off 116th Street and up the ladder of success, social reality begins to displace her dream world. "The trouble was with her," she and the narrator conclude in retrospectively examining her consciousness. "She had built up a fantastic structure made from the soft, nebulous, cloudy stuff of dreams. There hadn't been a solid, practical brick in it, not even a foundation. She had built it up of air and vapor and moved right in. So of course it had collapsed. It had never existed anywhere but in her mind" (191).

Although some critics see the sensationalism of the denouement as a weakness, it is consistent with the naturalism of Dreiser and Wright and with Petry's use of symbols of confinement and contrasting images of the white and black worlds to give structural and thematic coherence to the novel (Schraufnagel 42; Bone 185). The wide, quiet, treelined, sunny main street of Lyme, Connecticut, where the Chandlers live in gracious luxury is contrasted with the drab, violent, overcrowded streets where Lutie's economic, racial, and sexual circumstances trap her. "From the time she was born, she had been hemmed into an ever-narrowing space until now she was very nearly walled in and the wall had been built up brick by brick by eager white hands" (200–01). The implied author and narrator are in ethical agreement that the white world had a different set of values from those her grandmother had taught her. It was a strange world in which money was more important than people and young black women were considered potential whores. Her grandmother had warned her so often about the lust of white men for black women that she found them repulsive. Thus, when Boots Smith, a black musician, attempts to persuade her to exchange sexual favors with Junto, the Jewish owner of the major clubs and whorehouses in the black community, for the two hundred dollars she needed to help keep her boy out of reform school, the reader is sympathetic toward her internal and dramatic physical resistance to sexual exploitation and male abuse. "Junto has a brick in his hand. Just one brick. The final one needed to complete the wall that had been building up around her for years, and when that last brick was shoved in place, she would be completely walled in" (262). Angrily responding to Boots's actual and threatened violence, she beats his head into a bloody pulp with an iron candlestick, realizing afterward that "a lifetime of pent-up resentment went into the blows" (266).

Although the story is told by a disembodied third-person, omniscient narrator, Petry allows Lutie's consciousness to dominate the narrative and scrupulously avoids moralizing. The action and setting are subordinated to Lutie's impression of their impact on black women and the black family, thus encouraging our sympathy for her and other black women, who incredulously have no contact with the black church. Except for the denouement, the author-narrator explores the social evils of segregated communities, white and black, with restraint and objectivity. But it is clear that neither Petry nor her protagonist simplistically and stereotypically blame black men for the broken homes, poverty, and hopelessness that characterize too many urban black communities. The cause of these social problems, characterized as pathologies by black and white social scientists such as E. Franklin Frazier and Daniel Moynihan, respectively, is not black men like her alcoholic father and adulterous husband, nor black women like Mrs. Hedges, the whorehouse madam, but white people like Junto and the Chandlers, whose prosperity is based on the economic exploitation of blacks. If it is impossible to escape the corruption and despair of the black inner city, it is equally impossible, as the Chandlers reveal, to escape the degeneration and despair of small white towns.

In *Country Place* Petry moves beyond economic and racial determinism to explore the realities beneath the myths of rural small-town communities. In contrast to traditional stories and images of the beneficence, continuity, integrity, and homogeneity of values in small rural American communities, her narrative reveals the hypocrisy, violence, prejudice, and stagnation of a small post–World War II New England town. *Country Place* is a first-person, retrospective narrative with the town druggist, George Fraser, as the on-the-scene chronicler of events. In the opening five pages, the friendly, sixty-five-year-old narrator immediately establishes his reliability ("I am neither a pessimist nor an optimist"), the setting ("a quiet place, a country place, which sets at the mouth of the Connecticut River, at the exact spot where the river empties itself into Long Island Sound"), and the major theme: "wheresoever men dwell there is always a vein of violence running under the surface quiet" (1, 3, 4). Confessing his own petty prejudice against women, George is nevertheless sympathetic toward the townspeople, especially his friend Mrs. Gramby, and intimately knowledgeable about them and the "untoward events" that occurred during and after a storm the previous year when Johnnie Roane, the protagonist, returned home from the war.

The predominantly white characters of Lennox, Connecticut, are trapped by time, prejudice, and their own illusions. Refusing to sell land on Main Street to the Catholic church, ostracizing the Jewish lawyer Rosenthal, and impugning the moral character of the black maid Neola and her admirer, the Portuguese gardener Portulacca, who are only sketchily delineated, the townspeople belie the myth of the beneficent small town. Glory Roane, the protagonist's wife, and Lillian Mearns, her mother and daughter-in-law to the wealthy Mrs. Gramby, are shallow, covetous women, fighting futilely against time with diets and hair dye while cheating on their husbands and dreaming of inheriting the Gramby house and fortune. Mearns Gramby, the frustrated, middle-aged heir of the wealthiest family in town, is trapped by his mother's illusion of him as "the last of a long and honorable and distinguished family" (84) and by his addiction to vitamin pills and his marriage to a middle-aged, acquisitive bigot.

Only two major characters manage to transcend the moral and social stagnation of the town. The first is Johnnie Roane, who has outgrown the town while serving in the army and who returns there from the war only because of the love and memory of his wife, Glory. When, at the height of the storm that dramatizes the realities beneath the town's surface serenity, he discovers her infidelity with Lennox's middle-aged Lothario, Ed Barrell, Johnnie breaks free from his idealized past to pursue his dream of becoming a painter in New York. The second is Mrs. Gramby, who embodies the mythic virtues of New England Puritanism. She moves beyond the narrow-minded bigotry of her townspeople and the nostalgia of her personal dreams for her son to become the instrument for social change in the town. In death she herself becomes that instrument, for she wills land on the main street of town to the Catholic church; leaves her house, its contents, and money for its maintenance to her black maid, Portuguese gardener, and cook; and provides six thousand dollars to subsidize Johnnie's pursuit of his dream to become an artist. Marred by the melodramatic conclusion of the reading of the will following Mrs. Gramby's and Ed Barrell's fatal heart attacks, *Country Place* is nevertheless an imaginatively impressive, realistic modern narrative treatment of small-town life in New England in which time and place are more important thematically than color and class.

In *The Narrows* Petry moves even further beyond economic determinism as she continues to explore the impact of time and place on the shaping of character. The setting is the black community in Monmouth, Connecticut, another small, typically provincial, white New England town, during the era of Senator Joseph McCarthy's witch hunt for communists in the State Department. The red neon signs on Dumble Street tell the story of its change. We learn through septuagenarian Abigail Crunch's reverie that "it was now, despite its spurious early-morning beauty, a street so famous, or so infamous, that the people who lived in Monmouth rarely ever referred to it, or the streets near it, by name; it had become an area, a section, known variously as The Narrows, Eye of the Needle, The Bottom, Little Harlem, Dark Town, Niggertown—because Negroes had replaced those other earlier immigrants, the Irish, the Italians and the Poles" (5) Petry's exceptional craftsmanship is immediately apparent in the compelling manner that the structure, style, and theme of the narrative fuse as Abbie reflects in a series of open-ended conditional clauses on what in addition to the hate in the world has brutalized her adopted son, Lincoln (Link) Williams, the protagonist. "In Link's case—well, if they hadn't lived on Dumble Street, if the Major had lived longer, if Link had been their own child instead of an adopted child, if she hadn't forgotten about him when he was eight, simply forgotten his existence, if she hadn't had to figure so closely with the little money that she had [. . .] and eke it out with the small sums she earned by sewing, embroidering, making jelly. If" (13–14).

The modern existential theme, simply stated, is that our lives are shaped as much by chance and contingencies as they are by time and place. "On how peculiar, and accidental a foundation rests all of one's attitudes toward a people," Abbie invites readers to share sympathetically in her internal world. "Frances hears the word Irish and thinks of a cathedral and the quiet of it, the flickering light of the votive candles, the magnificence of the altar, and I see Irishwomen, strong in their faith, holding a family together. Accident? Coincidence? It all depended on what happened in the past. We carry it around with us. We're never rid of it" (235–36). The implied author develops this theme in the main plot of the love affair between Link, a black orphan and Dartmouth graduate, and Camilo Williams, the internationally known heiress to the wealth and power of Monmouth's most prominent white family, the Treadways—and the several tributary subplots. The movement of the main plot is clearly more psychological than chronological, for its pace is frequently interrupted by digressions and flashbacks some eighteen years to Link's childhood. The meeting of the couple in The Narrows, their falling in love, the discovery that she is rich and married, his rejection of her for betraying his trust and using him as a black stud, her revenge by claiming he attempted to rape her and thus appealing to traditional color and class prejudice are all influenced by chance and the historical past. The pattern of symbols and interior monologues suggest that the implied author and Abbie are in close moral and social agreement that the weight of their personal histories and the history of American racism and New England hypocrisy are too heavy a burden for their interracial love to survive. For breaking the American tribal taboo of interracial love and sex, Link is murdered by Camilo's mother and husband.

Petry dramatically represents Link, as his name suggests, as the major connection between the past and the present, the white world and the black, the rich and the poor; and it is his consciousness that dominates the third-person point of view of the narrative that shifts from character to character. Adopted when he was eight by Abbie and Major Crunch, and having grown up in Monmouth, Link, at twenty-six, has lost faith in himself and other people. Most of the modern plot unfolds in his and Abbie's minds. As the implied author shifts interior monologues, reverie, and flashbacks from Link and Abbie to the other characters, she weaves a gossamer, impressionistic pattern of events that suggests why Link is socially content to be a bartender at the ominously symbolic Last Chance although he was a star athlete and Phi Beta Kappa student at Dartmouth, where he majored in history. Abbie's urge to whiteness and New England respectability confused and frightened Link when he was young, making him ashamed of his color "as though he were carrying The Race around with him all the time" (138). These psychological feelings were reinforced in school, where he ambivalently accepted the role of Sambo in a minstrel show. But Bill Hod, the influential black owner of the most popular bar and whorehouse in town, and Weak Knees, his cook, who became Link's surrogate parents when Abbie forgot he existed for three months, taught him to be unashamed of his blackness and to defend himself against antiblack racist attacks.

Because Abbie and Bill betrayed his love and trust—Abbie by rejecting him during her depression over her husband's death and Bill by severely beating him after finding him in a whorehouse—Link's belief in his ability to control his life and his desire to conquer the world were destroyed. Although his love for Camilo revives his belief in himself and others, he again feels betrayed when he discovers that she has lied to him about her class and social status. When Camilo's mother and husband kidnap Link at the end of the novel, the implied author relies primarily on impressionism, reverie, and psychological realism to highlight Link's epiphany. Link remembers the sensational front-page pictures of a drunk Camilo and an escaped black convict under headlines that inflamed historical color and class prejudices by emphasizing that The Narrows bred crime and criminals: "So it was Jubine Lautrec's Harlot and The Convict by Anonymous that got me in this black Packard. That is one-quarter of the explanation. The other three-quarters reaches back to that Dutch man of Warre that landed in Jamestown in 1619" (399).

The frequency, length, and occasional remoteness to the events at hand of the digressions and flashbacks give complexity to the characters but annoyingly impede the progress of the plot as well as emotionally and psychologically distance the reader from the tragedy of the central character. This is most apparent in the denouement when Link is kidnapped and murdered. Equally passive but more strikingly individualized are Abbie and some of the minor characters. Abbie, a black New England Puritan, is an old widow who is driven by an ambivalence about black people and an obsession with aristocratic values. The minor characters include Major, her dead husband, who was a robust, sensitive mountain of a man who used to tell stories about the legendary members of his family, whom he affectionately called "swamp niggers"; Jubine, the "recording angel" of Monmouth, who is a man both with a deep compassion for "the poor peons" like himself and "who spent a lifetime photographing a river, and thus recorded the life of man in the twentieth century." Equally compelling representations by Petry are Malcolm Powther, a black Judas, who is a pompous, worshipful servant to rich white people, whose values he embraces, and to his sensual, promiscuous wife, whom he fears will leave him for another man, and Peter Bullock, the unprincipled owner and publisher of the *Monmouth Chronicle,* who is a slave to custom, to a house, to a car, to ulcers, and to the major advertisers in his paper, especially the Treadwell family. The *Monmouth Chronicle* has been transformed over the years from an antislavery newspaper into an antiblack tool of the white ruling class. Petry's use of symbolic characters like Cesar the Writing Man, the wandering poet who scribbles biblical verses on the sidewalk in Monmouth, is also dramatically effective. Early in the novel Cesar gives philosophical resonance to the characters, plot, and theme when he writes the following passage from Ecclesiastes 1:10 in front of the cafe where Camilo and Link rendezvous: "Is there anything whereof it may be said, See this is new? It hath been already of old time, which was before us" (91).

Petry, like Himes and Wright, is adept at complex modernist delineation of character, but her protagonists are cut from a different cloth than those of her two major male contemporaries. Rather than sharing the pathology of a Bigger Thomas or Bob Jones or Lee Gordon, Lutie Johnson and Link Williams are intelligent, commonplace, aspiring middle-class blacks, who, despite the socialized ambivalence resulting from racism and economic exploitation, are not consumed by fear, hatred, and rage. Petry's vision of black personality is not only different from that of Himes and Wright but is also more faithful to the complexities and varieties of black women, whether they are big-city characters like Mrs. Hedges in *The Street* or small-town characters like Abbie Crunch in *The Narrows*. Ann Petry thus moves beyond the naturalistic vision of Himes and Wright to a demythologizing of American culture and Afro-American character.

II

Nails, Snails, and Puppy-Dog Tails: Black Male Stereotypes in the Fiction of Toni Morrison, Alice Walker, and Terry McMillan

In addition to serving as the Fulbright senior adviser and chair of one of the panels in the International Symposium on Contemporary Literature of the African Diaspora at the prestigious University of Salamanca in 1996, I delivered "Nails, Snails, and Puppy Dog Tails: Black Male Stereotypes in the Fiction of Toni Morrison, Alice Walker, and Terry McMillan" as the keynote address. This semiautobiographical lecture valorizes American and African American vernacular culture by grounding its critical examination of black male stereotypes by celebrated contemporary black American women writers in a traditional folktale about gender differences. The symposium was organized under the dynamic leadership of Professor Olga Barrios, who, I was pleasantly surprised to discover, was a student of the blues as well as African American women writers. I believe that the overwhelming success of the extremely well-attended symposium established a precedent in African diasporic cultural and educational exchange for the University of Salamanca and Spain. Professor Barrios and I published selected papers from the symposium in Contemporary Literature in the African Diaspora *(1997).*

After a traumatic, inauspicious beginning with the theft of all my electronic and research materials, my spring 1996 experience as a Fulbright Senior Lecturer in nineteenth- and twentieth-century American and African American narratives at the University of Salamanca was one of the best of several international faculty appointments that I have enjoyed. The immensely exciting and enriching cultural experience of this Fulbright in Spain for my wife and myself would not have been possible without the early enthusiasm, sustained mutual professional respect, and personal generosity of the faculty, students, administrators, and staff in the Department of English Philology, especially Professors Catalina Montes and Juan Jose Coy.

My first trip back to Africa was on a Mediterranean cruise in 1955 as a nineteen-year-old U.S. Marine to protect our homeland—according to military authorities—from communism and to keep the world safe for democracy. My return two decades later to West Africa, my other historic and mythic homeland, was even more memorable and meaningful. In 1977 I imaginatively reversed the transatlantic scattering of my ancestors into slavery and the New World by journeying to Lagos, Nigeria, as a member of the Colloquium of the Second World Black and African Festival of Arts and Culture. As an African American scholar and literary critic, I was profoundly and palpably disturbed by feeling and being a racial insider yet cultural outsider in the homeland of my ancestors. I was at best ambivalent about the cultural, political, and psychological distance that I experienced between myself and my African "brothers" and "sisters," regardless of race, class, and ethnicity.

While housed as a U.S. official of the colloquium first in FESTAC Village and later in the Ikoye Hotel, for example, I was assigned a new Mercedes with an Ibo driver who insisted on calling me Bwana. Later, I was served meals in the hotel by immaculately white-jacketed waiters with crisply folded white napkins across their left wrists who, despite my requests to the contrary, insisted on serving me my salad and beverage after the other dinner courses. I was also addressed in different languages either deferentially or hostilely by people in the markets and streets. From the predictable response of the hotel desk clerk to my passport to the unpredictable responses of people in the street, I was made acutely aware that I was an American, not an African. Even more apparent was my feeling that I and the other African American participants in FESTAC, contrary to our intentions, were possibly complicitous in neocolonial cultural, political, and economic domination rather than activists in the emancipatory movement of pan-Africanism.

It is not only possible but also probable that black Americans have been complicitous in different degrees and for different reasons in perpetuating demeaning, disunifying stereotypes of ourselves and our culture. This has occurred primarily because of the legacy of colonialism, capitalism, and racism that informed the scattering of peoples of African descent from their homelands during the transatlantic slave trade and influenced the subsequent migrations north of emancipated slaves and free persons of color from the American South in the post–Civil War and pre–World War I eras. Specifically, some African American folklore and antiblack fiction by contemporary black women writers provide insidious, ironic, and representative examples of black American complicity in perpetuating colonial and postcolonial negative stereotypes of racial and gender differences that frustrate rather than facilitate our historical quest for intraracial unity.

While growing up in a single-parent household during the early 1940s near Seventh and T Streets in Washington, D.C., for instance, I was fascinated by the little black girls in my neighborhood who were more assertive than I. In response to my questions about the differences between these girls and me, my mother used to say, "No matter, son. Remember, girls are made of sugar and spice and everything nice, but boys are made of nails, snails, and puppy-dog tails." At six or seven years old, I was not about to question whether this folksaying about identity formation was fact or fiction. But clearly the authority of my mother conflicted with the authority of my very limited experience with the truth or fantasy of this saying.

In my preadolescent, black, male, working-class, female-centered, World War II context, was this folksaying realistic or romantic? Did it stereotype and, in postmodern jargon, essentialize females as naturally passive and males as naturally assertive? As I lost my innocence and acquired more varied experiences, I realized, as most of us do, that thinking and feelings based on simplistic, reductive binarisms and on the declared absolute truths of folksayings can be harmful to your health. This became most painfully clear to me when I was beaten and dumped into a tar barrel after school by an eleven-year-old black girl whose attentions I resisted as an eight-year-old student in Public School 3 in the South Bronx. This female was obviously neither physically nor emotionally nice to me even though she may have considered herself made of sugar and spice. On the other hand, as most of us know and as the reports of Sojourner Truth's "Ain't I a Woman" speech in a convention of white women in 1852 dramatically demonstrated, many black women, then and now, embody and express some of the assumed mutually exclusive traits of male dominance and female subservience. In any event, the resurgence of negative stereotypes of the character and identity of black males in the fiction of some contemporary black women writers reveals a close correlation with the decline of the 1960s Black Power and Black Arts movements and with the rebirth of the white Feminist movement. Of course, as social and cultural critics Paula Giddings in *When and Where I Enter* and bell hooks in *Ain't I a Woman* remind us, the history of the white Feminist movements has been as hypocritical and racist as that of many leading white male abolitionists, liberals, and Christians.

But in keeping the development of my thesis short and simple, let me begin with an outline of seven literary stereotypes of black character and the further reduction of black male stereotypes to the black revolutionary rapist popularized by Eldridge Cleaver and the black macho popularized by Michele Wallace. Turning next to a brief examination of male types, stereotypes, and archetypes in some of the realist and neorealist texts of Toni Morrison, Alice Walker, and Terry McMillan, I will conclude with a restatement of my implicit thesis: a man ain't nothing but a man. In 1933 Sterling A. Brown published the classic essay, "Negro Character as Seen by White Authors." "The Negro has met with as great injustice in American literature as he has in American life," Brown wrote. "The majority of books about Negroes merely stereotype Negro character. [. . .] Those considered important enough for separate classification, although overlappings do occur, are seven in number: (1) The Contented Slave, (2) The Wretched Freeman, (3) The Comic Negro, (4) The Brute Negro, (5) The Tragic Mulatto, (6) The Local Color Negro, and (7) The Exotic Primitive" (327). Marked by exaggeration and omissions, these stereotypes stress the divergence of African Americans from an assumed and ascribed White Anglo-Saxon Protestant social and cultural norm as justification of our subjugation, exploitation, and marginalization as a racial and ethnic group. They also "illustrate dangerous specious generalizing from a few particulars recorded by a single observer from a restricted point of view—which is itself generally dictated by the desire to perpetuate a stereotype" (S. A. Brown 328).

In 1971 literary critic Catherine J. Starke's *Black Portraiture in American Fiction* confirmed the validity and viability of Brown's list of stereotypes, which assumes that realism is the normative mode of modern American and African American fiction. Her list of seven familiar fictional images of blacks include: "A kindly old slave, an unhappy white-looking girl, a vicious brute, an exotic primitive, a comic show-off, a butt of prejudice, or a violently angry youth" (16). In "Images of Black Women in Afro-American Literature: From Stereotype to Character," a 1975 sketch of her book on the tradition of black women novelists, Barbara Christian adds the mammy and Sapphire to the gallery of literary stereotypes of black Americans.

In order to analyze and understand better the ironic implications of stereotypes of black males in the fiction of contemporary black women writers, three questions should be asked: How does the concept of stereotype relate to the meaning of type and archetype? How has the shift in power relations of the 1960s and 1970s that resulted from the changing social and cultural dynamics of race, class, and gender during the period influenced the contexts of their fictive constructions of these ideological and social formations? And how is the responsibility of the writer influenced by the politics of race, ethnicity, class, and gender in the production of cultural images?

According to C. Hugh Holman and William Harmon's *A Handbook to Literature*, a stereotype is a term derived from the printing trade that signifies "anything that repeats or duplicates something else without variation; hence something that lacks individualizing characteristics" (481). In other words, a stereotype is a commonly held, oversimplified mental picture or judgment of a person, character, race, issue, or event. In contrast to the generally pejorative connotation of stereotype, a type, as we are using it here as an epistemological sign of classification, is a "character [. . .] that embodies a substantial number of significant distinguishing characteristics of a group or class. Such a character becomes almost a kind of synecdoche, a representative of the whole of which he or she is a part" (Holman and Harmon 514). Unlike stereotype and type, the term *archetype* is derived from the depth psychology of Carl Jung. In literary criticism an archetype is "an image, a descriptive detail, a plot pattern, or a character type that occurs frequently in literature, myth, religion, or folklore and is, therefore, believed to evoke profound emotions in the reader because it awakens a primordial image in the unconscious memory and thus calls into play illogical but strong responses" (Holman and Harmon 36). Archetypes are thus transhistorical, transcultural symbols and images.

Assuming fallaciously that all narratives seek to reflect mimetically rather than reconstruct innovatively human characters and experiences, too many readers confuse these literary terms and misuse the term *stereotype* as a synonym for type and archetype in analyzing modern and contemporary innovative and experimental narratives. Even some feminist and postcolonial critics, aware of the stylistic and structural movement of most modern and contemporary novels beyond the conventions of social realism, directly correlate stereotypic expressions and archetypal representations of black women, as Madhu Dubey does in her provocative study of black women novelists and the Black Aesthetic movement. In contrast, after identifying Richard Wright, James Baldwin, Chester Himes, and Ralph Ellison as the four novelists who dominate the genre of the modern African American novel, Barbara Christian persuasively argues that "the black women that appear in the novels of these four literary giants come painfully close to the stereotypes about the black woman projected by white southern literature in the latter part of the nineteenth century" (*Black Women Novelists* 15).

What, then, are the major stereotypes of black males in the fiction of black women writers since 1970? Because we have neither the time nor space to undertake either a comprehensive survey or analytical examination of this topic, I will focus briefly on the texts of the three most celebrated female fiction writers since the 1970s: Toni Morrison, Alice Walker, and Terry McMillan. In several of the most realistic and neorealistic novels by these black women, we discover a rewriting and perpetuation of the following four negative stereotypes of black males: (1) the brute Negro, popularized by white authors of the nineteenth century; (2) the dog, represented in folk-sayings by many black women and even internalized by some men; (3) the existential black antihero, popularized in 1940 by Richard Wright as an amoral black American native son; and (4) the misogynist black revolutionary nationalist, popularized in 1968 by Black Panther leader Eldridge Cleaver and in 1978 by black feminist Michele Wallace as rapist of white women and abuser of black women.

Before looking at some of the texts by Morrison, Walker, and McMillan, let us first look at how social and cultural forces of the 1960s shaped fictive constructions of black males and sought to silence dissenting voices. For people in the United States, among the most significant social and cultural forces during the 1960s were the transformation of the Civil Rights movement into the Black Power, Black Arts, and Black Studies movements as well as the Women's Rights movement. As defined by leading black cultural nationalist Larry Neal, the Black Arts movement was "the aesthetic and spiritual sister of the Black Power concept. As such, it envisions an art that speaks directly to the needs and aspirations of Black America. In order to perform this task, the Black Arts movement proposes a radical reordering of the western cultural aesthetic. It proposes a separate symbolism, mythology, critique and iconology" ("Black Arts Movement" 272). Like the historical experiences and racial identities of black Americans, as most leading black cultural and revolutionary nationalists were well aware, the movements were neither homogeneous nor monolithic.

Although black nationalism in the United States ranges in definition from racial pride to various types of pan-Africanism, two major ideological groups that were frequently in paradoxical and fratricidal conflict in their struggle for unity and common struggle for liberation from the economic, cultural, and political hegemonic control of the white ruling class dominated the media of the period. On the one hand were the black revolutionary nationalists, who stressed class mobilization and masculine militancy over racial consciousness, and on the other hand were the black cultural nationalists, who stressed the need for an indigenous racial or pan-

African transformation of cultural consciousness before economic and political liberation could be achieved. Because both nationalist movements foregrounded and focused on black men while marginalizing and devaluing black women, many post–Black Power movement critics agree with black social historian and feminist Paula Giddings's classification of the 1960s as "the masculine decade" (314).

Just as the Abolitionist movement was a catalyst for the Women's Rights movement of the nineteenth century, the Civil Rights and Black Power movements of the 1960s were catalysts for the resurgence of the modern Women's Rights movement. But as in the past, the leading feminists as well as the majority of the women in that movement were and still are white and middle class. As bell hooks and others have noted, definitions of feminism range widely from individuals who advocate gender equality to a radical, committed political movement against sexist oppression of women and all systems of domination. Even so, the experiences and truths of black and poor women were generally ignored or glossed over when references were made to women and blacks. *All the Women Are White, All the Blacks Are Men; but Some of Us Are Brave* (1982) for example, is a popular anthology by, about, and for black women that cogently expressed both the irony of this marginalization and the paradox of the absence yet presence of black women in white feminist and black nationalist discourses.

"I became a rapist," black revolutionary leader Cleaver wrote in *Soul on Ice*. "To refine my technique and *modus operandi*, I started out by practicing on black girls in the ghetto [. . .] and when I considered myself smooth enough, I crossed the tracks and sought out white prey. I did this consciously, deliberately, willfully, methodically. Rape was an insurrectionary act," he declared in a commercially successful, self-serving attempt to elevate the stereotype of the brute Negro to the level of an archetypal political revolutionary. "It delighted me that I was defying and trampling upon the white man's law, upon his system of values, and that I was defiling his women—and this point, I believe, was the most satisfying to me because I was very resentful over the historical fact of how the white man has used the black woman. I felt I was getting revenge" (14). In the essay "The Primeval Mitosis" Cleaver reinforces this fusion and confusion of the stereotype and archetype in his sexual and political allegory of white males as Omnipotent Administrators and black males as Supermasculine Menials.

In *Black Macho and the Myth of the Superwoman* (1979), Wallace writes:

> White men were perversely obsessed with the black man's genitals but the obsession turned out to be a communicable disease and in the sixties

black men came down with high fevers. [. . .] Black men began to harp on the white man's obsession with their genitals and that was the very point at which their own obsession began to take hold. [. . .] Perhaps it was necessary for Huey Newton and the Black Panthers to make a public display of arming themselves. Their actions represented an unprecedented boldness in the sons of slaves and had a profound and largely beneficial effect on the way in which black men would regard themselves from then on. Yet the gains would have been more lasting if an improved self-image had not been so hopelessly dependent upon Black Macho—a male chauvinist that was frequently cruel, narcissistic, and shortsighted. (73)

In the introduction to her 1990 edition of the book, Wallace disavows "that Black Macho was the crucial factor in the destruction of the Black Power Movement." She acknowledges that her critique was based "upon a limited perception of it taken primarily from the mainstream media," from white writers such as Norman Mailer and Tom Wolfe and, more important, from black writers such as Wright, Ellison, Baldwin, Baraka, and Cleaver (xxi). Nevertheless, this image of black males has been dominant in the fiction of black women writers since the 1970s as their voices moved, sometimes with the vengeance of Gayl Jones's castrating protagonist in *Eva's Man,* from the margins to the center of the production, commodification, and consumption of black culture.

The most compelling and controversial images of black males arguably appear in the texts of Morrison and Walker. Although her characters are more often types and individuals than stereotypes, especially in *Beloved,* Morrison has been criticized for creating in *The Bluest Eye,* her first novel, some of the most vicious, morally grotesque black male abusers of black women and children in contemporary fiction, especially Charles "Cholly" Breedlove and Elihue Micah "Soaphead Church" Whitcomb. Abandoned on a junk heap while four days old, Cholly grew up to become a self-hating, brawling, alcoholic rapist and impregnator of Pecola, his eleven-year-old daughter. The confused mixture of his drunk memories of her resemblance to Pauline and "the doing of a wild and forbidden thing excited him," Morrison writes in one of the most graphic and offensive rape episodes in contemporary American literature, "he wanted to fuck her tenderly. But the tenderness would not hold. The tightness of her vagina was more than he could bear. His soul seemed to slip down to his guts and fly out into her, and the gigantic thrust he made into her then provoked the only sound she made—a hollow suck of air in the back of her throat. Like the rapid loss of air from a circus balloon" (128–29). The moral offensiveness of this episode is compounded for some readers by Morrison's rendering of the rape episode from the interiorized, sympathetic perspective of the incestuous male abuser rather than from the silenced, preteenaged female victim.

Soaphead Church is a West Indian spiritualist, misanthrope, and molester of children like the young, pregnant Pecola, who naïvely seeks his help in her tragic quest for blue eyes. Soaphead, writes Morrison with uncompromising ironic understatement, "could have been an active homosexual but lacked the courage. Bestiality did not occur to him, and sodomy was quite out of the question, for he did not experience sustained erections and could not endure the thought of somebody else's. [...] His attentions therefore gradually settled on those humans whose bodies were least offensive—children" (131–32). Because *The Bluest Eye* moves beyond the realism of the traditional bildungsroman to a hybrid form of poetic realism and Gothic fable, the representation of Soaphead and Cholly to many black readers correspondingly moves beyond the conventional stereotypic black male abuser to a more disturbing expression of the sexual perversity and social pathology of contemporary black American male character.

In her first novel, *The Third Life of Grange Copeland*, Alice Walker outlines in unrelenting graphic details the three lives of the patriarch of the Copeland clan. Ostensibly, the novel dramatizes how the birth of his granddaughter Ruth marked Grange Copeland's rebirth of self-respect after a youth and manhood of dissolution. But actually the narrative chronicles the social pathology that he passes on to his son, Brownfield, the brutish, self-hating black male abuser of black women and children. Walker catalogs episodes in the Copeland family life, especially Brownfield's, to arouse the reader's indignation at the price black women pay as the victims of economic, racial, and sexual exploitation and abuse. Like Grange, who drives his wife, Margaret Copeland, to drink, degradation, and death, Brownfield destroys his wife spiritually and physically by beating her every Saturday night, "trying to pin the blame for his failure on her by imprinting it on her face" (63).

Although more middle class and less physically violent, the black men of the 1960s in Walker's second novel, *Meridian*, are, with the exception of the father, similarly disloyal and despicable in their abuse of women. Truman, Meridian's conquering black prince and Walker's parody of the archetype—a French-speaking civil rights organizer and painter—impregnated her, but betrayed her to marry and then desert a white exchange student and his child. Tommy, a bitter black civil rights activist, rapes Truman's white wife, Lynne, in revenge for the arm he lost to a white sniper. And Alonzo, the apolitical black scrapyard worker, was so grateful for Lynne's invitation to sleep with her,

Walker writes with righteous political indignation, that he "licked her from her earlobes to her toes" (167). Like the omniscient narrator, Walker thus encourages the reader to see most of her black male characters in the limited moral category of the low-down dirty dog in the novel who impregnated the thirteen-year-old tragic Wild Child.

Except for Odessa's Jack, abusive and nonabusive black men in *The Color Purple* are also depicted stereotypically as dogs or frogs with no hope of becoming princes. Gender-role reversal, feminine domination of masculine principles and practices, or egalitarianism, however, does foster some redemption for some of the black men. Harpo, for example, not only acquires a love for housekeeping, especially cooking, but also becomes a house-husband while his wife works as a storekeeper. And the abusive Albert, whom Celie ironically calls "Mister," learns not only to make quilts, Walker's symbol for the independence, creativity, and integrity of women, with Celie but also to acknowledge Celie's independence and integrity as a person. Guided by the spirit and achievement of Hurston, Walker has Shug, the liberated bisexual moral center of the novel, to express one of the major themes of the book more poetically in the vernacular when she tells Celie, "You have to git man off your eyeball, before you can see anything a'tall" (168).

Like several of the black women in the narratives of Morrison and Walker, the black female protagonists in Terry McMillan's novels are usually victims of black male emotional, psychological, and verbal, if not physical, abuse. "Most of the black men couldn't find jobs," the sympathetic feminist, omniscient narrator in *Mama*, McMillan's first novel, tells us; "and as a result, they had so much spare time on their hand that when they were stone cold broke, bored with themselves, or pissed off about everything because life turned out to be such a disappointment, their dissatisfaction would burst open and their rage would explode. This was what usually passed for masculinity, and it was often their wives or girlfriends or whores who felt the fallout" (20). Some readers may therefore be politically or morally offended but not surprised when Crook, the protagonist's husband, beats her with a belt as he would a child. These readers may also ask along with the couple's young children who hear this violence, "Why they try to kill each other, then do the nasty?" (9).

In McMillan's best-selling *Waiting to Exhale*, four educated, independent, modern, urban African American women in their thirties—Savannah Jackson, Bernadine Harris, Robin Stokes, and Gloria Matthews—support one another like sisters as they romantically and ironically "wait," as the book jacket states, "for that man who will take their breath away." But, according to the following climactic dialogue among the four women at Gloria's thirty-eighth birthday, all black men are one type of dog or another:

> "Shit, I'm smart, I'm attractive, I'm educated, and my pussy's good, if I do say so myself. What happened to all the aggressive men?" Savannah asks. "The ones that aren't scared to talk to you? Where the fuck are they hiding?" "They're not hiding. They're just scared to make a damn commitment," Robin said. "They're with white women," Bernadine said. "Or gay," Gloria said. "Or married," Savannah said. "But you know what? They're not all with white girls, they're not all homosexuals, they're not all married, either. When you get right down to it, we're talking five, maybe ten percent. What about the rest?" "They're ugly." "Stupid." "In prison." "Unemployed." "Crackheads." "Short." "Liars." "Unreliable." "Irresponsible." "Too Possessive." "Dogs." "Shallow." "Boring." "Stuck in the sixties." "Arrogant." "Childish." "Wimps." "Too god damn old and set in their ways." "Can't fuck." "Stop!" Savannah said. "Well, shit, you asked," Robin said. (332)

In this negative stereotyping and commodifying of the sociohistorical and sociocultural battle of the sexes, especially among signifying black women and men, should we really be all that shocked when Snoop Doggy Dogg—whose name illustrates the ironic reinscription and internalizing of the neocolonial and post-Reconstruction popular black male stereotype—and other gangster rappers became millionaires by stereotyping and signifying on black women with similar vicious and playful invectives and epithets like "bitches" and "whores"?

Black feminist and womanist critics such as Mary Helen Washington in her introduction to *Black-Eyed Susans* and Barbara Christian in *Black Women Novelists* applaud the displacement of stereotypic with more realistic and diverse images of black women. But as I have attempted to remind readers, stereotypes of black males as dogs are not uncommon in black folksayings and in fiction by the most celebrated contemporary black women writers of the 1970s. Major writers like Morrison and Walker have moved beyond the conventions of traditional realism in their more recent contributions to a black female literary tradition, but some of their hybrid narrative constructions perpetuate rather than interrogate black male stereotypes. In short, by frequently repeating and reinforcing commonly held, oversimplified images and judgments of black males, celebrated black women writers of fiction like Morrison, Walker, and McMillan have been complicitous in different degrees in the neocolonial cultural and political domination of American males of African descent. In *Beloved*,

Morrison's most outstanding novel so far, for example, black men are not stereotyped as "low-down dirty dogs" like the incestuous rapist in *The Bluest Eye*, the nameless Assistant and Wild Child's anonymous impregnator in *Meridian*, Mister and even God in *The Color Purple*, and all of the men in *Waiting to Exhale*. Although circumstances in *Beloved* may reduce some of the black male characters to defiling or debasing themselves with cows, clabber, or the ghostly daughter of their lover, Baby Suggs, Sethe, Morrison, and this reader agree: a man ain't nothing but a man.

III

The Liberating Literary and African American Vernacular Voices of Gayl Jones

The editor of Comparative Literature Studies *invited me to write the following review essay of* The Healing *(1998) and* Liberating Voices *(1992) in 1998. Because of the mysterious drama of her personal life as well as the compelling, radical black feminist themes, style, and structure of Gayl Jones's experimental novels, I delightfully accepted the invitation. It was a welcome opportunity to begin draft chapters about post-1983 black novelists and novels for my new book,* The Contemporary African American Novel: Its Folk Roots and Modern Literary Branches. *But reading and looking back on writing "The Liberating Literary and African American Vernacular Voices of Gayl Jones," I have mixed emotions about my critique of her achievements in the two books that I examined.*

Although, as I say in the essay, I believe it was appropriate to assess the manner and degree to which the literary and African American vernacular voices in The Healing *are liberating by her own literary standards for excellence, I now believe that readers will find the style and tone of my initial criticism of* Liberating Voices *too rigorous and academic. The primary reason for its academic style is that I was focusing on developing the appropriate voice for the audience of my book in progress rather than for the audience of the refereed journal in which it would appear. I did not and do not intend for the tone of my criticism, which generally commented on what I perceived to be the inadequate context for some of her texts and authors, to disparage the merits of her comparative examination of the vernacular roots of distinctive national literatures. On the contrary,* Liberating Voices *is not only the first but also the best and most intellectually provocative extended critical comparison by a contemporary black woman writer of the oral foundation of African American literature with the similar vernacular roots of world literature.*

AFTER FIVE YEARS IN EUROPE, GAYL JONES HAS RETURNED TO THE UNITED STATES with a new attitude and two new books: *Liberating Voices,* a collection of essays, and *The Healing,* a novel. Like the blues women in her highly successful early fiction, she lives a life of quiet desperation, volcanic desire, male domination, and distrust of white Americans. From its tenor, tone, and texture, her writing seems to be her political liberation and spiritual salvation. Raw, sexually explicit and violent, psychologically dense and painfully poignant, the language of the vernacular voices that Jones uses to represent the lives of Ursa in *Corregidora* and Eva in *Eva's Man* transgresses thematic and stylistic conventions. In these early novels Jones fingers the jagged grain (Ellison's descriptive phrase for the blues) of the legacy of slavery and the politics of identity that black women in love and trouble on the margins of society struggle to transform as they tell their own stories and sing their own songs in African American vernacular voices.

Illustrative of the complex relationship between life, language, and literature, Jones abruptly resigned her professorship at the University of Michigan in a 1983 letter to President Ronald Reagan after her husband's violent confrontation with gay activists and his indictment for assault, taking flight to Europe with Robert Higgins, her husband. During their nearly six-year expatriation in Europe, the couple apparently lived mainly in France, as the celebrated author of such black feminist novels as *Corregidora* (1975) and *Eva's Man* (1976) immersed herself in the multilingual sounds and sense of transcultural experiences, continued to write fiction, and published a novel, *Die Vogelfängerin* (*The Birdcatcher*), in Germany. Returning in late 1988 to her hometown of Lexington, Kentucky, to care for her gravely ill mother, the extremely reclusive writer arranged with Beacon Press in her usual manner (by e-mail rather than in person) to have her recent fiction published. At the same time, an intermittent conflict in writing between the Joneses and the local authorities over alleged racial injustices toward the family, especially the hospital care of her mother, culminated in a violent confrontation with the police that resulted in Robert Jones cutting his throat and Gayl Jones being hospitalized for mental examination.

Many traditional specialists in comparative literature and some contemporary multiculturalists will find Gayl Jones's voices in *Liberating Voices dulce et utile* and in *The Healing* more experimental in theme, style, and structure yet less radically black feminist than her earlier fiction. A transhistorical, transcultural critical survey of literature, *Liberating Voices* focuses on the relationship of oral to written technique by African American writers and critics in their development of an indigenous literary tradition. Its thesis is that "the movement from the restrictive forms (inheritors of self-doubt, self-repudiation, and the minstrel tradition) to the liberation of voice and freer personalities in more intricate texts [. . .] links the writers of [the] African American literary tradition and is common to all literatures which have held (or assumed) a position of subordination to another literary tradition" (178). But Jones glosses over the fact that neither all subordination nor all liberation struggles are the same and that historical differences are fundamental to cultural distinctiveness. Organized in sections on poetry, short fiction, and the novel, the introduction, fifteen chapters, and conclusion of *Liberating Voices*—to my knowledge the first critical survey by a contemporary black woman writer that attempts an extended comparison of the oral foundation of African American literature with those of non–African American literatures—provide a provocative and important map of the oral or vernacular tradition in African American literature.

The primary importance of *Liberating Voices* is that in supporting the proposition that "the foundation of every literary tradition is oral, whether it is visible or invisible in the text," Jones gives extensive examples of "the freeing of voice" in literature from different times, places, and peoples. From Chaucer and Joyce to the Canadian writer Margaret Laurence on one hand and from Lady Murasaki's *Tale of Genji* to Amos Tutuola's *The Palm-Wine Drinkard* on the other, readers experience a cavalcade of stories and storytellers from around the world that move innovatively beyond the conventions of their time. "Like many of their Latin American counterparts," Jones writes in the introduction, "African American writers frequently combine aesthetics with social motive, so that art almost always conjoins humanity and society; thus, 'kinetic art' is mostly championed" (2). But the most frequent comparisons of the vernacular and literary voices are with Spanish authors and texts, especially Cervantes and Lorca, who, consistent with her emphasis, were more subversive in literary technique than in thematic and social practice.

In the conclusion Jones makes an interesting case for the validity of a blues standard by comparing it to some of the significant literary standards and "stylistic strategies" of the oral traditions in Africa and Asia that conflict with those of the West. In her efforts to situate the oral and literary tradition of African Americans in the global context of world literature, Jones provides the necessary sociohistorical and sociocultural contexts to illuminate the distinctiveness of the code-switching between dialects and between languages in the different texts that she briefly analyzes and uses to make broad generalizations in the short chapters on selected African American writers and texts. This is most apparent in what she calls the "movement from literary double-consciousness to literary 'true self-consciousness'" (178).

Jones does not, however, significantly support her theory with the most important recent African American vernacular studies that were basically inspired by the theories and practice of Ralph Ellison, especially *Shadow and Act* (1964). On one hand are those by such black academics and writers as Stephen Henderson, Bernard W. Bell, John Edgar Wideman, Houston A. Baker Jr., and Henry Louis Gates Jr.[1] On the other hand are those by such white academics as Lawrence Levine, Keith Beyerman, John Callahan, and Eric Sundquist.[2] Jones refers vaguely to the criticism of Wideman, Baker, and Gates, especially in the postscript and glossary, as well as to an essay by Callahan. But she chose not to ground her literary theory and criticism in the distinctive historical pattern of the journey of black Americans from Africa and slavery in the United States to freedom. This unfortunately weakens the authenticity and authority of her discussion of the importance of the complex relationship between black folk speech or dialect and minstrelsy.

Although her comparison of the creative use of language, especially the vernacular, by Henry James and Mark Twain is useful, an outline of the sociohistorical contexts would have enhanced readers' understanding of the complex dynamics of how specific racial, ethnic, gender, class, and regional power relationships were maintained or subverted by language. Specifically, more facts are needed to illumine the manner and degree to which texts during the Reconstruction and post-Reconstruction periods by James, the expatriate around 1876 to England, and Twain, the migrant around 1874 to New England, neglected, reflected, or reconstructed the principles and conventions of the romantic, plantation, minstrel, and realistic traditions of literary representation in the nineteenth and twentieth centuries. This information would enable readers to examine the tensions between Creole languages, regional dialects, and Standard American English in the struggle for freedom, literacy, and civil rights in different black communities in the South and North. These tensions include the role of publishing companies established by black churches beginning in 1817 and of black newspapers beginning in 1827, as well as the subsequent role of black literary clubs. Though Jones's analysis of "the links between dialect, perspective, character, and audience" in Dunbar's "The Lynching of Jube Benson" and in Sterling Brown's "Uncle Joe" are highly instructive, it would have been even more illuminating to know why and how the "realistic dialect" in the 1930s of critic and poet Brown contrasted with the "ridiculous dialect of the minstrel tradition" and contributed to the poetic "reappraisal of the folk as serious, complex, and multidimensional" (31).

Finally, Jones's comparison of Sherley A. Williams and Langston Hughes as blues poets is provocative but misleading. Williams's criticism of Hughes's conventional blues poem "Young Gal's Blues" as "an example of an oral form moving unchanged into literary tradition" is cited to demonstrate that Williams's own poem, "Someone Sweet Angel Chile," is more improvisational (38). This conclusion dramatically demonstrates, on closer examination, the dangers of hasty inductive leaps from inadequate evidence. Although her movement of black feminist critics and writers from the literary margins to the center is appropriately in tune with the 1980s, Jones misleadingly suggests, based on this single example, that Williams is a better blues poet than Hughes.

In contrast, her use of John Wideman's 1976 bicentennial essay "Frame and Dialect" and acknowledgment of the need for asserting personal and national identity through language are more insightful. But once again a clear, full definition of the historical and sociocultural differences among American, especially African American, dialects would have enhanced the contemporary significance of this issue. For example, a more extended definition would have enabled readers to understand better the relationship of her theory of a black literary voice to how these differences among dialects influence literary representations of African American character and culture during major art movements. Except for the distorting influence of minstrel humor on Paul Laurence Dunbar, this is most apparent in the literary voices of such writers as Harriet Beecher Stowe, Joel Chandler Harris, Thomas Nelson Page, George Washington Cable, and Mark Twain.

The sociocultural and sociopsychological tension between Jones's early education in Kentucky and elite college education in Connecticut and Rhode Island, as well as her years in Europe, explain much of the paradox of her liberating voice in fiction. It also explains in part why she fallaciously assumes in the postscript that African American literary criticism reverted between 1982, when she first wrote *Liberating Voices,* and 1991, when the book was first published by Harvard University Press, to "New Criticism" in reaction to the "prescriptive and proscriptive criticism" of the Black Arts movement of the 1960s and 1970s. But as the writings in the late 1970s and 1980s by such important black critics as Baker, Gates, Hortense Spillers, and Robert Stepto confirm, many celebrated black academic critics moved beyond the radical, nonacademic vernacular theories and practices of the Black Arts era. Earning their doctoral degrees from white institutions, they were primarily influenced by the reader-response criticism, structuralism, and poststructuralism of such continental theorists as Wolfgang Iser, M. M. Bakhtin, Roland Barthes, Jacques Lacan, Jacques Derrida, Michel Foucault, and Julia Kristeva. In the 1980s the aesthetic battle over literary voice and audience thus shifted once again from "art for people's sake" to the rhetoric and poetics of postmodernism.

In assessing the manner and degree to which the literary and African American vernacular voices in *The Healing* are liberating, it is appropriate to apply Jones's own literary standards for excellence. In her assessment of the dialect and folklore in the literary texts of Dunbar and Hurston, Jones asks, "How does one employ the language in order to return it to the elasticity, viability, and indeed complexity, 'intelligence and sensibility,' that it often has when not divorced from the oral modes and folk creators?" Although she does not consider the interference of the author's idiolect, the distinctive pattern of linguistic features of one's own speech behavior, in the literary representation of the speech of different characters with authority and authenticity, it is reasonable nevertheless for readers to examine "the elasticity, viability, and [. . .] complexity" of the language in *The Healing*. However, as Wideman reminds readers, "Once a convention for dramatizing black speech appears in fiction, the literary critic should be concerned not with matters of phonetic accuracy, but with tracing the evolution of a written code and determining how that code refers to the spoken language in suggestive, artful, creative ways" ("Frame and Dialect" 36).

How, then, should readers, especially literary critics, respond to the position of contemporary novelists and critics like Jones and Wideman in assessing the black voice in *The Healing*? Assuming that language is a system of signs for communicating ideas and feelings about reality and for establishing and maintaining relationships with others, many contemporary readers find that one of the most reasonable and appropriate responses is to address their concern by focusing on the problems of agency, authenticity, and authority in the text. As *The Contemporary African American Novel* explains more fully, in narratology an agent is the representation of a human being whose speech acts influence events. But as it is used here, agency, to paraphrase philosopher Charles Taylor, is the sociocultural and sociopsychological process by which the individual assumes a responsible political position in maintaining or changing the systems of language and power by which he or she constructs and represents a personal and group identity or subjectivity of authenticity and authority (Prince, ch. 1). Although in *Sincerity and Authenticity* Lionel Trilling explains authenticity "as a criterion of art and as a quality of the personal life which may be either enhanced or diminished by art" (134), Charles Taylor defines authenticity more broadly in *The Ethics of Authenticity*:

> Authenticity (A) involves (i) creation and construction as well as discovery, (ii) originality, and frequently (iii) opposition to the rules of society and even potentially to what we recognize as morality. But it is also true [. . .] that it (B) requires (i) openness to horizons of significance (for otherwise the creation loses the background that can save it from insignificance) and (ii) a self-definition in dialogue. That these demands may be in tension has to be allowed. But what must be wrong is a simple privileging of one over the other of (A), say, at the expense of (B), or vice versa. (66)

Authenticity thus implies both transcending or overcoming restrictive material conditions and transgressing or violating social and moral boundaries. In contrast, authority is basically the power to influence or command thought, opinion, or behavior. "Three grounds on which legitimate authority often rest," Marvin E. Olsen reminds us in "Power as a Social Process," "are (a) traditional values, beliefs, norms, and customs, (b) legal prerogatives established through more-or-less rational agreements, and (c) special expertise or knowledge relevant to the situation. To the extent that an actor draws legitimacy from three sources [. . .] his authority is especially strong" (7).

Although the black voice in *Corregidora* and *Eva's Man* was praised by such prizewinning writers as James Baldwin, Maya Angelou, James Updike, and John Wideman, Wideman's analysis is the most critically illuminating. "In [. . .] *Corregidora* there is no hierarchical relationship between black speech and a separate literary language, no implicit dependency," Wideman writes. "The norms of black oral tradition exist full-bodied in the verbal style of the novel: lexicon, syntax, grammar, attitudes toward speech, moral and aesthetic judgments are rendered in the terms of the universe they reflect and reinforce. The entire novel flows through the filter of the narrator's sensibility, and Corregidora's sensibility is constructed of blocks of black speech, her own, her men's, the speech of the people who patronize Happy's bar, the voices of her mother and the dead black women keeping alive the memories of slavery" ("Frame and Dialect" 36). But *The Healing* moves beyond her previous blues novels because, as Jones states, "they emphasized the narrowest range of subject matter—the man-done-her-wrong-type blues—and even the blues itself has more possibility and range. *The Healing* is meant to be a rejection of those earlier novels" (qtd. in Chambers 68).

The problems of agency, authenticity, and authority in *The Healing* are most productively explored by focusing on the residual oral forms of religious ritual, vernacular language, and music. Rather than a blues singer, the central character and principal narrator of *The Healing* is a faith healer, Harlan Jane Eagleton, who was formerly a beautician who gambled on horses and the business manager of a not-so-famous black rock-and-roll singer, Joan Savage, who is a bibliophile that "prefers to be called, Savage Joan the Darling Bitch" (148). We first meet Harlan in the frame story as she travels by bus to one of the "little southern and midwestern tank towns" where she performs her healing ritual with a gathering of believers and skeptics. Casually eating a tin of sardines in mustard sauce with a Bible on her lap, to the irritation of other bus passengers but with the class sympathy of the implied author, the narrator dramatically opens the novel in her vernacular voice. Picked up by Martha and a local welcoming committee, Harlan reflects on the relationship between language, knowledge, and power that is the primary theme of the novel. "The women in the backseat are still thinking how common I am, how full of chitchat, and my vocabulary sounds elementary, it don't even sound like that preacher-teacher woman that give that lecture, ain't that wondrous and fantabulous vocabulary them healers uses, and if I could really heal, wouldn't I already just know about them trains too? And I don't talk that revelation talk, that prophet passion. Just some ordinary woman, could be one of them, or one of their daughters, one of their own girls" (25).

After establishing the class, ethnic, gender, and moral authority and viability of the black female faith healer in the initial two chapters, the dialect becomes more elastic and complex as the story within a story shifts in flashbacks and increasingly shorter chapters to the relationship between Harlan and Joan. The agency and authority of Harlan, the protagonist/narrator, is challenged by other voices in her nonlinear, retrogressive, cyclical movement from healer to Joan's business manager, to beautician, and to her self-healing of a stab wound from a jealous, misguided Joan that transformed Harlan into the healing woman whom we meet in the opening chapter. The frame story enigmatically closes the forty-six-chapter, five-part novel with a two-page epilogue in the black dialect of a local hostess committee that welcomes Harlan, the healing woman, to yet another town. But in this town, Nicholas, the black security guard, does not tell the story that he observed of her healing powers. Instead of Nicholas, she discovers a male from her past whom she least expected waiting to bear witness to her healing powers. Stylistically and structurally, *The Healing* is compellingly and challengingly innovative to the end.

In moving beyond the conventional humorous or pathetic black dialect of the plantation and minstrel traditions and of the traditional frame structure for representing black American culture and character, Jones filters her novel through the sensibility of the protagonist/narrator, who transgresses the hierarchical relationship between African American Vernacular English (AAVE) and literary language and between foreign languages and Standard American English (SAE) dialects. Omitting all quotation marks for direct addresses and dialogue, as well as erasing all specific time markers in identifying specific episodes, Jones constructs a complex text of characters and events whose authority and authenticity are occasionally undermined by its ambitious elasticity and heteroglossia.

For example, after one of Harlan's healing rituals, we hear the following creative voices straining to encompass both the local and global, the oral and literate modes of knowing and being in the world with others:

> I can already hear 'em talking about me, those flibbertigibbets. She ain't no preacher woman or a teacher woman neither, she a faith healer, one of them others be saying. What's the difference? She look like she belong on a submarine or on a motorcycle. They don't allow womens on no submarine. On the modern submarine they do, 'cause this is the age of feminism. Her and that bum's jacket. It's what they call a bomber jacket. Anyway, I seen her heal someone in D.C. I seen her when she healed in Memphis and then again in Kansas City. She even healed folks in Milan, that's over there in Italy. Dottoressa is what they calls her there in that Milan. I seen this picture of her healing over there in Italy and she were surrounded by all these Italians who looked just liked colored people to me. Say she's even healed folks in Brazil. I know they's got colored people in Brazil. Curandera's what they call her in Brazil. (13)

On one hand, the nonstandard grammar, vocabulary, and pronunciation enhance the transgressive agency, epistemology, and ontology of the narrative as Jones juxtaposes at different times and to various degrees a wide range of voices that are orthographically, but not typographically, marked by hierarchical social and national distinctiveness. The author's innovativeness is most apparent in her use of neologisms, foreign words, and repetition to control the vitality and rhythm of the dialogue.

On the other hand, the authority and authenticity of the wide range of voices are diminished by anomalous and incongruous repetitions of words, catalogs of books, and sentences in different languages. Although Harlan was born in New Orleans and raised in Louisville, Kentucky, for example, people say that she has a Geechee or Gullah accent, which is characteristic of the residual African speech behavior of black Americans acculturated on the Georgia and South Carolina Sea Islands. "Don't sound like a accent to me, but other people call it a Geechee accent. Then some people tell me I got a blend of different types of accents" (43). The transgressive, experimental style and structure of *The Healing* suggest that crossing traditional national, cultural, social, and linguistic boundaries is the liberating healing for or faith in the promise of a new world order of what Bakhtin calls dialogism, which limits the potential conflict of heteroglossia with dialogue that achieves mutual understanding and respect for cultural unity and dialectal diversity for believers and disbelievers. Even so, the range of voices whose regional distinctiveness and social variations are not clear is wide. The range of dialects include Martha and her welcoming committee; Josef Ehelich von Fremd, the Afro-German thoroughbred horse owner and Harlan's lover; and Nicholas, his black security guard and the witness to Harlan's first healing. We also hear and see Joan, the well-read, multilingual black college graduate and socially misguided rock-and-roll singer; James, Joan's ex-husband with whom Harlan has a sexual encounter; and Norvelle, the medical anthropologist in Africa and Harlan's ex-husband. The most dramatic symbol of the legacy of the ancestors is Jaboti, the grandmother whose stories about the turtle shell that she was required to wear while performing in a carnival as the Turtle Woman symbolize the strategies of mask wearing and tricksterism that enabled black Americans, especially women, to survive the prejudice and domination by others.

In blending fact with fiction, nonstandard with Standard English, American with non-American languages, and vernacular with literary voices, Jones moves thematically and stylistically beyond national, cultural, and linguistic boundaries. In response to her apparent cultural provincialism and monolingualism, Harlan's Afro-German lover responds:

> I grew up speaking English as well as German. Most Europeans speak several languages. I speak English, French, German, Dutch, a little Portuguese. It's only you Americans who're stingy about language, who believe that your own language is the universal language. I guess it is the universal language. You've made it the universal language. You've made it so your language is identified with modernity, with internationalism. I even know some Americans, though, who've lived in Berlin for years, and in other European cities, and insist on speaking only English. Who insist on English only even when they're in other people's country. (46)

Clearly critical of Harlan's linguistic limitations, Jones, the implied author, is more sympathetic with Harlan's contesting of modern narrative practice and modern ways of knowing and being in the world with others.

Reflecting on the possibility that Nicholas, the Afro-German's bodyguard, would retire as her "confabulatory" witness, and foreshadowing his replacement in the epilogue, Harlan states:

> Course there's probably a lot of fakers that hires theyselves witnesses, y'all know like them evangelist fakers—there's true evangelists and there's evangelist fakers—and some of them probably do better witnessing than the true witnesses. you know, maybe one of them evangelist fakers have a true witness to thy healings, but the people don't believe the true witness so's they's got to hire theyselves a fake witness, 'cause the fake witness to they healings is more believable than the true witness. Now I'm wondering whether that would make the healer a faker, if the healings theyselves is real, but the healer got to hire a fake witness, 'cause even the true believers don't believe the true witness. 'Cause maybe the fake witness got more confabulatory imagination than the true witness that just got a knowledge of the healings. (11)

Insofar as truth is a fictive or imaginative construction in language that communicates the ideas and feelings of the speaker or writer about the nature of reality to an audience, storytelling is both an epistemological and ontological act of identity formation.

Nicholas, for example,

> usedta tell the tale with more fanfare, more flourish, more confabularooiness. And when he tells about that healing, it sounds like a true tale; it don't sound like no confabulatory tale. [. . .] And those people that come to faith healing most of them want to hear confabulatory-sounding stories, which don't mean they's confabulatory stories they ownself. It's just that when people come to be healed, they just likes to hear them confabulatory-sounding stories. And there's other folks that comes to them faith healings not to be heal'd but to be entertained, like it's a circus or a carnival rather than a faith healing. Them sorts you don't know whether there's true believers amongst them or not. (11)

Rather than provide a specific example of Nicholas's "confabulatory" storytelling, the ability to fill in gaps in memory by fabrication (*Webster's* 260), the entire text of *The Healing* is Jones's "confabulatory" tale.

Unlike her earlier novels, the language of the vernacular and literary voices in *The Healing* is neither raw, nor sexually explicit and violent, nor painfully poignant. Instead, the language with which Jones constructs the lives of Harlan Eagleton and Joan Savage aspires with uneven success to the narrative and sociolinguistic standards of elasticity, viability, and complexity that the novelist outlines in *Liberating Voices*. By grounding her text in the religious ritual of healing, the vernacular voices of a black healing woman, and the music of a college-educated black rock-and-roll singer, Jones moves beyond the cultural limitations of her blues voice in *Corregidora* and *Eva's Man*. In order to expand the varieties and complexities of agency, authority, and authenticity that mark *The Healing*, Jones explicitly contrasts the notorious Eva of her earlier novel with the identity formation of contemporary Americans of African descent, especially ordinary black women who are not "criminally insane." But only Jones's imaginative construction of Harlan bears witness to some of the levels of irony and paradox that mark the political and spiritual struggle of many black women to reconcile the double consciousness of their personal and group identities as people of African descent. Stylistically and structurally, the liberation movement of the novel is most apparent in the nonlinear, reflexive interplay between the past and present, the spoken and written language, and the vernacular and formal cultural forms of the characters. Regrettably, however, the liberating movement of the voices in *The Healing* disrupts a static, unitary, blues construction of black identity with a more confusing than compelling narrative vision of an emerging transracial, transcultural social order of multivalent ways of knowing and being black in the world with others. Even so, many readers, including the National Book Awards Panel that nominated the book as a finalist, may judge the vision and voices of *The Healing* more aesthetically bold, original, and "confabulatory" than other novels published in 1998.

Notes

1. Stephen Henderson, *Understanding the New Black Poetry* (New York: Morrow, 1973); Bell, *Folk Roots*; Bell, *Afro-American Novel*; Wideman, "Frame and Dialect" 33–37; John Edgar Wideman, "Defining the Black Voice in Fiction," *Black American Literary Forum* 2.3 (Fall 1977): 79–82; Baker; and Gates, *Signifying Monkey*.

2. Levine, *Black Culture*; Keith Byerman, *Fingering the Jagged Grain* (Athens: U of Georgia P, 1985); John Callahan, *In The African American Grain* (Urbana: U of Illinois P, 1988); and Eric Sundquist, *The Hammers of Creation* (Athens: U of Georgia P, 1992).

IV

Toni Morrison's Blues People in a Jazz World

My review of Jazz *has its roots in an ongoing political and cultural debate about affirmative action. Because Morton Kaplan, the editor and publisher of the* World & I, *wrote a hostile, conservative response to my May 1991 essay in support of affirmative action in the Currents in Modern Thought—Point/ Counterpoint: Affirmative Action section of the magazine, I was delightfully surprised to receive an invitation from the Book Review editor in July 1992 to review Toni Morrison's* Jazz. *"As our nation begins to celebrate the bicentennial of the Bill of Rights," I wrote in 1991 with scholarly conviction in "Keep the Faith: White Civil Rights and Black Affirmative Action," "the lessons of our ancestors [. . .] teach us to keep our hands on the plow and our eyes on the prize of freedom with justice and equality. They teach us to keep the faith. [. . .] Since the contradictory sanctioning of white freedom and black slavery in the Constitution and the promotion of the myth of America as the new Garden of Eden in the eighteenth century, the cardinal Christian principle of love and the constitutional guarantees of unalienable human rights have been perverted on a grand scale by the children of God and the citizens of the American republic. And still we wait" (517–18). The tenor and tone of my essay were apparently too progressive and provocative for the editors and publishers of the magazine. In any event, Kaplan, disappointed perhaps by the factual errors and specious reasoning in the usually commissioned counterpoint essay, "Affirmative Action and the Rise of Neotribalism," added his own reactionary editorial response, "The Tribalization of America," in the front of the magazine. In light of the history of the magazine, I was more flattered than surprised that my essay elicited a second attack by the editor/publisher. The* World & I *began in 1982 as an expensively produced, conservative international educational print magazine.*

It was a publication of a subsidiary company of News World Communications Inc. founded in 1976 by the controversial leader of the Unification Church, the Reverend Sun Myung Moon. The magazine is currently published only online.

As an African American scholar and activist, I am committed to an aesthetic that imaginatively seeks to challenge and change insidious contemporary language and other institutional manifestations of the system of antiblack racism, including representations of African American culture and character, in the United States. I deploy rhetorical, dialectal, and dialogical critical strategies to reexamine and reconstruct the relationship between conventionally and simplistically classified black and white cultures, especially their vernacular and literary traditions. I therefore welcomed the opportunity to examine Morrison's literary improvisation and imbrication in Jazz *of blues and jazz motifs and modalities in a black triangular Harlem love story in the 1920s. In polyphonic and antiphonic flights of prose, Morrison invites readers of* Jazz *to bear witness to the continuities and discontinuities, as well as the ironies and paradoxes, of valorizing the vernacular tradition of African Americans as the foundation of our distinctive national, racial, and ethnic literary aesthetic.*

"IF MY WORK IS FAITHFULLY TO REFLECT THE AESTHETIC TRADITION OF AFRO-American culture," Toni Morrison explained in 1984, "it must make conscious use of the characteristics of its art forms and translate them into print: antiphony, the group nature of art, its functionality, its improvisational nature, its relationship to audience performance" ("Memory, Creation, and Writing" 389). In her 1988 Pulitzer Prize–winning *Beloved*, Morrison keeps faith with the aesthetic tradition of African American culture by constructing a womanist neo-slave narrative of double consciousness set in post–Civil War Cincinnati, Ohio, that speaks in many compelling voices on several time levels of the historical rape of black American women and of the resilient spirit of black Americans in surviving as a people. In *Jazz*, her new novel, Morrison continues to explore this tradition as she improvises blues and jazz variations on the triangular love story of middle-aged Joe and Violet Trace and teenaged Dorcas Manfred in 1926 Harlem.

Although she mentions a "Trombone Blues" and several blues lyrics (e.g., "ain't nobody going to keep me down, you got the right key baby but the wrong keyhole, you got to get it, bring it, and put it right here, or else" [60]) in *Jazz*, some readers will be disappointed that Morrison employs neither specific well-known blues or jazz musicians as prominent characters nor a particular blues or jazz song as the dominant motif in her narrative. After all, the 1920s was the era of the classic unrelated blues "sisters" (Bessie, Mamie, Clara, and Trixie Smith) and legendary jazz innovators such as Louis Armstrong and Duke Ellington. Instead, Morrison introduces her narrative with a blues-based love story told in a retrospective vernacular voice by a dramatized, disembodied yet intimate narrator that sets up a polyphonic structure of call-and-response between old and young, past and present, rural and urban, and southern and northern voices of blues people in a jazz world:

> Sth, I know that woman. She used to live with a flock of birds on Lenox Avenue. Know her husband, too. He fell for an eighteen-year-old girl with one of those deepdown spooky loves that made him so sad and happy he shot her just to keep the feeling going. When the woman, her name is Violet, went to the funeral to see the girl and to cut her dead face they threw her to the floor and out of the church. She ran, then, through all that snow, and when she got back to her apartment she took the birds from their cages and set them out the windows to freeze or fly, including the parrot that said, "I love you." (3)

Insofar as Ralph Ellison's definition of the blues as a lyrical expression of "both the agony of life and the possibility of conquering it through toughness of spirit" (*Shadow and Act* 94) is valid, then the theme, characters, and mood of *Jazz* are bluesy. And insofar as jazz, like the blues, constructs a traditional melody or harmonic framework as the base for both subtle and strident improvisational flights, either solo or collective, then the structure and much of the style of Morrison's latest book is derived from the jazz tradition.

"I'm crazy about this City" (7), says the nameless first-person voice in a dialect that identifies her as an inner-city, street-smart, transplanted southern narrator in Harlem:

> Nobody says it's pretty here; nobody says it's easy either. What it is is decisive, and if you pay attention to the street plans, all laid out, the City can't hurt you. [. . .] I like the way the City makes people think they can do what they want and get away with it. [. . .] Do what you please in the City, it is there to back and frame you no matter what

you do. And what goes on on its blocks and lots and side streets is anything the strong can think of and the weak will admire. All you have to do is heed the design—the way it's laid out for you, considerate, mindful of where you want to go and what you might need tomorrow. (8–9)

Through subtle rhythmic shaping and blending of idea, tone, and imagination, Morrison probes the tragicomic reasons behind the craziness and absurdity of life and love for urban black Americans in the 1920s. "Risky, I'd say," her narrator calls for the imaginative cooperation of the reader, "trying to figure out anybody's state of mind. But worth the trouble if you're like me—curious, inventive, and well-informed" (137).

In lyrical, antiphonal flights of prose, Morrison evokes countryscapes, cityscapes, and interiorscapes. Whatever the problems with foul winter weather and fair-weather friends, transplanted southern migrants in the imagined black haven of Harlem became liberated, modern, urban New Negroes "on Lenox Avenue safe from fays and the things they think up; where the sidewalks, snowcovered or not, are wider than the main roads of the towns where they were born and perfectly ordinary people can stand at the stop, get on the streetcar, give the man the nickel, and ride anywhere you please, although you don't please to go many places because everything you want is right where you are" (10). In the judgmental words of the narrator, the "scandalizing threesome" (6) began on Lenox Avenue. For Alice Manfred, an emotionally and spiritually repressed "woman of fifty and independent means" (54), who was Dorcas's aunt and guardian, it was "the low down music" (56) of Harlem that drove Violet, whom she called "Violent," and other people wild with passion. "The dirty, get-on-down music the women sang and the men played and both danced to, close and shameless or apart and wild. [. . .] It made you do unwise disorderly things. Just hearing it was like violating the law" (58). Like many socially ambivalent members of the black middle class, Alice "knew from sermons and editorials that it wasn't real music—just colored folks stuff: harmful, certainly; embarrassing, of course; but not real, not serious" (59).

Probing into the souls of her black folk, especially the women, and the ironic, parodic tensions of the music of their modern urban world, Morrison illuminates their laughing-to-keep-from-crying survival strategies for sublimating their anger and alienation. "Yet Alice Manfred swore she heard a complicated anger in it," Morrison writes, something hostile that disguised itself as flourish and roaring seduction. But the part she hated most was its appetite. Its longing for the bash, the slit; a kind of careless hunger for a fight or a red ruby stickpin for a tie—either would do. It faked happiness, faked welcome, but it did not make her feel generous, this juke joint, barrel hooch, tonk house, music. It made her hold her hand in the pocket of her apron to keep from smashing it through the glass pane to snatch the world in her fist and squeeze the life out of it for doing what it did and did and did to her and everybody else she knew or knew about. (59)

What, then, are the intertwined stories behind the love triangle that complicate the violent passion and desperation of their midlife crisis and love? Joe, a fifty-year-old door-to-door cosmetics salesman, and Violet, a fifty-year-old door-to-door hairdresser, met in Vesper County, Virginia, under a walnut tree near the cotton field in which they worked. "They knew people in common, and they had at least one relative in common. They were drawn together because they had been put together, and all they decided was when and where to meet at night" (30). Charmed by his "two-color eyes" (96) and the light that she believed he carried inside him, Violet risked snakes, beatings, and extra work to meet Joe in the cane fields in the middle of the night. As the implied author reconstructs the historical northern migration of black Americans, she invites readers to join Violet and Joe in 1906 when they left the South for the North, joining "the wave of black people running from want and violence" to the city that seemed to love them and that they sought desperately to love back as it challenged them to discover "themselves: their stronger, riskier selves" (33).

Twenty years later, after they have "train-danced on into the City, they were still a couple but barely speaking to each other, let alone laughing together or acting like the ground was a dance-hall floor" (38). As Morrison's poetic prose shifts to represent their increasing alienation and emotional distance, a curtain of silence between them intensifies the emptiness of Joe's desire and soul, an inner void with which he has traveled since his "wild" natural mother's abandonment of him as an infant and her refusal to acknowledge or speak to him as a young man. "Violet takes better care of her parrot than she does me," he says in justification of his appeal to Malvino, an upstairs neighbor, to rent her apartment for his affair with Dorcas. "Rest of the time she's cooking pork I can't eat, or pressing hair I can't stand the smell of. Maybe that's the way it goes with people being married long as we have. But the quiet. I can't take the quiet. She don't hardly talk anymore, and I ain't allowed near her" (49).

Violet's agonizing retrospective interior monologues after Dorcas's death reveal the paradoxical, elusive nature of their love and her schizophrenic silence. Explaining her silence, she says, "I got quiet because the things I couldn't say were coming out of my mouth anyhow. I got quiet because I didn't know what my hands might get up to when the day's work was done. The business going on inside me I thought was none of my business and none of Joe's either because I just had to keep hold of him any way I could and going crazy would make me lose him" (97). Morrison dramatizes Violet's schizophrenic consciousness by the innovative use of interior monologue and syntax that stress the conflict between the two warring selves of her personality. After tea with Alice Manfred, Violet "sat in the drugstore sucking malt through a straw wondering who on earth that other Violet was that walked about the City in her skin; peeped out through her eyes and saw other things. [. . .] She forgot which way to turn the key in the lock, that Violet not only knew the knife was in the parrot's cage and not in the kitchen drawer, that Violet remembered what she did not: scraping marble from the parrot's claws and beak weeks ago" (90). Although Joe knows the emotional and psychological distance between them because of Violet's "private cracks," he does not know about her "public craziness" (22) until she tries to "kill" Dorcas's corpse in the funeral parlor.

Years earlier, we learn from one of the many background solos that punctuate and deepen the complexity of the blues texture and characterization of the novel, Violet created a public scene in the neighborhood when she mysteriously sat down in the middle of the street. Even more strange was her attempt to steal the baby that she was asked to watch by its older sister while the girl ran inside her house for a blues record. Joe's friends and neighbors never told him about these strange events involving the woman who "had been a snappy, determined girl and a hardworking young woman, with the snatch-gossip tongue of a beautician" (23) but who had also had more than two miscarriages, probable contributing factors of her kidnapping and violent episodes.

In her lyrical version of the psychological cracks that haunt Violet, Morrison develops an extended metaphor that the narrator calls

> dark fissures in the globe light of the day. [. . .] The globe light holds and bathes each scene and it can be assumed that at the curve where the light stops is a solid foundation. In truth, there is no foundation at all but alleyways, crevices one steps across all the time. But the globe light is imperfect too. Closely examined it shows seams, ill-glued cracks and

> weak places beyond which is anything. Anything at all. [. . .] Violet had stumbled into a crack or two. Felt the anything-at-all begin in her mouth. Words connected only to themselves pierced an otherwise normal comment. (22–23)

Gradually, Violet's silences finally depress Joe. "He is married to a woman who speaks mainly to her birds. One of whom answers back: 'I love you'" (24). The interplay of sounds—both music and speech—and silences are thus thematically and stylistically significant to the polyphonic narrative.

Morrison uses the canaries and parrot that Violet speaks to in their parlor cages as objective correlatives and symbolic riffs, as both stylistic extensions of and counterpoints to the theme, structure, and the mood of her jazz narrative: repetitions with an ironic or parodic difference. Introduced at the close of the initial paragraph of the book, the parrot, in whose cage Violet finds the knife for her futile attack on Dorcas, is set free outdoors by Violet immediately after the bizarre attack and the bird's "I love you" greeting. As she runs up and down the stairs searching desperately for Joe, the evicted, shivering bird, who has forgotten how to fly after its years of confinement in a cage, punctuates each trip with "Love you." After the parrot, a counterpoint to the love between Violet and Joe, disappears on the second morning, Violet remembers ruefully:

> And she had never named him. Had called him "my parrot" all these years. "My parrot." "Love you." "Love you." Did the dogs get him. [. . .] Or did he get the message—that she said, "My parrot" and he said, "Love you," and she never said it back or even taken the trouble to name him— and manage somehow to fly away on wings that had not soared for six years. Wings grown stiff from disuse and dull in the bulb light of an apartment with no view to speak of. (93)

This subtle bird leitmotif, which is repeated on an upbeat note at the end of the narrative, underscores the tragic irony of the Traces' love.

Even more tragic and haunting are the stories that elicit our understanding of Joe's love for Dorcas, if not our profound sympathy for either one. As Alice Manfred seeks to reconcile Joe's reputation as a "nice man" with her anger with him for seducing and murdering her niece, we discover the emotional void that Joe seeks to fill. Alice knew that he was also "a man store owners and landlords liked because he set the children's toys in a neat row when they left them scattered on the sidewalk.

Who the children liked because he never minded them. And liked among men because he never cheated in a game, egged a stupid fight on, or carried tales, and he left their women alone. Liked among the women because he made them feel like girls; liked by girls because he made them feel like women—which, she thought, was what Dorcas was looking for" (75–76). For Joe, Dorcas "had been his necessary thing for three months of nights," a new love with "sugar-flawed skin" (28) to whom he told things he never told his wife.

Most important, the implied author elicits the reader's sympathy for Joe by revealing the psychological rupture with his unstable mother. In retrospective narrative, Joe tells Dorcas about his quest as a boy to be acknowledged by some sign from his mother, a mysterious black woman who shuns people yet lives "close enough to scare everybody because she creeps about and hides and touches and laughs a low sweet babygirl laugh in the cane" (37). Deeply depressed after shooting Dorcas, Joe remembers the emotional and psychological void of not receiving any maternal sign of acknowledgment from his unstable mother, a void that only Dorcas filled. Maybe his mother did give him a cryptic sign thirty-six years ago when he called to her in the hibiscus-concealed cave in which he believed she lived, we learn from his melancholic interior monologue: "Maybe he missed the sign that would have been some combination of shame and pleasure, at least, and not the inside nothing he traveled with from then on, except for the fall of 1925 when he had somebody to tell it to. Somebody called Dorcas with hooves tracing her cheekbones and who knew better than people his own age what that inside nothing was like. And who filled it for him, just as he filled it for her, because she had it too" (37–38).

As the implied author shifts the narrative voice to Dorcas, readers discover that a similar painful void and quest for wholeness came from the horrific murder of her parents in the East St. Louis antiblack race riots of 1917. Her father was "pulled off a streetcar and stomped to death" by white terrorists, and her mother "had just got the news and had gone back home to try and forget the color of his entrails, when her house was torched and she burned crispy in its flames." Dorcas, who was sleeping across the street with her best girlfriend, saw but never spoke about the fire and the trauma of her parents' death. "She went to two funerals in five days, and never said a word" (57). She resisted her Aunt Alice's protection and discipline, which were no match for the call of the city, the music, the flesh, and Joe's whispered invitation to emotional, psychological, and sexual renewal when she was seventeen.

Readers experience the complexity of Dorcas's ambivalent character and fatalistic behavior through the interiority of the different narrators. For Joe, Dorcas's face in the photograph on the mantelpiece, which Violet's obsession with her nemesis has driven her to borrow from the aunt, is "calm, generous and sweet." For Violet, in contrast, "the girl's face looks greedy, haughty and very lazy" (12). For Felice, Dorcas's best friend and the agent of reconciliation between Joe and Violet, Dorcas used people and was cold in her pursuit of attention or excitement. She not only dumped Joe for a younger man but also, according to Felice's story, "let herself die. The bullet went in her shoulder. [. . .] She wouldn't let anybody move her; said she wanted to sleep and she would be all right. Said she'd go to the hospital in the morning. 'Don't let them call nobody,' she said, 'No ambulance, no police, no nobody'" (209). Despite this request, Felice tells the Traces, she called the ambulance twice, but it did not come until morning. Dorcas bled to death.

Morrison's most haunting and provocative stories in *Jazz* of the rural, repressed past focus on the tragic lives of black mothers and grandmothers who were not always successful in coping spiritually with slavery and racism, with hard times and cold hearts, with alienation and anger, which disrupted their families and their lives. As readers, we are challenged to retrace and reconstruct their lives with the fragmentary, elusive memories and reveries of the narrator and characters. Violet's mother, Rose Dear, was driven to suicide by poverty and desertion. Her grandmother, True Belle, as a slave, had to abandon her husband and daughters, including Rose Dear, in order to accompany the master's disowned, interracially pregnant daughter, Vera Louise Gray, into exile. In Baltimore, she midwifed Vera's baby, mothered for eighteen years her racially mixed son, Golden Gray, and then sent him in search of Henry Les Troy, his black father. Joe's mother was a mysterious, unstable, "berry-black woman" (144) who runs wild in the cane fields and attracts "redwings, those blue-black-birds with the bolt of red on their wings" (176). Dorcas's mother was burned alive in her own home by white anti-black rioters and terrorists. Raised by her grandmother, Felice saw her parents, who worked in Tuxedo, only forty-four days a year. "When they'd come home, they'd kiss me and give me things, like my opal ring, but what they really wanted to do was go out dancing somewhere (my mother) or sleep (my father)" (198). The men of these women, except for Joe, are either invisible, insensitive, or ineffectual bluesmen.

With Felice's slow-tempo "next year's news" (222) playing as counterpoint to Dorcas's frantic, desperate emptiness and as the bridge for the solo flights of silence and discordance between Joe and Violet, the long black song of *Jazz* closes on an upbeat melodramatic note. "It's nice when grown people whisper to each other under the covers," the nameless narrator reflects, their ecstasy is more leaf-sigh than bray and the body is the vehicle, not the point. They reach, grown people, for something beyond, way beyond and way, way down underneath tissue. [. . .] Breathing and murmuring under covers both of them have washed and hung out on the line, in a bed they chose together and kept together never mind one leg was propped on a 1916 dictionary, and the mattress, curved like a preacher's palm asking for witnesses in His name's sake, enclosed them each and every night and muffled their whispering old-time love. (228)

The Traces reclaim the pieces of their fragile yet thick love and reconcile the dialectic tensions of their lives by dancing together on the floor and beneath their time-worn patchwork quilt. Morrison's sensational blues-based Harlem love triangle and rhythmic antiphonal flights of fancy thus invite readers to participate in reconstructing and reaffirming the agony and ecstasy of loving and living in a jazz world.

V

Beloved: A Womanist Neo–Slave Narrative; or, Multivocal Remembrances of Things Past

Initially, I presented this essay as a lecture in 1989 in a conference at the University of Utah and in lectures in 2006 at Southwest University of Science and Technology and Sichuan Normal University in China. I then published a revised version in 1992 in the African American Review, *which has been reprinted in three different collections of critical essays on the novel. Convinced that* Beloved *was Morrison's most awesome novel stylistically and structurally, I began writing the essay in 1987 before my convictions of its outstanding merits were confirmed when the book received the American Book Award and Pulitzer Prize in 1988. Unlike univocal slave narratives in which plot rides character in the protagonist's journey of transformation from object to subject,* Beloved *is a haunting story of a mother's thick love that frames a series of interrelated love stories (maternal, parental, filial, sororal, conjugal, heterosexual, familial, and communal) by multiple narrators about the historical rape of black American women and of the resilient spirit of African Americans in surviving as a people.*

"WHAT IS CURIOUS TO ME," TONI MORRISON OCCASIONALLY SAYS IN HER lectures, "is that bestial treatment of human beings never produces a race of beasts." Since her childhood in Lorain, Ohio, she has been fascinated by the uncommon efforts of common black people to deal creatively with their tragicomic experiences and double consciousness. As first defined in 1897 by W. E. B. Du Bois in "Strivings of the Negro People," it was not the experience of all ethnic immigrants and hyphenated white Americans. Rather, it was the profound paradoxes and complex fate of Americans of African descent behind the veil of racial segregation whose humanity and culture had been historically devalued and marginalized by people of European and British descent. Arguably, it remains for many folks behind the veil the striving to reconcile one's ascribed identity with one's achieved identity; to reconcile the politics of race with the politics of sex; and to reconcile the condition of being an outsider with being an insider.

In an apparent rewriting of Du Bois's classic metaphor and sociologist Robert E. Park's 1928 theory of the marginal man (a racial and cultural hybrid or Creole), the term *socialized ambivalence* was coined in 1937 by anthropologist Melville J. Herskovits in *Life in a Haitian Valley* to signify the anthropological adjustment of Haitians to the sociopsychological conflict that resulted from the contradictory cultural imperatives of European colonialism and African traditions. In applying this model to the United States, one notes the ambivalence expressed by many modern Americans of African and interracial descent about ideologies of integration and separation and in our shifting identification between white hegemonic and black nonhegemonic cultural systems as a result of institutionalized antiblack racism. "Double vision," Ralph Ellison's 1964 rewriting in *Shadow and Act* of Du Bois's metaphor, is a fluid, ambivalent, laughing-to-keep-from-crying perspective toward life as expressed in the innovative use of irony, paradox, and parody in African American folklore and formal art.

How, then, do ordinary black people cope with the sexist customs, racist absurdities, and class exploitation of American life? Drawing on remembrances of her family's tradition of telling ghost stories and her long-standing fascination with literature, Morrison began attempting to answer this question creatively and expanded her commitment by joining a writers' workshop at Howard University in 1962. The short story she began in that workshop became the nucleus of *The Bluest Eye* (1970) and the apprenticeship for her major achievements in poetic realism and Gothicism: *Sula* (1973), *Song of Solomon* (1977), *Tar Baby* (1981), and the Pulitzer Prize–winning *Beloved* (1987).

Beloved contains Toni Morrison's most extraordinary and spellbinding womanist remembrances of things past. As Alice Walker's epigraphs to *In Search of Our Mothers' Gardens* suggest, *womanist* connotes "a black feminist or feminist of color" a woman who, among other things, is audaciously "committed to [the] survival and wholeness of entire people, male *and* female" (xi). As Afro-American literary critics Wilfred D. Samuels and Clenora Hudson-Weems remind us in their biocritical study *Toni Morrison,* because of the silences in the slave narratives due to authorial compromises to white audiences and to self-masking from a painful past, Morrison sees her role as a writer as bearing witness to "the interior life of people who didn't write [their history] (which doesn't mean they didn't have it)" and to "fill[ing] in the blanks that the slave narrative left" (97).

Unlike James Baldwin, who also defined his role as bearing witness, Morrison privileges the authority and epistemology of black and Third World women in America. "I use the phrase 'bear witness' to explain what my work is for," she told black interviewers and writers Steve Cannon and Ntozake Shange in 1977.

> I have this creepy sensation [. . .] of loss. Like something is either lost, never to be retrieved, or something is about to be lost and will never be retrieved. Because if we don't know [. . .] what our past is, [. . .] if we Third-World women in America don't know it, then, it is not known by anybody at all. [. . .] And somebody has to tell somebody something. (Qtd. in Samuels and Hudson-Weems 139)

As narrative strategy, remembrance, in Morrison's words, is "a journey to a site to see what remains have been left behind and to reconstruct the world that these remains imply" (qtd. in Samuels and Hudson-Weems 97). As in Marcel Proust's *Remembrance of Things Past,* the recovery of lost experience is triggered by some external, ostensibly insignificant event. For example, in *Beloved* Sethe

> worked hard to remember as close to nothing as was safe. Unfortunately her brain was devious. She might be hurrying across a field, running practically, to get to the pump quickly and rinse the chamomile

sap from her legs. Nothing else would be in her mind. [...] Then something. The plash of water, the sight of her shoes and stockings awry on the path where she had flung them; or Here Boy lapping in the puddle near her feet, and suddenly there was Sweet Home rolling, rolling, rolling out before her eyes, and although there was not a leaf on that farm that did not make her want to scream, it rolled itself out before her in shameless beauty. It never looked as terrible as it was and it made her wonder if hell was a pretty place too. Fire and brimstone all right, but hidden in lacy groves. Boys hanging from the most beautiful sycamores in the world. It shamed her—remembering the wonderful soughing trees rather than the boys. Try as she might to make it otherwise, the sycamores beat out the children every time and she could not forgive her memory for that. (6)

Sethe's voicing of her internal struggle with the repressed memory of the terrible price of the journey from slavery to freedom foreshadows the different voices of the will to survive enslavement by other characters in the novel.

On a sociopsychological level, *Beloved* is the story of Sethe Suggs's quest for social freedom and psychological wholeness. Sethe struggles with the haunting memory of her slave past and the retribution of Beloved, the ghost of the infant daughter whom she killed in order to save her from the living death of what Frederick Douglass called the tomb of slavery. On a legendary and mythic level, *Beloved* is a ghost story that frames embedded narratives of the impact of slavery, racism, and sexism on the capacity for love, faith, and community of black families, especially of black women, during the Reconstruction period. Set in post–Civil War Cincinnati, *Beloved* is a womanist neo–slave narrative of double consciousness, a postmodern romance that speaks in many compelling voices and on several time levels of the historical rape of black American women and of the resilient spirit of blacks in surviving as a people.

As the author has explained in interviews and as a sympathetic white minister's report in the February 12, 1865, issue of the *American Baptist* reveals (see Bassett), at the center of *Beloved* is Morrison's retelling of the chilling historical account of a compassionate yet resolute self-emancipated mother's "thick" love. Margaret Garner, with the tacit sympathy of her sexagenarian mother-in-law, cut the throat of one of her four children and tried to kill the others to save them from the outrages of slavery that she had suffered. Guided by the spirits of the many thousands gone, as inscribed in her dedication, Morrison employs a multivocal text and a highly figurative language to probe her characters' double consciousness of their terribly paradoxical circumstances as people and nonpeople in a social arena of white male hegemony. She also foregrounds infanticide as a desperate act of "thick" love (*Beloved* 164) by a fugitive-slave mother "with iron eyes and backbone to match" (9). "Love is or it ain't," Sethe, the dramatized narrator/protagonist, says in reproach to a shocked friend, Paul D. "Thin love ain't love at all" (164). Indignantly reflecting on Paul D's metonymic reprimand that she "got two feet [. . .] not four" (165), she later expands on their oppositional metaphors in reverie: "Too thick, he said. My love was too thick. What he know about it? Who in the world is he willing to die for? Would he give his privates to a stranger in return for a carving?" (203).

The implied author, the version of herself that Morrison creates as she creates the narrative (see Booth 70–75, 138, 151), brilliantly dramatizes the moral, sexual, and epistemological distances between Sethe and Paul D. After their first dialogue, a trackless, quiet forest abruptly appears between them. This metaphorical silence is an ingenious, ironic use of the technique of call-and-response that invites the implied reader—in Wolfgang Iser's words, that "network of response-inviting structures, which impel the reader to grasp the text" (34)—to pause and take stock of his or her own ambivalent moral and visceral responses to this slave mother's voicing of her thick love.

Thematically, the implied author interweaves racial and sexual consciousness in *Beloved*. Sethe's black awareness and rejection of white perceptions and inscription of herself, her children, and other slaves as nonhuman—marking them by letter, law, and lash as both animals and property—are synthesized with her nineteenth-century black feminist sense of self-sufficiency. Sethe reconciles gender differences with her husband, Halle Suggs, and later Paul D, in heterosexual, endogamous relationships that affirm the natural biblical principles of the racial and ethnic survival of peoplehood through procreation and parenting in extended families. Although the implied author blends racial and sexual consciousness, the structure and style of the text foreground the ambivalence of slave women about motherhood that violates their personal integrity and that of their families.

Foregrounding the theme of motherhood, Morrison divides the text into twenty-eight unnumbered mini-sections, the usual number of days in a woman's monthly menstrual cycle, within three larger, disproportionate sections. Within these sections, Sethe experiences twenty-eight happy days of "having women friends, a mother-in-law, and all of her children together; of being part of a neighborhood;

of, in fact, having neighbors at all to call her own" (173). Also within these sections, the passion and power of memory ebb and flow in a discontinuous, multivocal discourse of the present with the past. Unlike the univocal nineteenth-century slave narratives in which plot rides character in the protagonist's journey of transformation from object to subject, *Beloved* is a haunting story of a mother's love that frames a series of interrelated love stories (maternal, parental, filial, sororal, conjugal, heterosexual, familial, and communal) by multiple narrators. These stories begin in 1873 and end in 1874, but flash back intermittently to 1855. In the flashbacks and reveries, the omniscient narrator invokes ancestral black women's remembrances of the terror and horror of the Middle Passage. She also probes the deep physical and psychic wounds of Southern slavery, especially the paradoxes and perversities of life on Sweet Home plantation in Kentucky, and recalls Sethe's bold flight to freedom in Ohio in 1855. Freedom, as Paul D's and Sethe's stories most dramatically illustrate, is "to get to a place where you could love anything you choose—not to need permission for desire" (162).

The metaphors of personal and communal wholeness in the text heighten the psychological realism of its womanist themes of black kinship, motherhood, sisterhood, and love. Besides the structural analogue to a woman's natural reproductive cycle, the text frequently and dramatically highlights metaphors and metonyms for the agony and ecstasy, despair and hope, of loving, birthing, nurturing, and bonding. Heart, breasts, milk, butter, water, and trees—these recurring tropes first appear in the opening eight mini-sections as the vehicles for controlling the psychological, emotional, and moral distances among the narrators, characters, and implied reader who participate, on various levels, in Sethe's historical and mythic quest.

After the omniscient narrator introduces us to the restless, spiteful spirit of Sethe's two-year-old daughter Beloved, we are quickly and irrevocably drawn into the vortex of conflicting values and feelings of the text. On one hand, we are drawn emotionally and psychologically closer to Sethe through her unrelenting memory of the terrible price she has paid for loving her daughter so dearly; but on the other, like Paul D and Ella, we are at first morally repelled by her gory act of infanticide. When slave catchers and schoolteacher suddenly appear in the family's Ohio yard to return Sethe and her children to slavery, she not only cuts Beloved's throat with a handsaw and attempts to kill her other three, but she subsequently trades ten minutes of sex on her daughter's grave with an engraver, as his son watches, to pay him for carving the name *Beloved* on her daughter's headstone.

Our sympathies for Sethe are strengthened, however, through her grim reverie and dialogue with Paul D. Through them we discover that, earlier in 1855, while pregnant with Denver and before she could escape with her husband, Halle, to join their children in Ohio with the milk to nurse her baby girl, she was outrageously violated. "I am full God damn it of two boys with mossy teeth," she remembers, "one sucking on my breast the other holding me down, their book-reading teacher watching and writing it up." Weaving into her story the additional insufferable traumatic details provided eighteen years later by Paul D, who knew her from their shared years of slavery on the ironically named Sweet Home plantation, the horror continues:

> Add my husband to it, watching, above me in the loft—hiding close by—the one place he thought no one would look for him, looking down on what I couldn't look at at all. And not stopping them—looking and letting it happen. [. . .] There is also my husband squatting by the churn smearing the butter as well as its clabber all over his face because the milk they took is on his mind. And as far as he is concerned, the world may as well know it. (70)

Again we note the implied author's privileging of metaphor and metonym over black dialect to achieve just the right aesthetic balance between the poetics and polemics of the long black song of the many thousands gone that she skillfully orchestrates to engage our hearts and minds.

The collusion of many antebellum white women with the brutalization of black women is suggested by the ineffectual tears of the plantation mistress, Mrs. Garner, whom Sethe tells about the attack. In retaliation, Mrs. Garner's wryly named brother-in-law, who studies and treats slaves as animals, orders one of his nephews to whip Sethe. "Schoolteacher made one open up my back," Sethe tells Paul D, "and when it closed it made a tree. It grows there still" (17). The ugly scar on her back is described as having the trunk, branches, leaves, and blossoms of a chokecherry tree by Amy Denver, the runaway, ragged, and hungry indentured white girl who, in sharp contrast to Mrs. Garner, not only massages Sethe's swollen feet, but also helps to deliver her baby on the Ohio River bank. Unlike most of the black female narrators, Amy, whose quest for velvet rather than love is the principal sign of her racial, sexual, and class difference, is not raped, and she stands as the implied author's brightest ray of hope for black and white sisterhood. When Paul D hears about Sethe's stolen milk and bitter-fruit tree, he bends down behind her in the kitchen, "his body an arc of kindness," and holds her breasts in his hands as he "rub[s] his cheek on her back and learn[s] that way her sorrow, the roots of it; its wide trunk and intricate branches" (17). Symbolically, the chokecherry tree signifies the physical and psychic suffering of slavery that Paul D shares with Sethe.

As the text unfolds with the ebb and flow of characters, events, and memories, these figures of speech are developed in free association and free indirect discourse—the linguistic fusion of two narrative voices. Occasionally, the implied author's consciousness merges with the narrator's, the narrator/protagonist's with the characters', the past with the present, and the black female's with the male's. These techniques compel the reader viscerally and cerebrally to fill the gaps in the text of the fragmented yet complementary embedded stories and memories of Baby Suggs, Nan, Sethe's mother, Ella, Stamp Paid, and Paul D. The implied reader is moved by these illustrative comparisons and contrasts to reconstruct and reconsider the unspeakable human cost of American slavery, racism, and sexism, then and now—to whites as well as blacks, to men as well as women—and to sympathize with Sethe, black mothers, and black families in their struggle against white male hegemony to affirm their self-worth as a racial group.

The Gothic story of Sethe's loving and losing Beloved is thematically and emotionally emblematic of the historical struggle for survival with self-respect and love of black families that has been passed on orally and spiritually from generation to generation. "Not a house in the country ain't packed to its rafters with some dead Negro's grief," Sethe's sixty-year-old mother-in-law tells her. "You lucky. You got three left. [. . .] I had eight. Every one of them gone away from me. Four taken, four chased, and all, I expect, worrying somebody's house into evil" (5). Sethe tells her daughters the horror story of her mother as passed on to her by Nan, the one-armed slave wet nurse and cook who became her surrogate mother. For Sethe was nursed only two weeks by her mother, a field slave branded with a circle and cross under her breast, before she was turned over to Nan, who, along with Sethe's mother, had been raped many times by crew members during the Middle Passage. The children fathered by these and other whites, Sethe's mother threw away. "Without names, she threw them," Nan tells young Sethe in a pidgin tongue that implicitly valorizes the ancestral life-bestowing power of naming rituals, a tongue and ritual bonding that are only a dim memory for Sethe. "You she gave the name of a black man. She put her arms around him. The others she did not put her arms around. Never. Never" (62).

Ella, an agent on the Underground Railroad who twice rescues Sethe, believes in root medicine but not love. As a result of Ella's regular sexual abuse while in puberty by her master and his son, "the lowest yet," she considers sex disgusting and love a "serious disability." She remembers having delivered, "but would not nurse, a hairy white thing, fathered by 'the lowest yet'" (258–59). While she understands Sethe's rage in the shed, she regards Sethe's reaction as prideful and misdirected. Even so, "Ella didn't like the idea of past errors taking possession of the present [. . .] of sin moving on in the house, unleashed and sassy" (256). Morally and emotionally, the relationship of the past to the present is relative, not absolute.

Similarly, Baby Suggs, an "unchurched preacher" who is driven to bed to think about the colors of things by the un-Christian ways of white Christians, passes on the bittersweet wisdom of her years in stories she tells to her granddaughter Denver and her daughter-in-law Sethe. Baby Suggs's heart, her faith and love, began to collapse twenty-eight days after Sethe's arrival, when white slave catchers violated her home and terrorized Sethe into killing Beloved, the daughter of the only son Baby Suggs was allowed to mother, Halle. "What she called the nastiness of life," the empathetic implied author tells us in free indirect discourse,

> was the shock she received upon learning that nobody stopped playing checkers just because the pieces included her children. Halle she was able to keep the longest. Twenty years. A lifetime. Given to her, no doubt, to make up for *hearing* that her two girls, neither of whom had their adult teeth, were sold and gone and she had not been able to wave goodbye. To make up for coupling with a straw boss for four months in exchange for keeping her third child, a boy, with her—only to have him traded for lumber in spring of the next year and to find herself pregnant by the man who promised not to and did. That child she could not love and the rest she would not. "God take what He would," she said. And He did, and He did, and He did and then gave her Halle who gave her freedom when it didn't mean a thing. (23)

The double consciousness and double vision here (which some readers will recognize as analogous to Mikhail M. Bakhtin's theory of double-voiced or dialogic texts) are apparent in the interplay and interweaving of the represented discourse, time frames, and perspectives of the implied author and Baby Suggs.

In addition to the three basic types of represented discourse (direct, simple indirect, and free indirect), five different yet related linguistic codes and their concomitant ideologies (i.e., their implicit, related systems of beliefs and values) are present in *Beloved*: Standard American English, rural black vernacular English, black feminist discourse, black patriarchal discourse, and white male hegemonic discourse. The two dominant voices, however, are in Standard American English and black feminist discourse. For example, the implied author and the dramatized narrator/protagonist, Sethe, want Beloved and the implied reader to understand that far worse than Beloved's grisly death is

> that anybody white could take your whole self for anything that came to mind. Not just work, kill, or maim you, but dirty you. Dirty you so bad you couldn't like yourself anymore. Dirty you so bad you forgot who you were and couldn't think it up. And though she and others lived through and got over it, she could never let it happen to her own. The best thing she was, was her children. Whites might dirty *her* all right, but not her best thing, her beautiful, magical best thing—the part of her that was clean. (251)

The paradoxical simplicity yet profundity of "dirty" as a black feminist metaphor of the devastating psychological and physical dehumanizing potential of slavery is extraordinary. In contrast, Denver tells her sister Beloved in nearly as memorable Standard American English the legend of her birth and of the white girl with "no meanness around her mouth" whose name she bears (77).

In an apparent rewriting of Faulkner's narrative strategy in dramatizing Shreve and Quentin's reconstruction and reliving of Charles Bon and Henry Sutpen's fatal kinship in *Absalom, Absalom!*, Morrison imaginatively constructs Denver to voice the manner and degree to which the storyteller, story, and primary audience of *Beloved* share a concord of sensibilities in a residually oral culture that sanctions the dynamic coexistence of the spoken and written word, the metaphysical and physical, the mythic and historic:

> Denver was seeing it now and feeling it—through Beloved. Feeling how it must have felt to her mother. Seeing how it must have looked. And the more fine points she made, the more detail she provided, the more Beloved liked it. So she anticipated the questions by giving blood to the scraps her mother and grandmother had told her—and a heartbeat. The monologue became, in fact, a duet as they lay down together, Denver nursing Beloved's interest like a lover whose pleasure was to overfeed the loved. (78)

Near the end of the novel, in sections 22 and 23, the consciousness of Sethe, Denver, and Beloved merge in free indirect discourse and surrealism.

Unlike Morrison's *The Bluest Eye* and the womanist texts of Alice Walker, in *Beloved* black men are not stereotyped as "low-down dirty dog[s]," like the nameless Assistant and Wild Child's anonymous impregnator in *Meridian* (59–61, 24) and Mr. _____ and even God in *The Color Purple* (170, 164). Although circumstances may reduce some to defiling and debasing themselves with cows, clabber, or the daughters of their lovers, Baby Suggs, Sethe, and the implied author agree: "A man ain't nothing but a man" (23). Even Garner, the benevolent master of Sweet Home, stands out among his white neighbors for treating his slaves (Paul D, Paul A, Paul F, Halle, and Sixo) like men. "Bought em thataway, raised em thataway," he boasts with dramatic irony. Garner allows Halle to hire himself out on weekends for five years to buy his mother's freedom, allows his slaves to have guns, and even allows them to marry rather than breed them like animals. Thus, although Sethe was a desirable young girl of thirteen when she arrived on the plantation, the Sweet Home men, who were all in their twenties and "so sick with the absence of women that they had taken to calves," did not rape her. They "let the iron-eyed girl be, so she could choose" (10). Clearly, the theme, protagonist, structure, and style privilege a black woman's perspective, but sexual politics complements rather than dominates racial politics in the implied author's celebration of black people as more than the dehumanized victims of brutal social oppression.

In her multivocal celebration of the spiritual resiliency of black people, black men and women are physically and psychologically violated by slavery, racism, and sexism in the text. (These violations were exacerbated by the infamous Fugitive Slave Act of 1850, which legalized the kidnapping and enslavement of any black person anywhere in the United States.) With Garner's death, "schoolteacher broke into children what Garner had raised into men" (220). So after Paul F is sold, the other slaves attempt unsuccessfully to escape. Sixo is burned alive and shot; Paul A is hanged and mutilated; Sethe is raped and beaten; and Halle loses his mind after witnessing his wife's violation. Paul D is forced to wear a three-spoked collar and mouth bit while waiting to be sold down river where he and other black prisoners are terrorized with fellatio and death. Paul D's reverie explains his subsequent seduction by Beloved while he is Sethe's lover as "more like a brainless urge to stay alive" than a desire to have fun (264). Also "dirtied" by whites, Stamp Paid, the conductor on the Underground Railroad who ferries Sethe to Ohio and snatches Denver from death in a woodshed, was born Joshua. But "he renamed himself when he handed over his wife to his master's son. Handed her over in the sense that he did not kill anybody, thereby himself, because his wife demanded he stay alive. [. . .] With that gift, he decided that he didn't owe anybody anything. Whatever his obligations were, that act paid them off" (184–85). For the characters, narrator, and the implied author, the scars of sexual, racial, and class oppression on the soul—the price of the ticket for the journey from slavery to freedom and from object to subject—are more horrible than those on the body.

Even so, the struggle to survive with justifiable self-respect rather than inordinate self-esteem or self-debasement prevails for those who affirm ties to their ethnic community. When the community perceives excessive pride in Sethe and Baby Suggs, as illustrated by the former's "stand offishness" and the latter's extravagant blackberry party, it feels insulted and rejected—which is why no one from the community warns them about the slave catchers' approach. After sixty years of a life with less sunshine than rain, Stamp Paid reflects, "to belong to a community of other free Negroes—to love and be loved by them, to counsel them and be counseled, protect and be protected, feed and be fed—and then to have that community step back and hold itself at a distance—well, it could wear out even a Baby Suggs, holy" (177). But Ella and the community of thirty black women come praying and singing to Sethe's rescue after Denver reaches out to the community and after Beloved "t[a]k[es] flesh" in the world as a "devil-child" and nearly hounds Sethe to death (257–61).

The arrival, departure, and return of Paul D, however, provide the frame story for Sethe's realization of personal wholeness in the community and Morrison's synthesis of sexual and racial politics. With Paul D's arrival at Sethe's haunted house, she can suddenly "trust things and remember things because the last of the Sweet Home men was there to catch her if she sank" (18). In her mind's eye, "there was something blessed in his manner. Women saw him and wanted to weep. [. . .] Strong women and wise saw him and told him things they only told each other" (17). Paul D leaves Sethe after being shocked by her confession of infanticide and after responding insensitively about Sethe's number of feet. This remark is associated in the minds of the protagonist and, with mixed emotions, the implied reader with schoolteacher's belief and value systems as dramatized in his listing of Sethe's "characteristics on the animal side" (251).

Paul D returns to 124 Bluestone Road after Denver and the choral community of black women break Beloved's evil spell because he wants to take care of Sethe, who has withdrawn in despair to die in Baby Suggs's bed. As he proceeds to rekindle the will to live of the woman who, as Sixo said of his woman, is "a friend of my mind" by bathing her, he remembers how she "left him his manhood." As the frame story closes in a romantic vignette, he holds her hand and tells her that she is her best thing and that "we got more yesterday than anybody. We need some kind of tomorrow" (273). In her multivocal remembrances of things past, Morrison thus probes the awesome will to live of her characters in order to celebrate the truth and resiliency of the complex double consciousness of their humanity. What she passes on to generations yet to come in *Beloved* is an extraordinarily effective Gothic blend of postmodern realism and romance, as well as of racial and sexual politics.

5

Bearing Witness to the Changing Same

Representations of Black American Identity in American and African American Literature

I

Three Vernacular Theories for Teaching African American Literature for the Twenty-First Century

> In the case of the writer of African descent, her or his texts occupy spaces in at least two traditions: a European or American literary tradition, and one of the several related but distinct black traditions. The "heritage" of each black text written in a Western language is, then, a double heritage, two-toned, as it were. Its visual tones are white and black, and its aural tones are standard and vernacular.
>
> Henry Louis Gates Jr., "Criticism in the Jungle"

As the final chapter in this collection, the title of "Bearing Witness to the Changing Same" wryly represents the theme and tone of my professional journey as an African American scholar and activist. I first delivered this essay as a plenary lecture in a National Council of Teachers of English (NCTE) Conference in South Carolina in 1995. My wife, Carrie, reminds me that it was much too long and repetitious. I believe she was most concerned by the paradoxical refrain in my talk that "the more things change, the more they remain the same." This refrain underscored the fact in my opening anecdote that I recalled giving a similar lecture twenty-five years earlier to regional NCTE conferences in New England. In any event, assuming in my 1995 lecture that most of my audience of educators from primary schools to universities were already committed to preparing themselves and their students for change in a more culturally diverse twenty-first century, I divided "Three Vernacular Theories for Teaching African American Literature for the Twenty-First Century" into two major parts. First, I examined the sociohistorical and sociocultural contexts for the validity and viability of a rhetorical, dialectical, dialogical, and critical pedagogy. Second, I outlined three major vernacular theories by Henry Louis Gates Jr., Houston A. Baker Jr., and myself as recommended approaches to teaching African American literature and culture for the twenty-first century. Although I do not mention her in this piece, I would like to identify Gayl Jones's Liberating Voices: Oral Tradition in African American Literature *as an important transhistorical, transcultural critical comparison of the oral foundation of African American literature with similar vernacular roots of world literature. I examine her book closely in "The Liberating Literary and African American Vernacular Voices of Gayl Jones" in chapter 4. As a coeditor of* Call and Response: The Riverside Anthology of the African American Literary Tradition *(1997), which is a major reconstruction of the African American literary canon and its vernacular roots and which was in press at the time, I also indirectly promoted its pedagogical merits.*

BACK DURING THE DAYS BEFORE THE BROTHERS ON THE BLOCK BEGAN SINGING "I'm Black and I'm Proud" in the street with James Brown and before the sisters in the storefront church began bearing witness from the amen corner to James Baldwin's "No more water, the fire next time," many of us, then as now, were shaking our heads and saying with the resignation and resolution of our ancestors, "The more things change, the more they remain the same." Years ago, when I was head of the first and only consortium of departments of African American Studies at a major public university and four prestigious private New England colleges, I was invited to talk to the New England Association of Teachers of English (NEATA) about how to teach black American literature. "If we look at the young people of America— those under thirty-five—and their increasing rejection of racism and war," I said to my white Burlington, Vermont, audience,

> we see the handwriting on the wall. America is faced with a revolution, a revolution that challenges both the authority of the ruling class and

the legitimacy of traditional values, a revolution that is bound to change the lives of us all. But I am not about to go into the long history of the oppression of black Americans or to catalogue its tragic parallels in text books and teaching. [. . .] What I want to discuss is that body of American literature which until recently was omitted from the school curriculum and some methods of transmitting this literature to students. [. . .] Most importantly, as a result of the conspiracy of silence about the literary achievements of black Americans, our knowledge about America is at best incomplete and our qualifications for teaching black literature severely limited. What this means for the majority of teachers is that before they can educate others about the achievements of black writers they must first educate themselves. ("Black Literature" 3–4)

This talk appeared in April 1970 in a regional publication of the association.

Also in April 1970, my late colleague and fellow African Americanist Darwin Turner addressed the NCTE nationally in *College English* on two controversial issues in teaching African American literature: "1) the place of Afro-American literature in the curriculum, and 2) criteria for teachers and scholars of Afro-American literature." After affirming the academic value of African American literature and outlining three types of white teachers "who can be pitied" for the weaknesses they must overcome if they wish to teach African American literature well—"the unprepared, the subconscious racist, [and] the sentimentalist"—he is scornful of a fourth type. "He [or she] is the individual who views Afro-American literature as a vehicle for rapid promotion," says Turner. "He [or she] is the 'instant expert,' striving solely for grants and publications." Reinforcing the voices of our elders in historically black colleges and universities, Turner concludes with the caveat that "literature by Afro-Americans [. . .] needs to be taught, but only by teachers—black or white—who do all the homework which is required" (500, 505).

Today as yesterday, the more things change, the more they remain the same; the relationship of African American individual talent to tradition is as ironic, paradoxical, and complex as ever. Too many teachers, as Darwin Turner reminds us, are "thrust into a course in Afro-American literature after formal preparation of a summer or even less" (503). After only a single course with me as formal background on the subject, for example, one of my well-intentioned, reasonably intelligent white graduate students not only presumed to teach a summer college course on African American literature but was also hired without completing his degree the following semester to teach the subject in Scandinavia. Assuming that this audience is not only well-intentioned and intelligent but has already made a formal commitment to do all the homework required to teach African American literature well, let me divide my remarks today into two parts. First, I will outline the sociohistorical and sociocultural context for the validity and viability of a rhetorical, dialectical, dialogical, and critical pedagogy. Second, I will outline three vernacular theories of African American literature. If time and interest are sufficient, Professor Trudier Harris may join me in saying a few words about *Call and Response: The Riverside Anthology of the African American Literary Tradition,* a major project in reconstructing the African American literary canon that we are coediting with Patricia Hill, R. Baxter Miller, William Harris, and Sondra O'Neil and that is scheduled for publication by McGraw-Hill in December 1995.

As the contemporary Jensenites Richard Herrnstein and Charles Murray argue in *The Bell Curve: Intelligence and Class Structure in American Life,* Americans in our hip-hop nation and new world order of the 1990s still believe that black folks are inherently less intelligent than white folks. According to *Common Destiny: Blacks and American Society,* the 1989 updating by the National Research Council of Gunnar Myrdal's 1944 classic, though flawed, study, *An American Dilemma: The Negro Problem and Modern Democracy,* "The status of black Americans today can be characterized as a glass that is half full—if measured by the progress since 1939—or as a glass that is half empty—if measured by the persisting disparities between black and white Americans since the early 1970s" (Jaynes and Williams 4). This comes as no big surprise to my generation of socially aware and sensitive specialists in African American history and culture. Nor should it be a surprise to either my generation of educators or yours that, again according to *A Common Destiny,* most whites explain the causes of social and economic inequality between blacks and whites as individual lack of effort. "A 1981 national survey found that 65 percent of blacks rejected the claim that a lack of motivation or effort was responsible for black-white inequality, compared with 40 percent of whites," the editors report (151).

More recently, the *New York Times* reported on January 10, 1991, that the General Social Survey by the National Opinion Research Center of the University of Chicago found that the majority of whites still believe that "black and Hispanic people are more likely than whites to be lazy, violence-prone, less intelligent and less patriotic" ("Poll" B10). However, *A Common Destiny* concludes that "for many people low levels of support for affirmative action flow more from low levels of commitment to equality and a lack of awareness of social structural causes of inequality (coupled with prejudices) than from a high commitment to individualistic values" (Jaynes and Williams 153–54). In other words, although it is a fallacy to reduce the American racial pattern of progress and resistance exclusively to racial causes, "widespread attitudes of racism" among whites are responsible for "continuing resistance to full equality of black Americans" (155). The more things change, the more they remain the same.

How, then, should you teach black American literature to predominantly white or black college students in a time when and a place where white and black Republicans and some multiethnic Democratic conservatives approve a proposal by the Budget Committee of the House of Representatives to end all federal support for Howard University, the capstone of black academic institutions in the nation? At the same time as this draconian legislative action, a report by the Southern Education Foundation reveals that "statistics on college life in 12 states, all of which once operated *de jure* systems of segregation show that the proportion of black and Hispanic students at four-year colleges has remained at or below levels of the mid-1970s" (Healy A29). Should the fact that Gingrich, Dole, Gramm, and company use their political power (1) to argue disingenuously that federal affirmative action programs are no longer affordable or needed and (2) to pass a bill that subordinates the needs of the old, the sick, and the children of the poor to the desire for a tax cut by those taxpayers who earn less than $200,000 influence your pedagogy? Can, should, or ought you attempt to keep the politics of racial, ethnic, class, and gender differences out of institutional sites of learning?

My grandfather used to tell me that we may not get all we pay for in this life, "but Lord knows we sure enough pay for all we get." Educators should not only be committed to meeting the needs of students living in an historically racialized, hierarchically structured, multicultural society dominated by the hegemonic power of white people, especially men. They should also be enlightened enough to know and courageous enough to pursue their primary mission as educators to stimulate, challenge, and guide the development of critical intelligence in young adults and civic leaders of the twenty-first century. I therefore recommend that all phenomena and texts should be historicized, contextualized, and problematized. Was it Socrates who declared that the unexamined life isn't worth living? Political resistance to education that fosters understanding, tolerance, and respect for the differences as well as the commonalities of human culture should be contested. Among other things this means that through rigorous dialectic and dialogic methods of discourse the educator and student must situate themselves as well as the voices in the text under examination in a specific temporal, spatial, and sociocultural framework in order to deconstruct and reconstruct the deep as well as surface ideological meanings of the complex relationship of language, knowledge, and power in the text, in both its literary formalistic and anthropological semiotic sense.

Because of the protracted rite of passage of Americans of African descent, for example, our quest for national integration and racial/ethnic reintegration with full enforcement of our human and civil rights as African American citizens is still in progress. Our rite of passage, our quest for freedom, justice, and literacy with dignity as a people, began with the tragic irony of the enslavement of Africans by other Africans and our traumatic separation from Africa via the transatlantic slave trade, culminated in a devaluation of our humanity by Americans of British and European descent, and continues in a liminal experience of social marginality imposed by ceremonial acts of de facto racial discrimination, segregation, and lynching by the media as well as the mob. Perhaps the most ambivalent contemporary expression of our quest for freedom, justice, and literacy with dignity as a people is the move of middle-class blacks from inner-city neighborhoods after the raging urban revolts of 1968. The most pernicious and perverse expression is the intraracial, fratricidal gang-banging. And the most insidious and ironic are the desperate search for economic and psychological salvation in the drug culture and the commodification of hip-hop culture and glorification of thug life by gangsta rappers like Easy E, Tupac Shakur, Ice Cube, Dr. Dre, Ice T, and Snoop Doggy Dog, even though the latter four successfully turned their lives around in the entertainment industry.

The triumphs of the Civil Rights, Black Power, and Black Arts movements did not occur without the paying of heavy dues by many and the paying of the supreme price by too many, both black and white, young and old, male and female, upper class and underclass. Despite the Supreme Court's *Brown v. Board of Education* desegregation decision of 1954, the bombing deaths of four black girls in an Alabama church and the assassinations of Mississippi NAACP leader Medgar Evers and President Kennedy in 1963, of the murder of three civil rights workers in Mississippi in 1964, of the assassinations of Malcolm X in 1965 and Martin Luther King Jr. and Attorney General Robert Kennedy in 1968, the NAACP reports that "prior to Brown (1950), only 13.7% of blacks 25 or older were high school graduates. By 1991, that figure had reached 69.6%, but still 10% fewer than that of whites. Again in 1950, only 2.2% of blacks 25 or older were college graduates, one-third of the white rate. By 1991, 16.7% of blacks 25 or older were college graduates, compared to 22.2% of whites. [. . .] Further, the most segregated schools in America are now found in the Northeast, where in 1992 only 23.8% of minority children attended predominantly white schools and 50.1% attended 90–100% minority schools." A 1989 U.S. Department of Health and Human Services report reveals that blacks are twice as likely to die at birth, have twice the trouble getting jobs, are three times more likely to be poor, will endure more crime and divorce, and die six years sooner than whites. By virtually every official social index—mortality, health, occupation, income, education, and marital status—the racial inequality of African Americans, especially men, has stagnated or grown worse since the late 1970s. The more things change, the more they remain the same. This, in short, is the sociohistorical and sociocultural context in which texts by African Americans should be read and taught.

"The rhetoric of contemporary Afroamerican writers is revolutionary," I wrote in the winter 1969 issue of the *Massachusetts Review*.

> Its purpose is to destroy the myths and racial stereotypes of white America and to develop a viable aesthetic that reflects the point of view and affirms the cultural values of black Americans. In *Soul on Ice* Eldridge Cleaver recalls [...] the spontaneous reaction of a fellow prisoner to the Watts conflagration: "Baby," he said, "they walking in fours and kicking in doors; dropping Reds and busting heads; drinking wine and committing crime, shooting and looting; high-siding and low-riding, setting fires and slashing tires; turning over cars and burning down bars; making Parker mad and making me glad; putting an end to that 'go slow' crap and putting sweet Watts on the map—my black ass is in Folsom this morning but my black heart is in Watts!"
>
> The vitality of this rhetoric springs on the one hand from the shifting moods and tempos of the blues, spirituals, and jazz, and on the other from the dramatic tone, rich imagery, and wry humor of folk sermons and tales. It would be well, therefore, for those who are sincerely interested in understanding what black people are thinking and saying to begin by going to the source of the black American's culture—his folklore. ("A Key" 179).

Sparked apparently by the Watts riot or revolt, depending on one's ideological position, Lawrence W. Levine, with the aid of federal and private grants in 1965–66, began his reeducation in the field of African American history and culture, culminating in the 1977 publication of *Black Culture and Black Consciousness: Afro-American Folk Thought from Slavery to Freedom*, a major book in the field of African American Studies.

As I have noted here and elsewhere, a comparative methodology for interpreting African American literature has long been the prevailing wisdom of most specialists in the field. Every American writer of African descent speaks and writes with a dual voice that each inherits as part of his or her North American cultural legacy and that each develops, however marginally, in the elusive quest for status, power, and identity, both in the narrow Eurocentric sense of literary formalism and in the broader Afrocentric cultural sense. A Eurocentric worldview privileges Greece, Rome, and Europe as the birthplace of civilization and the universal standard of cultural excellence. In contrast, an Afrocentric worldview focuses on ancient Africa, including Egypt, as the more historically and archaeologically valid cradle of humankind and cultural diversity.

In "Tradition and the Individual Talent," T. S. Eliot argues for the Eurocentric imperative that writers must subscribe to and be assessed by canonical European literary standards and artists, ranging from Homer to those of their own time and place (49). In contrast, Richard Wright argues in "Blueprint for Negro Writing" that a dialectical European and African, white and black, formalistic and folkloristic perspective "should form the heritage of the Negro writer" (45). The point here is that black literary texts are sign systems whose referents are nonliterary as well as literary black and white texts that challenge readers to participate in reconstructing the meanings of the shared ironic and paradoxical experiences of black Americans' double consciousness, an aspect of African American identity that, as W. E. B. Du Bois explains in *The Souls of Black Folk* (1903), is both a burden and blessing.

Bakhtin's *The Dialogic Imagination* has complicated the distinctions among rhetorical, dialectical, and dialogical discourses between the different scholars of Artistotle's *Rhetoric* and Plato's *Phaedrus* and *Gorgias*. In "Dialogics as an Art of Discourse in Literary Criticism," my former colleague Don Bialostosky provides a lucid and cogent explanation of these distinctions that I have found useful for my examination of the Du Boisian double consciousness of African American literature. In Bialostosky's account,

> dialectic concerns impersonal relations among terms that are independent of those who hold them—relations of confirmation and contradiction, antithesis and synthesis, and the like. Rhetoric concerns relations of practical agreement and disagreement among persons—relations that may be effected, despite ideological differences in the formation of consensuses among divergent interests and parties. Dialogics concerns the relations among persons articulating their ideas in response to one another, discovering their mutual affinities and oppositions, their provoca-

tions to reply, their desires to hear more, or their wishes to change the subject. [. . .] Dialectic aims at discovering the truth of ideas or theses, rhetoric at determining the decisions of people, and dialogics at articulating the meaning of people's ideas, our own and those of others. As dialectic strives for conviction on a question and rhetoric for persuasion of an audience, dialogics strives for comprehensive responsiveness and responsibility to the consequential person—ideas of a time, culture, community, or discipline—that is, for the fullest articulation of someone's ideas with the actual and possible ideas of others. (789)

For an examination of double consciousness and double-voiced discourse in African American literature, the most important distinction here is between dialectics and dialogics. Although both are interpretive strategies that involve oppositional forces, the former signifies the dynamics of an historical process of inquiry for a truth that synthesizes partial, oppositional views and the latter the dynamics of a rhetorical process that acknowledges and articulates different voices.

A quick glance at the historical and social construction of the racial, ethnic, and national identities of African Americans by themselves and others illuminates some of the ironies and paradoxes of our continuing struggle for self-determination, justice, and social equality as human subjects and citizens rather than commodified objects. Too many teachers of American culture and character are either unable or unwilling to do the research necessary to discover that the first Americans of African descent did not arrive in the colonies with a monolithic group identity as "neegars," "nigras," or "Negroes" but with specific African ethnic identities. The majority were Ibo, Ibibio, Ewe, Biafada, Bakongo, Wolof, Bambara, Sere, and Arada. Unlike the first white immigrants to Massachusetts and their Mayflower Compact, they were the only people, as historian Lerone Bennett reminds us in *Before the Mayflower* (1971), that were brought in 1619 before the Mayflower to Virginia in chains, sold, and systematically deprived of their Old World cultural heritage and social systems in order to transform them from their initial fate as indentured servants into slave property for life. This development was the result of the interaction between institutionalized slavery and racism, for the increasing demand for cheap labor led to political acts and a social ideology of white supremacy and meritocracy that severely restricted or nullified the rights of blacks. Prior to the end of the seventeenth century, free blacks in Virginia could acquire property, including slaves, vote, and even intermarry with whites. But with the growth of slavery, the Black Codes of the eighteenth century reduced all blacks to a quasi-free lower caste. Christian and constitutional principles did not prevent the majority of Southerners and Northerners from arrogating to themselves supreme power over other human beings. And as Harriet Wilson reveals in 1859 in *Our Nig*, the first novel published by a black person in the United States, blacks, including servants, in the non-slave-based economies of the North, including many with white patrons and professed Christians, generally fared only a little better than their Southern brothers and sisters.

Etymologically derived from the Latin *niger* and the Portuguese and Spanish *negro* as the linguistic signs for the color black, "negro" was first used as a common noun for slaves by the Portuguese in 1441. Since the seventeenth century, the racial term has had many synonyms, spellings, and meanings, most frequently used as insults and slurs. In 1619 John Rolfe's journal identified the first enslaved Africans shipped to Virginia as "negars." By the end of the eighteenth century, the N-word, "nigger," became popular as a slur arguably as the result of institutional antiblack racism, as well as conscious and unconscious mispronunciation. The term "negro" became standard as a racialized socioeconomic concept by eighteenth- and nineteenth-century state laws that prohibited interracial marriage between whites and people with Negro ancestry or blood and was popular from about 1880 to 1960 (Poe 668–70). In 1930 the term became a proper noun, "Negro," as a result of the intervention of the interracial leadership of the NAACP. During the Black Power and Black Arts movements of the 1960s, "black," previously considered a badge of inferiority by most people of my pre–World War II generation, became popular with the help of the political action of the Student Nonviolent Coordinating Committee (SNCC) and the music of James Brown ("I'm Black and I'm Proud!") as a more prideful assertion of a broader and even diasporic racial and ethnic identity that affirmed both political and cultural distinctiveness and solidarity. "Afro-American" and "African American," believed by many folks as early as the 1920s to be the most accurate of the hybrid terms of biracial national identity with or without the hyphen, were also popular in the 1960s in affirming the common legacy of people of African descent in the United States, associating them with a specific place and past. Recently, the preference of many black intellectuals and artists is to use the name African American as a pronoun and noun without the hyphen as a sign of political, racial, and cultural affirmation. Until 1831, however, when the first convention of "People of Color" was held in Philadelphia to protest the revival of organized efforts by the American Colonization Society, founded in 1816 by a white minister, to send free blacks back to Africa, the most popular formal self-conscious group and institutional identity of free blacks was African: the

African Baptist Church (Silver Bluff, South Carolina, 1773–75; Williamsburg, Virginia, 1776; Savannah, Georgia, 1788), Free African Society (1787), New York African Free School (1787), African Mason Lodge (1787), and African Methodist Episcopal Church (1794).

"Language," literary theorists Rene Wellek and Austin Warren remind us, "is the material of literature as stone or bronze is of sculpture, paints of pictures, or sounds of music. But one should realize that language is not mere inert matter like stone but is itself a creation of men and is thus charged with the cultural heritage of a linguistic group" (22). African American folk or vernacular culture is the symbolic and material expression by black Americans of our relationship to nature, to our Creator, to our ethnic community, and to the white ruling class as we seek to change or maintain our environment and racialized hierarchical social structures in order to survive and thrive, both individually and collectively. Nationally, we find the roots of this culture in the Black Belt of the Deep South in the syncretism of residual Africanisms with elements of European and Native American culture, and in the dynamics of unequal, unjust racial, class, and ethnic differences. Culture thus signifies the constitutive social process by which people create specific, different ways of life as they adapt to environmental conditions and historical circumstances. For black Americans this process of acculturation has been shaped by a distinctive history: Africa, slavery, the Middle Passage, the Southern plantation, emancipation, Reconstruction, post-Reconstruction, northern migration, urbanization, industrialization, and most important, racism. The unique configuration of these historical experiences generated the interrelated processes of double consciousness, socialized ambivalence, and double vision that I believe best explain the complex, creative dynamics of African American culture and character.

As I have indicated in other lectures and studies, Du Bois defined the African American experience as the complex sociocultural and sociopsychological duality of Americans of African descent whose humanity and culture were institutionally devalued and marginalized by Americans of British and European descent. From a diasporic perspective, socialized ambivalence signifies a shifting identification between the values of the superordinate white and subordinate black cultural systems as a result of British and European imperialism, colonization, slavery, and institutionalized racism. In African American folklore and formal art, double vision refers to a tragicomic, wry perspective toward life as expressed primarily in the use of irony, paradox, and parody.

Having sociohistorically and socioculturally positioned myself as a senior black American specialist in African American cultural studies; having constructed my text as a dialectic and dialogic vernacular approach to reading and teaching African American texts; and having recognized you as an audience of predominantly white southern American teachers of American and African American literature, let me now focus more sharply on three vernacular theories of reading and teaching African American literature. As I've taken considerable time to explain as clearly and coherently as possible, the consensus of contemporary specialists in the fields of African American literary history and criticism is that the African American literary tradition is best understood and appreciated by interpreting its merits within the context of its own indigenous nature and function in the United States. Significant specialists and texts with this perspective to be consulted by teachers in the field include the following: Robert Stepto's *From Behind the Veil* (1979), which develops a structuralist approach to the intertextuality of call-and-response in canonical black texts; Barbara Christian's *Black Women Novelists* (1980), which traces the impact of negative stereotypic images on the narrative tradition of black women; Keith Beyerman's *Fingering the Jagged Grain* (1986), which focuses on the use of black folk materials in recent black fiction; Melvin Dixon's *Ride Out the Wilderness* (1987), which foregrounds ethnic spatial tropes as the distinctive feature of African American literature; Hazel Carby's *Reconstruction of Womanhood* (1987), which applies a cultural studies analysis to the nineteenth-century influence of black feminist discourse on the literary conventions of early black American women; and William Andrew's *To Tell a Free Story* (1988), which focuses on the uniquely self-liberating and empowering rhetorical strategies of black American autobiography.

Although all of these critical approaches are arguably responding on some level to the seminal work of Ralph Ellison's novel *Invisible Man* (1952) and collection of essays *Shadow and Act* (1964), the three vernacular theories by black American scholars that I believe are most pedagogically exciting and enlightening are by Houston A. Baker Jr., Henry Louis Gates Jr., and, so I modestly have been led to understand from colleagues and students, me. Baker's *Blues, Ideology, and Afro-American Literature* (1984) focuses on the blues as the key black vernacular trope; Gates's *The Signifying Monkey* (1988) privileges signifying and pastiche as the prototypical black vernacular and literary tropes; and Bell's *The Afro-American Novel and Its Tradition* (1987) interprets the African American novel as a socially symbolic act that formally encodes and wryly illumines the biracial, bicultural lives and residually oral tradition of African Americans.

Rather than the traditional approaches of historical survey, black classical texts, or images of black character in American literature, I have long been convinced that a systematic, rigorous dialectic and dialogic inquiry into the use of folklore or the vernacular in black American literature offers teachers the most challenging and effective method of stimulating and guiding students in the discovery of the complex relationship among language, power, and knowledge in their critical interrogations of the relationship of literature to life, fiction to fact, and myth to reality. The major difference in the vernacular theories of Baker, Gates, and Bell is that Baker focuses on music, Gates on language, and Bell on oratory, myth, legend, tale, and song as the principal cultural forms that generate the distinctive dialectic tension between oral and written African American literature.

Educated in the early 1960s as a specialist in Victorian literature at Howard University and the University of California, where he was a classmate of Addison Gayle Jr., Baker is one of the most distinguished and prolific living senior African American specialists in black American literary theory and practice in the world. His quest for an adequate theory of African American literature and culture began with teaching the subject at Yale in 1969. The quest continued with the publication in 1972 of his collection of essays, *Long Black Song*, and moved beyond the limitations of the folkloristic theory of black culture to the more richly complex "anthropology of art" of 1980 in *The Journey Back*. Shifting "from an exclusively symbolic to a more inclusively expressive perspective" in *Blues, Ideology, and Afro-American Literature*, the culmination of his quest, Baker argues that the blues is the essential vernacular trope for understanding both African American literature and American culture. "My quest during the past decade," he writes in the introduction,

> has been for the distinctive, the culturally specific aspects of Afro-American literature and culture. I was convinced that I had found such specificity in a peculiar subjectivity, but the objectivity of economics and the sound lessons of poststructuralism arose to reorient my thinking. I was also convinced that the symbolic and quite specifically the symbolically anthropological, offered avenues to the comprehension of Afro-American expressive culture in its plenitude. I discovered that the symbolic's antithesis—practical reason, or the material—is as necessary for understanding Afro-American discourse as the cultural-in-itself. My shift from a centered to a decentered subject [. . .] was prompted by the curious force of dialectical thought. (1–2)

This shift in rewriting his Eurocentric theory with an African American difference was inspired by close study of such scholars as Fredric Jameson, Hayden White, and Marshall Sahlins, as well as Hegel's *Phenomenology of Spirit.*

But how does Baker's use of the blues and vernacular theory provide him and readers of African American literature and culture with "a more inclusively expressive perspective"? Let's begin with his definition of vernacular. "The 'vernacular' in relation to human beings signals 'a slave born on his master's estate,'" Baker explains. "In expressive terms, vernacular indicates 'arts native or peculiar to a particular country or locale.' The material conditions of slavery in the United States and the rhythms of Afro-American blues combined and emerged from my revised materialistic perspective as an ancestral matrix that has produced a forceful and indigenous American creativity. The moment of emergence of economic and vernacular concerns left me [. . .] somewhere between symbolic anthropology and analytical strategies that Fredric Jameson calls the 'ideology of form'" (2).

Addressing the ideological anxieties of resisting readers, Baker assures us that Jameson's mode of inquiry "escapes all hints of 'vulgar Marxism' through its studious attention to modern critiques of political economy, and also through its shrewd incorporation of poststructuralist thought." To avoid naive, reductive analytical models and interpretations that directly correlate the economic base to its superstructure, current critiques of political economy interpret production and modes of production in semiotic terms. "To read economics as a semiotic process," Baker argues, "leads to the realization that ideological analyses may be as decidedly intertextual as, say, analyses of the relationship between Afro-American vernacular expression and more sophisticated forms of verbal art. If what is normally categorized as *material* (e.g., 'raw material,' 'consumer goods') can be interpreted semiotically, then any collection of such entities and their defining interrelationships may be defined as a *text*" (2–3).

But rather than interpret material in exclusive terms of semiotics, Baker focuses "directly on the living and laboring conditions of people designated as 'the desperate class' by James Weldon Johnson's narrator in *The Autobiography of an Ex-Colored Man.* Such people constitute the vernacular in the United States. Their lives have always been sharply conditioned by an 'economics of slavery' as they worked the agricultural rows, searing furnaces, rolling levees, bustling roundhouses, and pine-woods logging camps of America. A sense of 'production' and 'modes of production' that foregrounds such Afro-American labor seems an appropriate inscription of the material" (3). Even before explaining how the blues fits into Baker's vernacular theory and practice, I have already suggested that teachers who wish to appropriate and adapt his approach as a pedagogical model certainly have a lot more serious homework to do than just study black music. Perhaps this is one of the reasons that, unlike feminist literary criticism, African American literary criticism is neither taught in most graduate schools nor anthologized in current texts on critical theory. The more things change, the more they remain the same.

In any event, what is Baker's concept of the blues? Why and how is it a vernacular expression of America? Baker conceives of blues as a matrix. "A matrix is a womb, a network, a fossil-bearing rock, a rocky trace of a gemstone's removal, a principal metal in an alloy, a mat or plate for reproducing print or phonograph records," he writes. "The matrix is a point of ceaseless input and output, a web of intersecting, crisscrossing impulses always in productive transit. Afro-American blues constitute such a vibrant network. They are what Jacques Derrida might describe as the 'always already' of Afro-American culture. They are the multiplex, enabling *script* in which Afro-American cultural discourse is inscribed" (3–4).

Although, as Eileen Southern's invaluable scholarship establishes in *The Music of Black Americans* (1971), W. C. Handy was arguably the first man to compose a formal blues score in 1909 and the first to popularize the sale of blues scores in 1912, two blues pieces actually appeared prior to his "Memphis Blues" in 1912. The "Baby Seals Blues," written by the black rag-pianist Artie Matthews, appeared in August 1912 and "The Dallas Blues," written by the white songwriter Hart A. Wand, appeared the following month. Handy's "Memphis Blues" came out three weeks later, followed by his "Jogo Blues" in 1913, "St. Louis Blues" in 1914, and "Joe Turner Blues" in 1915" (339). In developing his vernacular theory of African American literature, Baker constructs an elaborate and complex philosophical definition of the blues that challenges the dominance of poststructural antiessentialist theories in Ivy League academies. "Rather than a rigidly personalized form," he writes, "the blues offer a phylogenetic recapitulation—a nonlinear, freely associative, nonsequential meditation—of species experience. [. . .] The blues are a synthesis (albeit one always synthesizing rather than one already hypostatized). Combining work songs, group seculars, field hollers, sacred harmonies, proverbial wisdom, folk philosophy, political commentary, ribald humor, elegiac lament, and much more, they constitute an amalgam that seems always to have been in motion in America—always becoming, shaping, transforming, displacing the peculiar experiences of Africans in the New World" (5).

Baker concludes his scholarly contemporary definition of the blues by classifying it as a code of African American cultural signifying and an equivalent to Hegelian "force." In the first instance, "The materiality of any blues manifestation, such as a guitar's walking bass or a French harp's 'whoop' of motion seen, is [. . .] enciphered in ways that enable the material to escape into a named or coded, blues signification. The material, thus, slips into irreversible difference. And as phenomena named and set in meaningful relation by a blues code, both the harmonica's whoop and the guitar's bass can recapitulate vast dimensions of experience. For such discrete blues instances are always intertextually related by the blues code as a whole. Moreover, they are involved in the code's manifold interconnections with other codes of Afro-American culture." In the second instance, analogous to Hegel's explanation in *The Phenomenology of the Spirit*, "Force is [. . .] defined as a relational matrix where *difference* is the law [. . .] and as an image for the investigation of culture, represents a *force* not unlike electricity. [. . .] The blues, therefore, comprise a mediational site where familiar antinomies are resolved (or dissolved) in the office of adequate cultural understanding." For Baker, the mediational site and trope for the blues is "an image of the black blues singer at the railway junction lustily transforming experiences of a durative (unceasingly oppressive) landscape into the energies of rhythmic song. [. . .] The singer's product, like the railway juncture itself (or a successful translator's original), constitutes a lively scene, a robust matrix, where endless antinomies are mediated and understanding and explanation find conditions of possibility" (6–7).

Turning to why and how the blues is a vernacular expression of America, Baker argues that "the blues should be privileged in the study of American culture to precisely the extent that inventive understanding successfully converges with blues force to yield accounts that persuasively and playfully refigure expressive geographies in the United States." For African Americans the railroad became the symbol of economic progress and, because of "the locomotive's drive and thrust, its promise of unrestrained mobility and unlimited freedom," of aesthetic expression. "The blues musician at the crossing [. . .] became an expert at reproducing or translating these locomotive energies," Baker writes. "With the birth of the blues, the vernacular realm of American culture acquired a music that had 'wide appeal because it expressed a toughness of spirit and resilience, a willingness to transcend difficulties which was strikingly familiar to those whites who remembered their own history.' [. . .] The signal expressive achievement of the blues, then, lay in their translation of technological innovativeness, unsettling demographic fluidity, and boundless frontier energy into expression which attracted avid interest from the American masses" (11). Teachers and readers who find Baker's blues vernacular theory and practice too intellectually and politically bold and difficult may either tailor it to suit their pedagogical situation or consider, among others, the approaches of Gates and Bell.

Although his education in British, African American, and African literatures at Yale and Cambridge Universities began in 1969, and although his first edited book, *Black Literature and Literary Theory*, was published in 1984, Gates did not significantly begin to realize his quest to locate "within the African and Afro-American traditions a system of rhetoric and interpretation that could be drawn upon both as *figures* for a genuinely 'black' criticism and as *frames* through which [. . . to] interpret, or 'read,' theories of contemporary literary criticism" until around 1977 (*Figures in Black* ix). Gates launched his professional career as an academic literary theorist, he admits in the introduction of his first book, *Figures in Black: Words, Signs, and the "Racial" Self* (1987), with polemical critiques published in 1979 of the three major academic Black Arts critics: Houston Baker Jr., Addison Gayle Jr., and Stephen Henderson. "If my analysis of the tautological dead end of their theories of black literature was accurate," Gates writes, "then I felt that I could use non-black theories to detour, or step around, a position about black criticism that held no promise for my work." Critical responses to what he subsequently considered "somewhat excessive and too polemical" arguments for formalism led to "a sustained interest in the black vernacular tradition as a source field in which to ground a theory of Afro-American criticism, a theory at once self-contained and related by analogy to other contemporary theories" (*Figures in Black* xxviii–xxix). The blueprint for his examination of the relationship between the African and African American vernacular traditions and black literature in *The Signifying Monkey* (1988) is included as the last chapter of his first book.

"Ralph Ellison's example of a thoroughly integrated critical discourse, informed by the black vernacular tradition and Western criticism, provided the model for my work," Gates writes in the preface of his magnum opus. "Ishmael Reed's formal revision and critique of the Afro-American literary tradition [. . .] helped to generate this theory, especially as Reed manifested his critique in the third novel, *Mumbo Jumbo*. It seemed to me that the relation of Reed's text to those of Ralph Ellison and Richard Wright, Jean Toomer and Sterling A. Brown, and Zora Neale Hurston, was a Signifyin(g) relation, as the Afro-American tradition would have it. Through Reed's character, Papa La Bas, I was able to construct a myth of origins for Signifyin(g) and its sign, the Signifying Monkey" (ix). Acknowledging *Blues, Ideology, and Afro-American Literature* as "subtle and insightful," he also states that "Baker's use of the black vernacular inspired my own approach to theory by assuring me that I was on the right path. My reading of his manuscript convinced me that in the blues and in Signifyin(g) were to be found the black tradition's two great repositories of its theory of itself, encoded in musical and linguistic forms. This book, in so many ways, was written out of my deep regard for Houston Baker's critical presence" (x). In contrast, Baker's trenchant criticism of Gates in *Black Studies, Rap, and the Academy* (1993) as an authority on rap in the criminal defense case of 2 Live Crew for their salacious rap performances further underscores that the more things change, the more they remain the same.

But what is the Signifying Monkey and its relationship to the language and literature of African Americans? Gates interprets the Signifying Monkey as the transplanted African trickster figure Esu-Elegbara:

> At first glance, these two tricksters would seem to have little in common. Esu, both a trickster and the messenger of the gods, figures prominently in the mythologies of Yoruba cultures found in Nigeria, Benin, Brazil, Cuba and Haiti, among others. The Signifying Monkey, it seems, is distinctly Afro-American. Nevertheless, the central place of both figures in their traditions is determined by their curious tendency to reflect on the uses of formal language. The theory of Signifyin(g) arises from these moments of self-reflexiveness.
>
> Whereas Esu serves as a figure for the nature and function of interpretation and double-voiced utterance, the Signifying Monkey serves as the figure-of-figures as the trope in which are encoded several other peculiarly black rhetorical tropes" (xxi).

Both tricksters represent certain principles of verbal expression, which Gates compares to reveal the forms of language each uses in the production of meaning in literature. He demonstrates "that the Monkey's language of Signifyin(g) functions as a metaphor for formal revision, or intertextuality, within the Afro-American literary tradition." He also attempts "to show through their functional equivalency that the two figures are related historically and are distinct aspects of a larger, unified phenomenon" (xxi). Because Gates does not draw this line of descent from "archeological evidence of a transmission process, but [. . .] from] their functional equivalency as figures of rhetorical strategies and of interpretation" (53), his theory is intriguing and useful, but problematic.

Relying on research by anthropologists, folklorists, linguists, sociolinguists, and literary artists, as well as drawing on materials by black folks, themselves, Gates explains how signifying as a rhetorical strategy emanates directly from the Signifying Monkey toasts or tales. As most black American males of my generation know from experience, the action represented in Monkey tales turns on the survival traits and tactics of three stock characters—the Monkey, the Lion, and the Elephant. "The Monkey—a trickster figure, like Esu, who is full of guile, who tells lies, and who is a rhetorical genius—is intent on demystifying the Lion's self-imposed status as King of the Jungle," Gates reminds us (56). Because the Monkey is no match for the physical prowess of the Lion and the Elephant is, the Monkey seeks to trick the Lion into a conflict with the Elephant, who is the true king of the jungle. "This the Monkey does with a rhetorical trick, a trick of mediation," Gates explains. "Indeed, the Monkey is a term of (anti)mediation, as are all trickster figures between two forces he seeks to oppose for his own contentious purposes, and then to reconcile. The Monkey's trick of mediation—or, more properly, antimediation—is a play on language use. He succeeds in reversing the Lion's status by supposedly repeating a series of insults purportedly uttered by the Elephant about the Lion's closest relatives (his wife, his 'mama,' his 'grandmama, too'). These intimations of sexual use, abuse, and violation constitute one well-known and commonly used mode of Signifyin(g)" (56). After the Lion confronts the Elephant, who deflates his kingly pretensions with a severe beating, the Lion returns to punish the Monkey for his deception. The Monkey then signifies on the Lion with a stream of witty, rhyming, rhythmic, vulgar verbal insults.

After providing a wide range of folk and academic explanations and examples of signifying by H. Rap Brown, Roger Abrahams, Thomas Kochman, and Claudia Mitchell-Kiernan, Gates draws on the classifications of sociolinguist Geneva Smitherman as the most explicit instructive typology: "For Smitherman, Signifyin(g) is a black 'mode of discourse' that is a synonym of 'droppin lugs; joanin; capping; [and] sounding.' For her, Signification has the following eight characteristics: 1. indirection, circumlocution[;] 2. metaphorical-imagistic (but images rooted in the everyday, real world[;] 3. humorous, ironic[;] 4. rhythmic fluency and sound[;] 5. teachy but not preachy[;] 6. directed at person or persons usually present in the situational context[;] 7. punning, play on words[; and] 8. introduction of the semantically or logically unexpected" (94). Emphasizing the importance of repetition and revision, parody and pastiche, in black language and literature, Gates convincingly concludes, "Rhetorical naming by indirection is central to our notions of figuration, troping, and of the parody of forms, or pastiche, in evidence when one writer repeats another's structure by one of several means, including a fairly exact repetition of a given narrative or rhetorical structure, filled incongruously with a ludicrous or incongruent context" (103). For readers and teachers prepared to do a lot of homework, Gates's move from a Eurocentric to an Afrocentric theory of

African American literary criticism is a challenging and instructive approach to reading and teaching African American literature.

Educated at Howard University and the University of Massachusetts, I began my quest for an indigenous theory of African American literature in 1958 under the mentorship of Professor Brown. (Both he and his wife, Daisy, were light, bright, and damn near white and both were proudly determined to be Negroes till the day they died.) In 1972 in the introduction to my first edited book, *Modern and Contemporary Afro-American Poetry,* I wrote, "Historically, Afro-American poetry has its roots in the African slaves' lyrical affirmation of life. It is to the black unknown bards of the spirituals and folk songs—a unique fusion of a centuries-old African sensibility and an inchoate Puritan American culture—that America is indebted for its most priceless music, those sorrowful and joyous songs that subtly yet forcefully decried oppression and celebrated the possibilities of the human spirit. And whatever is distinctively racial in the poetry of this generation of black poets is, it seems to me, attributable to the creative forces of this heritage" (1).

In 1974 in the third volume of the Broadside Critics Series' *The Folk Roots of Contemporary Afro-American Poetry,* I made a modest case for the importance of Herder's folk ideology on the quest of black writers for an indigenous art. "Major attempts by Afro-American academicians and artists to identify the strengths of Afro-American folk art and its potentialities for a Black American tradition of high art have been strikingly similar to the spirit if not the letter of Herder's folk ideology," I wrote. "I have found no documentary evidence that W. E. B. Du Bois, Alain Locke or James Weldon Johnson—the elder statesmen of the Harlem Renaissance of the Twenties—nor Richard Wright, Ralph Ellison or Imamu Amiri Baraka (LeRoi Jones)—the spiritual fathers of the Black Arts movement of the sixties—had read Herder. But there is more than adequate circumstantial evidence that they were familiar with Anglo-American interpretations of Herder's theory that folk art laid the base for high art and the corollary concept of folksong as a spontaneous, indigenous expression of the collective soul of a people" (20–21).

In an effort to move beyond the limitations of a prescriptive literary social realism and sociocultural romanticism in order to map the multiple dialectic conflicts and tensions in African American culture and literature—for example, between past and present, white and black, European and African, Euro-American and Afro-American, male and female, oral and print, the romance and the novel—*The Afro-American Novel and Its Tradition* (1987) employs an interdisciplinary approach that focuses on the complex sociohistorical, sociopsychological, and sociocultural folk roots and contemporary branches of the African American narrative tradition, especially the romance and novel. It is grounded in three basic assumptions. First, although the current orthodoxy is crossing boundaries, there has always been a cultural and social boundary in America beyond which black Americans could not go without great risk to their lives and liberty. "It was [. . .] from this position as the prototypical outsiders and marginal people of American culture and society," I wrote, "that representative black American novelists began exploring the literary possibilities of their residual oral Afro-American folk forms and Western literary tradition (their dual African and Western cultural heritages) for appropriate structures and language to construct their visions of the human condition as filtered through the prism of their particular time, place, and ethnic group." Second, "inadequate attention by readers and critics to such literary matters as genre, structure, style, characterization, and point of view has led to misunderstandings about the merits of individual Afro-American novelists as artists and about their use of the narrative tradition." Finally, "the Afro-American novel is not merely a branch of the Euro-American novel but also a development of the Afro-American oral tradition" (xii–xiii).

Since I've already outlined in the first half of my talk the important sociohistorical, sociopsychological, and sociocultural elements of my vernacular theory, let me conclude with a few remarks on the residually oral forms:

> Cultures in which oral forms compete with print, as in the case of the black American subculture, may be classified as residually or largely oral cultures. "The residual," Raymond Williams explains, [. . .] "has been effectively formed in the past, but it is still active in the cultural process, not only and often not at all as an element of the past, but as an effective element of the present. Thus certain experiences, meanings, and values which cannot be expressed or substantially verified in terms of the dominant culture are nevertheless lived and practised on the basis of the residue—cultural as well as social—of some previous social and cultural institution or formation." In contrast to literate cultures, residually oral cultures are basically aural, functional, collective, and direct. Like oral cultures, they stress performance, mnemonics, and improvisational skills. The tendency is to focus on the here and now, to employ some kind of formulaic mode of expression, and to subordinate the individual to the group or type. Whereas an oral culture relies primarily on sound, the spoken word, and a literate culture primarily on sight, the written

word, residually oral cultures rely on the interplay or dialectic between the two. (*Afro-American Novel* 20–21)

Several residually oral forms may be identified in the African American novel: oratory, including the vernacular; myth, including ritual; tale; and song. In contrast to the vernacular theories of Baker and Gates, I therefore propose five rather than a single vernacular form for reading, critiquing, and teaching the rich diversity of African American literature. But either of these vernacular approaches to teaching African American literature provides a comparative, dialectic strategy that can be creatively and critically expanded in any manner the instructor and students consider appropriate for their study of American cultural diversity.

Well, as the refrain of a once-popular R&B song reminds us, "mama said there'd be days like this, there'd be days like this, my mama said." But we also know that the more things change, the more they remain the same. The lessons of the ancestors and elders also remind us, as gospel singer Sam Cooke sang inspiringly, "It's been a long time coming, but I know a change's goin' come." What black folks and committed educators, black and white, know and need to do to turn things around, if not upside down, at this juncture, then, is to educate themselves better about African American literary theory and practice in order to take care of the business, as Ralph Ellison reminds us, of changing the joke and slipping the yoke.

II

Mark Twain's "Nigger" Jim: The Tragic Face behind the Minstrel Mask

In celebration of the centennial anniversary of the publication of Mark Twain's Adventures of Huckleberry Finn, *I received and accepted with excitement the invitation from Thomas Tenney, the editor of the* Mark Twain Journal, *to participate in the critical debate on the representation of slavery, Southern culture, African American character, and racial epithets in the novel. Professor Thadious M. Davis was the guest editor of the Fall 1984 special issue of the journal titled "Black Writers on* Adventures of Huckleberry Finn *One Hundred Years Later." It contained intellectually provocative and informative articles by eight black scholars, critics, and writers: Richard K. Barksdale, Rhett S.*

Jones, Julius Lester, Charles H. Nichols, Charles H. Nilon, Arnold Rampersad, David Smith, and Kenny J. Williams. My essay appeared along with seven additional black and white Twain critics and educators in the Spring 1985 issue. In 1992 fifteen essays by black critics, including the earlier eight and my own, were published by editors James S. Leonard, Thomas A. Tenney, and Thadious M. Davis with the title Satire or Evasion? Black Perspectives on Huckleberry Finn *to demonstrate the diverse range of interpretations of the novel by black educators and critics. The thesis of my essay is that the representation of the impact of slavery, Southern antiblack racism, and blackface minstrelsy on the complex identity formation of Jim and Twain, especially the compassion behind their comic, occasionally ironic, masks, can best be fully understood and appreciated by interpreting* Adventures of Huckleberry Finn *in its sociohistorical and literary contexts.*

WITH THE CRY THAT IT IS "RACIST TRASH" AND SHOULD BE BANNED FROM PUBLIC schools and libraries, the battle lines are again drawn. Even though it has been a hundred years since the publication of the *Adventures of Huckleberry Finn*, controversy still clouds the achievement of this tragicomic, satirical antislavery novel. Unlike nineteenth-century white readers and censors like the Public Library of Concord, Massachusetts, that condemned it as "trash and suitable for the slums" (Haight, *Banned Books* 57), many modern-day black readers are less offended by the vulgarity and delinquency of Huck, the rebellious teenaged narrator protagonist, than by the minstrel image of Miss Watson's runaway slave, Jim, his companion in "crime" against the conventional morality, religion, and respect for property of the period (Hentoff).[1] For some blacks the frequent (more than 150 times) use of the epithet "nigger" and general ridicule of Afro-American character for the enjoyment of whites are only the proverbial tip of the iceberg. Beneath the surface are the claims of white liberal scholars and commentators that Mark Twain, clearly a product of his time, place, and people, was, in the often-quoted phrase of his close friend William Dean Howells, a "desouthernized Southerner" (Howells 50).

Does the historical and literary evidence support the notion that America's most popular and representative nineteenth-century humorist and satirist escaped or outgrew the influence of the racial prejudice and discrimination endemic to the period? Born and bred in the antebellum Southwest, a volunteer in the Confederate militia, and an advocate of the delightful accuracy of minstrelsy, Twain, as we will see, struggles valiantly, like Huck, to reject the legacy of American racism and to accept his personal share of responsibility for the injustice of slavery, but never in the *Adventures of Huckleberry Finn* does he fully and unequivocally accept the equality of blacks. "Writing at a time when the blackfaced minstrel was still popular, and shortly after a war which left even the abolitionists weary of those people associated with the Negro, Twain," as Ralph Ellison noted in the 1950s during the public attack by blacks on the racial offensiveness of the book, "fitted Jim into the outlines of the minstrel tradition, and it is from behind this stereotype mask that we see Jim's dignity and human capacity—and Twain's complexity—emerge" ("Change the Joke" 50). The portrayal of the complex humanity of Jim and Twain—their pernicious, tragic racism as well as the compassion behind their comic, occasionally ironic, masks—can best be fully understood and appreciated as an American classic rather than trash by interpreting the *Adventures of Huckleberry Finn* in its sociohistorical as well as literary context. Let us begin, therefore, with the racial climate in which Samuel Langhorne Clemens, alias Mark Twain, lived and wrote and then examine the deployment of point of view in the novel to discover the tragic face behind Jim's minstrel mask.

Twain's Socialization in the Ethics of Jim Crow

The major achievement of *Huck Finn* is its realistic and humorous portrayal of the moral hypocrisy of antebellum life along the Mississippi River and its satirical attack on slavery. What clouds this achievement is Twain's moral ambivalence about the humanity of blacks. The principle source of this ambivalence and the ethics that inform the novel is his boyhood experience with racism and slavery in Hannibal, Missouri, the town in which his family settled in 1839, four years after his birth in Florida, Missouri. Although everybody in Hannibal was poor, Twain recalls in his autobiography, the small town "was a little democracy which was full of liberty, equality, and Fourth of July, and sincerely so, too; yet you perceived that the aristocratic taint was there" (qtd. in Paine 120). (The "aristocratic taint" in his own old Virginia and Kentucky family stock was mainly the legacy of his father, John Marshall Clemens—by profession a lawyer and by vocation a land speculator, storekeeper, justice of the peace, and slave-trader (J. Kaplan 15)—whose declining fortunes led to the family's move from Tennessee to Missouri and ultimate bankruptcy. The paradox of Twain's memory of his background—aside from revealing his penchant as a storyteller to stretch the truth and from suggesting the conflict in his character between being a poor old southwestern river man and a wealthy eastern writer, businessman, and world traveler—"was mainly due to the circumstance that the town's population had come from slave states and still had the institution of slavery with them in their new home" (Paine 120). Underscoring the fact that Twain's enlightened attitude "that slavery was a bald, grotesque and unwarrantable usurpation" came later in life is his confession that "In my schoolboy days, I had no aversion to slavery. I was not aware that there was anything wrong about it. No one arraigned it in my hearing; the local papers said nothing against it; the local pulpit taught us that God approved it; if the slaves themselves had any aversion to slavery they were wise and said nothing" (*Autobiography* 6). Explaining with unintentional irony why "our slaves were convinced and content," he tells us in his autobiography that there was nothing about the slavery of the Hannibal region to rouse one's dozing humane instincts to activity. It was the mild domestic slavery, not the brutal plantation article. Cruelties were very rare, and exceedingly and wholesomely unpopular. To separate and sell the members of a slave family to different masters was a thing not well liked by the people, and so it was not often done, except in the settling of estates (Paine 123–24). Growing up in what was actually an antebellum midwestern slave state (thanks to the Missouri Compromise of 1820), Twain, in short, was no better or worse in his attitude and behavior toward blacks than other self-proclaimed benevolent white supremacists of his region and class.

When, then, does Twain become the desouthernized southwesterner or reformed midwesterner with Southern values? Did leaving Hannibal in 1853 for New York arouse his "dozing humane instincts to activity"? Certainly not right away, for in a letter to his mother concerning the circumstances of free blacks he saw, he writes, "I reckon I had better black my face, for in these Eastern States niggers are considerably better than white people" (qtd. in Wecter 20). After working for four years in the East and Midwest as a printer and news correspondent, Twain went south to New Orleans and became a riverboat pilot on the Mississippi. It was while visiting his hometown of Hannibal in 1861, he tells us in the semiautobiographical sketch "The Private History of a Campaign That Failed," that he joined the local Confederate militia as a second lieutenant. In neither the sketch nor his autobiography does Twain express any moral concern about his defense of slavery; instead, he humorously claims that he "resigned" after two weeks because he "was 'incapacitated by fatigue' through persistent retreating" (*Autobiography* 102). But in *Mark Twain and Southwestern Humor* Kenneth S. Lynn more accurately tells us:

> Not long after his enlistment, a hayloft in which he and some of his soldiers were sleeping caught fire, and lieutenant Clemens was forced to

jump for the barnyard below. In the fall, he painfully sprained his ankle and had to be put to bed. By the time he was up and about, he had had enough of fighting for a cause he only half-believed in, so that when his brother Orion [. . .] was appointed Territorial Secretary of Nevada, Twain leaped at the chance to secede from the Secession and go along as secretary to the Secretary. (141)

In *Mark Twain: Social Critic* Philip S. Foner also points out that it was not antislavery sentiment but "a boil, a sprained ankle, and heavy rain" that hastened Twain's desertion from the Confederacy (255). When Twain went west in 1861, his experiences as a reporter, silver prospector, gold miner, and, later, world traveler certainly helped to democratize and deepen his humanity. But even after becoming a transplanted New Englander in 1871, publishing the deeply moving attack on the plantation tradition from the black perspective of Aunt Rachel in "A True Story" in 1875, observing firsthand the changes in the post-Reconstruction South in 1882, and developing, around the same time, a friendship with George W. Cable (a reformed Southern writer who was driven north for his criticism of the South), Twain never completely outgrew the racial prejudice and paternalism of his boyhood. Rather than an unequivocal commitment to egalitarianism, Twain's post-Reconstruction statement "that (bar one) I have no race prejudices, and I think I have no color prejudices nor caste prejudices nor creed prejudices. [. . .] All that I care to know is that a man is a human being—that is enough for me; he can't be worse" reveals the ambivalence and pessimism of his final years (*Autobiography* 237). Behind the comic mask that Twain wears in his writings, in other words, is the complex humanity of a southwesterner whose ethics were shaped by the racism that defined the possibilities and limitations of democracy and freedom in nineteenth-century America.

Lamenting in 1906 the death of "the real nigger show—the genuine nigger show, the extravagant nigger show—the show which to me had no peer and whose peer has not yet arrived, in my experience," Twain writes: "To my mind it was a thoroughly delightful thing, and a most competent laughter-compeller and I am sorry it is gone" (DeVoto, *Mark Twain in Eruption* 110, 115).

He saw his first minstrel show in Hannibal in the 1840s. "It was a new institution," he reminds us. "In our village of Hannibal we had not heard of it before, and it burst upon us as a glad and stunning surprise." Sharing the commonplace notion of white contemporaries that their imitation of black character and culture was realistic as well as funny, he writes:

> The minstrels appeared with coal-black hands and faces and their clothing was a loud and extravagant burlesque of the clothing worn by the plantation slave of the time; *not that the rags of the poor slave were burlesqued, for that would not have been possible; burlesque could have added nothing in the way of extravagance to the sorrowful accumulation of rags and patches which constituted his costume*; it was the form and color of his dress that was burlesqued. [. . .] *The minstrel used a very broad negro dialect; he used it competently and with easy facility and it was funny—delightfully and satisfyingly funny.* (DeVoto, *Mark Twain in Eruption* 111; emphasis added)

The buffoonery and extravagant comic arguments of Bones and Banjo, the stock minstrel characters, were believed to be particularly funny: "Sometimes the quarrel would last five minutes; the two contestants shouting deadly threats in each other's faces with their noses not six inches apart, the house shrieking with laughter all the while at this happy and accurate imitation of the usual and familiar negro quarrel"[2] (111; emphasis added). Since minstrelsy was a national symbolic ritual of debasement of blacks for petty profit and for the psychological distancing of whites from their personal responsibility in the tragic perversion of American principles, Twain's taste in humor reveals his socialization as an American, not merely as a southwesterner, in the ethics of white supremacy.

As an apprentice writer, Twain was also influenced by the offensive racism of southwestern humor. His notebooks reveal that he was familiar with Augustus B. Longstreet's *Georgia Scenes* (1835), Johnson J. Hooper's *Some Adventures of Captain Simon Suggs* (1845), Joseph G. Baldwin's *Rush Times in Alabama and Mississippi* (1853), and George W. Harris's *Sut Lovingood* (1867). These southwestern frontier humorists used coarse, violent humor in the oral tradition as an entertaining form of local color and irreverence for rank and respectability. The chief characteristics of their writings include the use of frame stories, monologues, puns, eye dialect, concrete details, incongruity, gross exaggeration, understatement, caricature, anecdotes, tall tales, and sharp common sense (Blair, *Native American Humor* 62–101). "In the decade of Dred Scott and bleeding Kansas," Lynn reminds us, "Southwestern jokes at the black man's expense reached an apotheosis of fury. George Washington Harris's Sut Lovingood delighted in humiliating and frightening slaves; while black men yelled with pain or terror, Sut stood by and snickered" (104). Twain's offensive remarks in a series of travel letters to the *Alta California* in 1869 about the odor of blacks and his caricature of Blind Tom, the celebrated black pianist, as a minstrel are early evidence of this influence (Lynn 145). In the same year, however, Twain wrote a satirical editorial in the *Buffalo Express* against the lynching of blacks. Later, behind the ironic mask of Huck and the comic mask of Jim we sense Twain's continuing moral conflict in acknowledging the humanity of blacks to a dual audience of white readers of the post-Reconstruction South and North.

Twain's Relationship to His Audience, Huck, and Jim

One of the best ways to clear up the confusion about the nature of the humanity behind the masks in Huck Finn is to address the three basic questions concerning the vantage point from which the author tells the story: (1) How is the story told? (2) When is it told? and (3) Where does the author stand in relation to his audience, narrator, and principal characters? Quite clearly, the story of the friendship and flight to freedom of a poor white boy and a runaway slave is told by a young, first-person, naïve narrator-protagonist: the thirteen- or fourteen-year-old "uncivilized" son of an antebellum frontier-town drunk. This is immediately evident in the narrator's colloquial, direct introduction of himself to us in the opening chapter. By identifying himself as one of the principal characters in *The Adventures of Tom Sawyer*, a book by "Mr. Mark Twain [. . .] which is mostly a true book, with some stretchers, as I said before" (DeVoto, *Portable Mark Twain* 193–94), Huck, reinforcing the irony of Twain's prefatory warning to readers searching for motive, moral, or plot in the book, suggests that the narrative is merely a humorous sequel to *Tom Sawyer*. But the gradual development of Huck's ironic struggle to free himself from the moral hypocrisy, romantic conventions, and racial stereotypes of nineteenth-century America reveals another more serious, essentially satirical thematic purpose, mode of characterization, and structural design. Called "a fool" by Miss Watson because he does not believe that "a body can get anything they pray for," and "a numbskull" by Tom Sawyer because he does not romanticize a Sunday-school picnic as "a whole parcel of Spanish merchants and rich A-rabs" (207), Huck struggles with the conflict between the ascribed identity as "poor white trash" and the affirmation of his essential humanity. Psychologically, the internalized community conventions are in conflict with his own natural impulses toward freedom, common sense, and compassion. He first tells us about this conflict and quest in the first chapter, suggestively titled "I Discover Moses and the Bulrushers": "The widow Douglas she took me for her son and allowed she would sivilize me; but it was rough living in the house all the time, considering how dismal regular and decent the widow was in all her ways, and so when I couldn't stand it no longer I lit out. I got into my old rags and my sugar-hogshead again, and was free and satisfied" (194). And then in the chapter "I Spare Miss Watson's Jim," we witness Huck's first dramatic evidence of sympathy for Jim when he promises not to turn him in: "People would call me a low-down Abolitionist and despise me for keeping mum—but that don't make no difference. I ain't a-going to tell, and I ain't a-going back there, anyways" (241).

As a naïve, unreliable narrator, Huck is unaware of the moral courage he demonstrates in his relationship to Jim, and, unlike the author and modern reader, condemns himself for his inability to conform fully to the norms of the Widow Douglas and Tom Sawyer, the representatives of conventional antebellum life along the Mississippi. As they escape (Huck from his father and the Widow Douglas, and Jim from Miss Watson) down the Mississippi on a raft, Huck and Jim help and protect each other. The cornerstones of their friendship are on one hand Jim's folk wisdom, woodsmanship, trust, and kindness, and on the other, ironically, Huck's lying, cheating, and stealing. For black readers Jim's humanity is mainly affirmed by his natural desire for freedom and love of his wife and children. Huck, however, wrestles with his conscience and responds ambivalently to Jim's humanity as they approach Cairo, the planned route north to freedom:

> Jim said it made him all over trembly and feverish to be so close to freedom. Well, I can tell you it made me all over trembly and feverish, too, to hear him, because I begun to get it through my head that he *was* most free—and who was to blame for it? Why, *me,* I couldn't get that out of my conscience, no how nor no way. It got to troubling me so I couldn't rest; I couldn't stay still in one place. [. . .] I tried to make out to myself that I warn't to blame because I didn't run Jim off from his rightful owner, but it warn't no use, conscience up and says, every time, "But you knowed he was running for his freedom, and you could a paddled ashore and told somebody." That was so—I couldn't get around that no way [. . .] I got to feeling so mean and so miserable I most wished I was dead. (307–08)

Finally, in chapter 31, the climactic episode, Huck's moral ambivalence compels him to write and betray Jim to Miss Watson. This makes Huck feel "good and all washed clean of sin for the first time," but before sending the letter, he recalls his relationship with Jim down the river:

> I see Jim before me all the time: in the day and in the nighttime, sometimes moonlight, sometimes storms, and we a-floating along, talking and singing and laughing. But somehow I couldn't seem to strike no places to harden me against him, but only the other kind. I'd see him standing my watch on top of his'n, 'stead of calling me, so I could go on sleeping; and see how glad he was when I come back out of the fog; and when I come to him again in the swamp, up there where the feud was; and such-like times; and would always call me honey and pet me and do everything he could think of for me, and how good he always was; and at last I struck the time I saved him by telling the men we had smallpox aboard, and he was so grateful, and said I was the best friend old Jim ever had in the world and the *only* one he's got now; and I happened to look around and see that paper. [. . .] I studied a minute, sort of holding my breath, and then says to myself: "Allright, then, I'll go to hell"—and tore it up. (450-51)

Most commentators cite this passage as the high point of Huck's moral triumph. They ignore or gloss over Huck's equal, if not more important, resolve, given Twain's belief in moral courage as independent action, "to work and steal Jim out of slavery again" (451). Although Huck's moral resolve degenerates into burlesque under the influence of Tom's romantic escape plan for Jim in chapters 34–43, some modern black readers are more inclined to identify with Huck than Jim. Ralph Ellison, for example, expressed the view of many when he wrote: "I could imagine myself as Huck Finn. [. . .] but not, though I racially identified with him, as Nigger Jim, who struck me as a white man's inadequate portrait of a slave" ("Change the Joke" 58).

Before looking more closely at the relationship of black readers to Jim and Twain, let us briefly address the significance of when Huck tells the story of his adventures. Textual reference to *The Adventures of Tom Sawyer,* which was published in 1876, and to the theme of slavery in the United States, which ended legally with the Thirteenth Amendment in 1865, indicates that Huck tells about his adventures more than eleven years after they have happened, thereby underscoring the problematic nature of his reliability. But Huck is not eleven years older in this ostensible sequel to Tom Sawyer. On the contrary, he and Tom are still adolescents. In addition, the epistolary form of direct address to the reader and of the closing ("The End, Yours Truly, Huck Finn") on the first edition of the book suggests a shorter span of time between the actual events of the narrative and their narration. Since we know from external evidence that the novel was essentially written in four sittings over a period of seven years (the initial sixteen chapters in 1876, chapters 17 and 18 between 1879 and 1880, chapters 19–21 between 1880 and 1883, and the remaining chapters in 1883; Blair, *Mark Twain and Huck Finn* 199), some black readers are at first intrigued but ultimately disappointed by Huck and Tom's imaginative embodiment of Twain's conflicting realistic and romantic impulses toward his own boyhood experiences in antebellum Hannibal, Missouri.

Most intriguing is Twain's chief technical achievement: the effective use of the adolescent Huck as the center of consciousness in the book. As Ellison has pointed out, "The historical and artistic justification for his adolescence lies in the fact that Twain was depicting a transitional period of American life; its artistic justification is that adolescence is the time of the 'great confusion' during which both individuals and nations flounder between accepting and rejecting the responsibilities of adulthood" ("Twentieth Century Fiction" 33). That Huck succumbs to Tom's influence and flounders in his responsibility as a friend to Jim in the final chapters of the novel is painfully disappointing to many readers. This is a serious but hardly fatal flaw in the novel; for rather than relying primarily on Huck's summary and exposition of characters and events, Twain lets them unfold before the reader like a drama or describes them in Huck's vernacular in the natural sequence of his perceptions and memory of them. Thus Huck's psychological and moral struggle with slavery and racism, especially his ambivalent response to Jim's humanity, is a realistic dramatization of the tragicomic education of a poor young white boy of his time, place, and class.

What, then, is Twain's relationship to his audience, Huck, and Jim? Since most of Twain's books were sold "by subscription only," Twain, by circumstance and choice, wrote to appeal to the tastes of his special primary audience. "Instead of the urban, literate reader," as Hamlin Hill has noted, "the subscription book aimed at enticing the common man, the masses, the rural, semi-literate, usually Midwestern customer who had rarely bought a book before" (287). Twain's Southern white stock, socialization in a border state, and literary apprenticeship in the southwestern tradition fostered a close racial, regional, and class identification with this group of post-Reconstruction readers. It is important to remember that these readers were passive or active participants in the rising tide of racial, political, and economic oppression, terrorism, and exploitation that swept the nation in the 1870s and 1880s, depriving Southern blacks of their civil rights and, in many instances, their lives. These readers, many of whom, like Twain, looked with nostalgia on the days before the war, expected a mixture of sensationalism and moralizing. Explaining his choice of this audience in a letter to Andrew Lang in 1890, Twain writes defensively:

> The thin top crust of humanity—the cultivated—are worth pacifying, worth pleasing, worth coddling, worth nourishing and preserving with dainties and delicacies, it is true; but to be caterer to that little faction is no very dignified or valuable occupation, it seems to me; it is merely feeding the over-fed and there must be small satisfaction in that. It is not that little minority who are already saved that are best worth lifting at, I should think, but the mighty mass of the uncultivated who are underneath. [. . .] Indeed I have been misjudged from the very first. I have never tried in even one single little instance to help cultivate the cultivated classes. I was not equipped for it, either by native gifts or training. And I never had any ambition in that direction, but always hunted for bigger game—the masses. I have seldom deliberately tried to instruct them but have done my best to entertain them. (DeVoto, *Portable Mark Twain* 772–73)

This passionate identification with the masses explains, in part, the ambivalence of the description of the aristocratic pretensions of the Grangerfords and of the minstrel image of blacks in Huck Finn.

While Twain's roots, heart, and guts moved him to identify with the popular tastes of his subscription audience, his New England family and friends encouraged him to appeal to the literary standards of the cultivated. His marriage in 1870 to Olivia Langdon, the genteel, frail, semi-invalid daughter of a wealthy New York coal-mine owner and philanthropist, Jervis Langdon, opened the door to financial security, the New England elite, and cultural ambivalence. Moving to Hartford, Connecticut, in 1871, he built one of the largest, most fantastically designed, and lavishly equipped mansions in the Nook Farm community. His neighbors were such genteel, middle-class, liberal writers as Harriet Beecher Stowe, Charles Dudley Warner, and the Reverend Joseph Twichell; his close friends were Twichell and the Bostonian William Dean Howells, the most influential advocate of the genteel tradition in American letters of the period. Howells and this Nook Farm community were, in effect, Twain's other audience. Critics have frequently pointed to the influence that Twain's wife and friends, especially Twichell and Howells, had on his writings. "After my marriage," Twain confessed about his wife, "she edited everything I wrote. And what is more—she not only edited my works—she edited me" (qtd. in Brooks, *The Ordeal of Mark Twain* 136). Referring to her mother's censorship, Susy, his oldest daughter, wrote in her biography of the family:

> Papa read *Huckleberry Finn* to us in manuscript, just before it came out, and then he would leave parts of it with mama to expergate [*sic*], while he went off up to the study to work, and sometimes Clara and I would be sitting with mama while she was looking the manuscript over and I remember so well, with what pangs of regret we used to see her turn down the leaves of the pages, which meant that some delightfully terrible part must be scratched out. (Clemens, *Papa*, first entry for February 12, 1886)

More influential as literary adviser than his wife was Howells. In a letter to Howells, Twain wrote, "I owe as much to your training as the rude country job-printer owes to the city-boss who takes him in hand and teaches him the right way to handle his art" (qtd. in Brooks, *The Ordeal of Mark Twain* 153). Twain's secondary audience, then, as Michael Egan suggests, "comprised the descendants of the original American revolutionary class, already beginning to sentimentalize their political heritage and edge towards conservatism and hypocrisy. Ten years earlier Twain had savagely attacked their dishonesties and double standards in *The Gilded Age;* by the time he came to write the later sections of *Huckleberry Finn*, however, he was merely their court-jester. This led [. . .] to pale burlesque and satire" (63–64).

The burlesque and satire in the early as well as late sections of *Huck Finn* illustrate Twain's relation to Huck and Jim. "Speaking through the mask of an 'irresponsible' boy," as Lynn notes, "Twain was somehow able to 'let himself go' [. . .] with the result that Huck is the one Twain hero who is not shut out from the pageantry of life by his fear of being taken in by it" (220). Emotionally and philosophically, in other words, Twain is close to his naive hero, but, as stated earlier, intellectually and morally he is, by virtue of Huck's ironic character, usually distant from him. Like Twain, Huck is unsentimental and uncultivated in behavior yet occasionally sensitive in his perceptions and use of the vernacular. Commenting on "the victuals" for supper at the Widow Douglas's, Huck tells us, "There warn't really anything the matter with them—that is, nothing only everything was cooked by itself. In a barrel of odds and ends it is different; things get mixed up and the juice kind of swaps around and the things go better" (DeVoto, *Portable Mark Twain* 194–95). Later, in describing the Mississippi after escaping from Pap, he appeals winsomely for our understanding: "Everything was dead quiet, and it looked late and *smelt late*. You know what I mean—I don't know the words to put it in" (231). Twain is sympathetic toward his protagonist as he underscores the hypocrisy of the widow by having Huck see her take snuff after refusing to let him smoke because "it was a mean practice and wasn't clean" (195). Huck's belief that "of course that was all right" stresses his ironic role, for it is apparent here and throughout the narrative that the author and reader are more intellectually and morally aware of the hypocrisy of the respectable characters than is the protagonist.

But the author and his protagonist are kindred spirits in their ambivalence about the humanity and equality of blacks. In response, for example, to the tarring and feathering of the duke and king, the comic confidence men, Huck is moved to sympathy for them in chapter 33. "Well, it made me sick to see it," says Huck, "and I was sorry for them poor pitiful rascals. [. . .] It was a dreadful thing to see. Human beings can be awful cruel to one another." Yet earlier when Aunt Sally Phelps asked in chapter 32 if anybody was hurt on the boat that Huck, impersonating Tom, said blew a cylinder, his insensitivity to the humanity of blacks ("No'm. Killed a nigger.") is as ironically racist as hers. ("Well, it's lucky; because sometimes people do get hurt.") Twain, like Huck, was a racist, fighting nobly yet futilely against the customs and laws of white supremacy. Even though while writing *Huck Finn* Twain financed the college education of two blacks "as part of the reparation due from every white to every black man" and recommended Frederick Douglass to president-elect Garfield as marshal of the District of Columbia, the burlesque and satirical chapters showing Huck's reluctant participation in Tom's bizarre plan to free Jim, whom Tom knows Miss Watson's will has already freed, from his imprisonment on the Phelps farm provide more than ample evidence of this tragic flaw in Twain as well as in American character and culture (Blair, *Mark Twain and Huck Finn* 323; Foner 282–83). On one hand, these chapters are a satirical treatment of the romantic books on prison life and escape by Casanova, Cellini, Dumas, Carlyle, Dickens, and other writers, books which, as Walter Blair notes, few readers have recognized. On the other, they return to the same ignoble minstrel image of Jim that we see in chapters 2–8. "The comedy," Blair continues, "is chiefly that of the Sut Lovingood school: hound packs streaming through Jim's cabin; menageries of bugs, spiders, caterpillars, and snakes discomforting Jim; snakes dropping from rafters onto Aunt Sally; butter melting atop Huck's head. Working notes show that Mark delighted in the elaboration" (*Mark Twain and Huck Finn* 350). Twain's training in the ethics of Jim Crow, especially his influence by southwestern humor, delights in minstrelsy, and paternalistic attitude toward blacks he knew on his uncle's Missouri farm explain, in part, the tragic face of humanity behind Jim's comic mask. In his autobiography Twain nostalgically tells us about his "faithful and affectionate good friend, ally, and adviser [. . .] 'Uncle Dan'l,'" who was the model for Jim. In the manner of plantation school writers like Joel Chandler Harris, whose Uncle Remus tales Twain also admired, he recalls Uncle Daniel as "a middle-aged slave whose head was the best one in the negro quarter, whose sympathies were wide and warm, and whose heart was honest and simple and knew no guile. [...] he has endured [...] with the patience and friendliness and loyalty which were his birthright" (qtd. in Paine 100). In giving imaginative shape to these memories of Uncle Daniel and appealing to the prejudices of his white readers, Twain creates the harmless, superstitious, childish character we first meet sleeping in chapter 2.

We are encouraged to laugh indulgently with the author at how Jim becomes a "monstrous proud," popular conjuror in the black community as a result of his interpretation of Tom's prank on him while he slept as the work of the devil and witches. Although Huck does not participate in the prank, he nevertheless concludes, with Twain's implicit agreement, that "Jim was most ruined as a servant, because he got so stuck up on account of having seen the devil and been rode by witches" (200). In chapter 4 Twain uses eye dialect and the magical powers of "a hair-ball as big as your fist, which had been took out of the fourth stomack of an ox" to burlesque Jim's prediction of Huck's fate with his father: "Yo' ole father doan' know yit what he's a-gwyne to do. Sometimes he spec he'll go 'way, en den agin he spec he'll stay. De bes' way is to res' easy en let de ole man take his own way. [...] Yo wants to keep 'way fum de water as much as you kin, en don't run no resk, 'kase it's down in de bills dat you's gwyne to git hung" (213).

Twain's introductory note that he "painstakingly" represents "the Missouri Negro dialect" as well as various others should be analyzed in the context of his belief in the authenticity of minstrelsy, of his influence by the eye dialect of southwestern humorists, of his delineation of other blacks in the novel as comic servants, of his own speech features, and of all the distinctive grammatical, lexical, and phonetic features of nineteenth-century black Missouri speech—not merely in terms of Jim's pronunciation (Tidwell 174–76).[3] On one level, then, the bond between Huck and Jim is strengthened by their unsophisticated speech and mutual belief in the supernatural. On another, it is reinforced by such white paternalism as Huck's feeling, like Twain's for Uncle Daniel, that Jim "had an uncommon level head for a nigger" (279). Indeed, the highest praise that Huck can give Jim is that "he cared just as much for his people as white folks does for their'n. It don't seem natural, but I reckon it's so" (384). And after Jim sacrifices his freedom to save Tom's life at the end of the novel, Huck concludes that Jim was "white inside." For the reconstructed Twain as for Huck, in other words, the social relationship between blacks and whites even in its most benevolent form is that of noblesse oblige, a mutual social bond of love and loyalty between the master and slave classes rather than a mutual natural respect for human rights and egalitarianism.

The ambiguity and ambivalence of Twain's relationship to Jim is vividly illustrated in chapter 15 when Jim violates the ethics of Jim Crow and noblesse oblige by reprimanding Huck for ridiculing him:

> When I got all wore out wid work, en wid de callin' for you, en went to sleep, my heart wuz mos' broke bekase you wuz los', en I didn' k'yer no mo' what become er me en de raf'. En when I wake up en fine you back agin, all safe en soun', de tears come, en I could'a got down on my knees en kiss yo' foot, I's so thankful. En all you wuz thinkin' 'bout wuz how you could make a fool uv ole Jim wid a lie. Dat truck dah is trash; en trash is what people is dat puts dirt on de head er dey fren's en makes 'em ashamed. (290)

Here Jim's deep moral indignation surfaces from behind the comic mask he wears defensively to conceal his true feelings and thoughts from Huck and other whites who pervert their humanity in demeaning or denying his. (The mask slips again when he vows to free his wife and children even if he must steal them.) Huck, in response, felt so bad that he "could almost kissed *his* foot to get him to take it back. It was fifteen minutes before I could work myself up to go and humble myself to a nigger—but I done it and I warn't ever sorry for it afterward, neither" (290). Huck's contrition here and subsequent resolve not merely to go to hell but to steal Jim out of slavery represent Twain's moral identification with Jim and Huck. For Ellison, "Huck Finn's acceptance of the evil implicit in his 'emancipation' of Jim represents Twain's acceptance of his personal responsibility in the condition of Society. This was the tragic face behind the comic mask" ("Twentieth Century Fiction" 33). While this perceptive interpretation certainly redeems the narrative and author from being the trash that some would consign them to, for me and many other readers, Twain's tragic face is his failure of moral courage in reducing the complexity of Jim's humanity to a minstrel mask in the closing chapters. Jim's compromise of his desire for freedom, love of family, and self-respect for the forty dollars Tom gives him for cooperation in the burlesque escape plan is the tragic face behind his minstrel mask. It is sad but true for many black readers that Twain's "Nigger" Jim is the best example of the humanity of black American slaves in nineteenth-century white American fiction. It is ironic, finally, as Ellison observed more than twenty-five years ago, that "down at the deep dark bottom of the melting pot, where the private is public and the public is private, where black is white and white black, where the immoral becomes moral and the moral is anything that makes one feel good (or that one has the power to sustain), the white man's relish is apt to be the black man's gall" ("Change the Joke" 48–50).

Notes

1. From an interview with John H. Wallace, Mark Twain Intermediate School, Fairfax County, Virginia, qtd. in Hentoff. For the Concord Library censorship quotation, see *Critic* 6 (March 28, 1885): 155; it has been widely reprinted in critical anthologies on Twain.

2. See also Robert C. Toll, *Blacking Up: The Minstrel Show in Nineteenth-Century America* (New York: Oxford UP, 1974).

3. See also Summer Ives, "A Theory of literary Dialect," *Tulane Studies in English* 2 (1950): 137–82.

III

"The Negro" as Metonym, Metaphor, and Marginal Man in William Faulkner's *Go Down, Moses*

This essay had its origins in a University of Massachusetts graduate course on Faulkner in 1969 with Professor Arthur Kinney, an internationally respected specialist in Renaissance literature as well as a William Faulkner scholar. Like many black scholars, critics, and writers, I was as ambivalent as I was intrigued by Faulkner's imaginative representation of African American culture and character in his novels, especially in the context of the controversy over William Styron receiving the Pulitzer Prize for his novel The Confessions of Nat Turner. *Professor Kinney's initial idea for his collection of critical essays on Faulkner was to examine the issue of miscegenation in the McCaslin-Beauchamp-Edmonds saga. After several difficult drafts, my essay appeared under the title "William Faulkner's 'Shining Star': Lucas Beauchamp as a Marginal Man" in Kinney's* Critical Essays on William Faulkner: The McCaslin Family *(1990). I delivered it with its current title as the keynote address at the Third International Conference on William Faulkner in Chongqing, China, in 2004. The thesis of the essay is that Faulkner's consummate use of myth, ritual, metaphor, and metonymy in* Go Down, Moses *gives mythopoeic force to his vision of Lucas Beauchamp and "the Negro" as a marginal man, a modern man of mixed blood and culture who must personally bear the burden, the moral responsibility, of his humanity.*

"The Negro" as literary sign is central to William Faulkner's modernist narrative vision and achievement. Born the year after the custom of racial segregation and the popular blackface minstrel image of African Americans as Jim Crow were encoded as the law of the land in the 1896 *Plessy v. Ferguson* decision by the U.S. Supreme Court, Faulkner, a native son of Mississippi, was torn sociopsychologically and socioculturally between the curse and blessing of his southern heritage. He felt compelled in his quest for personal wholeness and a unified artistic vision to come to terms with "the Negro" in the southern white psyche as, in novelist and cultural critic Ralph Ellison's words, "a malignant stereotype (the bad nigger) on the one hand and a benign stereotype (the good nigger) on the other" ("Twentieth-Century Fiction" 42). Contrary to Arthur F. Kinney's thesis in "Faulkner and the Problematics of Procreation" that Faulkner's imaginative vision of "the Negro" Lucas Beauchamp is as "a humbled sambo" at the close of *Go Down, Moses,* Lucas, as I demonstrated in 1990 in "William Faulkner's 'Shining Star': Lucas Beauchamp as a Marginal Man," is most memorable as a complex representation of "the Negro" as a metonym, metaphor, and marginal man.

When exploring the issues of miscegenation and the struggle of "the Negro" in the United States to affirm a biracial, bicultural identity—the complex sociopsychological state that the incomparable black public intellectual W. E. B. Du Bois called "double consciousness"—as an African American, Faulkner invariably created characters that range from the stereotypical Sambo and tragic mulatto to the rebellious marginal man. The fear and courage, guilt and innocence, shame and pride of mixed blood and interracial marriage, as *Absalom, Absalom!* and *Light in August* illustrate, involve the social and cultural issues of heritage as well as the sociopsychological myths of pure white supremacy and impure Negro inferiority. When, as in the case of Lucas Beauchamp, the individual of mixed blood rejects or is rejected by one social group or racial culture without achieving a satisfactory adjustment to the other, he finds himself on the margin of each but a member of neither. He becomes a marginal man.

After the American Revolution, miscegenation statutes governing cohabitation and marriage primarily between "white" and "black" people began to define "the

Negro" by two criteria: African ancestry or descent and percentage of Negro blood. Unlike the three fundamental racial categories of white, colored (Creole or mulatto), and black that characterized the social structure of the Caribbean, Jim Crow codes in the United States arbitrarily reduced the categories to white and Negro. Despite the unscientific nature and absurdity of racial classifications, Mississippi law in 1890 defined as Negro any person having one-eighth or more Negro blood. Prior to 1890, miscegenation laws were repealed in many northeastern and midwestern states. But by 1931 the only states with large Negro populations that had no such laws were Illinois, New York, and Ohio. That all such state laws were not nullified until the 1967 Supreme Court decision of *Loving v. Virginia* reveals the tenacity of the myth of white supremacy, of the power of Jim Crow codes, and of the rituals of miscegenation that inform the theme, style, and structure of Faulkner's most important novels.

Etymologically, "negro" is derived from the Latin *niger* and the Spanish *negro*, both signifying the color black in lowercase letters. According to the *Oxford English Dictionary*, the term was first used around 1441 by the Spanish and Portuguese to designate African slaves from below the Sahara Desert, thus tying color to race and blackness to slavery and degradation. Although such eighteenth-century organizations as the Free African Society and the African Methodist Episcopal Church rejected the white imposed term in naming themselves, "negro" was still the socially sanctioned, dominant racial classification at the turn of the twentieth century. In response to a campaign led by the NAACP in 1930, the *New York Times* and other media began to capitalize the term as a proper noun, which in the 1960s most black Americans displaced with Black, African, Afro-American, and African American. However, the concept and sign of "the Negro," "nigger," or "Sambo" in American racial discourse and in Faulkner's fiction and novels obscure, devalue, or mythicize the humanity and individuality of African Americans as stereotype, type, or archetype.

In *Go Down, Moses* (1942)—seven interrelated stories about the bondage and freedom of the white and black descendants of Lucius Quintus Carothers McCaslin—Faulkner's compulsion as a Mississippi modernist artist to understand "the Negro" drove him to create a world in which the rituals of miscegenation paradoxically reinforce and undermine the myth of white supremacy as well as the racial conventions of Jim Crow. This is particularly evident in the representation of Lucas Beauchamp—the bearer of the American tradition of miscegenation, incest, and probable rape—as "the Negro": a metonym for the southern legacy of slavery and racism, a symbol of the mixed identity of a marginal man, and a metaphor for the ambivalence and complex identity of modern man.

Introduced as a narrator-participant in *Go Down, Moses* and as a major character in *Intruder in the Dust*, Lucas is not merely the son of the slaves Tennie and Tomey's Turl. He is also a grandson and great-grandson of old Carothers McCaslin, one of the founding white patriarchs of Yoknapatawpha County. Unlike the tragic deaths of Joe Christmas, whose racial mixture is fatally ambiguous in *Light in August* (1932), and of Charles Bon, whose mixed ancestry evolves as a more fratricidal character flaw, in *Absalom, Absalom!* (1936), Lucas moves beyond the stereotypical fate of the tragic mulatto and succeeds realistically in asserting his complex individuality as a black McCaslin. More important, he also triumphs metonymically and symbolically as a marginal man, the modern and contemporary southern person of mixed blood who ambivalently straddles two cultures, and metaphorically as the sign of unrealized spiritual brotherhood fundamental to our modern paradoxical sense of human bondage and freedom.

Lucius Quintus Carothers McCaslin Beauchamp, who boldly renamed himself Lucas, is first introduced as a major character in "The Fire and the Hearth." He appears briefly in "The Bear," and is mentioned in "Pantaloon in Black," "Delta Autumn," and "Go Down, Moses." Initially, "The Fire and the Hearth" presents two melodramatic plots with stereotypical characters who make bootleg whiskey and hunt for gold. On a deeper level, the narrative introduces us to Lucas Beauchamp's quest for independence, power, and integrity as a man of biracial and bicultural heritage through temporal and spatial shifts of memory, reverie, and flashback. The marginal man, we are told, is, at sixty-seven years of age in 1941, "not only the oldest man, but the oldest living person on the Edmonds plantation, the oldest McCaslin descendant even though in the world's eye he descended not from McCaslins but from McCaslin slaves" (36).

As old Carothers McCaslin's great-grandson and grandson, Lucas and his relationship to old Carothers McCaslin represent an ironic affirmation of the myth of the Southern plantation as a harmonious, benevolent socioeconomic system. But it is also the major source of Lucas's personal independence, power, and integrity. He displays his self-confidence in opposing George Wilkins, the young black "interloper without forbears" who sets up a rival still and plans to marry Lucas's seventeen-year-old daughter, Nat. "If George had just stuck to farming the land which Edmonds had allotted him," Lucas reflects, "he would just as soon Nat married George as anyone else" (34). But Lucas will tolerate no competition from George, especially after he discovers gold. Reinforcing the popular demeaning image of "the Negro" as buffoon perpetuated in blackface minstrelsy, Faulkner depicts Lucas's discovery of a gold coin while he is burying his own whiskey still before informing authorities of George's still.

Lucas's discovery is a melodramatic complication of both his plot to have the sheriff get rid of George and his quest to affirm his manhood.

Already financially independent with more than $3,000 of inherited McCaslin money in the bank—money tripled and deposited not by old Carothers but by his twin sons Amodeus (Buck) and Theophilus (Buddy) for their half brother and Lucas's father, Terrel (Turl) Beauchamp—Lucas experiences a profoundly significant flashback of forty-three years as he pursues his resolve to expose George. The flashback to the 1890s—the period of the rise of Jim Crow, white terrorism, and the industrial New South—occurs when Lucas approaches Roth Edmond's plantation house and the memory of both Zack Edmonds, Roth's father and Lucas's boyhood companion, and Cass McCaslin. The memory of "the old days, the old time, and better men than these" gives dramatic immediacy to the rituals of ancestral miscegenation and spiritual kinship. Pride, honor, and ruthlessness were the values that old Cass, Zack, and Lucas shared. Cass, a maternal grandson, took "the land from the true heir simply because he wanted it and knew he could use it better and was strong enough, ruthless enough, old Carothers McCaslin enough" (44).

In an extended flashback, Lucas also manifests these values in his effort to kill Zack Edmonds, with whom he had grown up almost as a brother. He presumed Zack to be guilty of sexually violating Molly, Lucas's wife, thereby disrespecting and challenging Lucas's authority to maintain the integrity of his family and home, archetypically signified by the "fire in the hearth." During the night of a raging flood, Zack not only summoned young Molly from nursing her own child to deliver his but also sent Lucas across a dangerous river for a doctor. With the death of his wife in childbirth, Zack, faithful to the ethics of Jim Crow and the rituals of miscegenation, keeps Molly in his house as a nursemaid and homemaker. "It was as though the white woman had not only never quitted the house, she had never existed [...] his own wife, the black woman, now living alone in the house which old Cass had built for them when they married, keeping alive on the hearth the fire he had lit there on their wedding day and which had burned ever since though there was little enough cooking done on it now" (46). After nearly six months, however, of "himself alone keeping alive the fire which was to burn on the hearth until neither he nor Molly were left to feed it" (47), Lucas boldly confronts Zack and demands the return of his wife. "But I'm a man too. I'm more than just a man. The same thing made my pappy that made your grandpaw. I'm going to take her back" (47). Lucas asserts the authority of his manhood by invoking his white McCaslin paternity and familial birthright, thus revealing his racial ambivalence and marginality.

When Molly returns home and continues nursing the Edmonds's baby while apparently neglecting her own, Lucas's pride and shame, a legacy of his biracial marginality, cry out for vindication. Standing stereotypically with a razor in his hand over Zack in his bedroom, Lucas, "a McCaslin on his father's side," distinguishes between his responsibility as a man and that of Molly and Zack, who is "woman-made" because he is "a McCaslin only on his mother's side" (44). Lucas chauvinistically defines a woman as "a critter not responsible like men are responsible, not to be held like men are held" (52). Consequently, he resolves initially to kill Zack and accept death by lynching rather than accept dishonor as a man. But in confronting Zack, Lucas throws away the razor in defiance and challenges Zack to get his pistol from the dresser drawer. As they struggle for the pistol, Lucas pulls the trigger, but it misfires in Zack's side.

In reverie a year or so later, Lucas thinks of the irony of the misfired cartridge he has kept as large enough to have contained two lives. "*Because I wouldn't have used the second one. [. . .] I would have paid. I would have waited for the rope, even the coal oil. I would have paid. So I reckon I aint got old Carothers' blood for nothing, after all.*" As a young mulatto male plowing on the plantation and coping with the realities of white patriarchy and the myth of white supremacy, Lucas saw the supper smoke and knew that Molly "would leave his on the hearth for him when she went back to the big house with the children" (58). Amplifying his dilemma, he wryly asks as he watches her depart: "How to God [. . .] can a black man ask a white man to please not lay down with his black wife? And even if he could ask it, how to God can the white man promise he won't?" (59).

Metonymically, Lucas bears the sociopsychological burden of a marginal man, the southern legacy of a person of mixed blood who struggles to reconcile the double consciousness of his dual identity. Lucas explicitly subscribes to traditional patriarchal values, but this is made ambivalent by the myth of white supremacy and the corollary myth of black inferiority. Still he struggles to remain, foremost, a man. When much later Molly seeks a divorce with Roth's assistance because Lucas's obsession with hunting for gold results in the neglect of his family, home, and God, Lucas responds tersely and proudly to Roth's inquiry: "'I'm a man.' Lucas said. 'I'm the man here. I'm the one to say in my house, like you and your paw and his paw were the ones to say in his home'" (120). Significantly, Lucas's role models are white patriarchs, not black.

Lucas is the youngest of three children. His sister, Fonsiba, was born in 1869 and left the plantation in 1876 after marrying a Northern black man. His brother, James, was born in 1864 and migrated north in 1885. The father of three children

(Henry, born in 1898; an unnamed daughter who died in childbirth in 1915; and Nathalie, born in 1924), Lucas remained on the Mississippi plantation yet defied the ethics of Jim Crow and the stereotypical role of "the Negro." He bore the curse and blessing of the legacy of old Carothers McCaslin's blood. This legacy included a handmade beaver hat, gold watch chain, gold toothpick, rent-free house and land, and $3,000, as well as pride, courage, independence, ruthless individualism, faintly Syriac features, and an altered Christian name. These qualities are revealed as Lucas refuses to address whites, especially Zack, as mister; to trust whites financially or morally, including his cousin Isaac McCaslin, the trustee of his money; and to use a razor on Zack for dishonoring his rights and responsibilities as husband and father, for violating symbolically his fire and hearth. Sociolinguistically, as we learn in "The Bear," Lucas asserts personal and racial agency in the reconstruction of his identity by changing his name from Lucius to Lucas, "making it no longer the white man's but his own, by himself composed, himself selfprogenitive and nominate, by himself ancestored" (281).

In other words, for the omniscient narrator and Roth Edmonds, who was midwifed, nursed, and raised as a foster son by Molly much in the manner as Faulkner was nurtured by "Mammy" Caroline Barr, Lucas was archetypically impervious to time. "*He's more like old Carothers than all the rest of us put together, including old Carothers,*" Roth thinks. "*He is both heir and prototype simultaneously of all the geography and climate and biology which sired old Carothers and all the rest of us and our kind, myriad, countless, faceless, even nameless now except himself who fathered himself, intact and complete, contemptuous, as old Carothers must have been, of all blood black white yellow or red, including his own*" (118).

Although a practical, dominating, selfish man, Lucas, in giving up his obsessive search for gold, transcends his most negative traits and manifests the paradoxical interdependency and independence of modern man. At the end of "The Fire and the Hearth," he tells Roth to sell the divining machine that he used nightly in his search for gold because, he says with biblical resignation, "I am near to the end of my three score and ten, and I reckon to find that money aint for me" (131). Actually, the motivation for his transformation is primarily to save his forty-five-year marriage to Molly, to protect his fire and hearth. He dramatically demonstrates this by his sentimental gift of candy to his wife with the unsentimental remark, "Here. [. . .] You aint got no teeth left but you can still gum it" (130). Lucas, like most of Faulkner's major characters, is haunted and driven by memories of racialized slavery and segregation. Basically, the racial, economic, cultural, and moral complexities of this inner drive for Lucas are to be respected as a man and to affirm the biracial, bicultural bond of modern humanity.

Although the power of men as well as the complex kinship ties of the white and black descendants of old Carothers are further illustrated in the other stories in *Go Down, Moses,* the final story ironically rewrites the messianic theme of the mythic biblical story and black spiritual song of the same title. In Faulkner's version, Roth Edmonds is accused by old Mollie Worsham Beauchamp, Lucas's wife, of selling her young grandson Benjamin (Samuel Worsham Beauchamp) into bondage. Pleading for attorney Gavin Stevens's help, she chants, "It was Roth Edmonds sold him [. . .] Sold him in Egypt. I don't know whar he is. I just knows Pharaoh got him. And you the Law. I wants to find my boy" (371). In Mollie's unreconstructed belief in the myth of the plantation and pastoral traditions, the sin of slavery is identified with life in town and in the North. In his symbolic role as Moses, Gavin Stevens reveals a moral ambivalence and rhetorical excess that are more similar to Faulkner's own major characteristics than to the biblical Moses's traits. This paradox is most apparent when Stevens demonstrates the social interdependency of southern whites and blacks, the system of paternalism and noblesse oblige that was in reality more parasitic than symbiotic, by assuming most of the expense for burying Mollie's grandson, who was electrocuted in Chicago for killing a policeman. "Mr. Edmonds will want to help, I know," he tells Miss Belle Worsham, the last white descendant of the family that had owned Mollie. "And I understand that old Luke Beauchamp has some money in the bank" (377).

Because he values his authority and autonomy more than social ties and responsibilities, however, Lucas does not contribute to his grandson's funeral. Nor is he present when Miss Worsham and Gavin Stevens hear Mollie and her brother Hamp chant an improvisation of the traditional black spiritual song "Go Down, Moses" in the mourning "circle about the brick hearth on which the ancient symbol of human coherence and solidarity smoldered" (380). Because he is a living repudiation of the southern stereotype of "the Negro," Lucas is socially outside of and symbolically beyond the circle of solidarity that constituted the traditional ties of the human bondage and emancipatory struggle of blacks in the United States. Archetypically, Lucas is a marginal man, a product of the pride and shame of his mixed blood that socially and culturally provokes his ambivalence about both whites and blacks and that paradoxically affirms the complex multiracial, multicultural web of identity and kinship ties of modern and contemporary Americans of the twenty-first century.

IV

William Styron's Nat Turner: A White Southerner's Meditation on a Legendary Slave Revolt

As an invited contribution to the angry responses of black American readers to William Styron's controversial Pulitzer Prize–winning fictional meditation on Nat Turner's slave revolt, this essay was my first important publication on the stereotypic misrepresentation of African American culture and character in American literature and popular culture. Although historian John Henrik Clarke, associate editor of Freedomways, *invited me to submit an essay for* William Styron's Nat Turner: Ten Black Writers Respond *(1968), I missed the deadline for submitting it. Civil rights activists inspired by the Black Power, Black Arts, and Black Studies movements for social justice and equality in the late 1960s, the ten black writers (historian John Henrik Clarke, historian Lerone Bennett Jr., psychiatrist Alvin F. Poussaint, historian Vincent Harding, novelist John Oliver Killens, novelist John A. Williams, contributing editor of* Freedomways *Ernest Kaiser, freelance writer Loyle Hairston, political scientist Charles V. Hamilton, and essayist Mike Thelwell) argue polemically to general readers that Styron's novel ignores facts and distorts history in order to perpetuate the white bigoted stereotype of Nat Turner and slave revolts as demonically violent, lustful, and criminal. Styron was defended in book reviews by such white academic critics as Martin Duberman and Eugene D. Genovese. In his biography* William Styron: A Life *(1998), James L. W. West III, a Penn State University colleague, writes condescendingly, "To anyone educated to observe basic standards of logic and decorum,* Ten Black Writers *is an appallingly poor performance. Many of the essays are based on shaky scholarship, and most are flawed by emotionalism, some of it theatrical" (386).*

My culturally and politically informative late submission was subsequently published with Clarke's recommendation in American Dialog *(1968) and by request from the editor, in a shorter, revised draft in the* Michigan Quarterly Review *(1968) as a book review. Because "William Styron's Nat Turner: A White Southerner's Meditation on a Legendary Slave Revolt" first appeared as "The Confession of Styron" in* American Dialog *rather than in Clarke's collection, it did not receive the significant attention of the literary establishment of that era of radical change that it will hopefully receive from readers of this collection of essays.*

Since William Styron's *The Confessions of Nat Turner* (1967) is a fictional treatment of history, the reader assumes that the novelist is familiar with the major sources of information about his subject. The primary source for any account of Nat Turner's life is Thomas Gray's *The Confessions of Nat Turner* (1831). Although Gray, the white recorder at Turner's interrogation and the prosecuting lawyer at the trial, was himself a racist, his book is of dubious reliability yet paradoxically the most authoritative document available.[1] It contains the only biographical record of Turner's life that we have and, despite its racist reconstruction, purports to be an "authentic account" of the revolt, "acknowledged by him [Turner] to be such" (Aptheker, *Nat Turner's* 128). The most scholarly book on Turner is arguably Herbert Aptheker's *Nat Turner's Slave Rebellion* (1966). Aptheker reveals that Nat Turner was a "highly intelligent man" of profound religious sentiment who, in the "struggle for freedom," led a slave revolt in Virginia in 1831 that accelerated, but it did not initiate, such political movements in America as "colonization, repressive legislation, pro-slavery ideological development, abolitionist agitation [. . .] anti-Negro apprenticeship agitation and sectionalism within Virginia" (35). Aptheker's book also includes the full text of Gray's *Confessions*. The only other book at the turn of the century that focused solely on the Turner revolt was William Sidney Drewry's *The Southampton Insurrection* (1900), which, according to Aptheker, "for the truth of the Turner event it would have been better if Drewry had never published" (i). Other significant accounts of the revolt appear in Ulrich B. Phillips's racially conservative and influential *American Negro Slavery* (1918), Herbert Aptheker's radical *American Negro Slave Revolts* (1943), Kenneth Stampp's progressive *The Peculiar Institution* (1956), and contemporary periodicals, especially the *Richmond Enquirer* in 1831 and 1832.

Although Styron tells us in the introductory note to *The Confessions* that he is going to use "the utmost freedom of imagination" in his novel, he nevertheless pointedly claims that he has "rarely departed from the *known* facts about Nat Turner and the revolt." Since Styron himself raises the question of historical truth in his novel, and since our contemporary racial tensions give immediate significance to this interpretation of a man whom many readers may visualize as an archetype of black militancy, a careful analysis of the book should include a discussion of its historical as well as its fictional validity and what Gray considers "a kind of, uh, dignity of style" (42).

I suggest that as history the book is deficient because Styron, despite his explicit disclaimer, frequently ignores and distorts the known facts. Furthermore, because Styron uncritically accepts as true Phillips's view of slavery as benign, especially in Virginia, Drewry's view of Negroes as congenitally inferior, and Gray's view of Turner as a diabolic, gloomy fanatic, Styron does not convince me, as he seems to have done many other reviewers, of Turner's validity as a legendary slave personality, realized in his own time. On the other hand, the fact that Styron chooses to tell his story from Nat Turner's point of view through prolonged, deep reveries on the paradox of divine justice for the sins of slavery suggests that the novelist intends to involve the reader not only morally but also emotionally to create sympathy for his central character. However, the tortured rhetoric and sensational incidents in the book that Gray justifies as "a reconstitution and recomposition" of Turner's confession (42), undermine the credibility of the central character and alienate the sentiments of many readers for both Nat Turner and William Styron.

Given the world of the novel in general and the immediate circumstances of Turner's spiritual and physical misery in particular, the literary rhetoric observed in the informally educated slave's recollection of two fellow Negroes is out of character: "Then slowly the blessed nincompoops rearranged the sawhorses into a stack again, hoisted them up and continued their hunched, leadfooted pilgrimage across the field, two ragged silhouettes against a frieze of pinewoods and wintry sky, bound as if for nowhere on to the uttermost limits of the earth-black faceless paradigms of an absurd and immemorial futility" (327). Equally unconvincing as the actual feelings and thoughts of a hungry, cold slave awaiting execution in chains are the nostalgia, grandiloquence, and convoluted syntax of the following Turner description:

> The particular November day I met Jeremiah Cobb is clear in my memory! An afternoon of low gray clouds scudding eastward on a gusty wind, cornfields brown and sere stretching toward the distant woods, and the kind of stillness which comes with that time of autumn, the buzz and hum of insects having flickered out, the songbirds flown south, leaving the fields and woods to dwell in a vast gray globe silence; nothing

stirs, minutes pass in utter quiet, then through the smoky light comes the sound of crows cawing over some far-off cornfield, a faint raucous hullabaloo which swiftly dwindles off in the distance, and silence again, broken only by the scratching and scrabble of dead windblown leaves. (58)

The ominous mood of this passage is also a melodramatic contrivance, at the expense of characterization, to set the stage for Turner's meeting the judge who subsequently sentences him to death. Moreover, when Turner refers to the "daily grind of nigger work" and to "a sale which a weakness for irony impels me to remark was effected at the moment I reached my manhood" (54), the anomalous diction, which the Oxford English Dictionary reveals was first used in 1851, and the incongruousness of his sophisticated literary sentiments about irony are, of course, chronologically and logically out of character.

The most implausible characteristic of Styron's Negro narrator, however, is his gratuitous racial commentary. Early in the novel Styron, through his narrator, begins offering the reader such alleged revelations of the Negro psyche as "the contentment a Negro takes in a white man's misery, existing like a delicious tidbit among bleak and scanty rations, can hardly be overestimated" (68). Here the author himself has overestimated and overstated what he believes to be the manner in which not only Nat Turner but also all nineteenth-century Negroes responded to a white man's misery. Other gratuitous alleged insights into Negro character, which are actually stereotypic and preposterous, abound in the novel. Commenting on the wit and wryness of Hark, his rebellious slave friend, the narrator states that "it is impossible to exaggerate the extent to which white people dominate the conversation of Negroes" (63). The narrator also claims that "a white man's discomfiture observed on the sly has *always* been a Negro's richest delight" (59; my emphasis). Styron then has Turner express the most reprehensibly improbable and implausible advice on how to dominate the will of slaves to the hegemonic power of whites: "Beat a nigger, starve him, leave him wallowing in his own shit, and he will be yours for life. Awe him by some unforeseen hint of philanthropy, tickle him with the idea of hope, and he will want to slice your throat" (78). Any suggestion that these statements are intended as ironic hyperbolic comments only proves the unconvincing character of the narrator from another point of view, for Styron portrayed his narrator-protagonist as self-educated but lacking formal education and literary sophistication. Furthermore, other than Gray's allusion to the narrator's weakness for irony, no explicit or implicit evidence that irony is being employed is apparent to the careful reader.

When he looks closely at the fictional Turner's family, the discerning reader observes Styron manipulating and distorting history to create negative Negro stereotypes. Contrary to Gray's *Confessions*, Styron depicts Turner's grandmother as a savage American with "a mouth full of filed teeth and raised tattoos like whorls of scattered birdshot on her cheeks" (132) who died mad at the age of thirteen, after giving birth to Turner's mother, Lou-Ann. In Gray we are told simply that she "was very religious" and a person to whom Turner "was much attached" (133). Lou-Ann, moreover, is portrayed in Styron's novel as having been raped on the pantry table by Mr. McBride, the Irish overseer, an incident witnessed by Turner when he was nine or ten. Styron suggests the victim's basic willingness by having her to murmur "Dh-huh, aw-right" as the overseer promises her, "ye'll have earrings" (149). None of this appears in Gray; it only appears in Styron's stereotypic representation of the sexuality of slaves. That Turner is the product of a broken family because his father "done run off" is also Styron's invention, for in Gray we are told that young Turner was educated and trained by both parents. In addition, Styron represents the basis of the fictional Turner's informal education and religious sentiments as the result of the benevolence of his white master and the motherly teaching of his white mistress. Again Styron ignores the white recorder's *Confessions,* for Gray tells us that Turner had been taught to pray by both white and black and to read and write by his parents. Abusing his literary freedom, Styron often emphasizes Turner's alleged contempt for other Negroes with such racially demeaning vulgarities as "my black shit-eating people were surely like flies, God's mindless outcasts" (39), an attitude that is not supported by anything in Gray.

Although he interlaces his narrative with allusions to the Bible and frequent quotations by his central character of passages from the Old Testament, Styron melodramatically reconstructs Turner's religious visions as the hallucinatory results of his long periods of religious fasting and the repression of overwhelming sex drives. Before he saw his first vision, for example, Turner grows dizzy and weak from fasting and praying for five days:

> On the morning of the fifth day I awoke feeling sickly and strange, with an aching emptiness at the pit of my belly and a giddiness swirling about my brain. Never had a fast affected me with such weakness. It had grown wickedly hot. Smoke from the distant wildfires hung sulphurous in the air, so thick that the myriad shifting piney motes of it were nearly visible like dust, all but obliterating the round unwinking eye of a malign and yellow sun. Tree frogs in the oaks and pines joined with great legions of

cicadas to set up an ominous shrilling, and my eardrums throbbed at the demented choir. (278–79)

By such diction as "wickedly," "sulphurous," "malign," "ominous," and "demented," this passage suggests not only that Turner's visions were the result of fasting but also that the ensuing vision of "a black angel clothed in black armor with black wings outspread from east to west" (279) was diabolical in nature. Another oblique reference to the nature of Turner's religious visions occurs in his comment on the summer of 1825 as "a time of great inner confusion and turmoil for me since I was 'on the fence,' so to speak, toying with the notion of slaughter and already *touched* with the premonition of a great mission" (251; my emphasis). Thus Styron re-creates Nat Turner as driven to his fate by religious fantasy. Considering Gray's *Confessions,* the slave-breeding practices of Virginia,[2] and the other realities of slavery, a more reasonable and credible driving force for oppressed slaves, as David Walker's 1829 radical antislavery pamphlet *Appeal* demonstrates, is freedom for himself and his people.

More significant by far than the impact of religion on Nat Turner's character in Styron's novel is the impact of his sex drives. On no evidence at all, Styron ascribes Turner's primary motives for revolt to a stereotypic yearning to rape and brutalize white women. As a youth, his weekly masturbatory fantasies would involve "always a nameless white girl [. . .] with golden curls" (172). Equally obsessive is his attraction to Miss Emmeline, his twenty-five-year-old mistress. At first, he yearns merely to look at her white "pure, proud, astonishing smooth-skinned beauty" (177). After accidentally discovering this apotheosis of Southern white womanhood being sexually ravished by her cousin, however, Turner alters his entire vision of white women. Thereafter, says Turner,

> In my fantasies she began to replace the innocent, imaginary girl with the golden curls as the object of my craving, and on those Saturdays when I stole into my private place in the carpenter's shop to release my pent-up desires, it was Miss Emmeline whose bare white full round hips and belly responded wildly to all my lust and who, sobbing "mercy, mercy, mercy" against my ear, allowed me to partake of the wicked and godless yet unutterable joys of defilement. (181–82)

That Styron clearly "departed from the *known* facts about Nat Turner and the revolt" (author's note) in this stereotypic representation of the legendary slave leader's identity should at this late date be obvious to experienced critics and reviewers, which raises questions about the qualifications of the judges who awarded the novel the Pulitzer Prize. Although Turner probably had a black wife and children, Styron melodramatically represents the slave leader's sexual obsession with white women and contempt for Negro women. "Through the Lord's grace," Turner could not be tempted by the successes of the other Negroes in luring "some black girl of the town [...] behind a shed" for the purpose of "group fornication" (251). Almost as an afterthought, Styron allows Turner to envision a sexual experience with a Negro girl. But what a vision! The Negro girl is salaciously depicted as "a plump doxy, every nigger boy's Saturday piece," with whom Turner imagines his mouth "buried in her wet crotch" (330).

Turner's distracted thoughts about white women form the center of Styron's characterization. Having come to Jerusalem with his master, for example, Turner is portrayed ignoring other Negroes and reading his Bible, only to become aroused by a beautiful white woman crying in the streets:

> And even as I stood there trying to dominate and still this passion, which I knew to be abominable to the Lord, I sensed my thoughts had already run galloping beyond control, and in a swift fantasy I saw myself down on the road beginning to possess her without tenderness, without gratitude for her pity but with abrupt, brutal, and rampaging fury, watching the compassion melt from her tearstained face as I bore her to the earth, my black hands already tearing at the lustrous billowing silk as I drew the dress up around her waist, and forcing apart those soft white thighs, exposed the zone of fleecy brown hair into which I drove my black self with stiff merciless thrusts. (255–56)

It is neither unreasonable nor unrealistic to represent a slave fantasizing about sex with women while masturbating. But it is neither reasonable nor realistic to even naïve black readers to represent the primary motive of the major leader of American history's most dramatic slave revolt as sexual obsessions for white women rather than, as Gray's *Confessions* reveals, the spiritual visions of biblical justice for the sins of slavery.

At the center of *The Confessions of Nat Turner* is Styron's wholly imaginary relationship between Turner and Margaret Whitehead, his former young white mistress, and the only person the historical Turner is reported to have killed in the revolt. Styron's fictional Turner has ambivalent feelings of hate and lust toward

Margaret. These feelings begin when the seventeen-year-old, pantalets-clad girl bursts into the library in search of a book and surprises Turner while he is installing book shelves in the Whitehead library. Even though aroused by Margaret's "firm young bottom" and "fragrance of lavender," Turner is enraged by the girl's obliviousness to her immodest dress in his presence (322, 324). Later, while driving Margaret in a carriage to her friend's house, Turner can neither "refrain from stealing a glance again at the twin soft ridgelike promontories where her skirt drew tight across her thighs" (346), nor dispel thoughts of raping the girl. While in jail awaiting his execution, the memory of Margaret's lavender smell stirs Styron's Turner with longing and desire, influencing him to think that he would not kill Margaret along with the other whites if the revolt was yet to happen. Intending that readers neither overlook nor misinterpret the sexual fury that drove his Turner to revolt, Styron reconstructs him envisioning himself in the ecstatic throes of sex with Margaret two hours before his death. Obviously, there is no basis for this in the known facts. Indeed, the evidence in Gray's *Confessions* tells a different story. Unlike Styron, Gray is impressed by Turner's refusing to the end to repudiate his biblical mission in any of its phases. In response to Gray's question about his current feelings—whether he repented his folly—Turner compares his fate to that of Christ and the salvation of sinners: "Was not Christ crucified?" (Aptheker, *Nat Turner's* 138).

Still exercising the utmost freedom of imagination, Styron represents Will, the executioner in the revolt, as an animal whom Turner fears so much that he is bullied into letting Will join the band of rebels and goaded into killing Margaret Whitehead. In Gray, however, Will joins the revolt after expressing the noble view that "his life was worth no more than others, and his liberty as dear to him" (Aptheker, *Nat Turner's* 139). Again, the implied nobility of the historical Will is in sharp contrast to Styron's obscene, pathological killer. In the novel, Will, who has just run away from his white master after breaking the master's left arm and shoulder with a stick, threatens Turner in a distorted dialect as follows: "You shit me, preacher man [. . .] an' I fix yo' preacher ass! I isn't gwine hang out in de swamp no mo' eatin' huckaberries. I gwine git me some *meat*. I gwine git me some *blood*. So, preacher man, you better figger dat Will done jined deruction! You maybe is some fancy talker but you isn't gwine talk Will out'n dat!" (358).

At the Whitehead house during the revolt, Will, having already challenged Turner's leadership and having nearly decapitated Mrs. Whitehead in a single stroke, spots Margaret Whitehead and tells Turner, "Dar she is, preacher man, dey's one left [. . .]. An she all your'n! Right by de cellar do'! Go git her preacher man. [. . .] Ifn you cain't make de *red juice* run you cain't run de *army!*" (390). Thus Styron's Will is another stereotype: the archetypal "bad nigger" run amok.

The fictional Turner's leadership of the revolt also raises interesting questions about Styron's omissions of other vital facts. Why, for example, does Styron's Turner fail to escape from slavery when, in fact, the actual Turner ran away from his master and remained in the woods thirty days? Also, why does Styron fail to include in his novel the fact that Turner—to the astonishment and disgust of other Negroes on the plantation—voluntarily returned to slavery because, as he says in Gray's *Confessions,* "the Spirit appeared to me and said I had my wishes directed to the things of this world and not to the kingdom of Heaven, and that I should return to the service of my earthly master" (Aptheker, *Nat Turner's* 136). Perhaps these facts are omitted because Turner's resolute sense of divine mission on earth was incompatible with the kind of irresolute Negro leader Styron chose to reconstruct. Finally, why does Styron fail to mention the fact that Turner did not plan the revolt by himself? Apparently Turner's statement in Gray would have undermined the solitary and aberrant Negro leadership Styron wished to portray: "I communicated the great work laid out for me to do, to four in whom I had the greatest confidence (Henry, Hark, Nelson, and Sam)—It was intended by *us* to have begun the work of death on the 4th of July last—Many *were the plans formed and rejected by us,* and it affected my mind to such a degree, that I fell sick and the time passed without *our* coming to any determination how to commence—" (Aptheker, *Nat Turner's* 138; my emphasis). In short, Styron's meditation on history is a rhetorical mask for the fictional deconstruction of Nat Turner as a violent, pathological, repressed Negro slave rapist of white women.

What then does the discerning reader conclude about Styron's *The Confessions of Nat Turner*? Briefly stated, the character of the narrator-hero is simply improbable and implausible. Styron has created yet another stereotyped Negro character and leader. Indeed, he has distorted the historical character and spiritual nature of the most legendary black slave revolt leader whose actual deeds vigorously undercut the stereotypic image of the slave as a contented and docile child. Styron calls his book "a meditation on history," and it is clearly a meditation by and about a white southerner who, consciously or not, resurrects the myth of the plantation tradition and reinforces contemporary perceptions of black leaders as a pathological menace to the power and privilege of the white ruling class. *The Confessions of Nat Turner* is Styron's own dramatic confession that he still understands neither the core identity traits of Negroes nor the core principles of black leaders like Nat Turner.

Notes

1. The complete title of the book alerts the reader to the problem of reliability with the court record and subsequent narratives of the Turner revolt: Thomas R. Gray, *The Confessions of Nat Turner, the leader of the late insurrection in Southampton, Va. As fully and voluntarily made to Thomas R. Gray, in the prison where he was confined and acknowledged by him to be such when read before the court of Southampton; with the certificate, under seal of the court convened at Jerusalem, Nov. 5, 1831, for his trial. Also an authentic account of the whole insurrection, with lists of the whites who were murdered, and of the Negroes brought before the court of Southampton, and there sentenced, & the right whereof he claims as proprietor* . . . (Baltimore: Lucas & Deaver, 1831); Eric Foner, ed. *Nat Turner* (Englewood Cliffs, NJ: Prentice Hall, 1971) 37–55.

2. See Stampp 245–51; Franklin 176–77.

V

Deconstructing the American Melting Pot and Literary Mainstream: Validating and Valorizing African American Literature in the College Curriculum

It can be argued that the study of English and the growth of Empire proceeded from a single ideological climate and that the development of the one is intrinsically bound up with the development of the other, both at the level of simple utility (as propaganda for instance) and at the unconscious level, where it leads to the naturalizing of constructed values (e.g. civilization, humanity, etc.) which, conversely, established "savagery," "native," "primitive," as their antitheses and as the object of a reforming zeal. A "privileging norm" was enthroned at the heart of the formation of English Studies as a template for the denial of the value of the "peripheral," the "marginal," the "uncanonized."

Bill Ashcroft, Gareth Griffiths, and Helen Tiffin,
The Empire Writes Back

> The literary history of the dominant white and male culture will only in a limited degree be a useful account of the development of the varied literary cultures of the United States. A full literary history of this country requires both parallel and integrated accounts of differing literary traditions and thus of differing (and changing) social realities.
>
> Paul Lauter, Canons and Contexts

This essay began as lectures in 1968 and 1969 to regional National Council of Teachers of English (NCTE) in Massachusetts and Vermont. Subsequent drafts were responses to the decline of administrative and academic support and funding for Black Studies in the 1970s with the reallocation of resources to such alternative rising interdisciplinary programs as Multiethnic, Women's, and Postcolonial Studies in colleges and universities. Disappointed by the increasing competitiveness for resources with the proliferation of interdisciplinary programs that frequently appropriated the historical struggle and rhetoric of African Americans to advance their own agenda while accusing proponents of Black Studies with reverse racism and identity politics, I became frustrated by the divide-and-delay tactics of reactionary traditional administrators in resisting changes in educational institutions mandated by affirmative action laws. So, I became increasingly vigorous and rigorous in revising drafts of this essay to develop more persuasive lectures on the imperatives of cultural diversity, academic excellence, and social responsibility in validating and valorizing African American culture and literature in the college curriculum. As a Fulbright scholar, I delivered the current draft of this essay as a lecture in 1996 at the University of Salamanca in Spain and in 2006 at Sichuan Normal University in the Peoples' Republic of China.

IN HISTORICALLY CONTEXTUALIZING THE DECLINE OF EMPIRE IN SPAIN, ROBERTO Fernandez Retamar satirically reminds us in *Caliban and Other Essays* that Britain has declined from the "Queen of the Seas" to "a provincial lady more closely resembling Agatha Christie's Miss Marple" (68). Expanding on the fact that Britain has declined as a dominant power in international affairs, the editors of *The Empire Writes Back* remind us that through the legacy of the British literary canon and through the standardization of "the English of south-east England as a universal norm, the weight of antiquity continues to dominate cultural production in much of the post-colonial world. This cultural hegemony has been maintained through canonical assumptions about literary activity, and through attitudes to post-colonial literature which identify them as isolated national offshoots of English literature, and which therefore relegate them to marginal and subordinate positions" (Ashcroft, Griffiths, and Tiffin 7). By postcolonial literature I am here referring mainly to writing by peoples formerly colonized by Britain.

In this sense, then, because I am an African Americanist, whose critical analyses are grounded in the sociohistorical and sociocultural specificity of the United States, rather than an Afrocentrist, whose critical analyses of African diasporic cultures centers on Africa, I agree with the editors of *The Empire Writes Back* that the "first post-colonial society to develop a 'national' literature was the USA. The emergence of a distinctive American literature in the late eighteenth century raised inevitable questions about the relationship between literature and place, between literature and nationality, and particularly about the suitability of inherited literary forms" (16). The experiences of Americans, especially black Americans of sub-Saharan African descent, and their attempts to produce and valorize a distinctive literature can therefore serve, and occasionally has served, as a model for other postcolonial writing.

"Whereas Afrocentricity is often dismissed as methodologically sloppy anti-intellectual identity politics, postcoloniality is affirmed as theoretically sophisticated oppositional discourse," writes African Americanist Ann du Cille. Identifying herself as neither a proponent of Afrocentricity nor an opponent of postcoloniality, du Cille argues that "the most critical factor in the current reception of these two resistance narratives may have more to do with market than with methodology—that is, with the academic merchandising of *different* difference. If postcoloniality is discourse—an exotic, foreign field whose time has come within the U.S. academy—Afrocentricity is 'dat course'—local color (homeboys and girls) whose foreignness has become all too familiar" (30). In a special issue of *Social Text*, Ella Shobat defines postcolonial as "a new designation for critical discourses which thematize issues emerging from colonial relations and their aftermath" (qtd. in du Cille 30). Primarily East Indian and Middle Eastern, the superstars of postcolonial criticism include Edward Said, Gayatri Chakravorty Spivak, Homi Bhabha, and Abdul JanMohammad.

But, as du Cille astutely reminds us,

> while the designation "postcolonial" may be new, the thematizing of relations of power between colonizer and colonized is not. In the U.S. black intellectuals such as W. E. B. Du Bois, Alexander Crummell, Pauline Hopkins, and Anna Julia Cooper engaged in such thematizing in the late nineteenth and early twentieth centuries. More recently, but still years—even decades—before the rise of postcoloniality as an academic discipline, black activists, scholars, writers, and theorists such as Marcus Garvey, C. L. R. James, Frantz Fanon, and Aimé Césaire explored and exploded colonial and postcolonial power relations. In current academic theaters Stuart Hall, Sylvia Wynter, Selwyn Cudjoe, Paget Henry, Paul Gilroy, Hazel Carby, and Cheikh Anta Diop are among the many African, African American, Afro-Caribbean and other scholars of African descent who continue to problematize and critique the relationship between Prospero and Caliban, metropole and province. (31)

Rather than blatant appropriation of the history, culture, and methodology of African American postcolonial and black cultural nationalism critics, the oppositional discourse of some East Indian and Middle Eastern postcolonial critics, as the deceased critic Edward Said explained in *Culture and Imperialism* (1993), is probably derived mainly from their own political, cultural, and literary history of struggle with colonialism.

Nevertheless, because of its ascendancy in the American academy as a more acceptable possible master narrative, postcoloniality, as one critic argues, "can be used within academia to displace those minority groups whose social struggles for inclusion, empowerment, and representation cleared the space within which postcoloniality operates" (qtd. in du Cille, 33). In some major universities postcoloniality has already displaced African American Studies. Attacks on the methodology of African Americanists and some Afrocentrists come from all directions, including from feminists, multiculturalists, postmodernists, and others who should have more respect for the field of study. For example, the white deconstructionist and former chair of the Department of African American Studies at Harvard University, Barbara Johnson, fallaciously assumes in her critique of a 1992 Henry Louis Gates lecture that the terms "black" and "white" not only "imply a relation of mutual exclusion" but also mark a reductive, oversimplistic racial binarism of "pure, unified, and separate traditions" (qtd. in du Cille 30). Werner Sollors, another former chair of the same department, and Maria Diedrich, the German editors of *The Black Columbiad* (1994) attempt to establish the authority of their international and transcultural contributors' and their own readings of African American texts by combining the specious and the self-evident in the following undocumented statement: "The genius and imaginative courage of New World black cultures are lost and the scarring quality of the African diaspora is denied in romantic or sentimental readings of these cultures that insist on African survivalism, on an uninterrupted continuity of the African and African American experience. In reality the relationship is much more complex, and involves appropriations, retrievals, inventions, and discontinuous, fragmented memories" (11). No respected African Americanists to my knowledge argue for "an uninterrupted continuity of the African and African American experience." On the contrary, all respected African Americanists acknowledge the complex relationship between the colonizer and the colonized.

When the late, venerable African American critic Jay Saunders Redding stated that "values and value judgments, ideas and ways of thinking about these ideas; customs, costumes and manners—all these and more, both abstract and concrete—are the same for Negro American and for white" ("Negro Writing" 9), it was fashionable to endorse the social myth and culinary metaphor of America as a melting pot of racial and ethnic groups, as well as the correlative yet conflicting cultural myth and organic metaphor of the literary mainstream to represent predominately white, Anglo-Saxon, Protestant male writers as canonical American literature. Popularized in 1908–09 by the "rarely read yet universally invoked play" *The Melting-Pot* by Israel Zangwill, "the melting pot," as critic Werner Sollors perceptively explains in *Beyond Ethnicity* "has been criticized sharply since the Zangwill era [...] yet the images of prophetic meltings, fusions, caldrons, American symphonies, and attacks on 'hard' hypocrites infected even Zangwill's opponents" (66, 97).

Equally tenacious and insidious in its hold on the imagination of popular and academic writers is the myth and metaphor of the mainstream. Following the lead of the *Oxford English Dictionary*, we can define mainstream as "the principal stream or current" or as "the prevailing direction of opinion, fashion, society, etc." In 1952 the editors of *New World Writing* expressed the prevailing view of the literary establishment that modern Negro artists, in moving out into the mainstream of American culture, should gain a sense of solidarity with both the national and general world of art. Even more illuminating and paradoxical is Ralph Ellison's statement in an American Academy of Arts and Sciences conference in 1965 that "the main stream of American literature is in me, even though I am Negro, because I possess more of Mark Twain than many white writers do" ("Transcript" 437). Metaphorically, the mainstream thus validates and valorizes the power and privilege of white Americans, especially males, as organic, natural, and normative.

Although Native American, black, ethnic, and women writers broaden and deepen the traditional narrow sense of the mainstream as canonical white male writers like Emerson, Thoreau, Twain, James, Hemingway, and Faulkner, the trope, as Americanist critic Paul Lauter observes in "The Literatures of America—a Comparative Discipline," misrepresents the cultural diversity and vitality of our national literary heritage. "The United States," as Lauter notes, "is a heterogeneous society whose cultures, while they overlap in significant respects, also differ in critical ways. A normative model presents those variations from the mainstream as abnormal, deviant, lesser; perhaps ultimately unimportant" (49). Attributions of marginality are thus contingent on assumptions of centrality. For, as Sollors writes in an unacknowledged confirmation of the opinion of such modern African American writers and critics as Sterling Brown and Ellison, "Though it is often regarded as a very minor adjunct to great American mainstream writing, ethnic literature is . . . prototypically American literature . . . and it is well worth it to interpret America not narrowly as immigration but more broadly as ethnic diversity and include the pre-Columbian inhabitants of the continent, the kidnapped Africans and their descendants, and the Chicanos of the Southwest—though they, too, are not classic immigrants" (*Beyond Ethnicity* 8). Lauter also proposes a comparativist model for the study of North American literature, but he does not suggest alternative tropes for the melting pot and mainstream. The consensus, however, of specialists in African American and multiethnic cultural and literary studies is that a gumbo, mosaic, tapestry, and patchwork quilt are more compelling, viable, and representative sociocultural metaphors of the unity with diversity of North American life and literature. Rather than reinforcing and perpetuating traditional racism and sexism as natural and normative, these revisionist tropes evoke the presence of women and nonwhite writers as a sociocultural construct of North American multiracial, multiethnic, and gender difference.

In his efforts to discredit mainly Black American Studies specialists whom he disputatiously calls "ethnic literary historians," Sollors, who, ironically, is a white German ethnic literary historian and specialist in Black American Studies, examines the historical trajectory of the racist sentiments involved in the origins in 1924 of the term "cultural pluralism" by cultural critic Horace M. Kallen. By comparing their antiassimilationist bias to that of the Ku Klux Klan, Sollors fallaciously argues that "the new ethnic literary historians may inadvertently become well-intentioned practitioners of Pluralism Klux Klan" ("A Critique of Pure Pluralism" 263). He also unpersuasively argues that "the melting-pot image is eminently dynamic" but "both mosaic and orchestra are static" (260). In the following lengthy but highly illuminating excerpt, Sollors conveniently summarizes his case for polyethnic or postethnic and postpluralist literary history and criticism for us:

> The birth of cultural pluralism was beset by ironies: a non-religious Jewish student was converted to Zionism by a Boston Brahmin professor who suffered from spells of repugnance brought about by race contact during dinners; the student denounces assimilation and endears himself to his professor by claiming the same feelings of repugnance toward a black fellow student (Alain Locke, the first black Rhodes Scholar in 1907) whom, with the help of his professor, he yet wants to protect against racism; and he views the young black intellectual, perhaps tongue-in-cheek, not as a fellow-philosophy student, but as an athlete and credit to the university. It seems strange, indeed, that Kallen singled out the early contact with Locke as the stimulus for pluralism when his own letters at the time of the incident make Kallen such an unlikely ancestor for contemporary pluralists. Upper-case "Cultural Pluralism" emerged in a world which also contained lower-case "negroes." (272)

But as Sollors admits and most senior African Americanists know, the tradition of cultural pluralism has changed significantly since 1924, especially since the post–World War II and post–civil rights eras.

More than twenty years ago, for example, in "Black Literature: What Happens to a Dream Deferred?" I first addressed the problems of the miseducation of American students and the misrepresentation of North American literature by the exclusion from the canon and curriculum of literature by Americans of African descent. I also outlined some prospects and methodologies for introducing this body of literature into the curriculum. Prior to the Black Studies movement of the late 1960s, the systematic exclusion of black writers from textbooks, anthologies, and surveys of American literature projected a false image of the cultural and literary ability and achievement of black Americans. In addition, it reinforced the historical antiblack racism and bigotry of white America. Most important, as a result of the conspiracy of silence about the literary achievements of black Americans, our knowledge as educators about America was at best incomplete and our qualifications for teaching black literature severely limited. What this meant for the majority of teachers was that before they could educate others about the achievements of black writers, they had an obligation to be serious and systematic in educating themselves about African American literature and cultural diversity in the United States. Today, in the wake of the Civil Rights, Black Power, Black Arts, Black Studies, and Women's Rights movements and of the most radical geopolitical, economic, and cultural developments since the Russian Revolution of 1917, we are on the threshold of what our globetrotting former president Bush Senior hailed as a new world order illuminated by the mystical thousand points of light generated by the Republican Party, which President Clinton misguidedly, if not blindly, reconstructed as the new American Dream. Despite notable advances over the past twenty years, enlightened revisionist educators and cultural workers are still resisting the dominance of Eurocentric standards of judgment in the validation and valorization of African American literature in the college curriculum.

The problems and prospects of validating and valorizing African American literature in the college curriculum may be conveniently and meaningfully discussed by examining the dual issues of academic resources and respect. By academic resources I mean the availability of committed, willing, qualified educators and administrators as well as adequate, appropriate, updated books and teaching materials, which, of course, all involve ideological and economic priorities in education and publishing. By academic respect I mean, first, the importance and value assigned to nonwhite people of sub-Saharan African descent in general and then to texts by black American authors, women and men, which, of course, involves both sociocultural ideology and literary theory, principles, and practices. Second, I mean the value accorded to those educators with demonstrated qualifications and serious professional commitments—as opposed to self-serving academic opportunism—to teaching and writing about these texts, which, of course, involves personnel and pedagogical policies and practices.

Responding both to the Civil Rights and Black Nationalist movements of the 1960s, especially the establishment of Black Studies departments and programs at many universities and colleges, and to the Women's Rights movement of the 1970s, some educators, administrators, and publishers began to revise traditional approaches to what and how American literature is taught. In 1967 several African American graduate students at the University of Massachusetts in Amherst, for example—including Nathaniel Sims, Michael Thelwell, and this author—began drafting proposals to develop African American Studies departments at the university and at Smith, Amherst, Mount Holyoke, and Hampshire Colleges. The major purpose of these departments was to critique, challenge, and change traditional white, male, Western ideological hegemony in the curriculum of these institutions.

This would be achieved by introducing, increasing, and validating the presence of black American, African, and Caribbean faculty, students, staff, and sources in the institution at all levels, as well as by developing alternative interdisciplinary methods and interpretations that moved Africa and peoples of African descent from the margins to the center in our pedagogy and scholarship. Similar efforts by black undergraduate and graduate students and their supporters at predominantly white institutions on both the East and West Coasts resulted in the establishment by 1970 of Black Studies programs, centers, institutes, or departments at most major and many minor colleges and universities. The influence of this movement and civil rights laws, especially affirmative action policies, was the belated, reluctant efforts of many conservative white integrationist academics who had historically denied the validity or denigrated the quality of black American life, literature, and history to introduce selected black courses, texts, and writers in their relevant traditional disciplines.

After decades of racism that influenced black educators and administrators at historically and predominantly black institutions of higher education to organize the College Language Association (CLA) in 1937, the Modern Language Association (MLA) asserted its political, economic, and cultural institutional dominance in the theory and practice of teaching languages and literatures in the United States by designating white Ivy League institutions as the primary site for reconstructing North American literature. The Committee on the Literature and Language of America, formerly the Committee on Minority Literature, advocated that "an adequate American literary history requires a model based on a multiethnic and multiracial, rather than a European theory of culture," that a new American literary history and pedagogy "requires radical inquiries about the relations between literature and national identity," and that a redefinition of American literary history "calls for an understanding that American literature is a patchwork quilt created by many hands" (Ruoff and Ward 2).

In the introduction to *Redefining American Literary History*, editors A. La Vonne Brown Ruoff, a specialist in Native American literature, and Jerry Ward, a specialist in African American literature, tell us about the role of the committee of the MLA in belatedly providing academic resources and respect for revising the curriculum. Beginning with the seminars in Native American and African American literatures that it cosponsored in 1977 with the National Endowment for the Humanities, its programs at annual conventions, and the volumes of critical essays and course designs published under its sponsorship, the committee advocated the reconceptualization of American literary history and the American literary canon. In addition to *Redefining*

American Literary History, edited by Ruoff and Ward, these seminars and programs resulted in the publication of three more volumes by the MLA: *Minority Language and Literature,* edited by Dexter Fisher; *Afro-American Literature: The Reconstruction of Instruction,* edited by Dexter Fisher and Robert B. Stepto; and *Studies in American Indian Literature,* edited by Paula Gunn Allen (Ruoff and Ward 1).

Because of the change of heart, mind, fortune, or job market—resulting mainly from the activism of civil rights and Black Power advocates—some educators, black and white, have become not only willing but eager overnight specialists in African American literature. Although most are unfamiliar with and unsympathetic to the problem of the color line between the MLA and CLA, which was most dramatically bridged with the election of Houston A. Baker Jr., one of the most distinguished African American critics in the nation, to the presidency of the MLA in 1991, some have taken a course or two, taught a course or two, or written a biocritical article or two for one of the many reference books on black culture that are currently in vogue. Others have even turned their backs on years of formal preparation for doctoral degrees in European or British literature to write dissertations on an African American writer—usually Alice Walker, Toni Morrison, or Zora Neale Hurston—and a British, African, or white American writer, usually a woman. The recruitment of these ostensibly well-intentioned but usually less than well-qualified individuals to develop African American courses is not as desirable as hiring educators with the extensive, highly respected academic commitment, background, and achievement in teaching, publishing, and service that recruitment and personnel committees generally require for appointments and promotions in the traditional disciplines at nationally respected institutions. Because the pool of committed, well-qualified black American teachers of African American literature with postgraduate academic credentials and experience is disappointingly and frustratingly small, largely because of vestigial institutionalized racism, many are called to teach African American literature, but few are chosen.

Although the resistance of many educators and administrators to a systematic, committed validation and valorization of African American literature in the curriculum is in part attributable to antiblack racism, for some it is neither the only nor the main reason for resistance to curricular reform. Some educators and administrators are reluctant to consider or even tolerate curricular changes because of personal insecurities and ignorance about other cultures than their own and their traditional relationship to Eurocentric canonical texts. Others may suffer professional anxiety about the probability of diminished student enrollment in their traditional specialities or the possibility of diminished administrative power and privilege. As Lauter notes in "Reconstructing American Literature: Curricular Issues," "Such ignorance can, of course, be overcome through study and experience, to which more and more of our colleagues have committed themselves in faculty development seminars, in institutes, and in their own changing research" (101).

Whether we call it a sluggish economic recovery, deeper economic recession, or imminent economic depression, times are hard for white-collar, blue-collar, and no-collar workers. As corporations, businesses, and municipal governments downsize, reorganize, and relocate jobs outside of the United States, many of these people are relegated to part-time, nonbenefit labor in service industries. Others are joining the hungry and homeless in trying to survive the harsh realities fostered by the trickle-down economics of Reaganism and the voodoo economics of Bush, who proclaimed himself the champion of national education reform while his secretary of education, William Bennett, began an unrelenting conservative attack on educational and curricular reform, especially multiculturalism. Former congressman Newt Gingrich and the Republican-controlled Congress threatened and then completed their attack with the dismantling and ultimate elimination of the Department of Education and the social reforms initiated by President Roosevelt's New Deal and President Johnson's War on Poverty. This means that it was and is even more imperative in reconstructing American literature to represent more accurately, truthfully, and justly the cultural pluralism and diversity of the United States and that legislators and administrators in control of purse strings search their souls and screw their courage to the sticking place in targeting this crucial educational need for sustained, if not increased, high-priority funding for curricular reform.

In addition to the problems and prospects of the human and material resources already discussed in the institutionalization of African American literature, publishers must be encouraged and supported in printing and keeping in print the necessary books and other pedagogical reference materials. As quiet as it is kept by the ruling class, black Americans published a substantial number of important books of literature before and after World War I. For example, such landmark publications as Booker T. Washington's *Up from Slavery* (1901); Charles W. Chesnutt's *The Conjure Woman* (1899) and *House of the Cedars* (1900); Paul Laurence Dunbar's *Lyrics of Lowly Life* (1896) and *The Sport of the Gods* (1902); W. E. B. Du Bois's *The Souls of Black Folk* (1903); James Weldon Johnson's *The Autobiography of an Ex-Colored Man* (1911; reprinted 1927) and *The Book of American Negro Poetry* (1922); Jean Toomer's *Cane* (1923); and Alain Locke's *The New Ne-*

gro (1925) appeared at the turn of the twentieth century and during the Harlem Renaissance era of the New Negro movement. However, "these facts," as Lauter confirms in "Race and Gender in the Shaping of the American Literary Canon," "were in no way reflected in the teaching of American literature, in general anthologies, or in most critical discussions by whites of the literature of the United States." Lauter continues with the facts to support his claim: "of twenty-one major classroom anthologies (and their numerous revised editions) produced between 1917 and 1950, nine contained no works by black artists; three include only a few spirituals; four contained one black writer each [...] two printed some spirituals and one black writer each. [...] Only three somewhat unusual anthologies include the work of more than one black writer—never more than three—as well as a few spirituals or work songs. General and classroom poetry anthologies reveal a similar pattern. [...] It took fifteen years after *Brown v. Board of Education* and a decade after the sit-ins began to achieve even token representation of black writers in contemporary anthologies" (24–27).

But even American literature collections of the 1980s by such publishers as Norton and MacMillan provide inadequate representation of black and women writers. In fact, it was not until the 1990 publication of the *Heath Anthology of American Literature* by general editor Paul Lauter and other editors that we find an appropriately balanced representation of cultural diversity in the United States. It includes 109 women writers of all races, 25 Native Americans, 53 African Americans, 13 Hispanics, and 9 Asian Americans. Even so, in teaching a graduate seminar on the Harlem Renaissance, I was frustrated to discover that essential primary and secondary sources such as Wallace Thurman's *Infants of the Spring* and Nathan Huggins's *Voices of the Harlem Renaissance* were out of print in spite of efforts by Thundermouth Press, reprint publishers, and reprinting series at several university presses. Although both of these texts are now back in print, such essential black contemporary texts as Ishmael Reed's *Mumbo Jumbo* are now out of print. And so, as a popular black folksaying goes, the more things change, the more they remain the same.

As my students know, my motto and mantra for enhancing the prospects for valorizing African American literature in the classroom and college curriculum is historicize, contextualize, and problematize the texts. While I disagree with those critics who disdain and decry periodicity and ethnicity as viable methods for contextualizing texts in the temporal and spatial matrix of dynamic social and ideological forces that influence the shifting sands of literary principles and practices, conventions, and canons, I am nevertheless mindful that any theory or method—whether diachronic or synchronic, dialectic or dialogic—is only as effective and enlightening as the sensitive, informed, and innovative reader or critic who employs it. Rather than a literary survey of images and masterpieces or an ahistorical, abstract postmodern approach, the most resourceful and revealing probable approach is to employ some comparative form of neocolonial or postcolonial dialectical or dialogical model that primarily illuminates the complex relationship of the production of texts in historically specific contexts to their consumption by readers and that then examines the linguistic dynamics of intertextuality, self-reflexivity, and multivocality. Thirty years ago, I used to require students to analyze the language, myths, and rituals of the American Dream and what happens to a dream deferred in texts by white and nonwhite Americans. This approach may be useful still for some teachers and students, depending on when, where, and how they choose to respond to the challenge of interrogating the dominant monocultural narratives of the American past and contrasting them with different multicultural narratives of an American past and future.

According to Robert B. Stepto, "The Afro-American pregeneric myth is the quest for freedom *and* literacy. Once this is absorbed, our instructor will be able to abandon freely most nonliterary structures exclusively from freedom myths devoid of linguistic properties, speak rarely to questions of freedom and literacy" (18). In contrast, I attempt to demonstrate in *The Afro-American Novel and Its Tradition* (1987) that beneath the apparent multivocality of the tradition the principal African American canonical story is the quest for life, liberty, and wholeness—the full, socially equal development and unity of the self and the black community—as a biracial, bicultural people, as hybrid American citizens of African descent.

Because of the colonial and postcolonial distinctive history and acculturation of Africans in the British colonies during the eighteenth-century North American revolutionary period, their literary tradition and texts are most meaningfully assessed by examining them in the context of the tension between African American attitudes and movements toward, on the one hand, integration and separation and, on the other, the oral and literate heritages of African Americans. In *The Roots of American Culture* (1942) Constance Rourke traces the folk philosophy of literature from Montaigne to Herder and concludes that Johann Gottfried von Herder's theory of folk art went unnoticed in North America until some of the Transcendentalists and Walt Whitman saw its major implications for their efforts to develop a national literature. Although it does not give adequate attention to the fact that among the earliest indigenous literary forms in the United States are African American folk songs and slave narratives, Gene Bluestein's *The Voice of the Folk* (1972) expands these observations into an intriguing thesis. According to Bluestein, Emerson and Whitman found the then radical notion of folk art, especially folk song, as the base of a nation's formal written literature compatible with their own ideas and efforts. Unlike Rousseau, who also emphasized the value of "primitive" cultures but included the corollary idea that civilization destroys them (which was a popular theory and practice during the Harlem Renaissance movement of the 1920s), Herder "does not suggest nostalgia for some irretrievable golden age; the importance of this point of view lies in his emphasis upon the persistence within contemporary society of folk traditions and his argument that a national literature can be attained only through building upon them" (7). In 1974 I rewrote this theory in *The Folk Roots of Contemporary Afro-American Poetry* from an Afrocentric perspective.

Although some contemporary Americanists turn to Horace Kallen's American Zionist theory of ethnicity in "Democracy versus the Melting Pot," which was first published in 1924, and some to Mikhail Bakhtin's Russian dialogic theory of the novel in "Discourse on the Novel," which was first published in 1934, for the significance of cultural pluralism and double-voiced texts, I turn instead to W. E. B. Du Bois's "Strivings of the Negro People," published in 1897, and *The Souls of Black Folk,* published in 1903. "It is a peculiar sensation this double-consciousness," Du Bois wrote in his frequently quoted metaphorical definition of the dual identity of black Americans, "this sense of always looking at one's self through the eyes of others, of measuring one's soul by the tape of a world that looks on in amused contempt and pity. One ever feels his twoness,—an American, a Negro; two souls, two thoughts, two unreconciled strivings; two warring ideals in one dark body, whose dogged strength alone keeps it from being torn asunder" (76). Clearly, for Du Bois the impact of racialized slavery and segregation was not the fate of all ethnic immigrants and hyphenated Americans. It was, instead, the complex fate of Americans of African descent whose humanity and culture had been historically devalued and marginalized by the political, social, economic, and cultural dominance of people of European and British descent. Because, as white feminist critic Elaine Showalter argues in "A Criticism of Our Own," some feminist, gay, and postcolonial critics see historical parallels between our quest and theirs, they employ similar critical metaphors and theories, "such as the notion of a double-voiced discourse, the imagery of the veil, the mask, or the closet" (349).

Insofar as Du Bois's prophecy that "the problem of the twentieth century is the problem of the color line" is valid and true, he would probably predict that the problem of the twenty-first century will be the problem of bicultural and biracial identity, the struggle of people to reconcile the sociopsychological and sociocultural tension between the individual's personal and ethnic group consciousnesses and between the individual's ethnic and national identities. When this problem has been historically and rhetorically addressed in most European countries, it has been benignly encoded as the problem of ethnic pluralism, but when addressed in most African countries, it has been pejoratively encoded as tribalism. However, by both signs the social referent it marks has tragically degenerated most recently into the genocidal wars of ethnic cleansing in Eastern Europe and Central Africa. The American motto *E Pluribus Unum*—unity with diversity or from many people, one nation—is, in contrast, mythologized in the sanctioned histories and mottoes of the former Union of Soviet Socialist Republics, as well as in such nations as Brazil, Portugal, Jamaica, Cuba, and Trinidad.

As for enhancing the respect for those educators with a demonstrated commitment to validating and valorizing African American literature in the college curriculum, institutions must do more than profess a commitment to cultural diversity and affirmative action as an integral part of their mission to educate an increasingly heterogeneous student body and social system. Arguably, among other things, colleges and universities should develop a five-stage model for the twenty-first century. First, an office of educational equity should be established to develop a five-year plan to implement federal and state affirmative action plans. Second, a minimum cultural diversity university requirement ought to be established for undergraduate students. Third, an office of curriculum development and enhancement that supports with grants and awards the introduction of new courses including a cultural diversity focus should be established in each college. Fourth, a well-funded, president-and provost-supported Center for the Recruitment and Retention of Minority Graduate Students, Faculty, and Staff should be established at each university under the directorship of a progressive, highly qualified academic administrator with experience in the Civil Rights movements. Finally, the affirmative action officer on each campus should also be proactive instead of reactive in monitoring vigorously the personnel, curricular, and pedagogical policies and practices concerning African American and other minority students, faculty, and staff.

"One concept that I wish we would get rid of," Ralph Ellison stated in 1965, "is the concept of a main stream of American culture—which is an exact mirroring of segregation and second-class citizenship. I do not think that America works that way at all. I would remind us that before there was a United States, a nation, or a form of a state, there were Negroes in the colonies. The interaction among the diversified cultural groups helped to shape whatever it is we are who call ourselves Americans" ("Transcript" 414). What I am suggesting, then, is that in order for students to develop a critical understanding and appreciation of the heterogeneity of American society and the world, educators and administrators need to be committed, sensitive, informed, and innovative agents of change for the future in institutionalizing African American literature in the college curriculum.

WORKS CITED

Achebe, Chinua. *The Chancellor's Lecture Series, 1974–1975.* Amherst: U of Massachusetts, 1975.

Andrews, William L. *To Tell a Free Story: The First Century of Afro-American Autobiography 1760–1865.* Urbana: U of Illinois P, 1988.

Anzaldúa, Gloria. *Borderlands/La Frontera: The New Mestiza.* San Francisco: Aunt Lute, 1987.

Appiah, Anthony. "The Uncompleted Argument: Du Bois and the Illusion of Race." *"Race," Writing, and Difference.* Ed. Henry Louis Gates Jr. Chicago: U of Chicago P, 1976. 21–37.

Aptheker, Herbert, ed. *A Documentary History of the Negro People in the United States.* 1951. New York: Citadel, 1965.

———. *Nat Turner's Slave Rebellion.* New York: Humanities, 1966.

Asante, Molefi. *The Afrocentric Idea.* Philadelphia: Temple UP, 1987.

Ashcroft, Bill, Gareth Griffiths, and Helen Tiffin, eds. *The Empire Writes Back: Theory and Practice in Post-Colonial Literatures.* London: Routledge, 1989.

Assefa, Hizkias, and Paul Wahrhaftig. *Extremist Groups and Conflict Resolution: The MOVE Crisis in Philadelphia.* New York: Praeger, 1988.

Bacon, Sir Francis. "Of Studies." *Essays or Counsels, Civil and Moral.* Ed. Brian Vickers. New York: Oxford UP, 1999. 114–15.

Baker, Houston A., Jr. *Blues, Ideology, and Afro-American Literature: A Vernacular Theory.* Chicago: U of Chicago P, 1984.

Bakhtin, Mikhail M. *The Dialogic Imagination: Four Essays.* Trans. Caryl Emerson and Michael Holquist. Ed. Michael Holquist. Austin: U of Texas P, 1981.

Baldwin, James. *The Fire Next Time.* New York: Dial, 1963.

———. *Notes of a Native Son.* Boston: Beacon, 1955.

———. *The Price of the Ticket: Collected Nonfiction 1948–1985.* New York: St. Martin's, 1985.

Barbour, Floyd B., ed. *The Black Power Revolt: A Collection of Essays.* Boston: Collier, 1968.

Bassett, P. S. "A Visit to the Slaver Mother Who Killed Her Child." *American Baptist* 12 Feb. 1856: n.pag. Rpt. *The Black Book.* Comp. Middleton A. Harris, Ernest Smith, Morris Levitt, and Roger Furman. New York: Random, 1974. 10.

Bell, Bernard W. *The Afro-American Novel and Its Tradition.* Amherst: U of Massachusetts P, 1987.

———. "Black Literature: What Happens to a Dream Deferred?" *New England Association of Teachers of English Leaflet* 69 (1970): 3–10.

———. *The Folk Roots of Contemporary Afro-American Poetry.* Detroit: Broadside, 1974.

———. "A Key to the Black Experience in America." *Massachusetts Review* 10.1 (1969): 179–82.

———, ed. *Modern and Contemporary Afro-American Poetry.* Boston: Allyn, 1972.

Berghahn, Marion. *Images of Africa in Black American Literature.* Totowa, NJ: Rowman, 1977.

Bhabha, Homi. *The Location of Culture.* New York: Routledge, 1994.

Bialostosky, Don. "Dialogics as an Art of Discourse in Literary Criticism." *PMLA* 101.5 (1986): 788–97.

Blair, Walter. *Mark Twain and Huck Finn.* Berkeley: U of California P, 1960.

———. *Native American Humor.* 1937. San Francisco: Chandler, 1960.

Blauner, Robert. "Black Culture: Myth or Reality?" *Afro-American Anthropology: Contemporary Perspectives.* Ed. Norman E. Whitten Jr. and John F. Szwed. New York: Free, 1970. 347–66.

Bluestein, Gene. *The Voice of the Folk: Folklore and American Literary Theory.* Amherst: U of Massachusetts P, 1972.

Bone, Robert. *The Negro Novel in America.* Rev. ed. New Haven: Yale UP, 1965.

Bontemps, Arna. Introduction. *Great Slave Narratives.* Ed. Bontemps. Boston: Beacon, 1969. vii–xix.

Booth, Wayne C. *The Rhetoric of Fiction.* Chicago: U of Chicago P, 1961.

Brawley, Benjamin Griffith. *The Negro in Literature and Art in the United States.* 3rd ed. New York: Duffield, 1929.

Brooks, Van Wyck. *The Ordeal of Mark Twain.* 1920. New York: Dutton, 1970.

Brown, Sterling A. "Negro Character as Seen by White Authors." *Journal of Negro Education* 2 (1933): 197–203. Rpt. *The New Cavalcade* 1. Ed. Arthur P. Davis, J. Saunders Redding, and Joyce Ann Joyce. Washington, DC: Howard UP, 1991. 607–39.

———. *The Negro in American Fiction.* New York: Atheneum, 1969.

Brown, Sterling N. *My Own Life Story.* Washington, DC: Hamilton, 1924.

Bruce, Dickson D., Jr. "W.E.B. Du Bois and the Idea of Double Consciousness." *American Literature* 64 (June 1992): 229–309.

Cade, John B. "Out of the Mouths of Ex-Slaves." *Journal of Negro History* 20 (1935): 294–337.

Campbell, Stanley W. *The Slave Catchers: Enforcement of the Fugitive Slave Law, 1850-1860.* New York: Norton, 1972.

Carretta, Vincent. "Olaudah Equiano or Gustavus Vassa? New Light on an Eighteenth-Century Question of Identity." *Slavery and Abolition* 20.3 (Dec. 1999): 96–105.

Census Bureau Facts for Features. 1999. http://www.census.gov/Press-Release/cb98-139.html.

Chambers, Veronica. "The Invisible Woman Reappears—Sort Of." *Newsweek* 16 Feb. 1998: 68.

Christian, Barbara. *Black Women Novelists: The Development of a Tradition, 1892-1976.* Westport, CT: Greenwood, 1980.

———. "Images of Black Women in Afro-American Literature: From Stereotype to Character." *Black Feminist Criticism.* By Christian. New York: Pergamon, 1985. 1–30.

Cleaver, Eldridge. *Soul on Ice.* New York: McGraw, 1968.

Clemens, Susy. *Papa: An Intimate Biography of Mark Twain.* Ed. Charles Neider. New York: Doubleday, 1988.

The Compact Edition of the Oxford English Dictionary. New York: Oxford UP, 1971.

Conrad, Joseph. *Heart of Darkness.* Ed. Robert Kimbrough. New York: Norton, 1963.

Delany, Martin R. *Blake; or, The Huts of America.* Boston: Beacon, 1970.

DeVoto, Bernard, ed. *Mark Twain in Eruption: Hitherto Unpublished Pages about Men and Events.* New York: Harper, 1940.

———. *The Portable Mark Twain.* 1946. New York: Penguin, 1979.

Douglass, Frederick. "What to the Slave Is the Fourth of July? An Address Delivered in Rochester, New York, on 5 July 1852." *The Frederick Douglass Papers; Series One: Speeches, Debates, and Interviews.* Ed. John W. Blassingame. Vol. 2: 1847–54. New Haven: Yale UP, 1982. 367–75.

Downing, Henry F. *The American Cavalryman: A Liberian Romance.* 1917. College Park: McGrath, 1969.

Dubey, Madhu. *Black Women Novelists and the Nationalist Aesthetic.* Bloomington: Indiana UP, 1994.

Du Bois, W. E. B. *The Autobiography of W.E.B. DuBois: A Soliloquy on Viewing My Life from the Last Decade of Its First Century.* New York: International, 1968.

——. "The Conservation of Races." *The Seventh Son: The Thought and Writings of W. E. B. DuBois.* Ed. Julius Lester. Vol. 1. New York: Vintage, 1971. 176–87.

——. "A Fellow of Harvard." *The Papers of W.E.B. Du Bois (1877–1963).* Comp. Robert W. McDonnell. U of Massachusetts, Amherst: Microfilming Corporation of America, 1981.

——. *The Souls of Black Folk: Essays and Sketches.* 1903. Greenwich: Fawcett, 1961.

——. "Strivings of the Negro People." *Atlantic* Aug. 1897: 194–98.

——. "The Talented Tenth." *The Negro Problem: A Series of Articles by Representative American Negroes of Today.* New York: Pott, 1903. 31–76.

——. "The Talented Tenth: The Reexamination of a Concept." *The Papers of W.E.B. Du Bois (1877–1963).* Comp. Robert W. McDonnell. U of Massachusetts, Amherst: Microfilming Corporation of America, 1981.

du Cille, Ann. "Postcolonialism and Afrocentricity: Discourse and Dat Course." *The Black Columbiad.* Ed. Werner Sollors and Maria Diedrich. Cambridge: Harvard UP, 1994. 28–41.

Dyson, Michael. *Reflecting Black: African American Cultural Criticism.* Minneapolis: U of Minnesota P, 1993.

Early, Gerald. *Lure and Loathing.* New York: Viking, 1993.

Eckman, Fern Maria. *The Furious Passage of James Baldwin.* New York: Evans, 1966.

Egan, Michael. *Mark Twain's* Huckleberry Finn: *Race, Class and Society.* 1977. Atlantic Highlands, NJ: Humanities, 1978.

Eliot, T. S. "Tradition and the Individual Talent." *The Sacred Wood: Essays on Poetry and Criticism.* 1920. London: Methuen, 1964. 47–59.

Elkins, Stanley M. *Slavery: A Problem in American Institutional and Intellectual Life.* New York: Universal Library, 1959.

Ellis, Trey. "The New Black Aesthetic." *Callaloo* 12.1 (38) (1989): 234–35.

——. *Platitudes.* New York: Vintage, 1988.

——. "Response to NBA Critiques." *Callaloo* 12.1 (38) (1989): 250–51.

Ellison, Ralph. "Change the Joke and Slip the Yoke." *Shadow and Act.* New York: Random, 1964. 45–59.

——. *Shadow and Act.* 1964. New York: Signet, 1966.

——. "Transcript of the American Academy Conference on the Negro American—May 14–15, 1965." *Daedalus: Journal of the American Academy of Arts and Sciences* (Winter 1966): 287–441.

———. "Twentieth-Century Fiction and the Black Mask of Humanity." *Shadow and Act.* New York: Random, 1964. 24–44.

———. "The World and the Jug." *Shadow and Act.* 1964. New York: Signet, 1966. 107–43.

Equiano, Olaudah. *The Interesting Narrative of the Life of Olaudah Equiano, or Gustavus Vassa, Written by Himself. Great Slave Narratives.* Ed. Arna Bontemps. Boston: Beacon, 1969.

Faulkner, William. *Go Down, Moses.* New York: Vintage, 1973.

Favor, J. Martin. "'Ain't Nothin' Like the Real Thing, Baby': Trey Ellis' Search for New Black Voices." *Callaloo* 16.3 (1993): 694–705.

———. *Authentic Blackness: The Folk in the New Negro Renaissance.* Durham: Duke UP, 1999.

Foner, Philip S. *Mark Twain: Social Critic.* 1958. New York: International, 1975.

Franklin, John Hope. *From Slavery to Freedom: A History of Negro Americans.* 4th ed. New York: Knopf, 1974.

Fuss, Diana. *Essentially Speaking: Feminism, Nature, and Difference.* New York: Routledge, 1989.

Gabbin, Joanne V. *Sterling A. Brown: Building the Black Aesthetic Tradition.* Westport, CT: Greenwood, 1985.

Gates, Henry Louis, Jr. *Figures in Black: Words, Signs, and the "Racial" Self.* New York: Oxford UP, 1987.

———. *Loose Canons: Notes on the Culture Wars.* New York: Oxford UP, 1992.

———. *The Signifying Monkey: A Theory of Afro-American Literary Criticism.* New York: Oxford UP, 1988.

Gates, Henry Louis, Jr., and Cornel West. *The Future of the Race.* New York: Knopf, 1996.

Gayle, Addison, Jr. *The Way of the New World.* Garden City, NY: Anchor, 1975.

Giddings, Paula. *When and Where I Enter.* New York: Morrow, 1984.

Gilroy, Paul. *The Black Atlantic: Modernity and Double Consciousness.* Cambridge: Harvard UP, 1993.

Gittleman, Edwin. "Jefferson's 'Slave Narrative': The Declaration of Independence as a Literary Text." *Early American Literature* 8 (1974): 239–56.

Gordon, Robert, and Bruce Nemerov, eds. *Lost Delta Found: Rediscovering the Fisk University–Library of Congress Coahoma County Study, 1941–1942.* Nashville, TN: Vanderbilt UP, 2005.

Haight, Anne Lyon. *Banned Books: Informal Notes on Some Books Banned for Various Reasons at Various Times and in Various Places.* 3rd ed. New Providence, NJ: Bowker, 1970.

Hammon, Jupiter. *Jupiter Hammon, American Negro Poet; Selections from His Writing and a Bibliography.* 1915. Ed. Oscar Wegelin. Miami, FL: Mnemosyne, 1969.

Harding, Vincent. *There Is a River.* San Diego: Harcourt, 1993.

Harrison, Paul Carter, ed. *Totem Voices: Plays from the Black World Repertory.* New York: Grove, 1989.

Healy, Patrick. "States Urged to Make New Efforts to End Persistent Segregation." *Chronicle of Higher Education* 26 May 1995: A29.

Hentoff, Nat. "Huck Finn Better Get Out of Town by Sundown." *Village Voice* 4 May 1982.

Herskovits, Melville J. *Life in a Haitian Valley.* New York: Knopf, 1937.

Hill, Hamlin. "Mark Twain: Audience and Artistry." *Mark Twain: Selected Criticism.* Ed. Arthur Scott. Rev. ed. Dallas: Southern Methodist UP, 1967. 286–302.

Hill, Patricia Liggins, Bernard W. Bell, Trudier Harris, William J. Harris, R. Baxter Miller, Sondra A. O'Neale, and Horace Porter, eds. *Call and Response: The Riverside Anthology of the African American Literary Tradition.* Boston: Houghton, 1998.

Hine, Darlene Clark. "In the Kingdom of Culture: Black Women and the Intersection of Race, Gender, and Class." *Lure and Loathing: Essays on Race, Identity, and the Ambivalence of Assimilation.* Ed. Gerald Early. New York: Penguin, 1993. 337–51.

Holloway, Joseph E. "The Origins of African American Culture." In *Africanisms in American Culture.* Ed. Joseph E. Holloway. Bloomington: Indiana UP, 1991. 18–38.

Holman, C. Hugh, and William Harmon. *A Handbook to Literature.* 6th ed. New York: Macmillan, 1992.

Holt, Thomas C. "The Political Uses of Alienation: W. E. B. Du Bois on Politics, Race, and Culture, 1903–1940." *American Quarterly* 42 (June 1990): 301–23.

hooks, bell. *Ain't I a Woman.* Boston: South End, 1981.

Hopkins, Pauline E. *Contending Forces: A Romance Illustrative of Negro Life North and South.* 1900. Miami: Mnemosyne, 1969.

Hord, Fred Lee (Mzee Lasana Okpara), and Jonathan Scott Lee, eds. *I Am Because We Are: Readings in Black Philosophy.* Amherst: U of Massachusetts P, 1995.

Howells, William Dean. *My Mark Twain: Reminiscences and Criticisms.* Ed. Marilyn A. Baldwin. Baton Rouge: Louisiana State UP, 1967.

Hughes, Langston. *The Big Sea.* New York: Hill, 1993.

Hull, Gloria, Patricia Bell Scott, and Barbara Smith, eds. *All the Women Are White, All the Blacks Are Men; but Some of Us Are Brave.* Old Westbury, NY: Feminist, 1982.

Hurston, Zora Neale. *Every Tongue Got to Confess: Negro Folk-Tales from the Gulf States.* Ed. Carla Kaplan. New York: Perennial, 2002.

———. *Mules and Men: Negro Folktales and Voodoo Practices in the South.* New York: Perennial, 1970.

Iser, Wolfgang. *The Act of Reading.* Baltimore: Johns Hopkins UP, 1978.

Jackson, Blyden. *The Waiting Years: Essays on American Negro Literature.* Baton Rouge: Louisiana State UP, 1976.

Jameson, Frederic. *The Political Unconscious: Narrative as a Socially Symbolic Act.* Ithaca: Cornell UP, 1981.

Jaynes, Gerald David, and Robin M. Williams, Jr., eds. *A Common Destiny: Blacks and American Society.* Washington: National Academy, 1989.

Jefferson, Thomas. *Notes on the State of Virginia.* Ed. William Peden. Chapel Hill: U of North Carolina, 1955.

Johnson, Charles. *Being and Race: Black Writing since 1970.* Bloomington: Indiana UP, 1988.

———. *Faith and the Good Thing.* New York: Simon, 1974.

———. *Middle Passage.* New York: Atheneum, 1990.

Johnson, Randal. "Pierre Bourdieu on Art, Literature, and Culture." Introduction. *The Field of Cultural Production: Essays on Art and Literature.* By Pierre Bourdieu. Ed. Randal Johnson. New York: Columbia UP, 1993.

Jones, Gayl. *Eva's Man.* New York: Random, 1976.

———. *The Healing.* Boston: Beacon, 1998.

———. *Liberating Voices: Oral Tradition in African American Literature.* New York: Penguin, 1992.

Jones, Howard Mumford. Foreword. *A History of American Literature, 1607–1765.* By Moses Coit Tyler. Ithaca, NY: Cornell UP, 1949.

Jordan, Winthrop D. *White over Black: American Attitudes Toward the Negro, 1550–1812.* Chapel Hill: U of North Carolina P, 1968.

Kaplan, Justin. *Mark Twain and His World.* New York: Simon, 1974.

Kaplan, Morton. "The Tribalization of America." *World & I* May 1991: 14–16.

Kaplan, Sidney. *The Black Presence in the Era of the American Revolution, 1770–1800.* Greenwich: New York Graphic Society, 1973.

Kelley, William Melvin. *A Different Drummer.* 1962. Garden City, NY: Anchor, 1969.

———. *Dunfords Travels Everywheres.* Garden City: Doubleday, 1970.

Keneally, Thomas. "Misadventures in the Slave Trade." Rev. of *Middle Passage*, by Charles Johnson. *New York Times Book Review* 1 July 1990: 8.

Kennedy, Randall. "My Race Problem—and Ours." *Atlantic Monthly* May 1997: 55–66.

Kinney, Arthur F. "Faulkner and the Problematics of Procreation." *Connotations* 83 (1998/1999): 325–37.

Kulpe, Oswald. *Outlines of Psychology*. Trans. Edward Bradford Titchener. New York: MacMillian, 1895.

Lauter, Paul. "The Literatures of America—a Comparative Discipline." *Canons and Contexts*. By Lauter. New York: Oxford UP, 1991. 48–96.

———. "Race and Gender in the Shaping of the American Literary Canon: A Case Study from the Twenties." *Canons and Contexts*. By Lauter. New York: Oxford UP, 1991. 22–47.

———. "Reconstructing American Literature: Curricular Issues." *Canons and Contexts*. By Lauter. New York: Oxford UP, 1991. 97–113.

Lester, Julius. "James Baldwin—Reflections of a Maverick." *New York Times Book Review* 27 May 1984: 22.

———, ed. *The Seventh Son: The Thought and Writings of W. E. B. DuBois*. Vol. 1. New York: Vintage, 1971.

Levin, Harry. Introduction. *The Scarlet Letter*. By Nathaniel Hawthorne. Boston: Houghton, 1960.

Levine, Lawrence. *Black Culture and Black Consciousness: Afro-American Folk Thought from Slavery to Freedom*. New York: Oxford UP, 1977.

Lévi-Strauss, Claude. *The Savage Mind*. Chicago: U of Chicago P, 1968.

Lewis, David Levering. *W.E.B. Du Bois: Biography of a Race, 1868–1919*. New York: Owl, 1994.

Locke, Alain, ed. *The New Negro*. 1925. New York: Antheneum, 1968.

Loggins, Vernon. *The Negro Author, His Development in America*. New York: Columbia UP, 1931.

Lynn, Kenneth S. *Mark Twain and Southwestern Humor*. Boston: Little, 1959.

Major, Clarence. "Licking Stamps, Taking Chances." Vol. 6 of *Contemporary Authors Autobiography Series*. Ed. Adele Sarkissian. Detroit: Gale, 1988. 175–204.

———. *Such Was the Season*. San Francisco: Mercury, 1987.

Manning, Margret. "Caputo in the Heart of Darkness." *Boston Globe* 12 Oct. 1980: 1.

Mason, Julian D., Jr., ed. *Poems of Phillis Wheatley.* Chapel Hill: U of North Carolina P, 1966.

McCaffery, Larry and Jerzy Kutnik. "'I Follow My Eyes': An Interview with Clarence Major." *African American Review* 28 (1994): 121–38.

McKay, Claude. *Banjo: A Story without a Plot.* New York: Harvest, 1929.

McMillan, Terry. *Mama.* Boston: Houghton, 1987.

———. *Waiting to Exhale.* New York: Viking, 1992.

Merriam-Webster's New Collegiate Dictionary. Springfield, MA: Merriam, 1981.

Mitchell, Samuel L. *Medical Repository* 3 (1817): 185–86.

Morrison, Toni. *Beloved.* New York: Knopf, 1987.

———. *The Bluest Eye.* New York: Holt, 1987.

———. *Jazz.* New York: Plume, 1993.

———. "Memory, Creation, and Writing." *Thought: A Review of Culture and Ideas* 59 (1984): 385–90.

Moses, Wilson Jeremiah. *Black Messiahs and Uncle Toms: Social and Literary Manipulations of a Religious Myth.* University Park: Penn State UP, 1982.

———. "The Poetics of Ethiopianism: W. E. B. Du Bois and Literary Black Nationalism." *American Literature* 47 (Nov. 1975): 411–26.

Neal, Larry. "The Black Arts Movement." *The Black Aesthetic.* Ed. Addison Gayle Jr. New York: Doubleday, 1971. 272–90.

New World Writing. Vol. 1. New York: New American Library, 1952.

Noble, David W. *The Eternal Adam and the New World Garden: The Central Myth in the American Novel since 1830.* New York: Braziller, 1968.

Olsen, Marvin E. "Power as a Social Process." *Power in Societies.* Ed. Olsen. New York: Macmillan, 1970. 2–10.

Outlaw, Lucius. "'Conserve' Races? In Defense of W. E. B. Du Bois." *W. E. B. Du Bois on Race and Culture.* Ed. Bernard Bell, Emily Grosholz, and James Stewart. New York: Routledge, 1996. 15–38.

Paine, Albert Bigelow. *Mark Twain: A Biography.* New York: Harper, 1924.

Park, Robert E. *Introduction to the Science of Sociology.* 2nd ed. Chicago: U of Chicago P, 1928.

Patell, Cyrus R. K. *Negative Liberties: Morrison, Pynchon, and the Problem of Liberal Ideology.* Durham: Duke UP, 2001.

Peters, Fritz. *Boyhood with Gurdjieff.* 1964. Baltimore: Penguin, 1972.

Petry, Ann. *Country Place.* 1947. Chatham: Chatham Bookseller, 1971.

———. *The Narrows.* Boston: Houghton, 1953.

———. *The Street.* 1946. New York: Pyramid, 1961.

Phillips, Ulrich Bonnell. *American Negro Slavery: A Survey of the Supply, Employment, and Control of Negro Labor as Determined by the Plantation Regime.* Baton Rouge: Louisiana State UP, 1966.

Plumerm, William S. "Mary Reynolds: A Case of Double-Consciousness." *Harper's* 20 (May 1860): 807–12.

Poe, Richard. "Negro: By Definition." *Negro History Bulletin* (1977): 668–70.

"Poll Finds Whites Use Stereotypes." *New York Times* 10 Jan. 1991: B10.

Pollitzer, William S. "The Relationship of the Gullah-Speaking People of Coastal South Carolina to Their African Ancestors." *The Legacy of Ibo Landing: Gullah Roots of African American Culture.* Ed. Marquetta L. Goodwine. Atlanta: Clarity, 1998. 54–68.

Posnock, Ross. "How it Feels to Be a Problem: Du Bois, Fanon, and the 'Impossible Life' of the Black Intellectual." *Critical Inquiry* 23 (Winter 1997): 323–49.

Prince, Gerald. *Dictionary of Narratology, Human Agency and Language.* Lincoln: U of Nebraska P 1987.

Proust, Marcel. *Remembrance of Things Past.* Trans. C. K. Scott Moncrieff and Terence Kilmartin. Vol. 1. New York: Vintage, 1982.

Quarles, Benjamin. "Historic Afro-American Holidays." *Negro Digest,* 16 (February 1967): 14–19.

Rampersad, Arnold. *The Art and Imagination of W. E. B. Du Bois.* Cambridge: Harvard UP, 1976.

Rawley, James A. "The World of Phillis Wheatley." *New England Quarterly* 50.4 (1977): 666–77.

Redding, J. Saunders. "Negro Writing in America." *New Leader* 16 (May 1960): 8–10.

———. *To Make a Poet Black.* 1939. Washington, DC: McGrath, 1968.

Retamar Fernández, Roberto. "Against the Black Legend." *Caliban and Other Essays.* By Fernandez Retamar. Minneapolis: U of Minnesota P, 1989. 56–73.

Robertson, James O. *American Myth, American Reality.* New York: Hill, 1980.

Robinson, William H., Jr., ed. *Early Black American Prose: Selections with Biographical Introduction.* Dubuque, IA: William C. Brown, 1971.

Ruoff, A. La Vonne Brown, and Jerry Ward, eds. *Redefining American Literary History.* New York: MLA, 1990.

Samuels, Wilfred D., and Clenora Hudson-Weems. *Toni Morrison.* Boston: Twayne, 1990.

Sapir, Edward. "The Status of Linguistics as a Science." *Languages* 5 (1929): 207–14.

Schraufnagel, Noel. *From Apology to Protest: The Black American Novel.* Deland: Everett/Edwards, 1973.

Schuyler, George. *Black and Conservative.* New York: Arlington, 1966.

———. *Slaves Today: A Story of Liberia.* New York: Brewer, 1931.

Scott, Joan W. "Experience." *Feminists Theorize the Political.* Ed. Judith Butler and Joan W. Scott. New York: Routledge, 1992. 22–40.

Showalter, Elaine. "A Criticism of Our Own: Autonomy and Assimilation in Afro-American and Feminist Literary Theory." *The Future of Literary Theory.* Ed. Ralph Cohen. New York: Routledge, 1989. 347–69.

Sleeper, Jim. "Toward an End of Blackness." *Harper's Magazine* May 1997: 35–44.

Sollors, Werner. *Beyond Ethnicity: Consent and Descent in American Culture.* New York: Oxford UP, 1986.

———. "A Critique of Pure Pluralism." *Reconstructing American Literary History.* Ed. Sacvan Bercovitch. Cambridge, MA: Harvard UP, 1986. 250–79.

Sollors, Werner, and Maria Diedrich, eds. *The Black Columbiad.* Cambridge: Harvard UP, 1994.

Southern, Eileen. *The Music of Black Americans.* New York: Norton, 1971.

Spillers, Hortense. *Black, White and in Color: Essays on American Literature and Culture.* Chicago: U of Chicago P, 2003.

Stampp, Kenneth M. *The Peculiar Institution: Slavery in the Ante-Bellum South.* New York: Vintage, 1956.

Starke, Catherine J. *Black Portraiture in American Fiction: Stock Characters, Archetypes, and Individuals.* New York: Basic, 1971.

Stepto, Robert B. "Teaching Afro-American Literature." *Afro-American Literature: The Reconstruction of Instruction.* Ed. Dexter Fisher and Robert B. Stepto. New York: MLA, 1978. 8–24.

Streitfeld, David. "The Facts of Art." *Washington Post* 9 Aug. 1992: x15.

Styron, William. *The Confessions of Nat Turner.* New York: Random, 1967.

Syrett, Harold C., comp. *American Historical Documents.* New York: Barnes and Noble, 1970.

Taylor, Charles. *The Ethics of Authenticity.* Cambridge: Harvard UP, 1991.

———. *Human Agency and Language.* Cambridge: Cambridge UP, 1985.

Tidwell, James N. "Mark Twain's Representation of Negro Speech." *American Speech* 17 (Oct. 1942): 174–76.

Toomer, Jean. "Blue Meridian." *The New Caravan.* Ed. Alfred Kreymborg, Lewis Mumford, and Paul Rosenfeld. New York: Macaulay, 1936. 633–53.

———. *Essentials.* Chicago: Lakeside, 1931.

———. "On Being American." Unpublished ms. Fisk U Library, n.d.

Trilling, Lionel. *Sincerity and Authenticity.* Cambridge: Harvard UP, 1971.

Turner, Darwin. "The Teaching of Afro-American Literature." *New Black Voices.* Ed. Abraham Chapman. New York: New American Library, 1972. 499–505.

Twain, Mark. *The Autobiography of Mark Twain: Including Chapters Now Published for the First Time.* Ed. Charles Neider. New York: Harper, 1959.

———. *King Leopold's Soliloquy.* New York: International, 1961.

Tyler, Moses Coit. *A History of American Literature, 1607–1765.* Ithaca, NY: Cornell UP, 1949.

———. *The Literary History of the American Revolution, 1763–1783.* 1897. 2 vols. New York: Ungar, 1963.

United States Department of Commerce. Bureau of the Census. *The Social and Economic Status of the Black Population in the United States: A Historical View, 1790–1978.* Special Studies Series P-23. No. 80:6–18, September 1993.

Walker, Alice. *The Color Purple.* New York: Harcourt, 1982.

———. *In Search of Our Mothers' Gardens.* New York: Harcourt, 1983.

———. *Meridian.* New York: Washington Square, 1977.

———. *The Third Life of Grange Copeland.* New York: Harcourt, 1970.

Wallace, Michele. *Black Macho and the Myth of the Superwoman.* New York: 1990.

Washington, Booker T. *Up from Slavery.* New York: Signet, 2000.

Washington, George. *Writings.* Ed. John C. Fitzpatrick. 39 vols. Washington, DC: GPO, 1931–44.

Washington, Mary Helen, ed. Introduction. *Black-Eyed Susans: Classic Stories by and about Black Women.* Garden City, NY: Anchor, 1975. ix–xxxii.

Weber, Max. *The Theory of Social and Economic Organization.* Trans. A. M. Henderson. Ed. Talcott Parsons. New York: Free, 1964.

Webster's New Collegiate Dictionary. Springfield, MA: Merriam, 1981.

Wecter, Dixon. "Mark Twain." *Mark Twain: A Profile.* Ed. Justin Kaplan. New York: Hill, 1967. 1–29.

Wegelin, Oscar, ed. *Jupiter Hammon, American Negro Poet; Selections from His Writing and a Bibliography.* 1915. Miami, FL: Mnemosyne, 1969.

Wellek, Rene, and Austin Warren. *Theory of Literature.* 1948. 3rd ed. New York: Brace, 1962.

West, James L. W., III. *William Styron: A Life.* New York: Random, 1998.

Wheatley, Phillis. *The Poems of Phillis Wheatley.* Ed. Julian D. Mason Jr. Chapel Hill: U of North Carolina, 1966.

Whitman, Walt. "Preface to the 1855 edition of *Leaves of Grass*." *The American Tradition in Literature*. Ed. George Perkins, Sculley Bradley, Richmond Croom Beatty, and E. Hudson Long. 6th ed. Vol. 1. New York: Random, 1985. 1667–68.

Wideman, John Edgar. "Frame and Dialect: The Evolution of the Black Voice in Fiction." *American Poetry Review* 5.5 (1976): 33–37.

———. *Two Cities*. Boston: Houghton, 1998.

Wiggins Jr., William H. *O Freedom! Afro-American Emancipation Celebrations*. Knoxville: U of Tennessee, 1987.

Williams, John A. *The Man Who Cried I Am*. New York: Signet, 1968.

Wilson, Charles Morrow. *Liberia: Black Africa in Microcosm*. New York: Harper, 1971.

Wilson, Harriet E. *Our Nig; or, Sketches from the Life of a Free Black, in a Two-Story White House, North, Showing That Slavery's Shadows Fall Even There*. New York: Vintage, 1983.

Wilson, William J. *Power, Racism, and Privilege: Race Relations in Theoretical and Sociohistorical Perspectives*. New York: Free, 1976.

Wright, Richard. "Blueprint for Negro Writing." *New Challenge* 2 (Fall 1937): 53–65.

———. "Blueprint for Negro Writing." *Richard Wright Reader*. Ed. Ellen Wright and Michael Fabre. New York: Harper, 1978. 36–49.

———. *The Long Dream*. New York: Ace, 1958.

Yerby, Frank. *The Dahomean*. New York: Dell, 1971.

Yetman, Norman R. *Life under the "Peculiar Institution": Selections from the Slave Narrative Collection*. New York: Holt, 1970.

Young, Al. "God Never Drove Those Cadillacs." *New York Times Book Review* 13 Dec. 1987: 19.

INDEX

Abolitionism, 91, 105, 115, 171, 201
Abrahams, Roger, 257
acculturation, of Africans in the colonies, 13, 74, 76, 78, 80, 86, 101, 175, 176, 249, 304
Achebe, Chinua, 17, 125, 126; on "Heart of Darkness," 111–12
Acholonu, Catherine Obianuju, 86
Adams, Samuel C., 13
"Address to Those Who Keep Slaves, and Approve the Practice" (Allen and Jones), 33
aesthetic, African American, 5; and African American novel, 8; in art, 171; Black Arts vernacular aesthetic, 173, 180–84; blues aesthetic, 5, 22n4, 149–54; cultural nationalist aesthetic, 175, 200–201; neo-hoodoo aesthetic, 171, 172–73; New Black Aesthetic, 83, 172–73, 175
Afesi, Dovi, 22n8
affirmative action, 68, 218, 243, 300, 306
Africa: images of in African American novel, 111–26; mainly oral culture in eighteenth century, 87; white images of in Western culture, 112–14
Africa, John, 150, 152, 153–54
African American culture, defined, 75–76
African American identity: authority of, 179; bicultural and biracial, problem of, 306; centrality of roots, return, and journey to identity construction, 70; and storytelling, 216–17; transcultural identity formations, 177. *See also* double consciousness, African American; hybrid cultural identity, African American
African Americanists, 294; attacks on methodology of, 295
African American literary criticism, lack of attention to, 253
African American literature: appeals by African Americans for freedom from oppression, 76–77; autobiography, 250; colonial, 110; contemporary critical studies of, 84–85; and distinction between dialectics and dialogics, 247; irony, paradox, and parody, 27, 29, 35, 52, 56, 76, 90, 115, 121, 173, 201, 217, 228, 249; literary texts, 75; poetry, 81–83; sign systems with reference to nonliterary and literary texts, 75, 246; as socially symbolic linguistic construct, 69, 85, 173, 250; tension between dual African and European and oral and literary heritages, 74; theater, 84; typology of, 76; writers, 85–110. *See also* African American literature, teaching of; African American novel; African American women writers; double consciousness, African American
African American literature, teaching of: and academic resources and respect, 299; and contextualizing of texts, 303; criteria for teachers and scholars of African American literature, 241; lack of teacher preparation, 241–42; and place of African American literature in the curriculum, 241; pool of teachers, 301; validation and valorization of, 299–307; vernacular theories for teaching, 250–60
African American ministers, eighteenth-century, struggle for freedom of worship, 96–97
African American novel: avoidance of direct treatment of African heritage, 125; dominant aesthetic tradition, 8; drama of white versus black, 80; focus on mulattos in antebellum and postbellum periods, 176; as hybrid form, 79; messianic and jeremiadic themes, 80; nineteenth-century novelists, 80; post-Black arts movement, 174; pre-Black Arts movement, 174; quest for personal and communal freedom, 81; as residually oral form, 260; socialized ambivalence and double consciousness in, 125; as symbolic sociocultural

African American novel (*cont'd*)
act, 79; twentieth-century novelists, 79–81; use of oral forms to establish authority of identities, 179. *See also* African American novel, images of Africa in

African American novel, images of Africa in, 111–26; early nineteenth century, 114–16; post–World War II, 119–25; pre–World War II, 116–19; revealed by narrative setting, color symbolism, character, and point of view, 114; and tensions in novelists' self-image, 125

African American Review, 227

African Americans. *See also* entries under "black"

"African American," use of term, 75

African American Vernacular English (AAVE), 7, 15, 46, 151, 235. *See also* African American vernacular tradition; code-switching

African American vernacular tradition, 3, 8, 21, 76, 157–58, 178, 180, 214, 249; African American vernacular tropes, 85, 250, 251–54, 255–58; Black Arts vernacular aesthetic, 173; Du Bois and, 55; historical roots of, 4, 69; oral forms of, viii, 4, 8, 67, 173, 259–60; vernacular theories for teaching African American literature, 250–60. *See also specific authors*

African American women writers: and image of black macho, 202, 203–4; impact of negative stereotypic images on, 250; negative stereotypes of black men, 197, 198–206; underrepresentation in American literature anthologies, 303

African Americentric, defined, 7

African Baptist Church, 249

African Mason Lodge, 75, 87, 249

African Methodist Episcopal Church, 75, 87, 249, 277

African Society, 87

African stereotypes: African as Barbarian, 125; African as Noble Savage, 125; Noble Savages, 113, 118

African survivals, 32, 78, 212, 249, 296

"Afro-American," 75, 248

Afro-American Anthropology: Contemporary Perspectives. "Introduction" (Whitten and Szwed, eds.), 217

Afro-American Literature: The Reconstruction of Instruction (Fisher and Stepto, eds.), 301

"Afro-American Literature at the End of the Twentieth Century" (conference), 173

Afrocentrism, 13, 246, 294; attacks on methodology of scholars, 295; defined, 7, 74

agency, 65, 173, 174, 183, 211; defined, 179–80

Akan, 84

Alabama church bombing, 244

Allen, Paula Gunn, 301

Allen, Richard, 33, 97

All the Women Are White, All the Blacks Are Men; but Some of Us Are Brave (Hull, Scott, and Smith, eds.), 201

Alsberg, Henry G., 12

Alta California, 265

American Baptist, 230

American Colonization Society, 75, 248

American Dialog, 283, 284

American Dream, myth of, 186, 189

American enlightenment, 31

American literature anthologies, inadequate representation of black and women writers, 303

American Literature Center and American Studies Center, School of English and International Studies, BEIWAI, 170

American Negro Academy, 45

American Studies, pan-American comparative theory, 171

Americo-Liberians, 116, 117

Amistad revolt, 115, 164

Amsterdam News, 187

Anderson, Sherwood, 128

Andrews, William L., 34; *Critical Essays of W. E. B. Du Bois*, 41; *To Tell a Free Story: The First Century of Afro-American Autobiography, 1760–1865*, 85, 250

Angelou, Maya, 83, 137, 145, 212

Anzaldúa, Gloria: *Borderlands/La Frontera: The New Mestiza*, 172

Appiah, Anthony: "The Uncompleted Argument: Du Bois and the Illusion of Race," 52

Aptheker, Herbert, 17, 89, 90; *American Negro Slave Revolts*, 284; *A Documentary History of the Negro People in the United States* (ed.), 77; *Nat Turner's Slave Rebellion*, 284, 290, 291

Arada, 87, 247

archetype, defined, 199

Aristotle: *Rhetoric*, 43, 246

Armstrong, Louis, 82, 220

art, African Americentric and Afrocentric aesthetic in, 171

Asante, Molefi: *The Afrocentric Idea*, 180, 184n2

Ashcroft, Bill, 292

Assefa, Hizkias, 153

assimilation: cultural, 52, 88, 94, 182; racial, versus solidarity, 27, 28, 46; social, 88, 92, 110

Association for the Study of Negro Life and History, 10, 11
Atlanta Cotton Exposition of 1895, 11
Attaway, William, 185
Attucks, Crispus, 89, 100
authenticity, 174, 184, 211–12; defined, 65, 178–79; struggle for, 173
authority, 174, 212; of African American identity, 179; defined, 66, 179; struggle for, 173
autobiography/biography, 76, 77
Awkward, Michael, 185

Bacon, Francis, viii
Baker, Houston A., Jr., 67, 209, 240, 255, 301; *Blues, Ideology, and Afro-American Literature,* 85, 250, 251, 255; blues as key black vernacular trope, 250, 251–54; blues code, 253–54; concept of the blues as a matrix, 253–54; criticism of Gates in *Black Studies, Rap, and the Academy,* 256; definition of vernacular, 252; "the desperate class," 252; *The Journey Back,* 53; *Long Black Song,* 251
Baker, Josephine, 82
Bakhtin, Mikhail, 174, 211; *The Dialogic Imagination,* 43, 57–58, 246; dialogism, 177–78, 215, 235, 305; "Discourse on the Novel," 305
Bakongo, 87, 247
Baldwin, James, ix, 79, 199, 202, 212, 240; advocacy of civil rights and black nationalism, 144; "Alas Poor Richard," 143; *Another Country,* 144; as artist of redemptive love, 142–44, 147; "Autobiographical Notes," 143; *Blues for Mister Charlie,* 84, 138; comparison to Elie Wiesel, 146–47; dialectic tension in, 141; "Down at the Cross," 140, 142; "Fifth Avenue Uptown," 147; *The Fire Next Time,* 2, 138, 142, 147; *Giovanni's Room,* 144; *Go Tell It on the Mountain,* 52, 138, 143, 144, 147; *If Beale Street Could Talk,* 144; *Jimmy's Blues,* 138; *Just Above My Head,* 144; legacy of, 147–48; messianic love for American Republic, 146; "My Dungeon Shook," 142; *Nobody Knows My Name,* 143; *Notes of a Native Son,* 138, 143; *The Price of the Ticket,* 138, 139, 141, 143, 147; and Richard Wright, 143; role as righteous witness, 144–48, 229; "Stranger in the Village," 140; *Tell Me How Long the Train's Been Gone,* 144; white writers identified as witnesses by, 146
Baldwin, Joseph: *Rush Times in Alabama and Mississippi,* 265
Bambara, 87, 247
Banneker, Benjamin, 33, 77
Banner, William, 20
Baraka, Amira (LeRoi Jones), 26, 83, 137, 171, 176, 202, 258; "The 'Blues Aesthetic' and the 'Black Aesthetic': Aesthetics as the Continuing Political History of a Culture," 22n4; *Dutchman,* 84; *The Slave,* 84
Barbour, Floyd B., 3, 21
Barksdale, Richard K., 260; *Praisesong of Survival,* viii
Barr, Caroline, 280
Barrios, Olga, 195
Barthes, Roland, 211
Beatitude, 83
Beatty, Paul, 173, 174
Bell, Bernard W., 41–42, 209; "The African American Jeremiad and Frederick Douglass's Fourth of July 1852 Speech," 26; *The Afro-American Novel and Its Tradition,* ix, 4, 6, 26, 41, 73, 85, 144, 169, 175, 185, 250, 258–59, 259–60, 304; "The Afro-American Novel and Its Tradition" (doctoral dissertation), 17, 126–27; "Anger in the Novels of Ralph Ellison, John O. Killens and James Baldwin" (master's thesis), 16; "Black Literature: What Happens to a Dream Deferred?", 241, 298; "Booker T. and W. E. B.: The Authority, Authenticity, and Agency of African American Double Consciousness" (lecture), 64; "Cane: A Portrait of the Black Artist as High Priest of Soul," 127; *The Contemporary African American Novel: Its Folk Roots and Modern Literary Branches,* ix, 1, 4, 5, 169, 183, 206, 211; and establishment of African American Studies departments, 299–300; *The Folk Roots of Contemporary Afro-American Poetry,* viii, 18, 26, 41, 81, 258, 305; "Jean Toomer's 'Blue Meridian': The Poet as Prophet of a New Order of Man," 127; "Keeping the Faith: White Civil Rights and Black Affirmative Action," 163, 218; "A Key to the Poems in *Cane*," 18, 127, 245; "Looking Through a Glass Darkly: The Philosophical Legacy of Du Boisian Double Consciousness" (lecture), 41; *Modern and Contemporary Afro-American Poetry* (ed.), vii, 18, 258; "Oral Culture, Afro-American Folklore, and the Function of the Literary Artist," 111; "Slave Mutiny with a Difference," 163; "Trey Ellis's Voice of the New Black Aesthetic in Platitudes" (lecture), 169; vernacular theory of African American literature, 250, 258–60; "W. E. B. Du Bois's Struggle to Reconcile Folk and High Art," 41; "William Faulkner's 'Shining Star': Lucas Beauchamp as a Marginal Man," 275, 276

The Bell Curve: Intelligence and Class Structure in American Life (Herrnstein and Murray), 242
Benjamin, Playthell, 22n8
Bennett, Lerone, Jr., 283; *Before the Mayflower,* 247
Bennett, William, 302
Bercovitrch, Sacvan, 29; *The American Jeremiad,* 30–31
Berghahn, Marion: *Images of Africa in Black American Literature,* 114, 120
Berlin Conference, 116
Bestes, Peter, 89
Bethel African Methodist Episcopal Church, 97
Beyerman, Keith, 209; *Fingering the Jagged Grain,* 84, 149, 250
Bhabha, Homi, 172, 294; "Third Space," 174
Biafada, 87, 247
Bialostosky, Don: "Dialogics as an Art of Discourse in Literary Criticism," 43, 246–47
Bible: black/white symbolism, 115; as principal tool of African American cultural adaptation, 110
bicultural and biracial identity, problem of, 306. *See also* double consciousness, African American, biracial and bicultural state of being
bidialectalism, 4
Big Table, 83
"black," history of usage, 248
black and white, in Western symbolism, 113
Black Arts movement, 75, 83, 171, 177, 197, 200, 210, 244, 248, 258
Black Arts vernacular aesthetic, 173; Ellis's satire of, 180–84
black Atlantic culture, 7, 171
black beat generation, 83
Black Belt, 249
black churches, publishing companies established by, 209
Black Codes, 51, 68, 87, 247–48
The Black Columbiad (Sollors and Diedrich, eds.), 295–96
black cultural nationalist aesthetic, 175, 200–201
Black Diaspora, 171
blackface minstrel tradition, 9, 10, 13, 210, 262, 276, 278
black literary clubs, 209
black macho stereotype, 198, 202
black male stereotypes, 198, 200
Black Nationalism, 119, 299; and African religious retention, 32; domination by black revolutionary nationalists and black cultural nationalists, 200–201; focus on black men and marginalizing of black women, 201
Black Nationalist: Reconsidering Du Bois, Garvey, Booker T. and Nkrumah, 64
black newspapers, 209
Black Panthers, 202
Black Power movement, 16, 71, 75, 83, 119, 125, 197, 200, 201, 248
black revolutionary nationalists, 200
black revolutionary rapist stereotype, 198
Black Studies, ix, 12, 14, 17, 106, 171, 200, 297, 298; Afrocentric programs, 174; consortium, vii; establishment of, vii, 299–300; search in the 1960s and 1970s for a pan-African movement in, 171
Black Womanist movement, 173
Blair, Walter, 272; *Mark Twain and Huck Finn,* 269, 272; *Native American Humor,* 265
Bland, Alden, 185
Blary, Lilliane, 111
Blassingame, John W., 9; *Slave Community,* 14; *Slave Testimony,* 14
Blauner, Robert, 68
blues, as key black vernacular trope for understanding African American literature, 250, 251–54
blues aesthetic, 5, 22n4
blues code, 253–54
blues "sisters," 220
Bluestein, Gene: *The Voice of the Folk,* 305
blues voice, 149–54
Bone, Robert: *Negro Novel in America,* 185–86, 189
Bontemps, Arna, 12; Introduction. *Great Slave Narratives,* 105–6
Boston Massacre, 100
Boston Tea Party, 76
Botkin, Benjamin A., 9; *Lay My Burden Down,* 13–14
Bourdieu, Pierre, 7, 8–9
Brawley, Benjamin: *The Negro in Literature and Art in the United States,* 98
Broadside Critics Series, viii, 41, 258
Brooks, Gwendolyn, 82, 171; *Annie Allen,* 83
Brooks, Van Wyck, 174; *The Ordeal of Mark Twain,* 270, 271
Brown, H. Rap, 257
Brown, James, 240, 248
Brown, Sterling A., vii, 4, 9, 12, 13, 15, 255, 297; "Negro Character as Seen by White Authors," 114, 198; "Uncle Joe," 209
Brown, William W., 78, 79; *Clotel,* 78
Brown v. Board of Education, 244, 303

Bruce, Dickson D., Jr.: "W.E.B. Du Bois and the Idea of Double Consciousness," 44
Brute Negro stereotype, 198, 200, 201
Bryan, Andrew, 97
Buffalo Express, 266
Burundi, 171
Bush, George H. W., 299, 302
Butcher, Margaret, 20

Cable, George Washington, 210, 264
Cade, John B., 9, 11; "Out of the Mouths of Ex-Slaves," 11
Callahan, John: *In the African American Grain,* 209
call-and-response, 84, 220, 231, 250
Call and Response: The Riverside Anthology of the African American Literary Tradition (Hill, et al., eds.), 240, 242
Calloway, Cab, 6
Canales, Jose Ferrer, 20
Cannon, Steve, 229
Caputo, Philip: *Horn of Africa,* 112
Carby, Hazel, 295; *Reconstructing Womanhood,* 85, 250
Carmichael, Stokely, 16, 119
Carretta, Vincent, 86; "Olaudah Equiano or Gustavus Vassa? New Light on an Eighteenth-Century Question of Identity," 105
Caruthers, William A., 10
Center for the Recruitment and Retention of Minority Graduate Students, Faculty, and Staff, 306
Cervantes, Miguel de, 208
Césaire, Aimè, 295
Chaucer, Geoffrey, 208
Chesnutt, Charles W.: *The Conjure Woman,* 302; *House of the Cedars,* 302; *The Marrow of Tradition,* 51
chiliasm, 30
Christian, Barbara: *Black Women Novelists,* 84, 199–200, 205, 250; "Images of Black Women in Afro-American Literature: From Stereotype to Character," 198
Christian fundamentalism, 55
Christianity, image of Africans and their descendants, 113
Civil Rights Act of 1964, 142
Civil Rights movement, 71, 200, 201, 244, 299
Clarke, John Henrik, 283
Cleaver, Eldridge, 198, 200; "The Primeval Mitosis," 201; *Soul on Ice,* 201, 245
Clemens, John Marshall, 262

Clemens, Samuel Langhorne. *See* Twain, Mark
Clemens, Susy, 270–71
Clinton, William Jefferson, 68, 299
closet metaphor, 305
Cobb, Charlie, 16
code-mixing, 172
code-switching, 4, 7, 172, 174; Ellis's *Platitudes,* 175, 180–81; Jones and, 208–9; Wideman and, 150, 152
Cohen, Elliott, 143
Cole, Johnetta, 17
College English, 241
College Language Association (CLA), 300
colleges and universities, five-stage model for, 306
Collins, Albert, 149
Colloquium of the Second World Black and African Festival of Arts and Culture, Lagos, Nigeria, 196
Colombia, 171
color symbolism: and images of African in African American novel, 114; and myth of white supremacy, 115
Comic Negro stereotype, 198
Commentary, 143
Committee on the Literature and Language of America (formerly Committee on Minority Literature), Modern Language Association, 300–301
A Common Destiny: Blacks and American Society (Jaynes and Williams, eds.), 242–43
Compromise of 1850, 33
Congo, 171
Conjuring: Black Women, Fiction, and Literary Tradition (Pryse and Spillars), 185
Conrad, Joseph: *Heart of Darkness,* 111–12, 125, 126
consciousness, 43–44
Constitutional Convention of 1787, 91
Contented Slave stereotype, 198
Cooke, John E., 10
Cooke, Sam, 260
Cooper, Anna Julia, 9, 47, 295
Cortez, Jayne, 83
Count Basie, 6
Cox, Courtland, 16
Coy, Juan Jose, 196
Coyle, Martin, 73
Craft, William and Ellen, 78
Creole, 164
Crews, Frederick: *The Critics Bear It Away: American Fiction and the Academy,* 171
Crisis, 187

Cronyn, George, 12
Crummell, Alexander, 47, 295
Cruse, Harold: *Crisis of the Negro Intellectual*, 17
Cuba, occupation of, 67
Cudjoe, Selwyn, 295
Cullen, Countee, 82, 142
cultural assimilation, 52, 88, 94, 182
cultural capital, 7
cultural hybridity, 171, 172, 174, 228, 304
cultural mulattos, 173, 175
cultural nationalism, 119–20
cultural pluralism, 164, 167, 169, 172, 174, 297–98, 302, 305
Cultural Revolution of 1967, 170
culture, defined, 86
Currents in Modern Thought, 163
curriculum development and enhancement, office of, 306

Davis, Arthur P., 20
Davis, Chester, 22n8
Davis, David Brion: *The Problem of Slavery in Western Culture*, 112
Davis, Thadious M., 260, 261
Declaration of Independence, 27, 39, 47, 86, 110; deletion of all references to slavery, 91
de facto racial discrimination, 244
Delany, Martin, 65, 79, 119, 125; *Blake; or, The Huts of America*, 115; *The Condition, Elevation, and Destiny of the Colored People of the United States, Politically Considered*, 77
DeMott, Benjamin, 145
Denain, Pierre, 111
Department of Education, 302
Derrida, Jacques, 211, 253
DeVoto, Bernard: *Mark Twain in Eruption*, 264–65
dialectic, 43, 246
Diallo, Amadou, 68
dialogics, 43, 57–58, 246–47
Dickens, Charles, 146
Diedrich, Maria, 295
Diop, Cheikh Anta, 295
Dixon, Melvin, 111; *Ride Out the Wilderness*, 84–85, 250
documentary, 76
Dodson, Owen, 20, 83
Dog, black male stereotype, 200, 205
Dogon, 84
Dole, Bob, 243

Donaldson, Ivanhoe, 17
Dostoyevsky, Fyodor, 146
double consciousness, African American, viii, 4, 7, 13, 21, 27–29, 88, 187, 228; biracial, bicultural state of being, ix, 29, 41, 51, 61, 71, 85, 161, 172, 250, 276, 282, 304, 306; and code-switching, 4, 7, 150, 152, 172, 174, 175, 180–81, 208–9; as coping method, 67; as diagnostic term in psychological discourse, 44–45; expressed in irony and paradox of African American folk and formal art, 27, 29, 35, 52, 76, 78, 90, 115, 121, 125, 156–60, 173, 201, 217, 228, 249; in Morrison's *Beloved*, 219, 229, 230–31, 235; as product of cultural retention, reinterpretation, and syncretism, 148n1; as product of unique historical experiences, 68, 76, 148n1, 249; shared ironic and paradoxical experiences of, 246; and techniques grounded in transcultural black music, 171; and the transcendentalist, 44; trend toward repudiation of, 65; and urban male, 149. *See also* Du Bois, W. E. B., theory and trope of double consciousness
double vision, 28, 52, 69, 71, 76, 102, 141, 228, 235, 249. *See also* double consciousness, African American
Douglass, Aaron, 82, 128
Douglass, Frederick, 21, 78, 109, 272; 1863 article on Emancipation Proclamation, 26, 27; *The Heroic Slave*, 163, 164, 165–67; on human struggle for liberty, 3; on Martin Delany, 64–65; *Narrative of the Life of Frederick Douglass, an American Slave, Written by Himself*, 77; on "tomb" of slavery, 230; "What to the Slave Is the Fourth of July? An Address Delivered in Rochester, New York, on 5 July 1852," 33, 34–40, 77
Dove, Rita, 83
Downing, Henry: *The American Cavalryman: A Liberian Romance*, 114, 116–17; image of African in novels of, 125
Dr. Dre, 244
Dreiser, Theodore, 186, 189
Drewry, William Sidney: *The Southampton Insurrection*, 284, 285
drug culture, 244
Duberman, Martin, 283
Dubey, Madhu, 199
Du Bois, W. E. B., 4, 9, 32, 70, 258, 295; *The Autobiography of W.E.B. DuBois: A Soliloquy on Viewing My Life from the Last Decade of Its First Century*, 49; *Black Reconstruction in America*, 10,

12; "The Conservation of Races," 27, 45–47, 51; *Darkwater: Voices from Within the Veil,* 61; death of, 16; definition of race, 47; *Dusk of Dawn: An Essay Toward an Autobiography of a Race Concept,* 61; "A Fellow of Harvard," 43, 53–57; *The Gift of the Black Folk,* 10; metaphor of the veil, 28, 49, 51, 59, 68, 70, 228; "Of Our Spiritual Strivings," 51; "Of the Coming of John," 43, 53, 57–61; prediction of color line as problem of twentieth century, 42, 306; *The Souls of Black Folk,* 4, 28, 49–50, 54, 57, 58, 60, 70, 75, 246, 302, 305; "Strivings of the Negro People," 27–28, 49, 228, 305; *The Suppression of the African Slave Trade to the United States of America, 1638-1870,* 10; "The Talented Tenth," 27, 46, 48, 56, 66–67

Du Bois, W. E. B., theory and trope of double consciousness, viii, 27, 41, 65, 67–68, 88, 110, 141, 276; classic definition of psychological dualism of African American, 28–29, 49–50, 76, 249; critical challenges to, 171–72; double consciousness as mixed blessing, 71, 75, 246; double consciousness as unique vision to African Americans, 71, 228, 305; shift from rhetoric to dialectic and Dialogic discourse, 42–61, 67, 71

du Cille, Ann: "Postcolonialism and Afrocentricity: Discourse and Dat Course," 294–95

Dunbar, Paul Laurence, 210; ambiguous use of black speech and music, 82; "The Lynching of Jube Benson," 209; *Lyrics of Lowly Life,* 302; *Majors and Minors,* 82; *Oak and Ivy,* 82; "The Poet," 82; *The Sport of the Gods,* 302; "We Wear the Mask," 82

Dyson, Michael: *Reflecting Black: African American Cultural Criticism,* 66

Early, Gerald: *Lure and Loathing,* 62n4; "Toward an End of Blackness," 64
Early American Literature, 85
Easy E, 244
Eckman, Fern Maria, 142, 143
educational equity, office of, 306
educational opportunity, for African American and Hispanic students in southern states, 243
Egan, Michael, 271
Eliot, T. S.: "Tradition and the Individual Talent," 74, 246
Elkins, Stanley: *Slavery: A Problem in American Institutional and Intellectual Life,* 9, 10, 14, 16
Ellington, Duke, 6, 82, 220
Ellis, Pamela Fern, 175

Ellis, Trey, 173, 174, 179; *Home Repairs,* 175; "The New Black Aesthetic," 175, 176–77; "Response to NBA Critiques," 175, 177; *Right Here, Right Now,* 175; theory of a New Black Aesthetic, 175–77; *Tuskegee Airmen* (television movie), 175

Ellis, Trey: *Platitudes:* code-switching, parody, and culturally specific tropes, 175, 180–81; reconciling of double-consciousness through NBA, 184; representation of agency in, 183; satire of black aesthetic novels of 1960s and 1970s, 180–84

Ellis, William A. (father), 175
Ellis, William Arthur, III. *See* Ellis, Trey
Ellison, Ralph, 12, 42, 79, 145, 149, 174, 199, 202, 255, 258, 260, 297; "Change the Joke and Slip the Yoke," 262, 268, 274–75; concept of mainstream, 306–7; definition of the blues, 220; and double vision, 52, 68–69, 141, 228; on *Huckleberry Finn,* 262, 268, 269, 274; *Invisible Man,* 51–52, 165, 181, 250; and the "jagged grain," 207; *Shadow and Act,* 17, 52, 150, 209, 220, 228, 250; "Transcript of the American Academy Conference on the Negro American—May 14–15, 1965," 296, 307; "Twentieth-Century Fiction and the Black Mask of Humanity," 276

emancipation, 68, 249
Emancipation Proclamation, 26, 27, 76
emancipatory narratives, 77, 79
Emerson, Everett: *American Literature 1764-1789: The Revolutionary Years* (ed.), 85
Emerson, Ralph Waldo, 297, 305; "The Transcendentalist," 44
The Empire Writes Back (Ashcroft, Griffiths, and Tiffin, eds.), 292, 293–94
Encyclopedia of Literature and Criticism (Coyle et. al), 73
Equiano, Olaudah, 87, 92, 110; *The Interesting Narrative of the Life of Olaudah Equiano, or Gustavus Vassa, the African, Written by Himself,* 77, 105–9, 164
Erzgräber, Willi, 26
"Essay on Negro Slavery" ("Othello," pseud.), 32–33
essence, defined, 66
essentialism, 66
Esu-Elegbara, 53, 256
ethnic cleansing, 306
Eurocentricism, 7, 74, 246
Everett, Percival, 154–55, 173, 174
Evergreen Review, 83
Evers, Medgar, assassination of, 244

Ewe, 87, 247
existential black antihero stereotype, 200
Exotic Primitive stereotype, 198
Extremist Groups and Conflict Resolution (Assefa and Wahrhaftig), 153
eye dialect, 273

Fabre, Genevieve, 111
Fabre, Michel, 111
Fanon, Frantz, 295; *Wretched of the Earth*, 17
Faulkner, William, 173, 297; *Absalom, Absalom!*, 236, 276; *Intruder in the Dust*, 278; *Light in August*, 276, 278; "the negro" as literary sign, 276
Faulkner, William: *Go Down Moses*, 277–82; "The Bear," 278, 281; "Delta Autumn," 278; and double consciousness, 280; "The Fire and the Hearth," 278, 281; and marginal man, 277, 278, 280, 282; "Pantaloon in Black," 278; southern system of paternalism and noblesse oblige, 282
Favor, J. Martin, 177; *Authentic Blackness: The Folk in the New Negro Renaissance*, 178, 183
Federal Emergency Relief Administration (FERA) interview project, 11
Federal Writers' Project (FWP), Slave Narrative Collection program, 11, 12–13, 14, 22n6
feminism: black feminist discourse, 235–36; varying definitions of, 201; white Feminist movement, 197–98
Fernandez Retamar, Roberto: "Against the Black Legend," *Caliban and Other Essays.*, 293
Fernando Pocacao plantation, 116
First African Baptist Church of Savannah, 75, 97
Fisher, Dexter: *Language and Literature*, 301
Fisher, Rudolph, 174; *The Conjure-Man Dies*, 119
Fisk University, 11
Five-College Executive Committee of African American Studies, 17
Flowers, Arthur: *De Mojo Blues*, 172–73
folk art, Herder's theory of, 304–5
folklore, African American, 52, 74, 82, 197, 211, 228, 245, 249, 251, 7612
folk medicine, 55
folk songs, 81, 258, 305
Foner, Philip S.: *Mark Twain: Social Critic*, 264
Ford, Nick Aaron: *Black Studies: Threat-or-Challenge?*, 17
Foucault, Michel, 211
The Fourth of July: Political Oratory and Literary Reactions, 1776–1876 (Goetsch and Hurm, eds.), 25

Franco, Francisco, 6
Frank, Waldo, 174
Franklin, Benjamin, 186–87, 189
Franklin, John Hope, 9; *From Slavery to Freedom: A History of Negro Americans*, 10, 91
Frazier, E. Franklin, 20, 190; *The Negro Church in America*, 32
Fredrickson, George M.: *The Black Image in the White Mind: The Debate on Afro-American Character and Destiny, 1817–1914*, 112
Free African Society, 75, 249, 277
free blacks: "African" as most popular group and institutional identity of, 248–49; eighteenth-century organizations, 87; reduced to quasifree lower caste by black codes, 87
Freedman, Samuel G.: "Bearing Witness: The Life and Work of Elie Wiesel," 126
Freedomways, 283
"freeing of voice," 208
Freeman, Sambo, 89
Freund, Jurgen, 26
Frost, Robert, 128
Fugitive Slave Act of 1850, 33–34, 35, 38, 237
Fugitive Slave Act of 1793, 33
fugitive slave laws, 68
Fuller, Charlie: *A Soldier's Play*, 84
Fuss, Diana: *Essentially Speaking: Feminism, Nature, and Difference*, 6

Gabbin, Joanne V.: *Sterling A. Brown: Building the Black Aesthetic Tradition*, 12, 13
Gage, Thomas, 90
Gaines, Ernest, 79
gang-banging, 244
gangsta rappers, 244
Gardner, John, 164
Garfield, James, 272
Garrison, William Lloyd: "The Triumph of Freedom," 39
Garside, Peter, 73
Garvey, Marcus, 295
Gates, Henry Louis, Jr., 42, 67, 145, 209, 240, 295; *Black Literature and Literary Theory* (ed.), 255; "Criticism in the Jungle," 239; *Figures in Black: Words, Signs, and the "Racial" Self*, 255; *The Future of the Race*, 2; importance of repetition and revision and parody and pastiche in African American language and literature, 257; *Loose Canons: Notes on the Culture Wars*, viii; signifying and pastiche as key black

vernacular tropes, 250, 251, 255–58; *The Signifying Monkey*, 73–74, 79, 85, 250, 251, 255–58; Signifying Monkey as transplanted African trickster figure Esu-Elegbara, 256
Gayle, Addison, Jr., 251, 255; *The Way of the New World*, 186
Genovese, Eugene D., 283
George, David, 97
Ghana, 119
Giddings, Paula: *When and Where I Enter*, 198, 201
Gilroy, Paul: *The Black Atlantic: Modernity and Double Consciousness*, 7, 171, 295
Gingrich, Newt, 243, 302
Giovanni, Nikki, 83
Gittleman, Edwin, 86
Goetsch, Paul, 25, 26
Goode, Wilson, 150
goophering, 55
Gordon, Robert, 13
Gordone, Charles: *No Place to Be Somebody*, 84
Gossett, Thomas: *Race: The History of an Idea in America*, 112
Gramm, Phil, 243
Gramsci, Antonio: *Selections from the Prison Notebooks*, 2, 21n1
Grand Boulé, 48
Granger, Gordon, 26
Gray, Thomas: *The Confessions of Nat Turner*, 284, 285, 286, 288, 289, 290, 291, 292
"The Great Chain of Being," 113
Greene, Graham, 112
Griffiths, Gareth, 292
Griggs, Sutton, 79
Grosholz, Emily, 41–42
Guam, 67
Guellal, Cherif, 17
Guerard, Albert, 111
Gullah culture, 13, 69, 180, 215
Gullah Jack, 32
Gurdjieff, George Ivanovitch, 128, 130, 131, 132, 134, 136, 137
Guy, Buddy, 154

Haight, Anne Lyon: *Banned Books: Informal Notes on Some Books Banned for Various Reasons at Various Times and in Various Places*, 261
Hairston, Loyle, 283
Hall, Perry A.: *In the Vineyard: Working in African American Studies*, 17

Hall, Stuart, 295
Hamer, Fannie Lou, 145
Hamilton, Charles V., 283
Hammon, Briton: *A Narrative of the Uncommon Suffering and Surprizing Deliverance of Briton Hammon a Negro Man, Servant to General Winslow*, 77, 106
Hammon, Jupiter, 92, 110; *An Address to Miss Phillis Wheatley, Ethiopian Poetess, in Boston, Who Came from Africa at Eight Years of Age, and Soon Became Acquainted with the Gospel of Jesus Christ*, 93–94; *An Address to the Negroes of the State of New York*, 96; "A Dialogue Intitled the Kind Master and the Dutiful Servant," 95; *An Essay on the Ten Virgins*, 94; *An Evening's Improvement. Shewing the Necessity of Beholding the Lamb of God*, 95; *An Evening Thought. Salvation by Christ, with Penetential Cries: Composed by Jupiter Hammon, a Negro Belonging to Mr. Lloyd of Queen's Village, on Long Island, the 25th of December, 1760*, 93; *A Winter Piece: Being a Serious Exhortation with a Call to the Unconverted: and a Short Contemplation on the Death of Jesus Christ*, 94–95
Handy, W. C., 253
Hannibal, Missouri, 262
Hansberry, Lorraine: *A Raisin in the Sun*, 84
Harding, Vincent, 65, 283
hard-line messianism, 31
Harlem Renaissance, 5, 82, 119, 176, 177, 258, 303, 305
Harmon, William: *A Handbook to Literature*, 199
Harper, Francis E. W., 79, 109; *Poems on Miscellaneous Subjects*, 82
Harper, Michael, 83
Harris, George W.: *Sut Lovingood*, 265
Harris, Joel Chandler, 10, 210, 272
Harris, Trudier, 242; *Black Women in the Fiction of James Baldwin*, 145
Harris, William, 242
Harrison, Paul Carter, 17, 84; *The Great Mac Daddy*, 84
Hawaii, 67
Hayden, Robert, 1, 82; "Runagate Runagate," 83
Hayes, Roland, 82
Heath Anthology of American Literature (Lauter, ed.), 303
Hegel, Georg Wilhelm Friedrich: *The Phenomenology of the Spirit*, 252, 254
Hemingway, Ernest, 297

Henderson, Stephen: *Understanding the New Black Poetry,* 209, 255
Henry, Paget, 295
Henson, Josiah: *The Life of Josiah Henson, Formerly a Slave, Now an Inhabitant of Canada, as Narrated by Himself,* 77
Hentoff, Nat: "Huck Finn Better Get Out of Town by Sundown," 261
Herder, Johann Gottfried von, viii, 18, 41; theory of folk art, 304–5
Hernton, Calvin, 185
Herrnstein, Richard, 242
Herskovits, Melville J., 9, 13, 32; *Dahomey: An Ancient West African Kingdom,* 123; *Life in a Haitian Valley,* 52, 228; *Myth of the Negro Past,* 13; and socialized ambivalence, 141
heteroglossia, 214, 215
Higgins, Robert, 207
Hill, Hamlin, 269
Hill, Patricia, 104, 242
Himes, Chester, 185, 195, 199
Hines, Darlene Clark, 42
hip-hop culture, commodification of, 244
Holbrook, Felix, 89
Hollander, Lee M., 121
Holloway, Joseph E., 4
Holman, C. Hugh, 199
Holt, Thomas C., 51
hooks, bell, 42; *Ain't I a Woman,* 198; on varying definitions of feminism, 201
Hooper, Johnson J.: *Some Adventures of Captain Simon Suggs,* 265
Hopkins, Pauline: *Contending Forces: A Romance Illustrative of Negro Life North and South,* 114–15, 115, 295
Hord, Fred Lee (Mzee Lasana Okpara), vii
Howard-Pitney, David: *The Afro-American Jeremiad: Appeals for Justice in America,* 29
Howard University, 243
Howells, William Dean: *My Mark Twain: Reminiscences and Criticisms,* 261, 270, 271
Hudson-Weems, Clenora, 229
Huggins, Nathan: *Voices of the Harlem Renaissance,* 303
Hughes, Langston, 82, 174; *The Big Sea,* 4–5; "Mother to Son," 1; *The Weary Blues,* 82; "Young Gal's Blues," 210
Huntingdon, Countess of, 100, 101, 102, 106
Hurm, Gerd, 25

Hurston, Zora Neale, 12, 79, 174, 186, 255; *Mules and Men: Negro Folktales and Voodoo Practices in the South,* 55; *Their Eyes Were Watching God,* 80
hybrid cultural identity, African American, viii, x, 2, 4, 5, 7, 13, 21, 51, 53, 67, 69, 75, 112. *See also* cultural hybridity; double consciousness, African American
hybridization, 174

Ibibio, 87, 247
Ibo, 87, 247
Ice Cube, 244
Ice T, 244
idiolect, 211
imaginative genres, 76
imagists, 128
imperialism, 7, 249
India, 171
industrial education *vs.* higher liberal education, 54–55
industrialization, 76, 249
Institute for the Harmonious Development of Man, 128
institutionalized racism, 52, 59, 71, 76, 78, 249
integration, defined, 88
integration movement, 119
International Symposium on Contemporary Literature of the African Diaspora, University of Salamanca, 1996, 195
irony, 27, 29, 35, 37, 52, 56, 76–217, 77, 79, 90, 115, 121, 159, 161, 173, 219, 249
Iser, Wolfgang, 211
Iser, Wolfgang: *The Act of Reading,* 26, 231

Jackman, Harold, 128
Jackson, Blyden: *The Waiting Years: Essays on American Negro Literature,* viii
Jacobs, Harriet (Linda Brent): *Incidents in the Life of a Slave Girl, Written by Herself,* 77, 78
James, C. L. R., 295
James, Darius, 173, 174
James, Henry, 146, 209, 297
James, William, 48; *The Principles of Psychology,* 44
Jameson, Frederic: *The Political Unconscious: Narrative as a Socially Symbolic Act,* 55, 252
Jan-Mohammad, Abdul, 294
Jarfe, Gunter, 26
Jarrell, Randall, 143
Jauss, Hans Robert, 26

Jay, Gregory S.: *American Literature and the Culture Wars*, 171
Jaynes, Gerald David, 242–43
Jefferson, Thomas, 38, 91; belief in white supremacy, 32, 107; *Notes on the State of Virginia*, 31–32, 33, 77, 104–5, 107; on Phillis Wheatley, 104–5; view of Americans as living lives of slaves under British rule, 86
Jehlen, Myra: Introduction, *Ideology and Classic American Literature* (ed.), 171
jeremiad: black abolitionist tradition of, 33; black tradition of, 32–33; defined, 30; Frederick Douglass's July 5 address as, 32–33; Puritan tradition of, 30–31; sacred and secular origins of, 29–32; themes of in African American novel, 80
Jeremiah, 30
Jesus of Nazareth, 30
Jim Crow, 6, 11, 49, 67, 276, 277, 279
Joans, Ted, 83
"Joe Turner Blues," 253
"Jogo Blues," 253
Johnson, Barbara, 295; "Metaphor, Metonomy and Voice in *Their Eyes Were Watching God*," 42
Johnson, Charles S., 9, 173, 174; *Being and Race: Black Writing since 1970*, 164–65; cultural dualism and pluralism, 164, 167, 169; *Faith and the Good Thing*, 164; *Middle Passage*, 165–69; *Oxherding Tale*, 164; *Shadow of the Plantation*, 11; *The Sorcerer's Apprentice*, 164
Johnson, James Weldon, 258; *The Autobiography of an Ex-Colored Man*, 51, 252, 302; *The Book of American Negro Poetry*, 302
Johnson, L. B., War on Poverty, 302
Johnson, Randal, 7, 8–9
Joie, Chester, 89
Jones, Absalom, 33, 97
Jones, Gayl: assessment of dialect and folklore in Dunbar and Hurston, 211; comparison of Sherley A. Williams and Langston Hughes, 210; and complexities of agency, authority, and authenticity, 211–12, 217; *Corregidora*, 207, 212, 217; *Die Vogelfangerin (The Birdcatcher)*, 207; *Eva's Man*, 202, 207, 212, 217; "freeing of voice," 208; *The Healing*, 202, 207, 208, 211, 212–17, 217; *Liberating Voices: Oral Tradition in African American Literature*, 207–8, 240; and relationship of oral to written techniques in African American literature, 208; transgression of relationship between vernacular and literary language and between foreign language and Standard American dialects, 213–17
Jones, Hettie, 176
Jones, Howard Mumford, 110
Jones, Kellie, 176
Jones, Lewis Wade, 13
Jones, Lisa, 176
Jones, Rhett S., 260–61
Jones, Robert, 207
Jordan, June, 83
Jordan, Winthrop D.: *White over Black*, 112, 113
Journal of Negro History, 10
Joyce, James, 173, 208
Juneteenth, 26
Jung, Carl, 199

Kaiser, Ernest, 283
Kallen, Horace M.: "Democracy versus the Melting Pot," 305
Kaplan, Amy: "'Left Alone with America': The Absence of Empire in the Study of American Culture," 171
Kaplan, J., 262
Kaplan, Morton A.: "The Tribalization of America," 163, 218
Kaplan, Sidney: *The Black Presence in the Era of the American Revolution*, 16, 17, 89–90, 92
Kaufman, Bob, 83
Kelley, William Melvin, 79, 112, 120, 174; *A Different Drummer*, 121–22; *Dunfords Travels Everywheres*, 121; image of Africa in novels of, 120, 121–22
Kelsall, Malcolm, 73
Keneally, Thomas: "Misadventures in the Slave Trade," 164
Kennedy, John F., assassination of, 244
Kennedy, Randall: "My Race Problem--and Ours," 64, 65
Kennedy, Robert, assassination of, 244
Killens, John Oliver, 174, 283
King, Martin Luther: assassination of, 244; "I Have a Dream" speech, 71, 142
King, Robert, 109
King, Rodney, 62n4, 68
King, Woodie, 84
Kinney, Arthur: *Critical Essays on William Faulkner: The McCaslin Family*, 275; "Faulkner and the Problematics of Procreation," 276
Knight, Etheridge, 83
Kockman, Thomas, 257

Kreymborg, Alfred, 129
Kristeva, Julia, 211
Ku Klux Klan, resurgence of in 1920s, 118
Kulpe, Oswald, 44
Kutnik, Jerzy, 162

Lacan, Jacques, 211
Lang, Andrew, 269
Langdon, Jervis, 270
Langdon, Olivia, 270
language: code-switching, 4, 7, 150, 152, 172, 174, 175, 180–81, 208–9; defined, 211; hybridized, 174; indeterminacy of, 155; in relation to knowledge and power in identity construction, 44, 65, 66, 180, 211, 213, 244, 251; and Signifying Monkey, 256–57; vernacular as, 5. *See also* African American Vernacular English (AAVE); African American vernacular tradition; Standard American English (SAE)
Language and Literature (Fisher, ed.), 301
Larsen, Nella, 128
Latinos, 170–71
Laurence, Margaret, 208
Lauter, Paul: *Canons and Contexts,* 293, 297, 302, 303; "The Literatures of America--a Comparative Discipline," 297; "Race and Gender in the Shaping of the American Literary Canon," 303; "Reconstructing American Literature: Curricular Issues," 302
law enforcement, brutality against African Americans, 68
Lawrence-Lightfoot, Sara: *I've Known Rivers,* 70
legend, 67, 173
Leonard, James S., 261
Leopold II, 116
Lester, Julius, 22n8, 261; "James Baldwin—Reflections of a Maverick," 143, 145, 146; *Lovesong: Becoming a Jew,* 138; *The Seventh Son: The Thought and Writings of W.E.B. DuBois,* 27
Levin, Harry, 125–26
Levine, Lawrence W.: *Black Culture and Black Consciousness: Afro-American Folk Thought from Slavery to Freedom,* 32, 67, 209, 245
Lévi-Strauss, Claude, 87
Levitas, Saul, 143
Lewis, R. W. B.: *The American Adam: Innocence, Tragedy, and Tradition in the Nineteenth Century,* 29
Lewis, Sinclair, 186; *Main Street,* 187

Liberia, 116
Lincoln, Abraham, 27, 187
literate orientation, 88
Little, John, 9
Lloyd, Henry, 92
Local Color Negro stereotype, 198
Locke, Alain, 258, 298; *The New Negro,* 4, 302
Logan, Rayford, 20
Loggins, Vernon, 88
Lomax, Alan, 12, 13
Lomax, John, 12
Longstreet, Augustus B.: *Georgia Scenes,* 265
Lorca, 208
Lost Delta Found (Gordon and Nemeroy), 13
Louima, Abner, 68
Lovell, John, 20
Loving v. Virginia, 277
Lucas, Curtis, 185
Lynch, Acklyn, 22n8
lynching, 49, 71, 244
Lynn, Kenneth S.: *Mark Twain and Southwestern Humor,* 263–64, 265–66

Mackey, Nathaniel, 173, 174
MacKinnon, Catherine, 42
MacMillan, 303
Madhubuti, Haki (Don Lee), 83
magical realism, 171
Mailer, Norman, 202
mainstream, myth and metaphor of, 296–97
Major, Clarence, 83, 154, 173; *The Dark and Feeling: Black American Writers and Their Work,* 155; "Licking Stamps, Taking Chances," 160; *Some Observations of a Stranger at Zuni in the Latter Part of the Century,* 160
Major, Clarence, *Such Was the Season*: black intellectuals and professionals, 161; and blues tradition, 158; and double consciousness, 156–60; homecoming voice in, 154–63; narrative structure, 155–56
Malcolm X, assassination of, 244
Mann, Horace, 33
March of Washington, 1963, 16
marginal man: in Faulkner's *Go Down Moses,* 277, 278, 280, 282; theory of, 52, 228
Mark Twain Journal: "Black Writers on *Adventures of Huckleberry Finn* One Hundred Years Later," 260
Marrant, John, 102; *A Narrative of the Lord's Wonderful Dealings with J. Marrant . . . Taken*

Down from His Own Relation. Arranged and Corrected, and Published by the Reverend Mr. Aldridge, 106
Marshall, Paule, 21
mask wearing, 82, 215, 229, 261–62, 266, 272–74, 305
Mason, Julian, Jr., 97, 98, 99, 103
Mason-Dixon line, 14
Massachusetts Anti-Slavery Society, 39
Mather, Cotton: *Rules for the Societies of Negroes,* 88
Matthews, Artie: "The Baby Seals Blues," 253
McCaffery, Larry, 162
McCarthy, Joseph, 192
McCosh, James, 48
McHenry, Jerry, 34
McKay, Claude, 12, 82; *Banjo: A Story without a Plot,* 118–19; *Home to Harlem,* 118
McMillan, Terry, 200; male types, stereotypes, and archetypes, 198, 204, 205; *Mama,* 204; *Waiting to Exhale,* 204–5, 206
"melting pot" concept, 296
Melville, Herman: "Benito Cereno," 15, 163, 165, 166; *Billy Budd,* 163, 164, 165, 166, 168; *Moby Dick,* 163, 164, 165
"Memphis Blues," 253
messianism, 29–30, 31, 80
Michigan Quarterly Review, 283
middle-class African Americans, move from inner-city neighborhoods, 244
Middle Passage, 68, 76, 108, 249
Miles, Ray, 22n8
millenarianism, 30
Miller, Kelly, 20
Miller, Perry, 29; *The New England Mind: The Seventeenth Century,* 30
Miller, R. Baxter, 242
Mills, Florence, 82
Milner, Ron: *What the Wine Sellers Buy,* 84
mimetic art, 155
miscegenation statutes, 276–77, 279
misogynist black revolutionary nationalist stereotype, 200
Missouri Compromise, 263
Mitchell, Samuel L., 44
Mitchell-Kiernan, Claudia, 257
Mkalimoto, Ernest, 22n8
Modern Language Association (MLA), 300
Montaigne, Michel de: "Of Cannibals," 113
Montes, Catalina, 196
Moon, Sun Myung. *See* Sun Myung Moon

Morrison, Toni, 79, 137, 145, 173, 174, 179; *The Bluest Eye,* 202–3, 206, 229; *Jazz,* 218, 219–27; male types, stereotypes, and archetypes, 198; "Memory, Creation, and Writing," 219; self-defined role as bearing witness, 229; *Song of Solomon,* 229; *Sula,* 229; *Tar Baby,* 229
Morrison, Toni: *Beloved,* 52, 81, 202–3, 205–6, 227–38; black feminist discourse in, 235–36; call-and-response, 231; five linguistic codes and ideologies, 235–36; interweaving of racial and sexual consciousness, 231; metaphor and metonym, 232–34; portrayal of black men, 236–37; remembrance as narrative strategy, 229–30, 232, 238; structural analogue to woman's menstrual cycle, 231–32; womanist neo-slave narrative of double consciousness, 219, 229, 230–31, 235
Moses, Wilson J., 29; *Black Messiahs and Uncle Toms: Social and Literary Manipulations of a Religious Myth,* 29–30, 31, 32, 33; "The Poetics of Ethiopianism," 40, 44
Motley, Willard, 12, 185
MOVE, 150, 153–54
Moynihan, Daniel, 190
Muddy Waters, 13
Müller, Karl, 26
multiculturalism, 171, 172, 173, 174, 243, 282, 295, 302
multiple consciousness, 172
Mumford, Lewis, 129
Murasaki, Lady: *Tale of Genji,* 208
Murray, Charles, 242
Myrdal, Gunnar: *An American Dilemma: The Negro Problem and Modern Democracy,* 13, 242
myth, 155; of American Dream, 186, 189; defined, 186; of the mainstream, 296–97; as residually oral form, 67, 173, 260; of white supremacy, 32, 115, 247, 277, 280

NAACP, 75, 248, 277
Narratives of the Sufferings of Lewis and Milton Clarke, 77
Nation, 143
National Endowment for the Humanities, 300
naturalism, 189
Naumberg, Margaret, 134
Naylor, Gloria, 174
Neal, Larry, 83; "And Shine Swam On," 42; "The Black Arts Movement," 200
"Negro": defined, 75; as racialized socioeconomic

concept, 248; and tying of color to race and blackness to slavery, 277
Negro Ensemble Company, 84
Negro Renaissance, 82
Nemerov, Bruce, 13
neocolonialism, 119
neo-hoodoo aesthetic, 171, 172–73
neorealism, 171
neo-slave narratives, 172
New Black Aesthetic, 83, 172–73, 175
The New Caravan (Kreymborg et al.), 129
"New Criticism," 210
New England Association of Teachers of English (NEATA), 240
New Federal Theater, 84
New Leader, 143
New Negro movement, 4, 82, 303
New South, 66, 279
News World Communications, 219
Newton, Huey, 202
New World Writing, 296
New York African Free School, 75, 87, 249
Nichols, Charles, 261; *Many Thousand Gone,* 14
Nilon, Charles H., 261
Noble, David W.: *The End of American History: Democracy, Capitalism, and the Metaphor of Two Worlds in Anglo-American Historical Writing, 1880–1890,* 29, 31
Noble Savage image, 113, 118
Nook Farm Community, 270
northern migration, 68, 69, 76, 197, 222, 249
Northrop, Solomon, 78
Norton, 303

Occom, Samson, 102–3
Offord, Carl, 185
Old South Church, Boston, 99
Olsen, Marvin E.: "Power as a Social Process," 66, 179, 212
one-drop rule, 2, 71
O'Neil, Sondra, 242
oral forms, of African American vernacular tradition, viii, 4, 67, 173, 259–60
oral orientation, 88
oratory, 67, 173
"Oreo," 184
Ostendorf, Berndt, 26; *Black Literature in White America,* 42
Otis, James: *Rights of the British Colonies,* 89

Ottley, Roi, 12
Outlaw, Lucius: "'Conserve' Races? In Defense of W.E.B. Du Bois," 46

Page, Thomas Nelson, 10, 210
Paine, Albert Bigelow: *Mark Twain: A Biography,* 262–65
pan-African movement, 180
paradox: of African American folk and formal art, 29, 76, 90, 173, 219, 228, 249; of African American hybrid identities, viii, x, 21, 27, 35, 51, 71, 76, 172, 187, 228, 246, 247; of how the more things change the more they remain the same., 151, 239, 240, 241, 243, 245, 253, 256, 260, 303. *See also* double consciousness, African American
Park, Robert E., theory of the marginal man, 52, 228
parody, in African American folk and formal art, 29, 35, 52, 76, 79, 121, 180, 182, 203, 228, 249, 257
Partisan Review, 143
passive resistance, 119
Patell, Cyrus R. K., 172
Patterson, Orlando: *The Sociology of Slavery,* 32
Peck, John, 73
Pendleton, John, 10
Pennington, J. W. C., 78
Pentecostal church, 140
People's Voice, 187
Peters, John, 103
Peterson, Dorothy, 128
Petry, Ann: *Country Place,* 186, 187, 190–92; demythologizing of cultural myths, 186–95; and economic determinism, 187–90; and existentialism, 192; *The Narrows,* 186, 187, 192–95; *The Street,* 186, 187–90, 195; use of symbolic characters, 194
Pfaff, Françoise, 111
Phi Kappa Phi, 17
Philippines, 67
Phillips, Ulrich B.: *American Negro Slavery,* 9, 284, 285; *Life and Labor in the Old South,* 9
Phylon, 187
Pilch, Herbert, 26
Plato: *Gorgias,* 43, 246; *Phaedrus,* 43, 246
Plessy v. Ferguson, 10–11, 46, 49, 67, 276
Plumerm, William S., 44
Plumpp, Sterling, 83
pluralism: cultural, 164, 167, 169, 172, 174, 297–98, 302, 305; ethnic, 206
The Poetic Edda (Hollander, trans.), 121

poetry, African American, 81–83
police brutality, 8
Pollitzer, William S.: "The Relationship of the Gullah-Speaking People of Coastal South Carolina and Georgia to Their African Ancestors," 69
Pope, Alexander, 101
population distribution, African Americans, 69–70
Porter, Dorothy, 20
Posnock, Ross: "How It Feels to Be a Problem: Du Bois, Fanon, and the 'Impossible Life' of the Black Intellectual," 70
post–Black Arts movement, 171
postcolonial literature, 294–95
postcolonial studies, 171
postmodernism, 155, 171
post-Reconstruction, 68, 76, 249
poststructuralism, 210–11, 252
Poussaint, Alvin F., 283
Prince, Gerald, 65
Protestant ethic, 189
Proust, Marcel, 146; *Remembrance of Things Past*, 229
Pryse, Marjorie, 185
Puerto Rico, 67
Puritan jeremiad, 30–31

Quarles, Benjamin, 27

Raboteau, Albert J.: *Slave Religion*, 32
racial assimilation, versus racial solidarity, 27, 28, 46
racial inequality, increase in from 1970s to 1990s, 244–45
racial profiling, 8
racial redlining, 8
racial segregation, 3, 11, 49, 110, 148n1, 179, 228, 243, 244, 276, 281, 305, 307
racism, antiblack, 68, 76, 249; contemporary, 8; de facto and de jure, 52–53; defined, 52; in early twentieth century, 9–11; institutionalized, 52, 59, 71, 76, 78, 249; and lack of equality for African Americans in 1990s, 242–43; pseudoscientific and theological ideology, 52–53; and resistance to validation of African American literature, 301
Rahv, Philip, 143
Rampersad, Arnold, 44, 48, 261
Randall, Dudley: "Booker T. and W. E. B.", 63–64; Broadside Critics Series, 41
rap, 244, 256
Rawick, George P., 9; *From Sundown to Sunup*, 14
reader-response criticism, 210

Reagan, Ronald, 207
Reconstruction, 68, 76, 249
Reddick, Lawrence D., 9, 11
Redding, Jay Saunders: *To Make a Poet Black*, 100; "Negro Writing in America," 296
Redefining American Literary History (Ruoff and Ward), 300–301
Redmond, Eugene, 83
Reed, Ishmael, 79, 83, 154, 155, 171, 173, 174, 179; *Flight to Canada*, 80; *Mumbo Jumbo*, 74, 80, 172, 255, 303; *Yellow Back Radio Broke-Down*, 80
reinterpretation, 13, 148
residual Africanisms, 32, 75, 78, 212, 249
retention, 13, 32, 148
revisionist scholarship, 12, 13–14, 16
Revolutionary War, 91
Reynolds, Mary: "A Double Consciousness, or a Duality of Person in the Same Individual," 44
rhetoric, 43
Richards, Olufemi, 22n8
Richmond Enquirer, 284
Roach, Max, 17
Robertson, James O.: *American Myth, American Reality*, 186, 187
Robeson, Paul, 82
Robinson, William H., Jr., 82
Rochester Antislavery Sewing Society, 77
Rodgers, Carolyn, 83
Roosevelt, F. D., New Deal, 302
root healing, 55
Rosenfeld, Paul, 129
Rourke, Constance: *The Roots of American Culture*, 304
Rousseau, Jean-Jacques, 305; *Emile*, 113
Rubin, Steven, 111
Ruoff, A. La Vonne Brown, 300–301

Sahlins, Marshall, 252
Said, Edward, 294; *Culture and Imperialism*, 295
Sambo identity, 14
Samuels, Wilfred D., 229
Sanchez, Sonia, 83
Sapir, Edward, 29, 67
satire, 173
Satire or Evasion? Black Perspectives on Huckleberry Finn (Leonard, Tenney, and Davis, eds.), 261
Savoy, Willard, 185
school desegregation, 119
Schraufnagel, Noel, 189

Schuyler, George: image of African in novels of, 125; *Slaves Today: A Story of Liberia*, 114, 116, 117–18
Scott, Joan W., 42
Sea Islands, 69
segregation, 244
Seller, Cleveland, 16
Senegambia, 97
"separate but equal" racial segregation, 3, 11, 46, 49
separatism, 28, 51, 71, 86, 88, 89, 174
Sere, 87, 247
Sewall, Joseph, 99
Sewall, Samuel, 99
sexism, 78
Shadrack, 34
Shakur, Tupac, 244
Shange, Ntozake, 229; *for colored girls who have considered suicide / when the rainbow's enuf*, 84
sharecropping, 55
Sheffrey, Ruth T.: *Trajectory*, viii
Shepp, Archie, 17
Shobat, Ella, 294
Showalter, Elaine: "A Criticism of Our Own: Autonomy and Assimilation in Afro-American and Feminist Literary Theory," 305
Signifying Monkey, 53, 256–58
Sims, Nathaniel, 299
slave mutinies, accounts of, 164, 165–167
slave narratives, 11, 77, 105–9, 164, 172, 229, 305
slave revolts, 283
slavery, 2, 29, 68, 71, 76, 179, 249, 288; in Africa, 107–8; and African American jeremiad, 32–40, 95; apology for, 68; deletion of references to in Declaration of Independence, 91; Elkin's study of, 10, 14; Frederick Douglass on the "tomb" of, 230; impact on culture and character in Johnson's *Middle Passage*, 167–69; interaction with color, 277; interaction with racism, 87, 247; Jefferson and, 32, 86, 104; justified on notions of cultural and racial superiority, 113; radicalization and growth of, 87; revisionist scholarship on, 10, 16; romanticized representations, 10, 13; sanctioning of in U. S. Constitution, 91, 139, 218
slaves: deprived of Old World heritage and social support, 68, 87, 247; early petitions for permission to purchase their freedom, 89–90; population by 1790, 91–92; specific African identities, 87, 247
slave trade, transatlantic, 7, 197, 244
Sleeper, Jim: "Toward an End of Blackness," 65

Smith, Adam, 47
Smith, Bessie, 82, 220
Smith, Clara, 220
Smith, David, 261
Smith, Gerrit, 3, 33
Smith, Henry Nash: *Virgin Land: The American West as Symbol and Myth*, 29
Smith, Mamie, 220
Smith, Trixie, 220
Smith, William Gardener, 185
Smitherman, Geneva, 257
Snoop Doggy Dogg, 205, 244
Snowden, Frank, 20
social assimilation, 88, 92, 110
socialized ambivalence, 52, 53, 76, 125, 141, 187, 195, 228, 249
Social Text, 294
Socrates, 243
soft-line messianism, 31
Soitos, Stephen: *The Blues Detective: A Study of African American Detective Fiction*, 121
Sollors, Werner, 26, 295–96; *Beyond Ethnicity: Consent and Descent in American Culture*, 296, 297; "A Critique of Pure Pluralism," 297–98
song, 67, 173, 260
Sorrentino, Gilbert, 175
South Africa, 171
Southern, Eileen: *The Music of Black Americans*, 253
Southern plantation tradition, 68, 76, 249
Southern University, Louisiana, 11
Southworth, Emma: *The Hidden Hand*, 78–79
Sowell, Thomas: *Black Education: Myths and Tragedies*, 17
Spanish Civil War, 6
Spiller, Robert, 85, 86
Spillers, Hortense, 185, 210; *Black, White, and in Color*, viii
spirituality, residual African, 46, 48, 55
spirituals, 81
Spivak, Gayatri Chakravorty, 294
Sri Lanka, 171
Stampp, Kenneth M., 9; *The Peculiar Institution: Slavery in the Ante-Bellum South*, 10, 14, 284
Standard American English (SAE), 7, 54, 150, 158, 180; in *Beloved*, 235–36
Starke, Catherine: *Black Portraiture in American Fiction*, 198
Stepto, Robert, 42, 210, 301; *From Behind the Veil*, 84, 250; "Teaching Afro-American Literature," 304

stereotypes: of African American men in works of African American women writers, 197, 198–206; of African Americans as biologically and culturally inferior, 9–10; of African Americans in Styron's *The Confessions of Nat Turner*, 287, 288–89; of African Americans in white American literature, 14, 114, 198; defined, 199; held by white Americans toward African Americans in 1990s, 242–43; held by whites toward Africans, 125
Stevens, Nelsen, 17
Stevenson, William: *The Ghosts of Africa*, 112
Stewart, James B., 41–42
"St. Louis Blues," 253
Stoephosius, Rita, 26
storytelling, 3, 19, 20, 80, 160, 216–17
Stowe, Harriet Beecher, 210, 270; *Uncle Tom's Cabin*, 142
Streitfeld, David, 154
Strickland, William, 22n8
structuralism, 210
St. Thomas African Episcopal Church, Philadelphia, 97
Student Nonviolent Coordinating Committee (SNCC), 248
Studies in American Indian Literature (Allen, ed.), 301
Styron, William: *The Confessions of Nat Turner*, vii, 14, 16, 275, 283–92; archetypal black male brute, 290–91; distortion of history to create negative black stereotypes, 287; imaginary relationship between Turner and Margaret Whitehead, 289–90; implausibility of narrator, 291; narrator's gratuitous racial commentary, 286; narrator's literary rhetoric, 285–86; narrator's religious visions, 287–88; narrator's stereotypic desire to rape white women, 288–89; stereotypical representation of sexuality of slaves, 287
subscription books, 269
Sumner, Charles, 33
Sundquist, Eric: *The Hammers of Creation*, 209, 218n2
Sun Myung Moon, 219
survivals, African religious and cultural, 32, 75, 78, 212, 249
symbolic capital, 7
syncretism, 13, 29, 46, 55, 75, 148n1, 249
Syrett, Harold C., 91
Szwed, John F., 217

tale, 67, 173, 260. *See also* storytelling
Tanner, Obour, 98, 103

Taylor, Charles, 65; *The Ethics of Authenticity*, 65, 178, 211–12; *Human Agency and Language*, 179–80
Tea Act, 101
Tenney, Thomas A., 260, 261
Terry, Esther, 22n8
Terry, Eugene, 22n8
Terry, Lucy: "Bar's Fight," 76
theater, African American, 84
Thelwell, Michael, 16, 17, 283, 299
Theroux, Alexander, 175
Theroux, Paul: *Girl at Play*, 112
Third International Conference on William Faulkner, Chongquing, China, 275
Thoreau, Henry, 297
Thornton, John, 102–3
Three-Fifths Compromise, 91
Thundermouth Press, 303
Thurman, Wallace, 128; *Infants of the Spring*, 303
Tiananmen Square student revolt, 170
Tiffin, Helen, 292
Till, Emmett, 152
toast traditions, 53
Tolson, Melvin, 82
Toni Morrison (Samuels and Hudson-Weems), 229
Toomer, Jean, 18, 82, 137, 174, 255; "Blue Meridian," 128–36; *Cane*, 51, 128, 129, 302; *Essentials*, 129; "November Cotton Flower," 161; "On Being American," 128; "Outline of the Story of the Autobiography," 128; self-image as cultural aristocrat, 127–28; synthesis of new forms and themes, 128; use of concrete symbols, 134
Toure, Askia, 83
tragic mulatto, trope of, 176, 198
transatlantic slave trade, 7, 197, 244
transcendentalists, 44, 45, 304
transcultural border crossing, ix, 172
tribalism, 306
trickster, 53, 215, 256
Trilling, Lionel: *Sincerity and Authenticity*, 65, 178, 211
Truth, Sojourner: "Ain't I a Woman" speech, 197
Tucker, George, 10
Tucker, Nathaniel B., 10
Turner, Darwin, 127; "The Teaching of Afro-American Literature," 241
Turner, Frederick Jackson, 171
Turner, Nat, 16, 32
Tutuola, Amos: *The Palm-Wine Drinkard*, 208
Tuveson, Ernest, 29

Twain, Mark, 173, 209, 210, 297; *The Adventures of Tom Sawyer*, 266, 268; *The Autobiography of Mark Twain*, 263, 264; desertion from Confederacy, 263–64; dual audiences, 269–71; *The Gilded Age*, 271; and the minstrel show, 264–65, 272, 273; moral ambivalence about humanity of blacks, 262, 266, 267, 272–75; "The Private History of a Campaign That Failed," 263; and racism of southwestern humor, 265–66, 272, 273; socialization in ethics of Jim Crow, 262–66, 272; "A True Story," 264; and William Dean Howells, 271

Twain, Mark: *The Adventures of Huckleberry Finn*, 260, 261–62, 266–68; Huck's moral struggle with slavery and racism, 269; time-frame of story, 268–69; Twain's ambivalence of relationship to Jim, 272–75; Twain's close racial, regional, and class identification with audience, 269–70; Twain's reduction of Jim's humanity to minstrel mask, 274; white paternalism, 273

Twichell, Joseph, 270

2 Live Crew, 256

Tyler, Moses Coit, 86, 110; *A History of American Literature, 1607–1765*, 109–10; *The Literary History of the American Revolution, 1763–1783*, 97–105

type, defined, 199

Unification Church, 219

Union of Soviet Socialist Republics, 171

Updike, John, 212; *The Coup*, 112

urbanization, 68, 76, 249

U.S. Constitution, paradoxical sanctioning of freedom and slavery, 91, 139, 218

Van Vechten, Carl: *Nigger Heaven*, 118

Vass, Gustavus. *See* Hammon, Briton

veil, metaphor of, 28, 49, 51, 59, 68, 70, 228, 305

vernacular, 5. *See also* African American Vernacular English (AAVE); African American vernacular tradition

Vesey, Denmark, 32

Virginia, African American population, 88

von Goethe, Johann Wolfgang: *Faust*, 44; *Wilhelm Meister*, 127

W. E. B. Du Bois Department of Afro-American Studies, the University of Massachusetts, vii, 17

W. E. B. Du Bois on Race and Culture: Philosophy, Politics, and Poetics (Bell, Grosholz, Stewart, eds.), 41–42

Wagner, Richard: *Lohengrin*, 59

Wahrhaftig, Paul, 153

Walker, Alice, 79, 83, 200; black male redemption through gender-role reversal or egalitarianism, 204; *The Color Purple*, 80, 204, 206, 237; male types, stereotypes, and archetypes, 198, 204; *Meridian*, 203–4, 206, 237; *In Search of Our Mothers' Gardens*, 229; *The Temple of My Familiar*, 74; *The Third Life of Grange Copeland*, 203

Walker, David: "Walker's Appeal in Four Articles Together with a Preamble to the Colored Citizens of the World but in Particular and Very Expressly to Those of the United States of America," 33, 77, 288

Walker, Joseph: *River Niger*, 84

Walker, Margaret, 12, 82; "For My People," 83

Wallace, Michele, 198, 200; *Black Macho and the Myth of the Superwomen*, 201–2

Wand, Hart A.: "The Dallas Blues," 253

Ward, Douglas Turner, 84

Ward, Jerry, 300–301

Warner, Charles Dudley, 270

Warren, Austin, 75, 249

Warshow, Robert, 143

Washington, Booker T., 70; accommodationist support of social segregation, 49, 66; "Atlanta Compromise," 11, 46, 63; *The Negro Problem* (ed.), 48; *Up from Slavery*, 77, 302

Washington, George, 103, 104

Washington, Madison, 164

Washington, Mary Helen, 42; *Black-Eyed Susans: Classic Stories by and about Black Women*, 205; *Invented Lives: Narratives of Black Women, 1860–1960*, 62n1

Waters, Ethel, 82

Watterson, India: "Gorham Munson on Jean Toomer," 128

Watts riot, 245

Weber, Max, 179

Wecter, Dixon, 263

Wellek, Rene, 75, 249

West, James L. W., III: *William Styron: A Life*, 283

Western imperialism, 67

Wheatley, John, 98

Wheatley, Mary, 98, 103

Wheatley, Nathaniel, 100

Wheatley, Phillis, 92, 94, 97–105, 110; duality of identity and reception, 101–2; *An Elegaic Poem, on the Death of George Whitefield*, 100; "Goliath of

Gath," 101; "Hymn to Humanity," 101; "An Hymn to the Evening," 101; "An Hymn to the Morning," 101; "Isaiah LXIII," 101; "Liberty and Peace," 103; neoclassicism, 101; "Ode to Neptune," 101; "On Being Brought from Africa to America," 99–100, 101; "On the Death of the Rev. Dr. Sewell, 1769, 99; *Poems on Various Subjects, Religious and Moral,* 81, 100, 101; "To His Excellency General Washington," 103; "To Maecenas," 101; "To the King's Most Excellent Majesty, 1768, 99; "To the Right Honourable William, Earl of Dartmouth, His Majesty's Principle Secretary of State for North America, etc.", 101–2; "To the University of Cambridge, in New England," 98–99, 101; trip to England, 100–101, 102

Wheatley, Susannah, 98

Wheelock, Eleazer, 102

White, Hayden, 252

white American fiction, African American in, 14, 114, 198

white Americans: images of Africa, 112–14; persistent stereotypes of African Americans in 1990s, 242–43

white Feminist movement, 197–98, 201

Whitehead, Colson, 173, 174, 179

Whitehead, Margaret, 289–90

white supremacy, myth of, 31, 247, 277, 280; and color symbolism, 115; Thomas Jefferson's belief in, 32, 107

white terrorism, 279

Whitman, Walt, 128, 129, 133, 134, 304, 305

Whitten, Norman E., Jr., 217

Whorf, Benjamin Lee, 67

Wideman, John Edgar, 79, 173, 209; analysis of Jones's *Corregidora,* 212; blues voices, 149–54; "Defining the Black Voice in Fiction," 217; "Frame and Dialect: The Evolution of the Black Voice in Fiction," 210, 211; *Homewood Trilogy,* 150; *Philadelphia Fire,* 154

Wideman, John Edgar, *Two Cities,* 149–54; African American vernacular tradition, 150–54; blues voices, 149–54; code-switching, 150, 152; relationship of blues and African American vernacular tradition to Standard American English, 152–53

Wiesel, Elie, 138, 146–47; *A Beggar in Jerusalem,* 147; *Night,* 147

Wiggins, William H., Jr., 26, 40

Williams, John A., 79, 112, 120, 283; image of Africa in novels of, 120; *The Man Who Cried I Am,* 120

Williams, Kenny J., 261

Williams, Raymond, 259

Williams, Robin M., Jr., 242–43

Williams, Sherley A.: "Someone Sweet Angel Chile," 210

William Styron's Nat Turner: Ten Black Writers Respond (Clarke, ed.), 283

Willis, Susan, 111

Wilson, August: *Fences,* 84

Wilson, Charles, 116

Wilson, Harriet E.: *Our Nig; or, Sketches from the Life of a Free Black, in a Two-Story White House,* 78–79, 184, 248

Wilson, William J., 52; *The Declining Significance of Race,* 64

Wolfe, Tom, 202

Wolof, 87, 247

womanist, defined, 229

Women's Rights movement, 200, 299; focus on white middle-class women, 201

women's studies, emergence of, viii

Woodson, Carter G., 9; *The Negro in Our History,* 10

Work, John W., 13

World & I, 137, 138, 163, 218–19

worship, African American struggle for freedom of in eighteenth-century, 96–97

Wretched Freeman stereotype, 198

Wright, Richard, 12, 79, 112, 120, 185, 199, 202, 255, 258; *Black Boy,* 143; "Blueprint for Negro Writing," 74, 246; existential black antihero, 200; image of Africa in novels of, 120; *The Long Dream,* 120; *Native Son,* 51, 80, 143, 165, 186; naturalism, 189

Wynter, Sylvia, 295

Yeats, William Butler, 21

Yellin, Jean, 77

Yerby, Frank, 12, 112, 120; *The Dahomean,* 114, 122–25; images of Africa in novels of, 120, 122–25

Yetman, Norman R., 9, 11, 12; *Life under the "Peculiar Institution": Selections from the Slave Narrative Collection,* 14

Yoruba oral and literary traditions, 84

Yoruba trickster, 53

Young, Al, 83, 155

Young, Charles, 116

Yugoslavia, former, 171

Zangwill, Israel: *The Melting-Pot,* 296

www.ingramcontent.com/pod-product-compliance
Lightning Source LLC
Chambersburg PA
CBHW081945230426
43669CB00019B/2924